ENID YANDELL

ENID YANDELL

KENTUCKY'S PIONEER SCULPTOR

JUILEE DECKER

UNIVERSITY PRESS OF KENTUCKY

Scholarly publisher for the Commonwealth,
serving Bellarmine University, Berea College, Centre
College of Kentucky, Eastern Kentucky University,
The Filson Historical Society, Georgetown College,
Kentucky Historical Society, Kentucky State University,
Morehead State University, Murray State University,
Northern Kentucky University, Transylvania University,
University of Kentucky, University of Louisville,
and Western Kentucky University.

Editorial and Sales Offices: The University Press of Kentucky
663 South Limestone Street, Lexington, Kentucky 40508-4008
www.kentuckypress.com

Library of Congress Cataloging-in-Publication Data

Names: Decker, Juilee, 1968- author.
Title: Enid Yandell : Kentucky's pioneer sculptor / Juilee Decker.
Description: Lexington, Kentucky : University Press of Kentucky, [2019] | Series: Topics in Kentucky history | Includes bibliographical references and index.
Identifiers: LCCN 2019025069 | ISBN 9780813178639 (hardcover) | ISBN 9780813178646 (pdf) | ISBN 9780813178653 (epub)
Subjects: LCSH: Yandell, Enid. | Sculptors—United States—Biography. | Women sculptors—United States—Biography. | Kentucky—Biography.
Classification: LCC NB237.Y36 D43 2019 | DDC 730.92 [B]—dc23
LC record available at https://lccn.loc.gov/2019025069

This book is printed on acid-free paper meeting
the requirements of the American National Standard
for Permanence in Paper for Printed Library Materials.

Manufactured in the United States of America.

Member of the Association
of University Presses

For Enid

Contents

Figures

Introduction

Who is Enid Yandell? I pondered this question in 2011 as I stared at the name among a multipage printout of all of the works of art owned by Georgetown College, a small liberal arts school in central Kentucky where I served as a faculty member and oversaw the art galleries as well as the artifacts and permanent collection. Enid's name was as unfamiliar to me as the supposed work by her in our collection. With an artist name and description ("Bust of J. J. Rucker") as starting points but the location "unknown," I was determined to find the work on campus—a ritual familiar to anyone who has worked in a museum or conducted an inventory of anything. A few days later, with the gallery staff, we discovered the bronze tucked in one of the formal reception rooms in the student center. A check mark replaced the question marks on our printout. Simultaneously I was formally introduced to the work of Kentucky's "girl sculptor," a moniker in use when Enid created this likeness.

Fast forward a year. Conducting research on Kentucky's Civil War statuary, I was reintroduced to Enid's name, as I learned that she was initially selected to construct the monument to the Confederate dead of Louisville in 1894—a commission that was ultimately taken away from her. Upon realizing that Enid had won commissions for both of these monuments—one a bust in honor of the faculty member who fostered the education of young women, and the other a memorial to sons, brothers, husbands, and fathers lost in the Civil War—I became interested in Enid as a research topic. In preparation for a February 2012 talk on that Confederate monument and the work that was ultimately erected, I pored over the Yandell manuscript collections of the Filson Historical Society in Louisville, looking for answers to the myriad questions I had about Enid Yandell.

What became clear to me was that this Kentucky-born artist who spent most of her adult life outside of the Bluegrass State had a story that needed to be told. Yet to date no full narrative exists, even though Enid has been the subject of three biographical studies over the past thirty-plus years, including Desiree Caldwell's 1982 exhibition and catalogue text for the Museum of Art at the Rhode Island School of Design; historian Nancy Baird's brilliantly detailed account in the *Filson Historical Quarterly* (1988); and Stephanie Darst's exhibition and catalogue for Louisville's Speed Museum (1993). Each of these scholarly endeavors has contributed much to our understanding of Enid as a seminal figure who created public statuary and private works in the United States and Europe from the 1890s and managed an art school on Martha's Vineyard from 1908 until her death in 1934.

While the previous research has provided the framework for understanding Enid's life and work at various times over those decades, no account to date has woven together her life and work across a persistent theme. Nor has any study taken a multifaceted approach to her life, work, and cultural milieu. In this volume, the theme of "pioneer" emerges just like Daniel Boone from the wilderness: out of a wilderness of details has been woven a narrative about how Enid worked and how she navigated the world around her. In particular, this biography acknowledges the multitude of influences on Enid's life and work, as well as her relationships with men and women over the years. The theme of the pioneer guides the discussion of Enid's longtime friendship with Reuben T. Durrett, who owned and shared relics of Boone; Enid's earliest monument to Boone for the Columbian Exposition (1893) and subsequent versions; and the overall creation, display, and dissemination of Boone as part of Enid's sculptural identity throughout the next forty years. Beyond the connection to Boone, Enid took on the subject of other pioneers—from women's education reformers J. J. Rucker and Emma Willard to A. D. "Pap" Ruff, an English expatriate cycling enthusiast who biked his way to Yellowstone in 1893. Moreover, Enid herself was referred to as a pioneer on several occasions, as documented in the following chapters.

To examine Enid's life is to bring together accounts of her public life that are recorded in reviews of her work, news of sculptural competitions, self-promotional material, and reports of philanthropic work that appeared in the periodical press from 1885 through her death in 1934. A thorough examination of Enid's personal and private life, however, has yet to be written, due in part to the dearth of extant primary documents written by her, as a number of the letters written by Enid were collected by her grandmother at the family estate in Nashville only to perish in a fire.[1] The largest collection of letters and documents concerning Enid's life, however, is housed in the Yandell Family Papers and the Enid Yandell Collection at the Filson Historical Society in Louisville, Kentucky.[2] Individual letters written by Enid and associated ephemera have been found in other autograph collections or records; however, no complete list of such documentation exists, thus making the search for details of Enid's personal life a difficult task. Complicating the research is the frequent misspelling of her first and last name (variations of Enid include Enie and Ella, while numerous variations of Yandell included Tandell, Yandle, Yandel, and Yardell) as well as the intentional and unintentional subsuming of her identity. Thus, constructing such a narrative is an endeavor that must focus chiefly on Enid's artistic accomplishment as an integral part of, even if inseparable from, her private life.

This volume presents a fuller biographical treatment of Enid Yandell than has been offered to date, introduces new information from archival materials, and seeks to foster new scholarship around Enid and her sculptural milieu. The publication is timed to coincide with the 150th anniversary of her birth—a year that has been variously misidentified as 1870 through 1875—as a means of firmly establishing what should be an easily identified biographical fact. However, if such basic facts are misconstrued, it is easy to see the difficulties in constructing a narrative over Enid's sixty-five years in her multiple studios and living quarters in Louisville, Cincinnati, Chicago, New York, Paris, and Martha's Vineyard. Though a worthy, if challenging, endeavor in its own right, the construction of *a* narrative of Enid's life and work from her earliest mud pies to her final pieces, highlights Enid's artistic accomplishment, private life, and legacy.

Misspellings, factual errors, and geography aside, a fourth complication arose in understanding the nuances of occupational identity vis-à-vis the status of women as sculptors at this historical moment. Put simply, barriers inhibited women's participation and achievement in the field of sculpture during the late nineteenth and early twentieth centuries: the very act of shaping a substance and forcing its aesthetic form is a physically demanding practice. This was especially true in the American South, where notions of feminine propriety and potential persisted in the postbellum period and the first half of the twentieth century. The story of Enid Yandell provides a framework for examining the limitations female artists confronted during that period and for acknowledging how she overcame barriers to make significant contributions to contradict the prescriptive understanding of what it meant to be a woman sculptor. Enid's experiences reflect how the education and professionalization of women sculptors relied heavily upon the encouragement of male sculptors and the endorsement of established institutions to attract international acclaim. And while Enid was successful in garnering global recognition, her Southern roots informed her oeuvre and outlook. They forged Enid's occupational identity.

In considering Southern identity, scholar Katherine A. Burnett approaches the literary South as a genre, understood as a series of conditions that produce "cultural, social, and artistic tropes, characteristics, or [formal] patterns."[3] This assessment can certainly be applied to the cultural production from the South as well, the region's art being another endeavor in which particular cultural, historical, and economic patterns are explored and disseminated. Burnett describes this promulgation as a "spore" paradigm.[4] Being Southern, however, is not a physical attribute that is easily put on—or shed. It is, rather, a strong emotional and cultural connection to place that serves as nourishment for a creative practice. Born in Louisville, Kentucky, in 1869, Enid retained ties to the Bluegrass State even as she traveled and relocated, domestically and abroad, for training, further education, and employment from 1887 onward. In doing so, she established a professional identity that transcended geographical boundaries, all the while retaining an affinity for and anchors in the South.

Beyond regional consideration, Enid challenged convention in other ways. She built upon the advancement of women sculptors from the previous generation, harkening back to a group that traveled to Rome in the mid-1860s, described by writer Henry James as a "strange sisterhood of American 'lady sculptors' who at one time settled upon the seven hills in a 'white marmorean flock.'"[5] Enid also exercised autonomy in defining the roles that men played in her life, whether as mentors, colleagues, or otherwise. She worked as an enterprising emerging artist to gain traction in a competitive arena before claiming agency as an independent professional. Further, she skillfully navigated shifts in position and rank, as student or teacher, and negotiated various stylistic attributes, such as classical, modern, realistic, idealized, abstract, or stylized. In short, she cast her own identity and legacy by breaking the molds that society and the art establishment had imposed upon so many women artists in the late nineteenth and early twentieth centuries.

Enid's story, then, is told through primary sources and works of art and their connections to contemporary cultural and historical contexts, and through analysis of her work through the lenses of public art and spectacle, exhibition theory and studies, Southern studies, and women's studies. Beginning with a chapter on Enid's birth and ending with an epilogue focused on her legacy, the text is arranged chronologically. Some overlap does occur across chapters. For instance, Chapters 4, 5, and 7 all begin in the late 1890s, although each chapter takes a particular point of view: large-scale commissions for civic projects as well as world's fairs from the Centennial in Nashville onward; dramatic, expressive works related to themes of love, loss, and companionship; and activism in the service of national and international causes. Through Enid's story, it is possible to understand what it meant to be a woman sculptor at this historical moment—an age of world's fairs and monument building that saw also the carnage and loss of total war—and to draw attention to the legacy that such an occupational identity has spawned.

Chapter 1 addresses Enid's early life, including her education in Louisville and Cincinnati. Particular attention is paid to her friendship with Colonel Reuben T. Durrett, a lawyer and amateur historian who served as the first president of the Filson Club, and her association with Charles C. Bickel, a businessman who supported Enid's career financially in the form of a $10,000 commission. The next chapter, "Caryatids and Clay," addresses Enid's life and work in Chicago as well as her identity as artist and author. The title of this chapter refers to Enid's award-winning contribution to the Woman's Building at the Columbian World's Fair and her preferred medium at the time. Chapter 3, "Commemoration and Controversy," situates Enid's artistic abilities, educational training, and social connection, particularly her parents' southern roots and her father's war service, relative to what would become her earliest significant commission, the monument to Kentucky's Confederate dead. Although this commission was ultimately revoked, attention is also paid to the manner in which Enid's name later became associated with the monument, even if erroneously. Chapter 4 addresses Enid's studio output from New York and Paris—the capitals of the art world at the time—which resulted in her colossal *Athena* for the 1897 Centennial Exposition in Nashville, the largest work ever created by a woman artist at the time, and submissions to subsequent fairs at Buffalo (1901) and St. Louis (1904). The next chapter, "Passions and Pursuits," addresses three key works: a silver cup designed by Enid; a memorial fountain for which Enid won a competition among a pool of nineteen international applicants; and a tabletop sculpture of two centaurs, male and female, given to Enid by a fellow sculptor. Chapter 6 situates the latter third of the volume by providing a glimpse of Enid's years on Martha's Vineyard from 1908 to 1934, defining the role that Edgartown played in Enid's life and work. Chapter 7, "Advocacy and Activism," focuses less on Enid's creative output and more on her work on behalf of causes, specifically women's rights, suffrage, and relief work for French artists, soldiers, and families impacted by the Great War. Chapter 8, "Pioneer and Promoter," examines subjects Enid portrayed as means of retaining, if not invigorating, her connection to the Bluegrass State while she operated studios in New York and Edgartown between visits to Paris during the last two decades of her life.

The Epilogue synthesizes the themes of the previous chapters: Enid's shaping of her occupational identity as an independent sculptor educated and working alongside male contemporaries; her documented success regardless of medium, size, and purpose; and her establishment of studio practices in Louisville, New York, Paris, and Edgartown. Woven into this narrative are the persistent ties that Enid held to the Bluegrass State, which helped construct her legacy.

Every chapter offers a springboard for further study, in terms of both Enid's life and work and the larger world of which she was a part—whether that was her family's home on Broadway, her grandmother's estate at Burlington, the world's fairs environs, her studio in New York, or her studio at Edgartown. My hope is that this volume fosters continued attention to Enid's life and legacy, attuned to Burnett's characterization of Southern studies simultaneous within and beyond the South—attention that Enid's life and legacy so deserve.

In sum, *Enid Yandell: Kentucky's Pioneer Sculptor* documents Enid Yandell's life and work as she transitioned from being a Southern dilettante, the daughter of a Confederate officer, and a mentee of men to an internationally recognized sculptor of large-scale, award-winning works, an independent woman engaging in art and activism. In short, she was a pioneer.

1

Cider and Cigars

In the spring of 1892, living as an early-career professional artist working at the Columbian Exposition in Chicago, Enid Yandell penned a note of gratitude to Reuben Thomas Durrett, a lawyer and amateur historian of Louisville's Filson Club. Having sipped some of Durrett's special-recipe cider, she wrote: "The box and cider came safely and we have drunk part of it with great glee—They all agree it is the finest cider they have ever tasted, and you may be sure we had drunk your very good health, happy days, and long life many times." The twenty-two-year-old artist further commented on her friendship with Durrett, a relationship that fostered her occupational identity as Kentucky's pioneer artist. For even as he befriended the Yandell family, Durrett seemed to have taken on another role as father figure to Enid in 1884.[1]

Born on October 6, 1869, in Louisville, Kentucky, Enid Bland Yandell was the eldest of four children of Louise Elliston Yandell (1844–1908) and Confederate veteran, surgeon, and medical doctor Lunsford Pitts Yandell II (1837–1884). A prominent, conservative, and Southern family, the Yandells lived in a comfortable Victorian home on Broadway, between Third and Fourth Streets (today the site of Brown Theatre). Prior to living there, the family had a smaller home on the southeast corner of Seventh and Magazine, near the Medical College where Lunsford worked, which was followed a residence at 206 West Chestnut near the city hospital at Chestnut and Floyd. For forty years this tract of land between Chestnut and Broadway served as headquarters for the Yandell family. Lunsford's medical office was just to the west of Enid's childhood home. The family attended Christ Church and one of its ten sister Episcopalian parishes, St. Paul's, where Enid earned a punctuality award for regular attendance in Sunday school during the first three months of the year in 1883. The family also served those in the community through participation in faith-based and benevolent groups that lent support to orphans and the infirmed. Interspersed among the medical buildings, churches, and social welfare and humanitarian societies were businesses and entertainment venues, including Solger's Confectionary, Candy Kitchen, and Macauley's Theatre—all of which the budding sculptor frequented, if not for her own pleasures, for those of her siblings. Enid's taste for such consumables was moderate, while sister Maude loved to eat, make, and share candies of all types, and the third in line, Elsie, had a penchant for theatre and performance.[2]

Enid found her passion in art: she began dabbling in mud as early as age three, attempted form at age four, and took to carving by age twelve. The earliest known letter from Enid's hand—dated June 17, 1878, and written in Louisville—detailed the eight-year-old's affection for her paternal grandmother, Eliza B. Yandell, who had recently moved from Louisville to a family home in Mason Depot, Tennessee. In her letter, Enid explained the issues she faced at home—being an active, affectionate, and communicative young girl who missed her grandmother sorely, especially at bedtime. To remedy this, Enid had her desk brought downstairs to her room so that she could still earn $5 for being quiet after bedtime: "I am working to make five dollars by going to bed at 9 o'clock and if I speak another word after 9 o'clock I will loose [*sic*] it." In her letter, she also mentioned her attendance at nearby St. Paul's Church. Enid's affection for her grandmother continued as a young girl, as documented by her writings, which extolled the immeasurable quality of this love. "I love you more than tongue can tell" was a common exchange between Enid and her grandmother and is especially quaint when seen in a child's handwriting on the letterhead of her father's medical office.[3]

Two years later, Enid tells her grandmother of her visit to Lexington in August 1880, writing how the city was "a large place" where she enjoyed the company of her siblings and the Desha and Breckinridge families. The city was not unfamiliar to the Yandells: Enid's grandfather had taught chemistry at Transylvania Medical College in Lexington before moving west to establish the Louisville Medical Institute. Relatives continued to reside in Lexington and play host to the Louisville clan. In 1883, fourteen-year-old Enid detailed her studio work and the effort she put forth: "I went to a time[d] sketch at the studio on Saturday. I worked very hard and got very tired." This earliest personal account of a studio practice

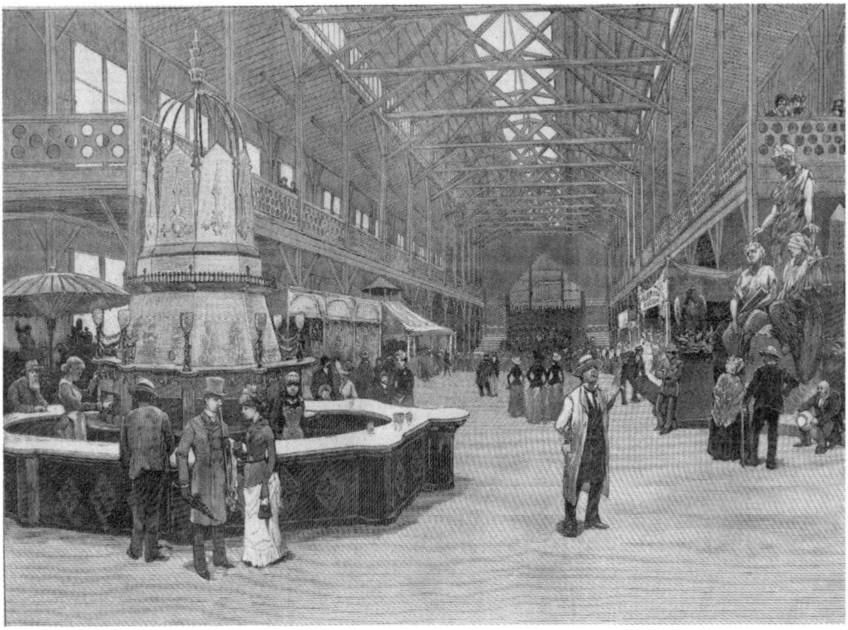

The central nave of the main building of the Louisville Southern Exposition. Visiting the Exposition was among Enid's favorite pastimes as a youngster. In the absence of a city art museum, it would have provided ample opportunity for Enid to see art and to learn from it directly. (Print Collection, PR400.0033. The Filson Historical Society, Louisville, KY.)

evidences her devoted pursuit of art by her early teens, the result of persistence and accomplishment as much as a reward for praises bestowed upon her thus far.[4]

In tandem with Enid's budding art interests and prior to any formal matriculation to learn art, which she undertook in 1887, Enid enjoyed attending public spectacles, such as the Southern Exposition. At this annual event, held from 1883 to 1887 in her home city, Enid learned about art and cultural affairs. The idea for the exposition was tied to an emphasis on central agricultural products, including cotton. By the time the fair was inaugurated, an expanse of forty-five acres, with an adjacent park (referred to as Central Park) covering eighteen acres manicured with forest and flowers, offered several buildings themed according to various exhibits: natural products (including cotton); machinery and implements; manufactured products; transportation; power, via animal, electricity, steam, and wind; and creative endeavors, including literature, music, and art. In the absence of a city art museum, this exposition functioned as a major exhibition venue for the budding artist in her hometown.[5]

Contemporary to the Exposition, the death of Enid's father in March 1884 left Enid's mother, Louise, to care for four young children, the eldest of whom intended to pursue an independent livelihood as a sculptor. Even as Enid's role within the family seemingly increased in importance with her age and as a result of her father's death, her letters to her grandmothers indicate her interest in art and sports rather than familial responsibility. Thus, continuing studio practice in Louisville and attending the Exposition were priorities for her, even if her siblings had to be included as part of the activities.

Enid attended the Exposition as early as 1885. "I am glad you have had so much pleasure attending the Exposition," her grandmother wrote, continuing that she knew Enid would enjoy getting back together with the girls from school. Further encouragement to attend came from Enid's mother. In 1886, while Enid was on a fishing excursion with friends, Louise encouraged Enid to return home for the Exposition. The following year, her mother indicated that a family friend, "Uncle Breck," could acquire tickets for Enid and her sister Maude, even though Enid should take up a season ticket so that she might come and go freely. For Louise, the significance lay in seeing the spectacle, as well as the exhibition space for art. For Enid, interest lay in access to cultural treasures in her hometown—a city that was becoming known for its appreciation of art.[6]

Reflecting on the first Exposition and its related art exhibit, the writer for the *Art Union,* a scholarly publication focused on American art, noted that Enid's hometown was "a city where art appreciation was so clearly indicated . . . [by] the sales of pictures in Louisville last year, [which] resulted in the formation of probably the finest collection of American pictures ever taken out of New York [C]ity." The writer remarked on the impact of the exposition in building the city's art coffers:

> Probably no loan exhibition ever held in this country has had a greater influence than the art exhibition held last year in connection with the Southern Exposition at Louisville, Ky. Nearly a million persons visited the Exposition, and most of them found the Art Department its most attractive feature. Visitors from all por-

> tions of the South, carried home with them new ideas of art, and a new appreciation of the beauties in Art and Nature. The influence of the gallery upon the citizens of Louisville was such, that at the close of the exposition, a popular subscription was raised, and ten thousand dollars worth of pictures were purchased for the nucleus of a permanent public gallery for the city.[7]

Without a doubt, such a display was impressive.

High-quality works were on display in the art gallery at the Exposition in a floor-to-ceiling fashion, like the galleries in larger cities in Europe and America. A number of paintings, some of which were borrowed from local collectors and others secured from artists' studios, contributed to the exhibits. Sculpture took center stage in the form of *Woman Triumphant* (ca. 1877), a depiction of a "sublime, ideal woman" by Kentucky's popular Neoclassical sculptor Joel T. Hart; and Randolph Rogers's *Nydia, the Blind Flower Girl of Pompeii,* which illustrates a young woman's heroic attempt in the wake of the eruption of Mount Vesuvius to lead companions from the destruction of Pompeii. Such contemporary sculpture shared the stage with Neoclassical and copies of ancient sculpture. A number of other sculptures, including those by Antonio Canova, an eighteenth-century Italian Neoclassical sculptor whose work both epitomized the Classical Revival that was praised by art lovers and admired by art students. Drawing attention to likeness over inspiration, copies of famous works, such as the Venus di Medici (on loan from the Polytechnic Society), epitomized the beauty and attraction of classical sculpture with its matte white surface, attention to anatomical detail, and sensual (yet modest) expression. Such signature works, even if copies, were on view along with busts of civic leaders, including veterans. What's more, the works were illuminated with "a large cluster of electric lights" hanging above "several pieces of fine statuary" situated on a raised platform with "broad-leaved tropical plants grouped about them." In short, women were on display through the exhibition of carved, evocative works.[8]

The assemblage made an impression on Enid, prompting her frequent visits to the Exposition. These visits supported her long-standing ambition to create and exhibit her own works of merit, as recounted a few years later. A July 5, 1891, *Louisville Courier-Journal* article traced the highlights of her early training: "There is a legend in the family to the effect that Miss Yandell, when only three years old, presented to her mother a composition representing the temptation of Eve, in which the figures were modeled on a board from the material generally used for mud pies and that she early manifested a predilection for artistic pursuits." Enid cultivated such pursuits through her attendance at the Exposition as well as formalized training in art.

The decision for Enid to undertake serious art study came after her father's death, although the two events should not be considered cause and effect. Rather, her decision to take up art was a long time coming. In fact, any family influence may be attributed to the passing of a torch from mother to daughter. The arts were practiced by young girls of Enid's status, though a woman was not assumed to be a serious practitioner but rather a dabbler in paint—that is, one with only a fancied interest even if skill were present. Enid's sister Maude reported on her own sketching endeavors while Enid was away at school, noting that she had been using a publication she borrowed from the corner candy store to build her skills. Using the images in the journal as a guide, Maude made drawings that she intended to send on to Enid, perhaps to evaluate or to pass along to others. Beyond the tools of her trade, Maude noted the friendship she found among girls of her sort. In a letter to Enid around November 6, 1887, she wrote: "but as I am the youngest 'Studio girl' I get the kisses and pet names. I have taken flowers several times every time I get a kiss—She [the instructor, Miss Radford] says I get splendid effects of light, call[s] me 'Little Turner' . . . Love from all the girls at the Studio is sent to you." Maude also reported her own contributions to civic duty: she made candy and put it up for sale at the Woman's Exchange, a newly formed club (established in 1885) that filled in the liminal spaces between charity and entrepreneurship.[9]

More significantly than Maude's attempts at drawing and confections, however, Enid's mother had at least one professional commission to her credit, copying a portrait of lawyer and politician Robert Crittenden that hung in the home of his widow in Frankfort. Less interested in oil and inks, Enid showed skill in modeling clay (or "mud") at a very early age. She was encouraged by her mother to pursue education and a professional career in art. Yet sculpture was beyond the pale because it required strength, necessitated working with unclean materials, and was simply too masculine a field for young ladies of the nineteenth century.[10]

A second track of familial influence, the dexterity of working with one's hands—requisite for a sculptor's craft—Enid later attributed to her father's surgical skill. A further connection from the technical side may have been to her maternal great-grandfather, Joseph Thorp Elliston, a silversmith of note. Even with the dexterity imparted from father and great-grandfather and the support of her mother and grandmother, however, Enid was seen as liberal in her ideas and in her notion of having a career, particularly one that involved working with her hands. Her uncle, David Yandell, who was a well-known and established physician with ties to Lexington and Louisville, noted that she was the "first woman of the name to make a dollar for herself." And for that he was not pleased.[11]

Art Education in Louisville

Despite such disdain, Enid pursued formal art education in two phases: as a teenager at Hampton College in Louisville, then in Cincinnati in 1887, where she took up more serious study in sculpture and carving. Enid's early education, however, was confined to her home city. Because her skills were extolled at an early age, Enid took art seriously early on. She eked out an existence until matriculating as a teenager to Hampton College in Louisville for further training. Hampton College was a private female academy with fourteen faculty and a student body of approximately 280. The "Ninth Annual Catalogue of the Hampton College" (1886–1887) detailed the school year and faculty. Classes were in session from mid-September to early June. Subjects included math and metaphysics, English literature, physics and chemistry, botany and physiology, history, vocal music, German, French, drawing, and painting.[12]

Miss Bartlett, who taught painting and drawing, "gave a cordial welcome to the thin stream of lecturers who came to us in the early days, and many of them spoke in her large gymnasium. In the studio above it, Miss Bartlett's enthusiasm planted and fostered the first seeds of arts knowledge [in the community] and made them flourish and bear fruit[,] and her pupils have handed on the torch." In addition, the gymnasium served as a venue for philanthropic benefits, thus conjoining two spheres of women's work, dilettante arts and benevolence, while the community of women students navigated the world beyond Louisville, as recounted by notices of women taking excursions as far away as Mammoth Cave.[13]

Hampton served as a boarding and day school for young women; in terms of artistic practice, the college provided an important outlet for women of the city in terms of both education and exhibition. While classes consisted of students from the age of eleven on up, the exhibition opportunities were opened to all current and former students of the school. It was through exhibition that notice was drawn to Enid's work, as told through an announcement that appeared in the *Louisville Times* (1885), which stated that "the wood-carving and modeling in clay of 15-year-old Miss Enid Yandell seems the most advanced of that of all of the pupils" and that "her mechanical skill is equal to her exceptional ability to design artistic figures." The *Louisville Courier-Journal* also took notice of the exhibition and remarked, "Miss Enid Yandell has gone rather further than her fellow-students in the practical application of her knowledge, as she has done some excellent wood-carving and some very good modeling in clay." Praise was given to her abilities to create forms by looking at plaster casts (known as "the antique") and to her own abilities of invention, such as her treatment of ivy leaves, a fish, and a stone wall.[14]

While the intent of the articles was to frame the students' achievements in art as limited, Enid's interest in modeling led to something greater, at least in her own mind. Remarking that the works were appropriate for demonstrations of Miss Bartlett's method, the *Courier-Journal* article noted the limits to ambition: "For while ambition in art is commendable, impatient ambition which o'erleaps itself is the cause of more worthless production than even ignorance itself." Yet it held out promise for the art of the South through exhibitions such as this one: "all these facts are an encouragement to those who hope to see a development of the high arts in the South. There is as much talent and feeling for art here as elsewhere, and it only needs impulse, encouragement and direction."[15]

Enid graduated from Hampton College in 1887, one of a class of 19 students from a total enrollment of primary and preparatory students numbering 230. At Hampton, Enid excelled in acting as well as academics, particularly her performance in *Mlle de la Grandmaison*. Her ambition and focus were noticed widely: "By the time [Enid] graduated from school [she] had become so infatuated with the work that she went to Cincinnati to begin the serious study of sculpture and carving." She was putting aside any other pursuits, like theatre, for art.[16]

Art Education in Cincinnati

Enid's decision to undertake art education in Cincinnati was related to proximity as well as the rising status of the Queen City as an art center. In the early part of the nineteenth century, art education occurred in academies and studios where artists directly supervised their pupils. In 1869, the practice was formalized through the opening of McMicken School of Design, which was transferred in 1884 to the Cincinnati Museum Association; the school later changed names, becoming the Art Academy of Cincinnati in 1887. Based at the museum, this educational model, which extolled the virtues of simultaneously seeing art and creating art, became the model for art instruction in larger cities throughout the United States.[17]

In September 1887 Louise Yandell made an inquiry to the Art Academy of Cincinnati to seek her daughter's admission. Enid matriculated that fall and, through this expansion of her educational opportunities, and poised with her own ambition and love for the subject, positioned herself to gain a range of technical abilities in addition to her already established repertoire. For instance, while Enid evidenced abilities in clay before matriculating, one of her contemporaries contended that only at Cincinnati did she find both opportunities for clay work and respect as an artist, noting that she "discovered the world held the thrilling adventure of modeling in clay." For her part, Enid gained access to an established faculty and an expanded curriculum.[18]

Information on classes and general experience in the studio at Cincinnati may be derived from Academy records, reporting in the newspaper during Enid's first year at the academy, as well as biographical details by Janet Scudder, a classmate of Enid's, whose biography *Modeling My Life* offers a glimpse into the studio. Members of the inaugural class of students, the two young women joined the academy's first season of 400 co-ed students in October 1887 even as finishing touches were still being put on the school building, just north of the museum proper. The *Cincinnati Enquirer* reported on the setting:

> The rooms [were] all large and spacious and beautifully lighted. . . . Adjoining is the library, a room 16 x 22 [feet] containing for the most part works of reference. The next room is devoted to

> the class in wood-carving, and here were massive specimens of doors and tables, articles of virtu[e] and orn[a]ment, the carving of which was both exquisite and artistic. . . . Adjoining is the students' dining-room, with ample culinary attachments. Opposite is Prof. Humphreys' department devoted to decorative art, a large room, 48 by 32 feet, and separated into three divisions by arches.[19]

The article also mentioned the sculpture studio, at 32 by 40 feet, outfitted with casts as well as "a tank for dipping" and making plaster molds. Additional rooms included a lecture room and studios with skylights and blackboards. The third floor contained the "antique room" for storage of casts and space for displaying and copying them. This seemingly static space was accompanied by the life classroom and airy, well-lighted studios. It was as if the structure of the building itself offered a commentary on the hierarchy of design. Drawing from the nude and drawing from the antique—requisite skills for any medium and undertaking at the Academy—were elevated literally and figuratively, with their studio spaces on the third floor. Such an organization, and truly an elevation of particular techniques, stood in contrast to the organization of classes and practice of the regional art colleges, such as Hampton in Louisville, which valued but did not have strict adherence to sequencing of courses and required tenure in a particular discipline. For instance, at the Academy, sculpture students had to enroll in four sequences of drawing in order to understand how to model form.

This hierarchy also bore out in the annual exhibition of student work: the lower floors were reserved for students' work in pen-drawing, watercolor, and decorative design; the second floor contained work of the beginning classes undertaking drawing; and the third floor contained the work of the advanced students and that of the life classes. In addition to the hierarchy, sheer volume played a role in the exhibition and presentation of student work. In June 1889, the final exhibition in which Enid participated, the *Cincinnati Enquirer* noted that the quality was "the best that [Superintendent Thomas Noble had seen] for many years," with 473 drawings and a large number of oil and watercolors on view, alongside 50 sculptures and wood carvings.[20]

Instruction was delivered in a co-educational setting, with drawing as requisite and electives offered in painting, sculpture, and decorative arts, including woodcarving and ceramics. As told through her letters home, Enid participated in the life-drawing classes (drawing from the nude or partially draped figure) as a means of modeling form—converting a three-dimensional object in life into a drawn or painted surface that achieved the appearance of dimensionality. Such manipulation of line and chiaroscuro contributed to Enid's skills as a sculptor—to crafting a form (human, animal, or mythological) in three dimensions. While only a few drawings survive of Enid's practice, a few sketches on scraps of paper and backs of envelopes and annotations on photographs over the entirety of her career offer some clues to her creative process, which took root as a student in Cincinnati.[21]

Enid enrolled in two full years of wood carving and sculpture and one year of drawing, the "Second Grade—Day Class" in drawing and perspective, taught by L. H. Meakin, which focused on detached features of the face, hands, and feet in outline and detached features of the face, hands, and feet shaded before students advanced to the outline drawing of skull, studies of light and shade from masks, and busts in outline. The drawing-course students were given access to a model from which to draw the head for an entire week each month. This was the first opportunity for life drawing afforded Academy students, after which the access and duration of opportunities increased. For instance, students in the third grade were given "life room" (that is, drawing from a model) access three days per week, with an emphasis on anatomical and antique figures. All students had the opportunity to create impromptu sketches from life, using one another as models, in order to practice rapid, freehand drawing.[22]

During 1887 and 1888, Enid also enrolled in the "Fourth Grade—Day Class" and the "Fourth Grade—Night Class" in sculpture taught by Louis Thomas Rebisso (1837–1899), an Italian expatriate who became known for his casts of the "hero on a horse," or monumental statuary of males, in the post–Civil War era. Her undertaking coursework in the fourth grade indicated that Enid had learned the skills offered in the lower-division courses, such as casting from clay in plaster of Paris and creating plaster facsimiles of fruits, ornaments, and casts of the human body (first grade); creating the more advanced architectural ornament and modeling busts and fragments from cast (second grade); and completing anatomical studies, modeling animals and the entire human figure from the antique, both draped and nude. Because she had been enrolled at this level, Enid would have gained access to third-grade opportunities, including drawing the entire figure from life and nude, an opportunity she had never had previously.[23]

Enid also gained access to the encouragement of her teacher. While Enid appears not to have documented Rebisso's personality or teaching demeanor directly, her classmate Janet Scudder offered a sense of his personality and belief in his students. When Janet queried her professor of her ability to "ever be a sculptor" and to become a "real sculptor—a great one" like him, Rebisso "took my hands in his—both his and mine were sticky with clay—and held them while he looked straight into my eyes. 'I'm going to tell you something. You've got it in you—the feeling for clay—the understanding—the—well—whatever you want to call it! One of these days you will be a much greater sculptor than I am. You are going way beyond me.'" Such encouragement laid the foundation for women to believe in their abilities with a medium that was, for many, unfamiliar yet held promise for the future.[24]

Making progress throughout her first year, Enid submitted works to advance to subsequent levels of study. These included a bust of Voltaire modeled from the work of French Enlightenment sculptor Jean Antoine Houdon, whose works exhibited personality, vibrancy, and simplicity as if done from life. During her second year of study (1888–1889), Enid created, of her own design, a four-foot-tall sculpture that represented her interpretation of Shelly's translation of Homer's fable about Mercury (Hermes), messenger of the gods. The story told of the theft of Apollo's cattle and the invention of the lyre, Enid's intention being to offer a figure that was "both strong and graceful."[25]

Wood carving, in particular, was among Enid's interests and pursuits. Her interest coincided with the rise of the carved-furniture movement and Cincinnati's excellence in education in this arena. She undertook carving with British expatriate Benjamin Pitman (Benn Pitman) (1822–1910), who began his tenure as an instructor at the Academy in 1883, just a few years before Enid arrived. From him, Enid learned how to execute designs in small and large scale, from mirror frames and clock cases to furniture.[26]

Coursework in carving began with surface, incised, and low-relief carving (first grade), including forms of leaves, flowers, and all-over decoration, nature and geometric forms, and the use of oils, gum, and resin to protect and beautify the works. Second-grade courses furthered skills in relief and added instruction in lettering for inscriptions and monograms. Adept in these skills, Enid enrolled in the third-grade class in wood carving taught by Benn Pitman, from whom she learned higher relief. Pitman's teaching extolled the virtues of nature as a motif, and Enid, along with the many women enrolled alongside her, undertook carving based upon nature, as well as geometric detailing. In addition, Enid attended weekly lectures on the historical development of decoration, cultural motifs, and the application of these to carving.[27]

As an instructor, Pitman advocated for the place of such decorative arts in daily life, thus advancing the ambition of his student artists to seek gainful employment. Pointing to Cincinnati's annual Industrial and Art Exposition, where his wife and daughter first exhibited carved furniture work, as the origins of the academy, he noted that two aims of the academy were to develop and disseminate ideas of American decorative art and to "widen the scope of woman's work, giving interesting and useful occupation to girls during the period intervening between leaving school and marriage." He hoped his students would carry their work further by becoming "teachers, and disseminat[ing] the theories and handicraft acquired in the school."[28]

Pitman used the work of his students as illustrations for a publication heralding decorative arts in support of the Cotton States International Exposition held in 1895 in Atlanta. Pitman outlined the forms of decoration: "Decoration, to the cultured mind, must have a meaning, illustrative or symbolic; it must have pleasing or historical associations, and must possess that beauty which is never separated from truth of form." For him, decoration had purpose. Just as Pitman instructed his students to find that purpose and realize it, the public should desire to include decoration as part of their everyday lives. Recognizing that design had changed and, in his opinion, evolved over time, Pitman commanded his students to "set good examples before the people, that shall interest and improve the public taste, and so raise the national standard, that worthless and ignoble art shall be recognized and despised."[29]

Given her work during this period and immediately following, Enid may have dabbled in the fourth-grade lessons that focused on the carved furniture elements by which Cincinnati had built its reputation—that is, mantles and furniture of original execution. Toward the end of her coursework or perhaps in 1890, she designed and executed a fifteen-foot-long carved desk with an Italianate motif for a Louisville business office. An undated clipping (ca.1889–1890) described the item:

> Decidedly the most elaborate piece of furniture in Louisville is a fifteen-foot desk just completed by Miss Enid Yandell for the office of Barbee & Castleman. The desk is in the style of the Italian Renaissance. Nine carved panels and all the other ornamentations are in adapted forms of the Acanthus leaf—the whole the result of three months' labor. The desk is not yet mounted and will not be on exhibit before the fifteenth of this month; but I am told by some of Miss Yandell's friends that this is her happiest work, and certainly the most laborious that she has yet undertaken.[30]

Ceramics was also offered at the Academy; such courses would have come in handy for Enid's pursuits as a sculptor, given the need to create three-dimensional forms in a variety of media as preparation for creating sculptures in a finished medium. Models of such works are referred to as *maquettes*. In other words, Enid would have benefited from familiarity with clay and ceramic glaze and coloring, undertaking preparatory works in clay (a softer medium), then translating the form into plaster (which could be worked additively and/or subtractively as it was molded and/or chiseled) before finalizing the work in stone or metal, usually marble or bronze. Moreover, the manner in which ceramics were hardened, whether by air or through heat, simulated sculptural practices in plaster, an area in which Enid worked throughout her entire career as a medium of preparation as well as finished compositions.

In addition to developing Enid as an artist in terms of skill and practice, Cincinnati afforded her the opportunity to engage with other artists. She worked alongside her fellow art students and exhibited her work with theirs in the students' annual exhibition, thereby becoming part of a community of artists who exhibited their work to an increasingly interested public. Attending the academy in Cincinnati also afforded Enid ample opportunity to view works of art firsthand. Students had "privileges of the museum," allowing them entrance to the exhibition galleries by showing proof of enrollment. Students were allowed to copy paintings, drawings, and other objects in the museum; they could even request that an attendant change the position of an object they were copying (a luxury by

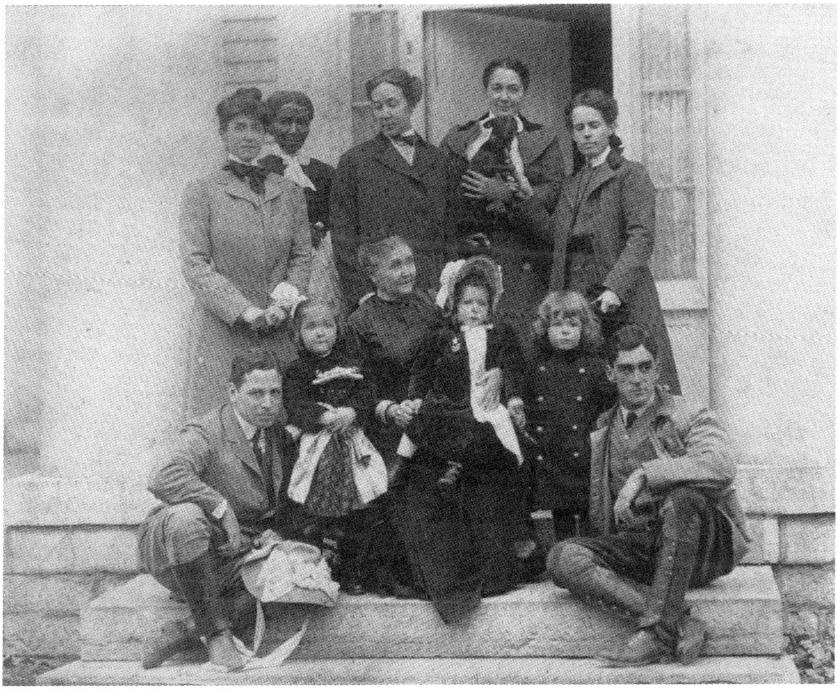

Members of the Yandell family gather around Mrs. Yandell (seated, center). Enid stands in the doorway. Her sister-in-law, Elizabeth Hosford Yandell, stands to the far right. In front of Elizabeth are two of her children, Hope Gay Yandell (seated) and Lunsford Pitts Yandell IV, who touches his father's shoulder. Enid's sister, Elsie, stands on the far left. Sitting on the step is Elsie's husband, Donn Barber, and between them is one of their children. (Enid Bland Yandell Photograph Collection, 987PC52X.047, Box 7. The Filson Historical Society, Louisville, KY.)

any educational standard!). In addition, she was exposed to works of art that had garnered attention across the United States. For instance, upon Enid's arrival in Cincinnati, Paul Philippoteaux's cyclorama, a panoramic painting of multidimensional illusion, of the battlefield at Gettysburg was on view in the city "after four years of continued success, [with] no less than 1,000 persons attend[ing] daily." The version in Cincinnati was the third iteration of this highly successful work, which showed the Confederate attack on the Union forces on July 3, 1863—an event that took place shortly before Enid's birth, and perhaps one of particular interest in her Confederate household, given her father's role as a surgeon in the Southern army.[31]

Enid's interest, ambition, and success at higher education was recognized within the family, beyond her mother. On January 1, 1888, Enid's cousin Farrell wrote from the family estate at Burlington, near Nashville, that he wanted to see Enid, as he had "been waiting for a long time to see a live,-sure-enough-non-Egy[p]tianed sculptor(ess I suppose)." The letter mentioned family matters and a desire to see his cousin. Such heartfelt sentiment for the family to come together may be at odds with Enid's self-identification as a sculptor who needed to separate from the family for work. Enid was coming into her own.[32]

That same year, Enid's sister Maude also identified her as a sculptor: "My first book shall be dedicated to my beloved sister the sculptor of unrivaled genius." Her brother, Lunsford, went so far as to compare Enid with a sculpture, and in fact, one that she had created, the Minerva (Athena) for the Centennial Exposition in Nashville. Lunnie wrote, "As for our young Minerva, Enid[,] she is a chrysalis up to this writing so far as my (—blind) eyes can see. . . . Enid is a treasure." Enid's maternal grandmother supported Enid's efforts as well, through encouragement and funding, relaying a dream in a letter of January 24, 1888: "Your mother's imagination readily anticipated the time when you would have a studio on 4th Avenue, you standing in the centre, surrounded by works of art the productions of your own brain &c&c. With the hope that all these hopes may be realized, I send you this $5.00 bill Your affectionate Ma." Later, "Ma" recalled Enid's earliest works in clay: "I need not tell you with how much interest I have followed you in your work, ever since you made 'Eve and the serpent' in mud, when you were four years old."[33]

While at school, Enid stayed at Miss Foster's boardinghouse, a living situation that was adequate, although certainly not up to her mother's standards. Such judgment may be gleaned from letters Enid wrote to her mother, as well as reports from friends who traveled north and relayed accounts to Enid's mother and grandmother. Louise pored over every detail as a means of affirming her daughter's decision to move and take up education in (eventual) pursuit of a career. Ultimately, Enid's move away from the family caused anxiety in her mother.[34]

The week following Enid's eighteenth birthday, which she presumably spent amid her new artist community, Louise forecast the responsibility Enid must assume with the departure from her family and pursuit of her own life and career. Enid's mother wrote, "You were never before thrown on your own responsibility to determine important questions on your own judgment. . . . my confidence in you is supreme—but it has so long been my pleasure to determine for you, that I can't help feeling as if I had sent [?] you out in the world alone. That you will always act as is becoming your father's daughter I am sure—& your love for me will always guard you against doing any wrong."[35] The household in Louisville was replaced by a community of boarders at Miss Foster's, friends with whom Enid could attend evening class and move about the city outside of class.[36]

In October 1887, Louise wrote to Enid asking for the details of her daughter's room so that she could imagine her (actually, "picture" her) as "[she] sit[s] in there at work." Enid and her mother corresponded over details of Enid's setup; for instance, Louise remarked that she could not find the red bedspread that Enid had requested and hoped that her daughter's other items sent from home would suffice. Enid was, for the most part, on her own.[37]

Over the course of Enid's first year at Cincinnati, the family's pride grew; they conceived of Enid's talent as worthy of attention at home. Even though she was an afternoon's journey away, living under another's roof, and pursuing her own career, Enid was warned against distractions. Louise cautioned her against taking up too many pursuits outside of art: "I think you had best begin your German & see how much leisure time you will have before you start with Guitar lessons. . . . Your Art work is most important just now—& you must save time enough for plenty of out of doors exercise." In a letter of February 21, 1888, Enid's sister Maude informed her that their mother was enthusiastic about redoing the studio (at home) and that Maude herself hoped to come out in the world as someone of merit, "with a boom louder than yours . . . Perhaps my debut shall be as a Poet, or a Psychologist, a Metaphysical or some thing of the kind."[38]

In October 1888 Louise noted: "It is very important to my happiness that you be comfortable and satisfied. Nothing but the fact that you are so reconciles me to you being away from me. If it be necessary to pay your model 5.00 a week, I will manage to do it. I am determined that you shall have every advantage in your art study whatever the sacrifice may be to me—and this I can easily arrange." After learning from Enid that her clothing was "uncomfortably tight" (perhaps due to her building muscle as a result of continuous practice at the Academy, or as a result of trying to work in clothing not suited for an all-day studio affair), Louise recommended that Enid purchase a skirt to work in and offered to mend clothes that had ripped as a result of their constricting seams. Increasingly over the course of her career, Enid avoided clothing that contained constricting darts, buttons, and seams in favor of cuts and closures that enabled a full range of movement.[39]

Such advantages that Enid's mother wanted for her daughter extended beyond payments for tuition, additional fees, acquisition of materials, and letters of encouragement. Louise supported Enid's desire to seek further education despite the burden the family bore for having to extend financial, and even emotional, assistance to Enid at a distance. Her mother wrote, "I am sorry you are having such a time with your model—I imagined there was a little tone of sadness in your letter. You must be bright for the only thing which reconciles me to being separated from you is the fact that you are happy & doing what you wish to do." But even happiness in one's work had its constraints, as Enid's mother warned her about "manish" tendencies and cautioned against some of the behaviors that had been reported to Louise in Louisville by Enid's grandmother in Nashville.[40]

Even with all of the inspiration from the galleries and time spent drawing from plaster casts and figures in class, Enid was in search of a model. As her grandmother recounted in a letter to Enid's mother, a friend of theirs "says she saw Enid in Cin[cinnati] riding in a buggy, with a pistol in her lap, looking for a 'Model.' Joe says she supposes she intended to shoot him, if he resisted." Thus, in this note to Enid, Louise reminded her not to "carry [her] pistol *conspicuous* if I were you. It does not look *lady like*. Remember to guard yourself against your masculine tendencies—you know I do not admire manish women in the least—nothing is so fascinating in a woman as femininity." Such passages, which occur within the context of reporting the daily and weekly events within and outside of the family circles, speak to the limitations placed upon women socially and culturally, but also suggest the restraints placed upon them in educational endeavors. Enid's search for a model, whether facetious or not, reflected her desire to secure a male model in order to create from a live model rather than the plaster casts that Enid and her colleagues had been using in the academy.[41]

Eventually, Enid's practice shifted again. She grew to favor modeling her own forms, an additive method, over carving, a subtractive one.

She stated this preference for the medium as well as the method: "I do a great many things for fun, but I devote myself to one thing in earnest. I paint, for instance, for amusement. I love to dabble with a brush in colors. But when I settle down to work, I always turn to clay." Skills of clay were transferable to plaster and staff—an inexpensive composite material made with concrete, plaster, and hemp or other readily available organic filler that would be used to construct large-scale works for temporary exhibition. Much later, Enid embraced bronze and other cast metals.[42]

Enid's concerted effort in sculpture over all other art forms was an investment that paid off through tenacious effort. She noted, "I have always stuck to one thing patiently and tirelessly and I believe that is one reason for my success. If you dissipate your talents, you will succeed in nothing." Indeed, press coverage of Enid's more formal work began in 1889, with mention of her work in a store-front window:

> There is in Escott's window a remarkable work of art from the hand of a daughter of Kentucky, Miss Enid Yandell; and, to judge from her achievements thus far, one with a brilliant future. This work is a high relief head in bronzed plaster, the result of three hours' work, in which the young artist has portrayed the mythological Phaeton, the child of Phoebus, as he is whirling through space behind the fiery chargers that draw the chariot of the Sun. As almost all elegant literature is permeated with mythology, and, as art, from the earliest ages, has rendered in finest form the fables of the ancients and wrought into tangible realities the myths of olden times, Miss Yandell has sought a subject in this infinite field of the imagination.

The article did not treat the work as an object of humility, but instead attributed boldness and confidence to it. The review offered an overview of the appearance of the work to guide the viewer and closed with a commentary on Enid's association with the Art Academy: "The mind was bright and the fingers deft and rapid that, within the appointed time (or any time), could give so striking a suggestion. It is a rare subject and wonderfully well treated. Miss Yandell stands second to none in the Cincinnati Art School, where she is studying."[43]

Throughout her education, Enid proved to be a focused and ambitious student, covering a four-year program in two, thereby completing her time at the Academy within the years 1887 through 1889. Thus, Enid's pursuit of art training was a six-year journey that began in Louisville and shifted to Cincinnati before moving abroad, when Enid sail for Europe with her mother and two sisters, Maude and Elsie, as a form of informal education. Over this period, then, Enid's education was cultivated through informal and formal means: her time at Hampton College and the Art Academy was supplemented by two phases of observation, learning, and engaging with art (at the Southern Exposition and abroad), which overcame the constraints of her limited firsthand access to art while growing up.[44]

Freedom of Travel

In June 1889, following the completion of her academic studies in Cincinnati, Enid set sail on an adventure that was part and parcel of the artist's experience: to see works of art firsthand. Her journey and self-study with her sisters and mother were also part of a growing interest in European travel by Americans, who were eager to see Paris following its successful world's fairs in 1867 and 1878, after which other expositions had been modeled, in the United States. Having taken in the Louisville's Southern Exposition on several occasions, Enid was ready to experience her first international exposition, the Exposition Universelle in Paris in 1889.[45]

For many, Paris meant fashion, jewelry, decorative arts and interior design, and luxury. Through an artist's eyes, the city promised artistic fulfillment. In Paris, access to art education and professional opportunities, while still limited for women, were vastly ahead of what female artists of the previous generation experienced. In addition to the abundance of collections, with originals as well as copies to foster direct observation—which Enid had experienced on a far smaller scale in Louisville at the Exposition and when she was at school—Paris offered ease of access to models, artists to help with production and acquisition of materials, and both peers and mentors in sculpture. Enid may also have viewed this experience as a calling card for future work, namely the Chicago World's Fair.[46]

Travel gave Enid freedom from the constraints of home, including the restrictive norms of polite society amid the land of cider and cigars. In Paris, life was comfortable, even familiar, rather than shocking and fascinating, as it was seen to be in Louisville or Cincinnati or her grandmother's home in Nashville—all places of her youth. Paris and its environs became home to Enid on and off from 1889 through 1933, the year before her death.

Spectacle: Satellites of Mercury

Following her pursuit of art education and the reward of travel, Enid engaged in a spectacle of a different sort, through her reign as Queen of the Satellites of Mercury, an unusual and short-lived social event and annual celebration in Louisville that began in 1888 and ran each fall for five years as the final event of the month-long Industrial Jubilee Celebration (also known as the Fall Commercial Celebration). Serving in some ways as a continuation of the Southern Exposition, the festival was intended to promote Louisville's growing material prosperity. Celebrations of this sort were established to bring business to the city after the depression arising from the destruction brought on by a tornado in 1890, although they lost support by the time of the financial panic of 1893. Even so, during its heyday, who better to rule over the festival than Mercury, the Roman mythological god of commerce. The "Satellites" were Louisville businessmen, whose identities were kept secret, as were the parade routes.[47]

The celebration schedule varied from year to year. In 1888, an elaborate barge, featuring Mercury on a steamboat, was accompanied by a court and the Satellites. The following evening, a torchlight parade with bands, floats, and horses was followed by a ball at the Galt House, a hotel and hall that was an anchor of Louisville social life. From 1889 to 1892, the carnival and ball grew more elaborate, including an annual theme. In 1890, for example, the theme was to be Ben-Hur, a fictional character from contemporary literature.[48]

While there is no evidence to suggest that Enid ever took an interest in this annual pageant, the year 1890 is of particular mention: that was the year she was named Queen of the Satellites.

As part of the festivities, the identity of the Queen was kept secret from the city's residents, although hints were given out in the days leading up to the pageant. Reports acknowledged the status of the mystery woman and her cosmopolitan nature:

> The Queen of the Carnival has been selected by the King. Who she is remains quite as much a mystery as does the identity of his majesty. Of course there will be a great deal of speculation as to the name of the lady thus honored, but nothing can be told concerning it, though, if any one wants to take a pointer, it can be obtained in a general way from the fact that her Majesty is a lady who, though connected with a prominent family, has not been much known in what is called society. She is *wealthy, educated, traveled and beautiful.* A goodly portion of her time has been spent abroad, and it is principally for this reason that she has not been prominent in social events in this city.[49]

Indeed, Enid's education had taken her away from her native city—first to Cincinnati and then abroad with her mother and sisters. Her absence from Louisville for long spells did not deter her city's residents from electing her Queen. Perhaps, in fact, Enid's travel and education fostered her receipt of this honor.

Or perhaps a contributing factor for her nomination was tied to her beauty and attractiveness. Enid's long brown hair, which she swept back or in a bun with a part down the middle, countered her creamy complexion and almond eyes. She was of medium build and had gained muscle not only from her work in the studio, but also from her love of sport, including tennis. In addition, she was a skilled horsewoman. While none of these activities are mentioned in contemporaneous accounts, newspapers did comment upon the appearance of the nominees. The *Twice-a-Week Messenger* of Owensboro compared the beauty of candidates and printed possible outcomes from *The Critic* and *Truth. The Critic* predicted that Miss Mattie Thompson would take the crown, as she was famous "not only in Kentucky, but all over the East for her beauty." Such a call opposed the *Truth's* declaration "with equal positivety [*sic*] that Miss Enid Yandell, of Louisville, will have that honor."[50]

By the time the winner for 1890 was announced, it was the day of the pageant of Mercury and His Satellites, a street theatre production with floats to illustrate Lew Wallace's story of Ben-Hur. That evening, the newly named Queen joined the parade. Candelabra illuminated the floats as they began the route from Third and Oak Streets at 7:30 p.m. with the destination of Broadway. Marching ahead of and between the floats

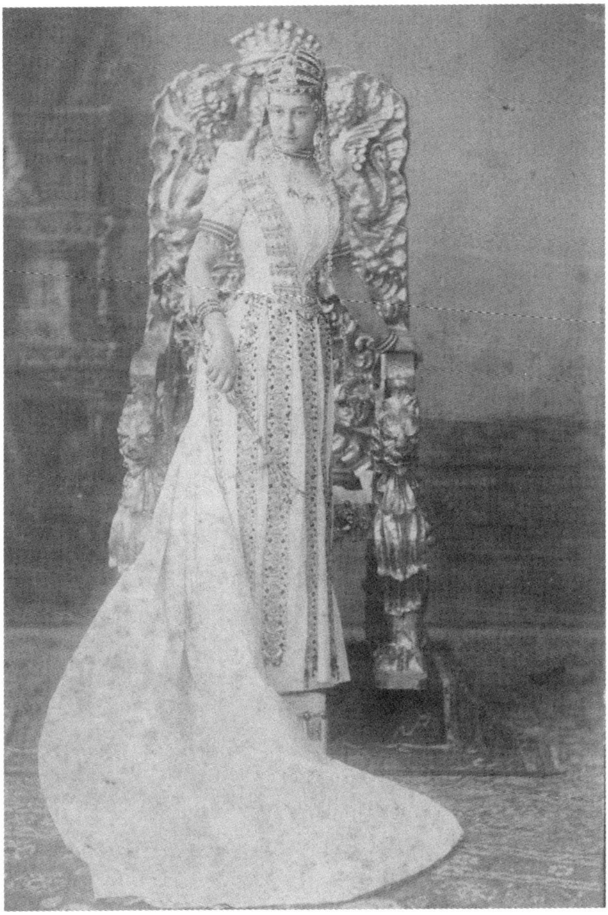

Upon returning from school and after her travels abroad, Enid engaged in a spectacle of a different sort, through her reign as Queen of the Satellites of Mercury in 1890. (Enid Bland Yandell Photograph Collection, 987PC52X.038, Box 1, Folder 7. The Filson Historical Society, Louisville, KY.)

were the Satellites (the Maids who supported the Queen and King), all of whom were dressed in royal costume. The floats were followed by a band and drum corps. Enid rode on the first float with the King, both of whom were mounted on a water lily and illuminated by incandescent electric lights, which "shed green rays upon the occupants, and gave the foliage something of the look of natural." Nineteen floats with people, plants, and animals followed. Costumes and decorations reflected the intersection of Egyptian, Greek, and Roman contexts for this street performance, which drew upon Biblical references, including one of the Magi (an Egyptian, Balthasar), enslaved Egyptians, a childhood friend of Ben-Hur who was a Roman tax collector, and Greek pirate ships as well as Roman vessels in the Aegean. Enid's costume included an elaborately encrusted staff; jewel-encrusted bracelets, neckband, and headwear; and a gown, also elaborately embroidered. Pleats and cinching emphasized Enid's curves in a way that no sculptor's garb—not even the ill-fitting garments she brought from to the Academy as a student—could.[51]

Clearly, though she was not quite twenty-one years old, Enid was attracting attention as a young woman of Louisville. Her reign as Queen brought attention despite her interest in, and pursuit of, art as a career. Her position within the social milieu would change as she began to assert her occupational identity as a sculptor. Being wealthy, educated, traveled, and beautiful were qualities that were essential to her climb up the social ladder, while being educated, traveled, skilled, and tenacious were requisite for her undertaking serious study in sculpture and establishing a career of her own.

Beyond the Academy

Enid's commitment as a sculptor and promise for success came on the heels of her degree from Cincinnati in 1889 and her notoriety as a pageant queen the following year. Determined to take up her own practice and get her name out to clients, she sent out invitations on July 3, 1891, to view her work at her newly established Louisville studio. The family's big, comfortable Victorian house on Broadway served as her home, studio, and exhibit venue at least during that year. Notice appeared in the paper affirming the space, Enid's talent, a queue of work to produce, and her potential for fame:

> Mrs. Lunsford Yandell has fitted up a handsome studio of three rooms adjoining her residence on Broadway, for her daughter Enid, who has developed such remarkable talent as a sculptress. Miss Yandell has several commissions to execute. She is especially endowed as an artist, and, with her advantages and careful mental

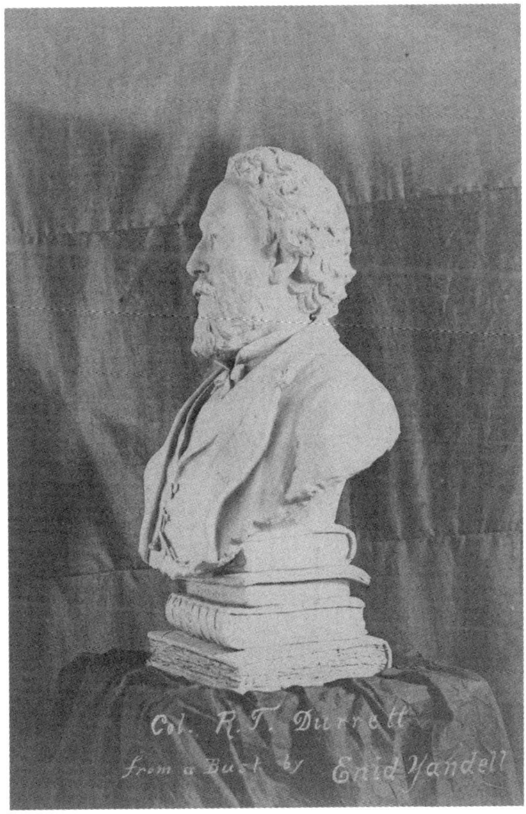

Enid captured Colonel Reuben Durrett's physical appearance, at nearly seventy, in 1891. Books serve as a fitting pedestal for this image of the historian and bibliophile. This plaster bust is now in the collection of The Filson Historical Society. (Enid Bland Yandell Photograph Collection, 987PC52X.253, Box 2, Folder 26. The Filson Historical Society, Louisville, KY.)

> training, it will not surprise me to see her win exceptional fame in the line of work she has chosen.[52]

With such resources at her disposal, Enid brandished business cards and offered viewing hours for her work. Her efforts led to increasing interest in her abilities and creative output.

One of Enid's earliest commissions was on view at her studio display: a bust of Colonel Reuben Durrett, "which faithfully portrays the massive head and broad, strong brow of that scholarly gentleman. The work is accurately executed and the features wonderfully portrayed." Enid captured Durrett's physical appearance at nearly seventy years old, with wavy hair and a neatly trimmed beard, dressed in a three-piece suit of which the top of the jacket and single-breasted vest are visible, along with a tie. Enid attended to Durrett's interests as well, depicting his pocket watch chain, complete with T-bar and double chain—one for the watch in his left pocket and the other to hold his cigar cutter, indicative of her subject's penchant for cigars. Five somewhat precariously stacked books form a pedestal, the literal foundation of Durrett's work as historian and bibliophile. The volumes Enid chose to depict included histories of Great Britain, the United States, and Kentucky, as well as local history: Durrett's sketch of John Filson and *Filson's History,* the first publication of the Filson Club, the historical association over which Durrett presided. Collectively, the volumes reference Durrett's impressive library, which was estimated to total some 50,000 items, and for which at the time the only catalogue was "the owner's memory."[53]

Enid's attention to detail in portraiture and veristic handling of form gave her works a certain authority. An article appearing in the *Courier-Journal* about the exhibition at Enid's Louisville studio noted what was on view: the Durrett, a statue of Hermes, a sketch for a bust of George Rogers Clark, and a bust of Mrs. Locke (Nannie Sherley), a medallion of Lillian Langham, and a sculpted gargoyle. The breadth and depth of Enid's body of work—combining veracity and truthfulness of depiction alongside the fantastic and invention—bore witness to her experience, accomplishments, and continued pursuits. The reporter noted, "One can not talk with Miss Yandell five minutes without seeing that her art is a serious business with her, and that she does not shrink from the labor that is essential to the satisfactory working out of even the swiftest inspirations. It is this earnestness more than the accomplished work, though this is by no means inconsiderable, that gives promise of future achievement."[54]

Beyond portraiture (the bust of Durrett) and mythological subjects (such as her Hermes of 1889), Enid took up architectural decoration in the early part of the 1890s. She developed ornamentation for the new Louisville Trust Building in 1891. Located several blocks from Enid's studio in the family home on Broadway between Third and Fourth Streets, the Trust building was designed by Louisville architects Mason Maury and William J. Dodd in a style with which Enid would have been familiar—the "Chicago School" of architecture, which she would have seen on her visit to the city in 1886 and with which she would have grown more accustomed when she took up work there later in 1891. The architectural plan for Louisville Trust took cues from the Chicago School, in particular the work of Louis Sullivan, who espoused the relevance of ornamentation in metal and stone as part of the character of modern, high-rise buildings.[55]

On the façade of Louisville Trust, ornamentation abounds. A first story of polished and pen-hammered granite develops a program of repetition and contrast: two low arches are flanked by square piers and are also separated from each other by two acanthus-topped capitals. Each level introduces another treatment, with round arches, radiating voussoirs, bays, and alternating courses of thick and thin blocks. It is unclear just what elements Enid had a role in designing and implementing. Nonetheless, the opportunity to collaborate with two of Louisville's most talented architects afforded her the ability to make connections with their circles. She remained in contact with both Maury and Dodd and would collaborate with Dodd a few years later for a monumental commission in Louisville in 1894.[56]

Clearly, by the early 1890s Enid had attracted attention through exhibition of her work in formal and informal settings—from a storefront and her Louisville studio to the Cincinnati Museum—while also enriching the work of others, as in her ornamentation work on the Louisville Trust building.[57]

Travel and Companionship

When traveling further afield, or even between Louisville and Cincinnati, Enid felt constrained in public; in private, and in particular in nature, she reveled in restorative solitude. For instance, she remarked upon the horror of the locals in northern Kentucky when she was seen ordering alcohol at a local establishment. It wasn't the fact that she was drinking alcohol that was alarming to the locals, but rather that she had the audacity to order it herself—among women friends, and not in the company of a man.[58]

Away from the city, Enid found peace in the country. One such place was the Dinsmore Homestead in Boone County. Here Enid enjoyed a place of education and retreat, as well as friendship. While visiting the matriarch, Julia Stockton Dinsmore (1833–1926), a well-educated friend of the Yandell family, Enid felt as though she were staying with family. In fact, the earliest mention of Enid's stays there appears to have been 1888, while she was making frequent trips to and from the Art Academy in Cincinnati, which she attended from 1887 to 1889. At Dinsmore, Enid found the pleasures of home without trekking all the way to Louisville. In particular, she remarked upon the food, with

> fried chicken heaped on a plate, brown and crisp, like "fore the war"—potatoes boiled and baked, ham and eggs, snap beans and bacon, peas . . . cabbage and ochre [okra], and such tomatoes and cucumbers with a dash of Corn pudding and corn bread, sweet milk and butter milk right on the table in great crocks. The vegetables fresh from the garden, "the chickens from the coop"; and for desert, a blackberry pie;—he who has not eaten a Boone blackberry pie, has not lived. Thus it is every day in Kentucky.[59]

In addition to the feast of food, a visual feast lay in store upon visiting Dinsmore, where a journey "across the fields, through woods, over streams, and after a two-mile walk" led to a view of nature like no other. "The sun was setting, and the sky picture of God only added to the beauty of his footstool, the earth. Before us lay the Ohio winding away east and west, a golden serpent. Here and there a boat sent a long black line of smoke athwart the sky—or with its tall smoke stacks, and puff-puff of its engines, made life in the country real." It was here that Enid could retreat, and she called upon the power of this place in contrast to her busy life in Cincinnati as an art student: "All mankind would be benefited, if once a year every one would live for awhile thus naturally, and think of nature and nature's God. The life of cities is feverish and unnatural, and dulls all our finer senses and love of nature."[60]

Visits to Dinsmore Homestead were not the only connection with Julia Dinsmore that Enid held. Over this time and their long friendship, Enid observed how Julia managed her affairs and presumably took cues from her, as evidenced by Enid's own scrupulous business practices later in life. The association between Enid and Julia may have come through family ties, as Enid's mother was friends with the Dinsmores. In fact, Louise is probably the person who gave Alice L. Williams's edited volume of poetry, *Treasures New and Old,* to Julia in 1884, the year that the volume was published and subsequently featured in the World's Fair at New Orleans. The friendship between Enid and Julia Dinsmore lasted from 1888 through 1920, with the two women sometimes traveling together.

One particular visit to Dinsmore, however, seems to have made quite an impact on Enid; it led to her first foray in writing about her experiences. In a short story, "A Corner in Kentucky," Enid recalls an invitation to visit "Boone," the name by which some referred to Dinsmore, to "come and spend two weeks with us" in July of an unspecified year. Although the piece is undated, with some assigning a date of around 1890, given that the text mentions Dinsmore as being twenty-five miles from where the author begins her story, it seems the piece was more likely written in the period 1887–1889, while Enid was in school in Cincinnati, most likely the summer of 1888, which may have been the time of Enid's first visit to Dinsmore.[61]

Throughout her story, Enid refers to details that resembled Dinsmore, but might also have been applied to any number of other estates in the area. For instance, her description of "an old-fashioned Kentucky house, square and roomy, built of logs covered with clap-boards; painted white, with green shutters" matched the 1842 timber-frame, Greek-revival dwelling built on a rectangular center-passage, and a "big hall ran through the middle, adorned with deer heads, and foxes' pads and brushes, and here and there the picture of a favorite hound or horse." Adventures during the visit included a game of tennis ("we had the only tennis court for a circuit of twenty miles") and opportunities to view the Ohio River from a river bank two miles away. In short, the country, specifically Dinsmore, was a place where Enid felt at home, where she felt comfortable enough to quench her thirst with beer one evening in public.[62]

The friendship between Julia Dinsmore and Enid expanded geographically when Julia traveled to Cincinnati in support of Enid's career. For instance, in October 1889 Julia visited "the art museum"—meaning the exhibition featuring Enid's *Hermes,* a product of her education at the Academy, on view at the Cincinnati Art Museum. The work is meticulously described in an article from the *Louisville Courier-Journal,* calling the sculpture "an original composition" representing "Hermes as he strikes the first perfect chord on his lyre, which he has made of a turtle shell and the horns of a goat." The article also points toward Enid's future study in Europe as well as the future life of this work, destined for near impermanence by being cast in clay "on Monday morning."[63]

Enid and Julia traveled together throughout the region and further afield in Kentucky. For instance, in September 1890 Julia went to Mammoth Cave and Cave City as part of a visit to other parts of the state before visiting with Enid. Julia wrote that "Enid met us and took us to lunch," thus suggesting that Enid was an independent woman of means who could afford pleasures for her friends. The two exchanged gifts of books, as noted in correspondence and extant volumes containing inscriptions from Enid, including a book that Enid gave Julia for Christmas in 1890. The following year, on her way to her first professional position in Chicago in 1891, Enid passed through Burlington. The two women were lifelong friends, as indicated by correspondence and documentation in Julia's diary.[64]

For fifty-four years, Julia kept a diary that documented the comings and goings of visitors and daily activity on the homestead. For instance, in May 1888, she mentioned Enid and a companion named Amy Campbell, who was traveling with Enid to Cincinnati. "Amy Campbell and Miss Enid Yandell of Louisville" visited, Julia noted in her diary, thus indicating familiarity with Campbell and an introduction to Enid. Julia's diary contained several such notations, even some chronicling less fortunate occurrences, such as a coach accident in 1897 that led to charges being made against Enid and Amy, as well as other friends in their circle. Enid, Julia, and Amy remained friends through at least 1920, when Julia sat for a portrait in New York City in the company of Amy.[65]

Like her friends Julia Dinsmore and Amy Campbell, from 1891 on Enid seemed to live the life of a "bachelor maid"—a term used in the late nineteenth and early twentieth century for a single woman who operated independently of men and managed her own business affairs. The term was officially applied to Enid in 1949, fifteen years after her death, in an article written by Louisville writer Melville O. Briney, who reflected that Enid's status as an unmarried working woman in the field of sculpture would have made the epithet apparent to her contemporaries once she left Louisville to take up artistic practice full-time.[66]

But hers was not a lonely road. At each of her educational endeavors prior to Paris (Hampton College and the Art Academy), Enid surrounded herself with female companions. After traveling to Paris with her mother and sisters in 1889, Enid returned to the United States to open her studio in Louisville. In 1891, she left for Chicago, where she spent two years before establishing a studio in New York and securing passage to Paris in 1894 with her sister Elsie and other companions. While in Paris, Enid

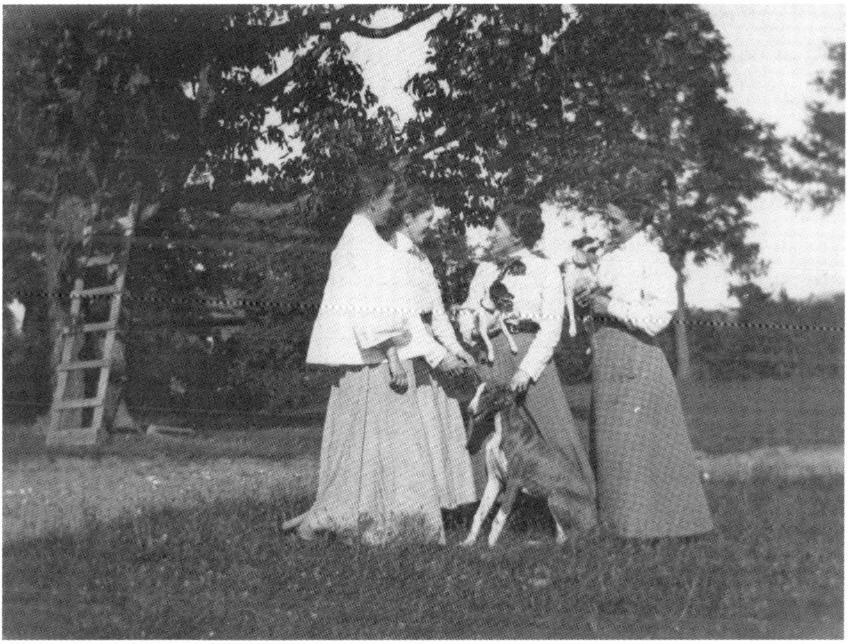

Enid (on the far right holding dog) is joined by Geysa de Braunecker (middle) and two unidentified women (at left) in this undated photo. Enid enjoyed traveling, female companionship, and visits to the country, even as she managed a studio practice in large cities following her tenure at the Chicago's World's Fair in 1891–1893. (Enid Bland Yandell Photograph Collection, 987PC52X.021, Box 1, Folder 3. The Filson Historical Society, Louisville, KY.)

befriended artists and performers of varying degrees of fame, paying heed to her interests in art, music, and theatre as well as the outdoors.[67]

One of Enid's female acquaintances in Paris, a Hungarian expatriate singer and musician who performed in Paris named Baroness Geysa Hortense de Braunecker (1869–1960), became Enid's longtime companion. The two roomed together in Paris from about 1895 through 1903, traveled to and from the United States on several occasions over these years, and were engaged in World War I relief efforts. Their relationship was long, compassionate, and relevant as a point of reference for understanding Enid's social circle and how she adapted to living on two continents and managing studios in Louisville (later New York) as well as in Paris.[68]

Letters from Geysa, or those that reference her, are numerous in the extant correspondence. For instance, a telegram from Geysa to Enid in January 1896 affirms support for Enid ("My Tender Thoughts Brace Up Dearest Shall Write—Geysa"). Later that year, Geysa wrote, "God bless you my own love! I hold you closely in my arms!" Geysa also served as an intermediary with Louise, Enid's mother, reporting on their goings on in Paris. Enid's mother also wrote to her daughter about Geysa: "My Darling Enid—I had a sweet letter from dear Geysa written on Thursday last telling of your search for a Studio—I hope you will before this reaches you have found what you want." In the same letter, Louise remembers the pair's visit home, noting, "Yours & Geysa's visit seems almost like a dream—Love & kisses to Geysa—& tell her to kiss you for me."[69]

The language used in these letters indicates the strength of the bonds between women at the time, for the female world was replete with varied and highly structured relationships. In the case of Enid and Geysa, the companionship endured, presumably until the end of Enid's life, in the form of art, travel, and friendship. In 1901, Enid exhibited a bust of Geysa at the World's Fair in Buffalo, and she continued to exhibit that work at least one more time, thus indicating persistent access to it. In addition to many instances recounted in letters, as to Geysa and Enid traveling together, newspaper accounts tell of their journeys, as was the custom of the day. For instance, Enid and Geysa traveled to Kentucky (Enid leaving Paris and Geysa coming from Paris) to meet their friend Pauline May in Louisville before venturing down to Boyle County. In 1906, for instance, when Enid had to undergo surgery for appendicitis, Geysa took it upon herself to communicate updates on Enid's condition to those in this close circle of friends, including Julia Dinsmore.[70]

Interpreting these relationships should be seen in the context of the Southern narrative after the Civil War as well as through the lens of overall relations with women as mothers, daughters, sisters, cousins, and friends. A term that has been used, though not specifically with regard to Enid and Geysa, is "Boston marriage," taken from Henry James's *The Bostonians* (1885), which situated freedoms and mutual growth through homosocial companionship. Indeed, Enid was afforded freedoms as an independent artist-in-residence after leaving her family's comfortable Victorian home in Louisville. Ultimately, social connections gave her opportunities and afforded her freedom (among these a drink of cider).[71]

Just as Enid was grateful for Colonel Durrett's gift of cider while she was away from Louisville earlier on, she thanked him again in 1899 on behalf of herself and Geysa for his latest gift box. Enid wrote of their joy and pleasure in receiving such bounty:

> The box and contents have come safely and yesterday your kind letter and the papers. To say thank you would hardly express our sentiments and you may be sure your health and long life has been drunk with "the grass in our grog." The Baroness was much touched that you sent her a bottle all for herself and threatens to take it to France. I am to again own some of this Old Crow and thanks again to the dear Colonel! . . . We have enjoyed the cider emensley [*sic*]. Non[e] like it anywhere!

The cider made such an impact that one of Enid's friends took her pen and added a postscript to the note, stating that even with the recipe Durrett provided them, she would "never be able to make cider like that but I am going to try very hard and follow your directions closely."[72]

While Enid's sculptural trajectory may be tied to cider and cigars, such intemperances speak to the larger narratives of the freedom that she enjoyed as an independent woman living in a big city—whether Louisville, Cincinnati, or Chicago—while maintaining her ties to the Bluegrass State. This chapter has highlighted Enid's relationship with her native state through her connections with people, foodways, and spectacle—the uniqueness of which were a function of her time and place—as well as her gender, her background, and her ambition. These factors built the foundation upon which Enid's career emerged. Like the pioneer Daniel Boone emerging from the woods, Enid came out of uncharted territory, primed for a lifelong career built upon public and private commissions from the 1890s and the Columbian Exposition, the subject of the next chapter.

2

Caryatids and Clay

Enid had a sweet tooth, so much so that candy made an impression on her during a visit to Chicago. She penned a note to her grandmother on her first visit to the city in 1886: "We spent a day in Chicago which I enjoyed very much. We bought a big box of Gunther[?] candy. Aunt Fannie gave me a box first before we started. Chicago is a very handsome city I am delighted with it." That delight was cemented in 1891, when Enid left the Bluegrass State and took a position with the World's Columbian Exposition, an international exhibit aimed at attracting tourists to Chicago and at showcasing international achievements in arts, science, and industry.[1]

To gain employment in Chicago, Enid enlisted the help of her mentor, Reuben Thomas Durrett, who was well connected to the Louisville elite through his roles as amateur historian, lawyer, publisher, and local philanthropist. To aid Enid in securing a position, Durrett wrote to Bertha Honoré Palmer, a businesswoman, socialite, and philanthropist originally from Louisville who served as president of the Board of Lady Managers in Chicago. Palmer was described as having "Southern vowels [that] flow like wine" and a "charming way of asking for the earth that you not only wish you could give it to her, but would like to throw in the moon as well." As president, Palmer facilitated the work of the women's governing body of the Chicago fair and authorized the creation of a separate building for women's exhibits, which came to be known as the Woman's Building.[2]

Durrett's recommendation, along with Enid's education and travels, secured a position for her at the fair. As part of her work, she was to reproduce the work of male sculptors and create works entirely of her own design. In this latter category, Enid designed a series of columns in the shape of classically draped female forms, called caryatids, for the roof of the Woman's Building. She also created the well-known statue of frontiersman Daniel Boone for the Kentucky state building. Enid navigated many worlds while at the fair: as an emerging professional, a Kentuckian, and a hired hand for a large-scale exhibition.

About the Fair

The Columbian Exposition was not the first time that the United States had held an international exposition. However, with this fair it seemed as though the world came to Chicago, with its chart-topping attendance: over six months, 27.5 million visitors attended. By comparison, 6 million people had visited London's Crystal Palace, also known as the Great Exhibition of the Works of Industry of All Nations, in 1851; 10 million had visited the Centennial International Exhibition in Philadelphia in 1876; and just over 6 million had attended the Exposition Universelle (in Paris, 1889), where the Eiffel Tower debuted. Even after its own incredible run, Chicago retained its prominence as the most popular fair compared to Buffalo's Pan-American Exposition in 1901, which played host to 8 million visitors, and St. Louis's Louisiana Purchase Exposition of 1904, which was attended by nearly 20 million.

To put this into perspective relative to Enid's life and work up to this point, Louisville and Cincinnati had populations of 161,129 and 296,908 in 1890 (in contrast to nearby Lexington, Kentucky with 21,567 residents as of 1890). Enid, in moving to Chicago, entered a city of over a million people (Chicago's population was 1,099,850 in 1890). There she witnessed, and became part of, a new form of art making, one anchored to a grand vision engineered by a team of architects. Already rebuilt just twenty years after the Great Chicago Fire that had destroyed three square miles, killed 300, and left 100,000 residents homeless, the city had rebounded and beat out New York, St. Louis, and Washington as the venue designed to celebrate the most nationalist of all claims, the four hundredth anniversary of Columbus's discovery of America.

Enid was in the midst of all of it, from the everyday to the celebrity. Exhibits focused on agriculture and horticulture, manufacturing, and mining as well as innovation. On view at Kentucky's exhibits alone were Japanese persimmon, 154 varieties of apple, 25 of pear, and 4 of quince, along with oak, birch, ash, cheery, poplar, elm, and many other species of wood. Ciders, whiskies, and other alcohols were also exhibited, as were hemp, limestone, and racehorses. Visitors to the fair found the novelty of Aunt Jemima pancake mix, the sugary sweetness of Cracker Jack, and mass-produced chewing gum alongside architectural feats of the Ferris Wheel and a moving sidewalk.

On the Midway Plaisance (*plaisance* being French for pleasure) exhibits of materials and products were juxtaposed with exhibits of culture. On this mile-long pathway, new ways of seeing the world through customs, traditions, and products of global cultures and civilizations burst forth for the visitor. The path was "lined on both sides with so remarkable a collection of shows of one sort or another that one man could never hope to find them all in a lifetime were he compelled to search through the world for himself." Furthering the notion of spectacle that was reflected in the regional industrial expositions prior to Chicago, the city played host to representations of the world through the construction of "villages" of residents and structures from far-off lands, such as Egypt. Contrasts between "savagery" and "civilization" simultaneously lent an air of legitimacy to segregation. Such a varied display of customs and cultures contrasted with the cautiously crafted and manicured "White City," which was further illuminated, literally, through the use of Edison lighting.[3]

Bringing all the world together meant the gathering of a level of celebrity that intersected a number of fields, from Jane Addams, Susan B. Anthony, and Frederick Douglass to Clarence Darrow, Marshall Field, and a number of inventors, including Elisha Gray, George Westinghouse, and Thomas Edison. Just beside the grounds of the fair were a fifteen-acre site and 18,000-seat arena where Buffalo Bill lassoed in thousands for his "Wild West and Congress of Rough Riders of the World" show and camp. Walking through the gates of Buffalo Bill's site before the show, visitors would find a staff of hundreds, including Indians, soldiers, and other employees. Before the show, with its grand review of soldiers and weapon firings, visitors were greeted by pioneers: Christopher Columbus as "Pilot of the Ocean, the First Pioneer" and Bill himself as "Pilot of the Prairie, the Last Pioneer."[4]

With every day of the fair, a theme engaged audiences to celebrate, including Kentucky Day on June 1, 1893. With its art, architecture, attendance, and invention, the fair surpassed any spectacle in which Enid had engaged over her young life. The breadth and depth of the fair's spectacle and its ability to appeal to all led American journalist Richard Harding Davis to dub the Chicago fair "the greatest event in the history of the country since the [C]ivil [W]ar" with an "ability to please every one, to give each person some one thing which exactly fits his or her idea of what is beautiful in art or wonderful in execution which is all-satisfying and which justified the whole." Such rhetoric was emphasized in the fair's Dedicatory Oration delivered on October 21, 1892, by none other than the Honorable Henry Watterson, editor of the *Louisville Courier-Journal*, friend of the Yandell family and supporter of Enid. His talk broached politics, particularly the notions of nationhood and the republic, with his statement "The curse of slavery is gone. It was a joint heritage of woe, to be wiped out and expiated in blood and flame. The mirage of the Confederacy has vanished. It was essential bucolic, a vision of Arcady, the dream of a most attractive economic fallacy." Watterson called to mind recent political acts, "which constitute the real treaty of peace between the North and the South, and seal our bonds as a nation forever." After reviewing a long history of discovery and American exceptionalism, Watterson asked the audience to "hail, Columbus, discoverer, dreamer, hero, and apostle! . . . Neither marble nor brass can fitly form his statue. Continents are his monument, and unnumbered millions, present and to come . . . will reverently guard and preserve from century to century, his name and fame." Thus, the connection of the fair to the past, present, and future had been stated in words suited to the architecture of the surroundings.[5]

Setting Up Shop

During the summer of 1891, Enid left for Chicago to secure work. Although she was three hundred miles from home, she was not alone. She found herself among companions in her work to support the Exposition, including friends that she had made while studying in Cincinnati, among them Janet Scudder (1869–1940), as well as new friends, such as Jean Loughborough of Little Rock, Arkansas, a writer who was Bertha Palmer's record keeper and file clerk, and Laura Hayes of Chicago, who served as Palmer's private secretary. Enid also retained ties to her family, particularly her mother, as recounted in copious letters from this period. Accounts of Enid's experiences may also be gleaned from letters she sent to Durrett after she moved to Chicago.

On September 24, 1891, in a letter to Durrett, Enid noted how she had settled into her work in Chicago: "Mrs. Palmer has been most kind to

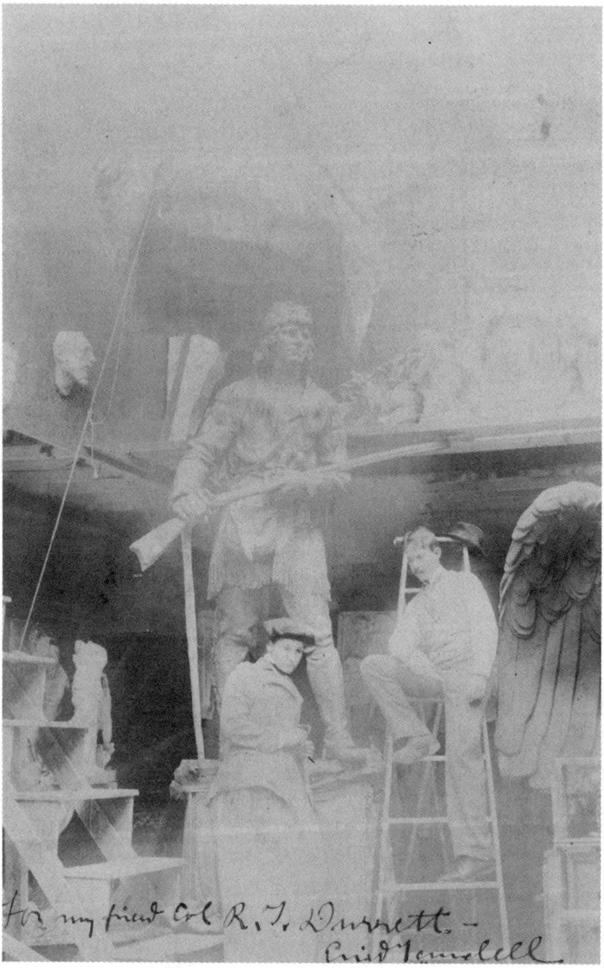

Taken in 1892 or 1893, this photograph shows Enid and Frederick MacMonnies in front of Enid's Daniel Boone statue, surrounded by preliminary works and studies. To keep Boone's rifle from falling, Enid propped the butt of the gun. In Enid's handwriting at the bottom, the inscription reads, "For my friend, Col. R. T. Durrett—Enid Yandell." Other versions of this studio photograph exist, with various inscriptions, suggesting that Enid distributed such images in order to promote her work as well as to document her depiction of Boone. (Enid Bland Yandell Photograph Collection, 987PC52X.050, Box 2, Folder 16. The Filson Historical Society, Louisville, KY.)

me and taken really a personal interest in me—I have made many charming friends here & some of them very influential. . . . I am very nicely fixed with some other girls who are also workers." In this same letter, Enid also recounted Palmer's invitation for Enid to address the women of the Board of Lady Managers on the topics of women's work and Enid's own work, in particular. Such a request seems to suggest the young artist's authority early on as being competent among her peers. A few months later, on April 15, 1892, Enid wrote to Durrett about her work ethic and drive: "I am studying hard and I hope daily becoming a better and big[g]er woman—if not a greater sculptor—But I know it is only by work one ever becomes great so I labor on steadily."[6]

In addition to offering encouragement to Enid, Durrett provided a subject for her work as Enid honed her skills in her profession. She created a bust of Reuben Durrett and exhibited it at the Art Institute Exhibition in 1891. She then used the portrait, with its evocation of personality and history, as a calling card. She wrote to the author and critic Edward Freiburger, inviting him to view her work: "I hope you will see and notice in your paper if it pleases you. Portraits are my forte and I hope to do several here." Thus wrapped up in this single bust is the trajectory of Enid's ambition after Chicago—portraits, history, and the higher forms of sculpture for which there was a sure market. Yet the portrait also called to mind a connection to home, family, and companionship. In addition to serving as family friend, mentor, and history tutor, Durrett supplied the artist with the familiar cider that he had prepared and shipped to her while she was in Chicago and thereafter.[7]

White Rabbits in the White City

Women's contributions to sculpture at the fair consisted of reproducing agreed-upon designs that contributed to the overall look of the "White City," as envisioned by Daniel Burnham, chief architect of the fair. Burnham's vision was for architecture and sculpture to work in tandem to celebrate the four hundredth anniversary of Christopher Columbus's arrival in the new world, thus informing the name of the fair as the World's Columbian Exposition. Burnham assembled a handful of local artists and architects along with others from the East Coast. The blending of the two talent pools was essential to the success of the fair, both in terms of meeting production goals and assuring buy-in from local politicians and civic leaders, who wanted to support Chicagoans only, whereas Burnham envisioned a cohort of professionals *not* from Chicago. An assembly of ten "starchitects," including Richard Morris Hunt, Charles McKim, William Mead, and Stanford White contributed plans for buildings, as did the firm of Adler & Sullivan, among other Chicago-based architects. Key to getting the assembly of ten architects was their collaboration with the lead landscape designer of the day, Frederick Law Olmsted, of Brookline, Massachusetts.[8]

Intentionally placed amid the meandering paths, bodies of water, and white, classical facades of the major fair buildings, the colossal sculptures by leading artists, including Daniel Chester French, Frederick MacMonnies, and Augustus Saint-Gaudens balanced and enhanced the overall plan. Burnham saw to the design and construction of a number of buildings in a neoclassical architectural style, emphasizing white stone and a plaster-like appearance, situated in a Beaux arts plan that included a large park adjacent to Lake Michigan. A harkening back to classical forms and their ethos informed the work of all artists, in particular those associated with the fair, who were adjusting to large-scale adoption of a Classical Revival style informed by an interplay between architecture and sculpture. In sum, Burnham's Beaux arts plan foregrounded the White City's neoclassicism and was intended to "civilize" and uplift attendees, an effect that would have long-reaching effects on future fairs as well as the public architecture of American cities. For even though much of the construction—in plaster, staff, and occasional stone—was ephemeral, the impact of the World's Columbian Exposition was long lasting. Sculpture was in its heyday at the fair, and myriad artists contributed to the implementation of the plan. The entire fair showcased sculpture, which likely inspired the establishment of the National Sculpture Society (a professional standards and recognition board) later that same year, 1893.

One of the sculptors responsible for carving and managing outdoor adornments, Lorado Taft (1860–1936), was asked to expedite production on the Horticulture Building. As faculty member at the School of the Art Institute of Chicago, Taft was familiar with the work of women sculptors and amenable to their contribution, and thus suggested to Daniel Burnham that he wanted to employ women among his assistants in order to complete the work on that structure. In response, Burnham supposedly replied, "Hire anyone who can do the work . . . white rabbits, if they will help out." Thus, the group of female assistants to Taft became known as the "White Rabbits," charged with the task of "pointing up" the statuary sent to Chicago, meaning that the models of the works were to be enlarged on site by these assistants. A description of this process comes from Enid's contemporary, Janet Scudder, who worked as one of the White Rabbits alongside Enid.

> The design for a group or statue is first made in a small sketch; from this sketch the sculptor models a very careful study in clay, usually one-fourth the size the finished work is to be; this is cast; over the plaster model is built a wooden frame, and from the top crosspieces strings are attached which fall to the floor. Beside this caged-in model is built another frame containing the iron armature—the framework on which the enlarged statue is to be built up. Then, by means of a compass, the distance from the strings to the clay model is measured, multiplied by four, and sticks reproducing this measurement are attached to the armature and extend to the point which is to be covered with clay. These sticks, with small metal pins at the end, serve as guides and are left uncovered until the work is finished, thus aiding in rectifying all mistakes and miscalculations. . . . After the armature is covered with the first application of clay, thus making a working foundation, little sharp-pointed wooden pegs with heads are stuck into the plaster, these heads at exactly the distance where the surface of the finished statue will end. When all the necessary points are established, the strings and the wooden frame are removed, and the work of building out the statue to the points indicated is commenced.[9]

Although several women artists were grouped together and called White Rabbits, little attention has been paid to the meaning of this term. However, unpacking it affords the opportunity to understand some of the complexities of language and meaning at the fair. First and foremost, the color white may have referred to the use of clay or staff in the production process, where the female sculptors would reproduce or enlarge works by male sculptors. The adjective was also in keeping with the overall aesthetic and to the nickname of the fairgrounds as the "White City." As for the noun, "Rabbits" bears witness to the biases at the fair among female and male professionals. In calling the female artists "White Rabbits," Burnham's gender and occupational biases were clear. The term conjures up an image of eager, playful animals known for their abilities at reproduction as opposed to skilled and able women attempting to make careers for themselves. Burnham's limited sense of the virtues and artistic accomplishments of the women sculptors he grouped so disparagingly with his term stood in stark contrast to Lorado Taft's privileging the women, both as an instructor and as the person who suggested the women be hired to complete the work. The designation also artificially constructed a group that sought to deny the women agency as independent artists.

In fact, in their independent pursuits at the fair, the women varied in age, educational background, style, iconography, and materials. Thus, we should view Enid as an individual rather than part of an anonymous group of artists of a particular time and place. Doing so enables us to gain a richer understanding of the women's occupational identity, their lives, and their work at the world's fair and beyond.

In addition, the pejorative terminology denied the reality of the obstacles that these women had already overcome just to be employed at the fair. Each woman's gaining employment required letters of introduction. In Enid's case, one of these came from Reuben Durrett. Even after securing a position, further endorsements were needed. Such recommendations came from Henry Watterson, Karl Bitter, Philip Martiny, and Thomas S. Noble, who taught in the Cincinnati Art Academy. Although it had been, by this point, four years since Enid attended the Academy, Noble offered a strong recommendation by commenting upon her abilities as well as her continued studies over the years since he had instructed her. In a letter dated February 27, 1893, Noble wrote: "Miss Yandell's membership in the Cincinnati Art Academy extended through two years in the class in Sculpture where she completed, with much credit, the prescribed course. This training was supplemented, immediately, by several months of travel amongst the galleries of the Old World. Of Miss Yandell's later work I have seen nothing. As, however, she has shown marked ability, I feel sure that her training, keen observation and continued work, have undoubtedly fitted her for the position she craves."[10]

Other Opportunities in Chicago

While "pointing up," female sculptors were permitted to secure independent work for the Woman's Building. In this capacity, Enid was awarded a contract to create unique work for the roof of the building. For this, she designed two dozen caryatids, column supports taking the form of a female in classical drapery.[11] Such statuary was aesthetic and functional, but also demonstrated artistic integrity given its reference to classical, in this case Greek, sculpture as source material—specifically, the Porch of the Maidens at the Erechtheion, an ancient temple on the north side of the Acropolis in Athens. Even with classical art as her precedent, Enid was careful to want to please her patron. In a letter to Bertha Palmer dated October 14, 1891, Enid wrote: "I have finished one of the Caryatides and would like very much for you to see it before it is cast. Will it be possible for you to come over Thursday morning to see it?" It is unclear if Palmer visited that day, although it is clear that Palmer took an interest in Enid throughout her stay in Chicago.[12]

This collection of columnar supports was Enid's largest work to date, at nine feet tall. For the design and implementation, Enid earned a Designer's Medal, one of only three given to women at the fair—tangible recognition of Enid's abilities, which she kept with her throughout her life. The recognition was not lost on Daniel Burnham, the chief architect of the fair, who acknowledged Enid's abilities in his letter of October 1892, in which he told her she was being given the award in recognition of the services of architects, artists, and designers of the fair. He invited her to attend the ceremony and went so far as to call her a colleague: "This is the first time in the history of the country that such services have been publicly recognized, and I most earnestly request your presence at the ceremonies in the Manufactures and Liberal Arts Building on October 21st, where I shall receive the medals from the President of the World's Columbian Exposition, and distribute them among those whom I am honored to call my colleagues. . . . It is scarcely necessary for me to add an expression of my conviction that the event is of the highest importance in the interest of the allied arts." Enid's work and the award of a medal were no small achievement for this young Louisville sculptor.[13]

Her choice of subject demonstrated Enid's authority over classical sub-

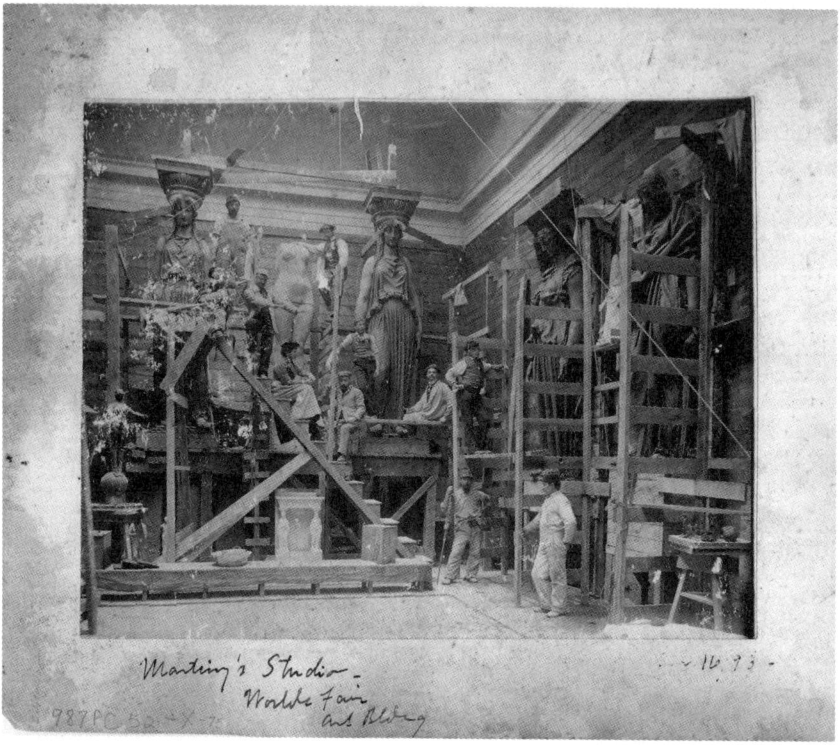

At the center of the photograph, wearing a beret, Enid is seated among a studio of men as they create myriad sculptural decorations for the World's Fair in Chicago. Notice the model for the caryatids beneath Enid and the large versions of the same work behind her. The annotations, in Enid's handwriting, as well as the wooden box on the platform in the foreground, identify the location: Martiny's Studio, World's Fair Art Building. (Enid Bland Yandell Photograph Collection, 987PC52X.075, Box 6. The Filson Historical Society, Louisville, KY.)

ject matter as well as evidence of her academic training and her independent pursuit of the arts while living in Louisville. While growing up, Enid had no access to public collections of art; however, she had passionately attended public spectacles such as the Southern Exposition, held annually from 1883 to1887 in her home city. There the Art Gallery exhibited works from finer collections along with curios and art of the past and functioned as a major source of study for the budding artist in her hometown.

What is often overlooked in the literature is that Enid's design for the caryatids was her "second effort," in that she had first applied to design the building. Her submission, along with nineteen others, was not chosen as the final design for the building's architecture. Nevertheless, the rejection letter from Susan G. Cooke, secretary of the World's Columbian Commission Board of Lady Managers, praises Enid's work and that of every other contributor for being as good as that of male contemporaries:

> The arrangements for the competition were such as to insure the most perfect fairness and impartiality, the designs being known to the committee only by number, so that each one was judged entirely upon its merit, and personal influence had no weight. . . . We hope that you, although failing to get the prize, will feel satisfied that the award was justly made, and that you will not be discouraged from future effort, because you were not successful in this case. We have been delighted with the interest taken in this competition by the women sculptors of the country, and we thank you for the assistance which you have given to the encouragement of art among women by contributing something of your own brain and handiwork. . . . The character of the work, taken as a whole, [w]as so good and showed so much serious study and originality of ideas that one of the gentlemen, afterwards chosen to act on the committee, happening to see the sketches for the first time without knowing that they were the work of young women, judged them by the most severe standards of art, and pronounced them good. When asked if he thought that young men of the same age could have done as well or better, he said he thought it doubtful, and that the result had more than justified the policy of the Board of Lady Managers in offering this competition to women.[14]

Comparing the work of women with that of men seems all the more satisfying when considered alongside the anonymity forced on the female assistants. It seems that in creative, innovative practice for large-scale work, women could compete with men.

Bertha Palmer called upon Enid to represent woman sculptors on at least one occasion: on August 29, 1891, Palmer informed Enid that members of the Board of Lady Managers were intending to visit the Woman's Building the following Wednesday. She requested Enid's presence on-site:

"I hope they will find you there at work. Please wear your blouse or apron or whatever you usually have on while modelling, for it will please me very much to have you give them a practical illustration of our women decorators at work. I believe the outfit of a sculptor is rather picturesque too—is it not?" In Enid, the president of the Board of Lady Managers had found her woman sculptor, a representative of the entire field of employees.[15]

Given her strong work ethic and building acclaim, Enid, like many of her female peers, were free to take on other commissions and, in doing so, made significant contributions to the sculptural work throughout the fair. In fact, after they were named White Rabbits and given the task of completing Taft's Horticulture Building, a handful of the women were hired on long-term, for an entire year, to work on the sculptural decoration. This assignment meant that the women's studio work moved from a one-story cluster to a full-fledged operation inside the Horticulture Building, with ten women and men working together—Enid and Janet Scudder among them. They lived at a hotel near the grounds of the fair so as to be near their work and formed a community of artists working all day, every day. They brought their "lunch in paper bags," Scudder later recalled, "and remained from eight in the morning until six in the afternoon; and when we got back to the hotel there was no question of what we would do in the evening; dinner and bed were the only things that appealed to us." Enid and her companions tracked the progress of their peers as they saw the statues and buildings come into focus over the months of work while the fair was under construction.[16]

For many, including Enid, fair work was the first time they had earned regular wages for sculpture. They expressed deep satisfaction upon receiving their first payments for their contributions. As Janet Scudder later wrote, "When the first month's work was finished and we took our place in line with hundreds of workmen to receive our pay envelopes, we were about the happiest white rabbits that ever existed. We rushed back to our rooms at the hotel, opened the envelopes and poured out the five-dollar bills—for some reason we were paid our one hundred and fifty dollars in five-dollar bills—and carpeted the floor with them. We wanted to see what it felt like to walk on money." Instead of paying to learn how to sculpt, Enid was now paid for how well she could sculpt.[17]

Enid's work in Chicago extended beyond the pointing up for the Horticulture Building and other Taft-managed projects; it included work on the caryatids for the Woman's Building and, significantly, the commission mentioned earlier—the sculpture that truly established her name among artists, patrons, and the public, a work that cemented her association with her home state of Kentucky.

Representing Kentucky: Enid Yandell and Daniel Boone

The historical society, the Filson Club, commissioned Enid to create a sculpture of Daniel Boone for the Kentucky State Building at the Chicago Exhibition. To fulfill the commission, Enid used props to prepare an authentic rendering by securing purported Boone relics, including his hunting shirt, flintlock rifle, tomahawk, knife, and powder horn, which were in the possession of Reuben Durrett. Given the shortage of likenesses of her subject, Enid also relied upon the Filson's portrait of Boone for the facial treatment. She also seems to have read and researched widely, relying upon historical accounts of Boone, such as *Collins' Historical Sketches of Kentucky* (1882).[18]

Over several letters, Enid and Durrett exchanged ideas on how to bring reality to an idea that she suggested to him in 1892, having observed firsthand how states were marketing themselves at the World's Fair. Enid applied what she had observed to her native state and, more broadly, to her own sculptural practice, thereby creating an opportunity for herself as the state sculptor. In May 1892, after working for a year on projects related to the Woman's Building, Enid wrote to Durrett, who fancied having a large-scale sculpture of Kentucky's forefathers in Louisville—a desire that he had expressed to Enid on more than one occasion. She wrote, "perhaps I have discovered a plan for the accomplishment of your pet scheme, now mine also, of having a statue of [George Rogers] Clark made and put in one of our parks. The different states are having figures of their great men made to go in their State buildings and Kentucky can boast of greater forefathers than any of them. Now should the park Commission join with the Fair commission they could have Stat[u]es of Clarke [*sic*], Boone, etc. made in Staff and sent to the fair, then afterward they could be cast in Bronze and marble and donated to the parks. . . . Now this is the time to arrange this thing and as the time is short it should be done as quickly as possible." Durrett agreed with Enid's suggestion and established a subscription fund through the Filson to pay her to create a statue of Daniel Boone.[19]

By the end of 1892 Enid had secured the commission to prepare a large Boone sculpture to be sited near the Kentucky Building, a colonial-inspired house plan designed on a grander scale by Maury & Dodd of Louisville. The two-story porticoed and columned structure measured 75 by 90 feet and offered grounds for sculpture. Enid answered the call for such work; the contract for Boone was written with her intentions in mind—allowing for the possibility of creating two busts, one of Boone and another of George Rogers Clark, military hero, surveyor, and founder of Louisville, or a single, life-sized statue of either man. Pledges were secured by December 1892, and the final contract was signed on January 28, 1893 between the Filson Club's committee and Enid Yandell, who was identified as "Sculptor, also of Louisville, Ky."[20]

Enid's commitment to the Boone project brought confidence: she was proud of the work, and her peers likewise had provided positive feedback on it. Moreover, the Boone work contributed toward her growth as an independent woman employed in sculpture. In a letter explaining her success to Durrett, Enid recounted that she had created a "sketch," or model in clay, of Boone and had intended for Durrett to see the work before committing it to plaster. Durrett replied to Enid's letters, offering support as well as asking questions. Promising to send photographs of the work to him, she remarked, "This is by far the best thing I have done and I hope it will meet with your approval. The gun & coat I have copied exactly and will return this week—The face is a combination of all the portraits and about 40 years old—in his prime—The artists who have seen it like it and I have new courage to go on working learning & doing better—I have made a great stride in my profession this year and am grateful to the Filson Club for this opportunity to show what I can do." Enid continued to work on the Boone alongside her contract work for other Chicago fair designs.[21]

Published accounts leading up to the unveiling recorded, with anticipation, what was forthcoming:

> Miss Enid Yandell's . . . Boone, which has just been completed in clay and which will be modeled in staff within a few days . . .

> is certain to win the praise of every son and daughter of the Blue Grass State, who will thus pay tribute to the memory of one of Kentucky's pioneers and add to the living glory of one of the State's fairest daughters. But not Kentucky alone will admire the splendor of Miss Yandell's latest and greatest achievement; for the work is one of such artistic and historic worth as to make it the theme of the praise of art students and connoisseurs from all over the world, who will find in this statue a new evidence of the ability of an American woman.

The article describes the sculpture, noting Boone's clothing, gun and tomahawk, watchful pose, and silent step. The exquisite handling and authentic lifelikeness demonstrated Enid's skill: "Miss Yandell has performed her task with fidelity, rare talent and grace, in, no sense, however betraying the woman's art. It is the best thing [she] has thus far done. . . . It shows a decided advance upon all her previous efforts and is a happy indication of what may be expected of her as the years advance and her art progresses. Ere long the figure will be cast in bronze and given a position in [Louisville's] Cherokee Park." Even before the work had debuted, it was destined for a life beyond the fair. In fact, it was envisioned early on as becoming a part of the Louisville parkscape. In other words, it would live a double life: at the fair before millions and then at home before the people of her city.[22]

Corresponding with Durrett about her successes and the Boone sculpture, Enid expressed a sense of her own competence and also sought intellectual stimulation from him: "I am sure you are right and very wise about my choosing American History as my field in Sculpture—and when I come home I hope you will give me some interesting history & biographies to read up—The Boone is cast and in place at the Ky Building—and I await further—instructions for the committee in regard to unveiling. . . . Awaiting your commands—Faithfully." Writing on May 20, 1893, Enid had little time for further enhancement to her Boone sculpture, as the final work arrived at the corner of the yard surrounding the Kentucky Building at the World's Fair on June 2, 1893.[23]

The life-sized Boone was created in staff, which was often used to construct large-scale works for temporary exhibition, such as at the World's Fair. Even if the intent was temporary, the artistic excellence was permanent. In short, Boone was highly celebrated at the fair. An issue of the *Chicago Herald* entitled "By Kentucky Belles" offered a sketch of the sculpture before its unveiling, draped by the American flag. Enid's depiction of Daniel Boone brought all those present into deeper association with Kentucky; as the *Chicago Herald* claimed, "Everybody present was a Kentuckian by birth, adoption or education and in the gathering was a goodly number of people whose progenitors made a considerable part of Kentucky history." By virtue of the likeness and the pioneer spirit that Enid had bestowed upon her sculpture of Daniel Boone, merely being in the presence of Enid's work caused people to draw an association to, and identify themselves with, Kentucky.[24]

At the sculpture's unveiling, politician William O'Connell Bradley offered an oration, which was followed by an address by Kentucky governor John Y. Brown. An article recounting their comments and the sculpture's debut drew attention to the interaction between the audience, the sculptor, and the sculpture: "As the orator finished speaking he grasped the ropes and, giving them a vigorous jerk, the American flag which had enfolded the statue parted and fell to its feet. A great shout went up and in it were calls for Miss Yandell, who appeared for a moment on the balcony overlooking her artistic creation. She was jauntily attired in a tailor-made suit of blue serge, wearing a white vest, standing collar, four-in-hand tie and black derby hat. Her eyes danced with pride, but she could not be induced to speak. She bowed her acknowledgments and, with Mrs. Potter Palmer, who accompanied her to the building, left the balcony and joined friends below."[25]

Several accounts of the sculpture's unveiling appeared in the *Louisville Commercial,* which repeated Bradley's and Brown's speeches, and pointed out that the work served as a tribute to Boone. A June 2, 1893, article in the *Louisville Commercial* closed with a "Tribute to Miss Yandell" and praised her brilliance in rising to the challenge to produce a Boone in motion. Such comments reflected how aptly Enid had succeeded in this endeavor: "It was reserved for the genius of a young Kentucky girl to have such a conception of the old pioneer and to embody it in a statue. The faithful young artist, trusting as little as possible to imagination, has reproduced the identical hunting shirt and rifle and tomahawk and scalping-knife and powder-horn used by Boone in life. We are reminded by the statue of the cautious step which makes no noise as the light foot touches the ground."[26]

Accounts of the Boone sculpture's unveiling further reflected how aptly Enid had succeeded in showing Boone in motion, emerging from the wilderness. The *Louisville Courier-Journal* recorded even more detail in its remark that as the flag covering the statue fell away "there stood Boone in the coat he wore and the gun he carried when he first saw the Kentucky River." After the unveiling, the band struck up "Dixie," a rather unusual anthem to honor a pioneer and frontiersman, but a suitable salute to postbellum Kentuckians, many of whom shared a Confederate past, as Enid had. From that moment forward, Enid Yandell was associated with Daniel Boone, pioneer and frontiersman.[27]

The plaster cast of Boone debuted at Chicago to great acclaim and was subsequently shown at several exhibitions. Copies were also made and exhibited by Enid for thirteen years before she found a patron who would enable her to cast the work in bronze. That commission came finally in 1906 for Louisville from the city's largest cigar manufacturer, C. C. Bickel. A permanent placement for Enid's frontiersman did not materialize until Bickel, manufacturer of the "Daniel Boone" brand cigar, donated $10,000 for the work to be cast in bronze. The dedication of this life-sized Boone emerging from the trees atop stone planks was held on June 15, 1906, a feature event of Kentucky Home-Coming Week. An estimated 50,000 people came to Cherokee Park to see the statue's unveiling, which was delayed by rain. Bickel's granddaughter pulled the ribbons that removed the drape over the form. The crimson covering landed in a puddle at Boone's feet, a reminder, perhaps, of Kentucky's nickname "dark and bloody ground," which referred to the fierce battles between Indians and frontiersmen. John Breckinridge Castleman of Louisville made the presentation address for Bickel, and the acceptance speech was made by Colonel Reuben Durrett, who had expressed to Enid some fifteen years earlier his desire of having such a work on view in the city.[28]

Enid also kept a small version of the Boone sculpture in her studio throughout her practice, thus demonstrating how her association with frontierism had been permanently affixed to her identity, giving her agency and contributing to her legacy. By sculpting Boone, Enid established her occupational identity as Kentucky's sculptor. Although born and raised in the state, she trained in Cincinnati, entered the profession in Chicago, and further trained and worked in studios in New York, Massachusetts, and France. She created public statuary and private works in the United States and Europe from the 1890s and managed an art school on Martha's Vineyard. However, throughout her lifetime she was praised and claimed by Southerners, fellow artists, and critics in the context of her Kentucky connection. An article entitled "American Women Sculptors" in 1899, for example, associated her with the state; and fellow artist Janet Scudder referred to Enid in her autobiography as "Kentucky's representative sculptor," clearly associating her with the Bluegrass state.[29]

Enid was from Kentucky, retained her ties to the state, and depicted Kentuckians and Kentucky themes in her work—taking up sculptures of Boone until the end of her life. Moreover, she hoped to secure patronage from the South by highlighting her Southern roots, as suggested by the article "A Southern Girl at the World's Fair," which told of her lineage, her father having served as a staff surgeon and medical inspector of Hardee's Corps during the Civil War. The article further commented on her pride "of being the daughter of a Confederate soldier" who had hoped "for her greatest patronage from the South."[30]

During the 1890s, Enid was characterized in publications as a "gifted sculptor, an American and Southern young woman." Shortly after Enid received her award at Chicago, the *Louisville Courier-Journal* called her a "Louisville sister of the Muses . . . going from triumph to triumph" and acknowledged that "the proudest leaf in Enid Yandell's wreath" was a measure of praise given by noted sculptor Augustus Saint-Gaudens (1848–1907), instructor at the Art Students League in New York and the most famous American sculptor of the day. Saint-Gaudens remarked, "If at her age I had done what she has done, I would have considered my title to fame assured." Such praise—particularly by an artist who was in no way affiliated with her education or training—attested to Enid's accomplishment at a young age and her prospects for future success. In closing, the paper called upon the public to watch her star rise, decreeing, "So let all men know that the climax of Enid Yandell's career is yet to come."[31]

Thus, even as she contributed to and supported the work of male contemporaries at the Chicago World's Fair, Enid challenged the field of sculptural practice, becoming a pioneer herself by creating colossal sculp-

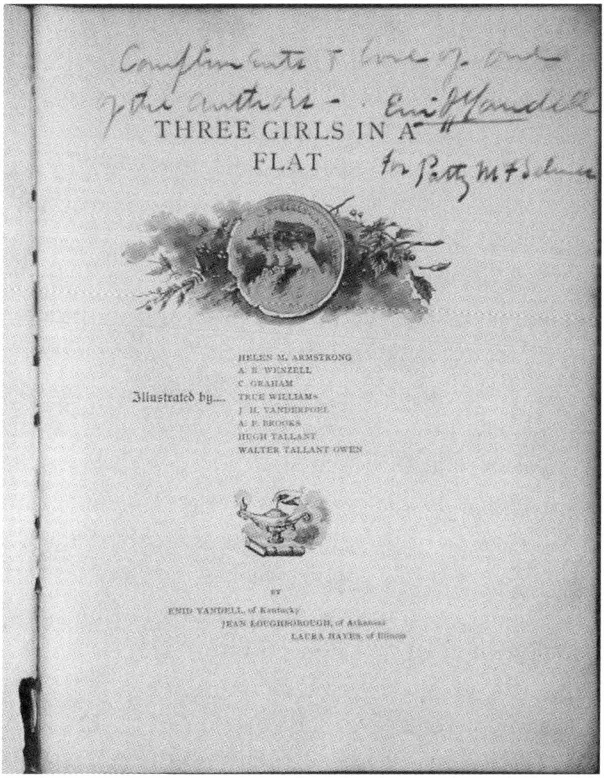

Enid was one of three authors of *Three Girls in a Flat*, a fictionalized account of the World's Fair in Chicago, published in 1892. Enid gave copies of the book to friends, including Reuben T. Durrett, and retained a copy herself. This particular volume was inscribed by Enid Yandell to Patty Selmes: "Compliments and love of one of the authors—Enid Yandell For Patty M. F. Selmes." The volume is in the collection of the Dinsmore Homestead. (Courtesy of Dinsmore Homestead, Burlington, KY.)

tures for world's fairs and in crafting life-sized representations of statewide heroes, such as Daniel Boone emerging from the wilderness.[32]

Women at Work: *Three Girls in a Flat*

Simultaneous with her sculptural work at the fair and her negotiation back and forth with Durrett, Palmer, and others, Enid also garnered attention through her writing. Along with two friends, Jean Loughborough (originally of St. Louis, later of Arkansas) and Laura Hayes (of Illinois), Enid wrote about her experiences at the fair in a semiautobiographical story entitled *Three Girls in a Flat,* which was published in 1892.

Though a work of fiction, this text, one of very few by contemporary artists, provided readers with an account of living and working at the Fair, and gave insight into the life of a bachelor maid. It was included among the 8,000 volumes of writing by women in the Woman's Library at the fair the following year, thus further extending Enid's influence there. A second literary effort occurred in 1893, when Enid recounted her description of sculpture at the fair. She also wrote about the profession of sculpture a few years later. Together these works demonstrated Enid's interest in writing, a pleasure and skill that she carried with her throughout her life. They also demonstrate her interest in both commemorating the experience of the Chicago fair through the eyes of an artist and documenting the work of artists for a wider population.[33]

Three Girls situated itself in relation to the actual Chicago World's Fair through its dedication: "To that noble body of women which is acting as advance guard to the great army of the unrecognized in its onward march toward liberty and equality—THE BOARD OF LADY MANAGERS of the WORLD'S COLUMBIAN EXPOSITION." The President of this board, Bertha Honoré Palmer, played a role in the novel's context as much as the fair. While giving such praise to the board, the authors critiqued the fair, its excesses, its limitations, and its environment overall. Moreover, they acknowledged the power and presence of women in this environment, an opportunity that had not been afforded to women at previous world's fairs. Through the world's fairs and expositions like Chicago, women gained agency through the construction of a shared identity and the ability to communicate that identity on a local, national, and global stage. Using gender as a framing device, women were able to organize themselves as well as the exhibits over which they took charge, to envision themselves, to communicate with an international public, and to share their similarities as much as their differences.[34]

The three central characters of the work—Marjorie, Virginia (or Gene), and Duke (or the Duke)—took their cues from each of the book's coauthors. Each held a profession, though the Duke was the most adamant and independent of these. Marjorie's profession was defined in the context of writing, making her a parallel to Laura Hayes, Palmer's private secretary. Gene's profession at a desk job is recounted in Chapter 12, while throughout the novel significant mention is made of her social engagements. This character paralleled Jean Loughborough, Palmer's record keeper and file clerk. The third character, the Duke, was a sculptor. Her association with Enid extended even to physical qualities (including her moderate build and long, dark hair) and attire. Also of note was the similarity in the character's last name, Wendell, which resembled Enid's surname as well as a family name. Moreover, the authors claimed that the story was their own, as noted in a review in the *New York World:* "the story is the personal experience of the writers. . . . These girls are self-supporting, interested in different lines of work, but endowed with artistic temperaments and keen appreciation of the refinements of life."[35]

Much of the text offered accounts of the experiences of the three and was on the whole a primer on the life of the active, social, professional, independent woman. Telling passages in the novel contrasted a married woman's role (as a slave to one's husband) to the ability of women to go out of the home to work, to travel to Europe, and to engage in social outings, such as the young women's attempt to visit a Turkish Bath or Sunday school, to attend entertainments and spectacles such as the opera, and to organize social engagements in their flat. The novel also highlighted the Duke's Kentucky roots. Through the character of Colonel Rogers, a connection is made between the Duke and Enid's own home state. In fact, Rogers resembled Colonel Durrett, a figure whom Enid had known all her life through her Louisville and Filson connections and family.[36]

Gendered perspectives emerge throughout the novel, not only in terms of its framework of the bachelor maid—the independent, self-supporting woman—but also in terms of its shorter narratives. For instance, in Chapter 2, the Duke asked Marjorie to open her diary and read about her time abroad. Marjorie obliged and selected a passage from June 29, 1891, which recounted a time when Mrs. Palmer received Mr. Theodore Stanton, who inquired as to the part that women were to play in the World's Fair. His inquiry prompted the narrator to assume that he had had early training in handling "the woman question with an ease and fearlessness that could only have come from deep conviction or early training." The narrator further discloses that Stanton, in addition to being a journalist, was the son of reformer Elizabeth Cady Stanton. Inclusion of such personalities and details thus served to illustrate the contours of the woman's point of view taken in the novel.[37]

In addition, passages recounted the history of the Woman's Building and other signal elements to be celebrated through the Chicago Fair, which would open in 1893, a year after the book's publication. For instance, Chapter 5 offered a history of the Woman's Building and served as an homage to its architect, Sophia Hayden. After this, Enid herself was mentioned as the creator of the caryatids (that she was also a coauthor of the book is not mentioned): "The clay models for these figures were designed and molded by Miss Enid Yandell, of Louisville, Kentucky, who at the early age of twenty-two has much reputation as a sculptor. This roof garden is one of the most charming places imaginable, with its high, arching palms, and the various ferns and flora that have been contributed through members of the Board of Lady Managers all over the country." This passage continued with an explanation of the building's purpose, that might also serve as one of the purposes of *Three Girls in a Flat:* "The Board of Lady Managers wished to emphasize particularly the progress of women in a business and professional way, and in this connection will show the finest work they have done in the various lines, such as illustrating, wood-engraving, painting, sculpture, wood-carving, designing for wall paper, carpets, fabrics, etc., as well as a complete showing of journalistic and literary work." Enid thus contributed to both the visual and the literary arts—contributions that greatly enrich our understanding of the bachelor maid and her context within the arts.[38]

Enid's persona in the form of the Duke also embodied the burgeoning pioneer spirit with which she would come to be associated. On the occasion of the unveiling of the Ulysses S. Grant monument in Lincoln Park—a stone and bronze monument by Louis Rebisso, the sculptor who served as Enid's teacher when she studied at Cincinnati—the Duke and the other protagonists encountered President Grant's widow, Julia Dent Grant, and thereby came into contact with an older woman's perspective on women and women's work. Despite being a guest of Mrs. Palmer on this day of celebration in honor of the Civil War general and former president, the Duke argued with Mrs. Grant, the lady of the hour, over the role of women, asserting the right of women to be employed.[39]

More to the point, however, is the right of women to be employed as sculptors. Julia Grant knew one other female sculptor, Lavinia (Vinnie)

Ellen Ream (1847–1914), who worked in Washington. But Mrs. Grant disliked Ream, just because of her particular profession and her holding a job: "I don't approve of women sculptors as a rule," Enid has her say in the novel; "every woman is better off at home taking care of husband and children. The battle with the world hardens a woman and makes her unwomanly." Perhaps this passage can be read in terms of differences between the North and the South, given Julia Grant's understanding of the South through her father, "Colonel" Frederick Dent, who gave service to the Confederacy and her husband's embattled war service for the Union, which led to his election to the presidency. However, it seems more likely that the distinction comes from her age and position as First Lady during Reconstruction. Confronting Julia Grant and winning her over to have her realize that perhaps there is room for women within professions, including sculpture, the Duke contends that cutting marble would enable a woman to develop "muscle to beat biscuit" when she kept house.[40]

Significant in the way that the book was received is an article about *Three Girls in a Flat* published in the *New York World*. It began by stating, "This clever little story wrote itself, and the writers beg us not to consider it in any way a literary effort." Following this absurd claim, which attempted to remove any agency from the authors, the true process was disclosed: "Each girl wrote six chapters the outgrowth of a daily journal. Every Friday night a chapter was read and submitted to the 'Flat' for approval. It was the importunity of friends to whom the chapters were read, friends who perceived in it the 'salable' quality that led to its publication." Praise was heaped upon the trio, according to the reporter, as women outside of this world wanted to know how they did "it"—meaning how they managed to build careers for themselves, how they managed to make their way as independent women, and how they managed to support themselves and one another.[41]

In addition to her publishing debut with *Three Girls in a Flat,* Enid also wrote an article, "Sculpture at the World's Fair," which appeared in *Current Topics* in April 1893 just prior to the opening of the fair. Unlike the fictional account (that had such verisimilitude), this essay documented the works on view at the fair, and in doing so demonstrated Enid's personal understanding of art at the time. One notice of Enid's article mentioned Enid's abilities and heritage. The *Buffalo Commercial* stated: "Miss Enid Yandell, who writes for *Current Topics,* Chicago, the article on 'Sculpture at the World's Fair,' is a daughter of the distinguished Dr. Lunsford Yandell, of Kentucky, whose recent death was a lamented loss to the world of science. Coming of a stock which has been distinguished for generations among the cultured families of Kentucky, Miss Yandell has added to great inherited talent a very unusual power of devoted study. Her achievements as a sculptor seem little short of astonishing when one learns that she is no older than 22 years."[42]

Thus, Enid's work for the Woman's Building and the Kentucky Building at the Chicago Exposition, when paired with her authorship of *Three Girls in a Flat* and her review of the women's work at the Fair, revealed robust beginnings as a professional artist. These contributions assured broad exposure for Enid's work, as such avenues offered the opportunity for women to identify with one another, showcase their work, and communicate with a mass public. Even so, the cards seemed to be stacked against the World's Fair sculptors, including those who had been awarded medals, as Enid had. In addition to the number of industrial achievements at the fair, the abundance of fine art on view flooded the market and colored perceptions as to the viability of those engaged in the work. Who among these artists would find fame? How could women compete with men, given the athletic ability required to work in sculpture, most notably clay?

Enid had to draw a distinction between herself and other artists. Thus, it was no surprise that she referred to her work in terms of manual labor, given the aforementioned anecdote by Enid's alter ego, Duke, in *Three Girls in a Flat* about whipping up the dough to prepare biscuits, a clearly domestic chore. Some years later, in an article about another large-scale composition for another world's fair, Enid remarked:

> The manual labor was more than you would think. Outsiders haven't any idea of the physical strength required by a sculptor. One reason there are so few women sculptors is because they can't stand the physical strain. In making busts and small things the only fatigue comes from standing so long, and one gets used to that, just as shopgirls do; but when one attacks big designs physical strength is a big feature of the undertaking. One sometimes handles 2,000 pounds of clay in a day. One pound wouldn't seem much to you, but, I tell you, 2,000 pounds make an impression

> on one's muscles. When I was working on the World's Fair things [1893] my hands and arms used to get so tired that they were perfectly numb and limp and I would have to stop using them for awhile. Now my muscles are hardened so they will stand a great deal.[43]

Through such assertive language, Enid offered her current thinking about sculpture, women's role in the field, and her ambition. First, she established for herself a hierarchy of sculptural output that happened to correspond to gender and that aligned with the current biases of the discipline. She authorized a distinction between the sculpture of women artists and those who make busts and small things, which cause fatigue only through standing and working with the form, much like a shopgirl attended to goods. Such seemingly passive activity contrasted with the activity required in heaving, manipulating, and "attacking" massive amounts of clay, the quantities required to build larger works. Enid both justified and authorized the presence of muscle on her body, the "manish" qualities that her mother found so problematic. Enid also proudly asserted her growth over time as an artist, and a competent one at that. She compared her current muscular form and abilities with clay as active, impressive, and measurable, different from her more malleable shape as a young, numb, and limp artist at the Chicago fair. Just as she could mold a caryatid out of clay, she could mold herself into a competent sculptor endowed with strength, tenacity, and ambition.

Enid's writing about, and justification of, the physicality of sculpture was an aspect of the work that no other woman sculptor had undertaken in the 1890s. Certainly, among her circle all women sculptors knew of the labor involved, because they were engaged in the act of *doing* the labor. Moreover, they were reminded of their limitations, as narratives that connected clay to the labor required to work with it resounded in articles about sculptors, rather than words from them. A 1904 issue of the *Richmond Item* mentioned the difficulties of modeling in clay. After identifying the scarcity of women in the field of sculpture, the article explained why they struggle in holding their "places against all competitors": "Modeling in clay is more difficult than painting. A girl must be strong enough to lift moderately heavy weights, to stand upon ladders and elevated platforms, to keep her hands for hours in the cold, wet clay she makes her images of and to consent to be covered oftentimes from head to foot with white dust and clay marks." The article continued, noting that commitment to the field requires labor, and if that work can be endured, then success will come. However, "if she is not willing to endure whatever comes in the shape of hardship, and endure it cheerfully, then she should let sculpture alone." While the call for cheerfulness may seem derogatory, the following statement draws attention to how and why women should not approach the field: "The adopting by women of a trade or profession, too often with inadequate preparation, then pursuing it in a half hearted, dabbling way, looking around to see how the world applauds them, has put back a full century the real progress of woman in the industrial world." Though it is unlikely that Enid would have seen this article, she likely would have reacted to it with a sense of her own accomplishment, given what she had achieved through her work in the first two decades of her career while also championing women in the field of sculpture generally.[44]

Public pronouncements by women artists about working in clay and as an affirmation of labor were rare. Enid chose to emphasize this aspect of her work in her writing and utterances, and even to equalize her abilities in comparison to the men whom she worked alongside. The earliest example of such assertion occurred in 1892 with *Three Girls in a Flat,* with the second occurring the following year with the article about sculpture for *Current Topics,* a popular periodical. A few years later, in 1898, Enid authored "Talent for Sculpture" for the publication *What Women Can Earn.* She began with an exclamation as to the importance of physical strength: "There is only one reason why women with a talent for sculpture should not reach the same pre-eminence in this art as in others, and that is they do not all have the muscular strength and physical endurance which sculpture in its largest form calls for." Enid continued by noting that women sculptors who dabble in small-form sculpture have the skills they need to accomplish much in that arena. Thus, in Enid's mind, distinction came through working in clay and working in large scale.

Yet Enid was, in 1898, holding the door open to fellow artists. Following the cursory note as to the challenges of clay, Enid explained in great detail the mechanical process of making sculpture and working with the medium. She defined terms such as "pointing up" (which she knew well from her years of service to the fair) and explained how a paper design was then converted to a 3-D skeletal framework before clay was applied.

Again, the predilection for the monumental was claimed: "If it is a portrait bust or a small figure, the clay model is made the actual size, but if it is a design for a monument, fountain, or anything else *of heroic proportions*, it is executed first in miniature."[45]

Enid's statements in "Talent for Sculpture" (1898) laid bare both the processes for working in sculpture and the challenges of this field while offering women particular advice on how to achieve success within it. For comparison, consider an account of the World's Fair and Industrial Art that appeared in *Engineering Magazine* in 1893. In the article, Alfred T. Goshorn, who had been the director of the Centennial International Exposition in Philadelphia, praised the work of the artists at the Chicago fair, but tempered these compliments in light of the movement that he had helped foster. Goshorn's undertaking at Philadelphia in 1876 spawned growth in the establishment of art museums and art schools in the United States. As a result, the market was becoming flooded in a multitude of ways. In his analysis of Chicago, however, Goshorn praised the work of painters and sculptors "whose work is frequently so far in advance of their time that it is encouraged neither by financial support nor even by intelligent comprehension" and drew comparisons between the excellence of industrial arts education in Europe and the needs of those seeking a profession in art in the United States. He asked for "schools for the teaching not only of drawing, painting, and modeling as fine arts, but of decorative art in all its applications, and for technical and scientific training in the purely mechanical processes of art. Further, a different conception of the value and dignity of the applied arts must be cultivated among our young men and women who are seeking occupation in art." A multitude of options existed to facilitate learning; however, Goshorn was quick to point out that enrollment in a program was no guarantee of success. "A large number of purely art schools are now firmly established and are prospering in many cities throughout the land. They are crowded with students, especially women, ambitious to become artists, *pursuing art with a restless hope of success and fame*. . . . It is a natural impossibility that all, or even a respectable minority of these students can become artists whose works shall have any permanent worth as fine art."[46]

In contrast to Goshorn's underestimation of the capacity of women artists in sculptural pursuits and his relegation of them to decorative spheres, Enid's advice to women was to study at home and to go abroad, as she did. She wrote: "I cannot too strongly urge American girls to make their first three years' study in their own country. It is worse than folly to go to France unprepared to work from life. . . . Six years' work in the schools ought sufficiently to prepare the young sculptor to take a studio of her own, where she may work on original models, getting criticisms from masters as she needs them. Her development is then a matter of time, ability, and opportunity."[47]

Thus, despite Goshorn's cautionary tale, or perhaps because of it, some artists were able to build names and craft a measure of fame for themselves. In Enid's case, she intended to do more than merely "pursue art with a restless hope of success and fame." She intended to *cast fame,* literally and figuratively, as evidenced by her design for the memorial "of heroic proportions" to the Confederate dead.

3

Commemoration and Controversy

Decoration Day was a highly regarded tradition in every postbellum Southern family. As Maude recounted in a letter of May 1888 to Enid while the latter was away at school, "Yesterday was the decoration of Confederate graves. We all went out. Elsie went first to the C's country place to get some roses for the decoration. She and Alice climbed cherry trees & ate as much fruit as possible then fill[ed] a box which Elsie brought home." This narrative, like so many of the period, utilized simple, single-sentence reporting that ultimately failed to convey the importance of any one event. As enticing as the cherry trees and ambitious climbs were that afternoon, the flowers for the graves at Cave Hill Cemetery were of significance. Enid would have understood what was important in her younger sister's laundry list of activities and events. She knew that Decoration Day was an important ritual for the entire Yandell family. They gathered their flowers with friends, in this case the Castlemans; visited the cemetery together with the wives, sisters, daughters, and mothers of other decedents; and paid homage to the sons of Kentucky who had given their lives for the Confederate cause. On this day, the deceased were treated as mythic figures who deserved monuments of heroic proportions.[1]

Although no one in Enid's immediate family had perished in the war, paying respect on this day was also a way to honor the service of all of Kentucky's sons who had fought for the Confederacy. They deserved to be memorialized in a more tangible, lasting manner; words and flowers were insufficient tribute to what the soldiers had given to the cause. Such men included Enid's father, Lunsford Pitts Yandell II, who had served in the battle of Belmont, "the first fought in the West," was staff surgeon and medical inspector of Hardee's Corps, and offered the account of the battle of Shiloh that became the record published by the federal government. Mention was made of this lineage when Enid was introduced to audiences. For instance, in reports on Enid's success at Chicago with the Boone sculpture, the *Confederate Veteran* noted, "The name, Yandell, is honored throughout our Southland. The family of doctors, of which three, David, Lunsford, and William, were conspicuous in the war and afterward." Such a lineage carried an expectation to contribute to the annual acts of commemoration, and perhaps through that effort to achieve true fame. The article continued, "She [Enid] is at present making studies for a magnificent Confederate monument, to be erected in one of our Southern States" and noted that she was "proud of being the daughter of a Confederate soldier." The use of the term "soldier" within this context was particularly important; for while Enid's father was an officer and surgeon, audiences of Southern statuary in the 1890s came to expect recognition of the ordinary soldier—so much so that over 60 percent of the Confederate monuments dedicated between 1886 and 1899 featured a solder rather than an officer.[2]

In addition to having the familial pedigree to pursue such a commission, Enid also had the professional one. She spent the first part of the 1890s building a name for herself. By the time she was awarded the commission to design the Confederate monument for Louisville, at age twenty-four, Enid had embarked upon her career. She had already established herself as a talented, competitive, ambitious sculptor who could work for as well as alongside male professionals. What is more relevant in terms of our understanding of Enid's life and art is to consider how the securing and eventual revocation of the commission for the Confederate monument offers a prism through which to discuss gender in a complex and nuanced way. Such a discussion requires consideration of Enid's identity as a Southern artist as well as the performative, proscriptive, and retrospective nature of monument building and memorial mania from the 1860s through the early part of the twentieth century.[3]

Postbellum Memorialization

In contextualizing early postbellum memorialization, historian Gaines Foster has noted an emphasis on "the process of bereavement: the creation of cemeteries, the erection of funereal monuments, and the springtime

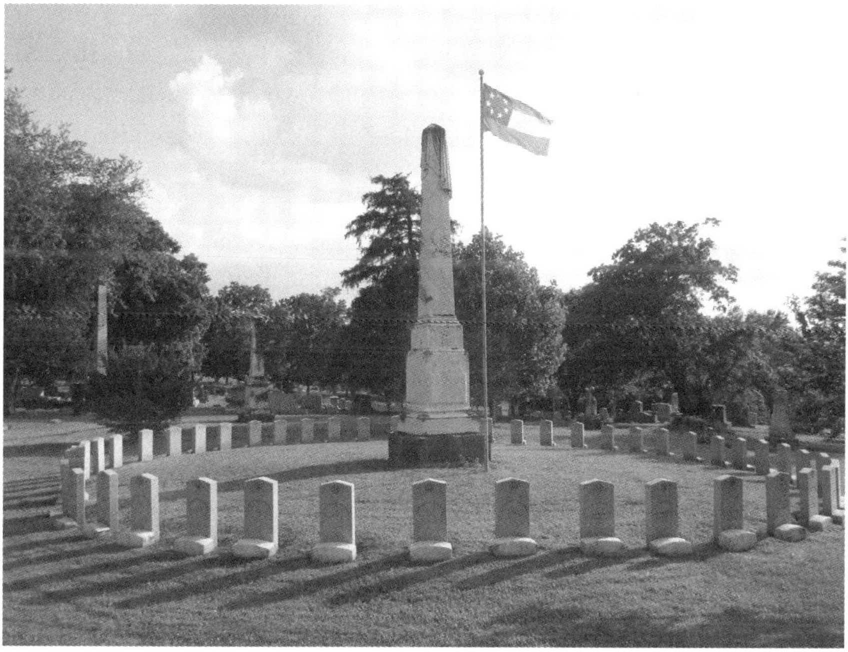

This Confederate monument, erected in 1869 in Cynthiana, Kentucky, is the oldest in the state. It features the geometric forms popular during the first phase of Confederate statuary in Kentucky. (Photo taken in June 2013, courtesy of the author.)

decoration of the graves." Memorialization was about those flowers from the home in the country that Enid's sisters picked alongside Alice Castleman and brought to the city to tend to the graves at Cave Hill Cemetery. Such commemorations were later accompanied by sculpture, as early monuments to the Confederate dead were constructed and placed in cemeteries shortly after the war. For these, the formal elements matched that of other grave markers. They had the trappings that symbolized death.[4]

Thus, the first phase of Confederate statuary in Kentucky was situated among the dead, for which the following three examples will suffice. The oldest Confederate monument in the state, in Harrison County, was erected in 1869 by the Cynthiana Confederate Monument Association, which commissioned a marble shaft to be placed in Battle Grove cemetery, the site of the last battle in Cynthiana and the ground established as a new cemetery that year.

The obelisk form draped at the top with a Confederate flag and placed within a circle of forty-seven Confederate soldiers' graves, used in Cynthiana, offered a prototype for several Confederate monuments in Kentucky over the next two decades. At Georgetown (1888), an unpolished granite obelisk featuring symbolic imagery (crossed cannons, crossed muskets, a drum, and flags) was surrounded by the graves of eighteen soldiers. The monument at Midway (1890) was a fifteen-foot-tall granite obelisk inscribed with the names of the dead. Eleven such monuments from the period 1869–1890 included an obelisk, shaft, or column as the primary element; were sited in a cemetery; and often included symbolic imagery, consisting of one or more of the following elements: weaponry of soldiers (swords, muskets, cannonball), symbols of victory, honor, and valor (such as the laurel wreath), or emblems of the Confederacy (such as the Confederate flag or the letters "CSA"). The form seemed prescriptive, given the subject and the lack of previous prototypes upon which to build.[5]

Beginning in 1892, however, the imagery used to commemorate the Confederate dead in Kentucky shifted abruptly. A figurative element became part of the Confederate memorial. That element took one form: the common soldier, or the "citizen-soldier," as discussed by scholar Kirk Savage. The inclusion of the figure marked a sharp contrast to the previous monuments to the Confederacy. According to Savage, "the entry of the common soldier into public sculpture created a profoundly different kind of sculptural body, a generic body." In other words, the figure represented an entire group of people, each of whom deserved to be recognized in statuary. Unlike commemorative statuary to specific individuals, the "citizen-soldier" was truly a generic embodiment. He was Everyman.[6]

From this point forward, examples of Confederate statuary in Kentucky reflected a choice in how to bear the burden of representation between the emblematic and the figurative. Three statues to the Confederacy that were installed from 1892 to 1894 illustrate this new trope of the citizen-soldier.

In the state capitol at Frankfort (1892), a common soldier stands atop four plinths and concrete footing in the Frankfort Cemetery. The figure of the soldier is made of marble, in contrast to the granite and limestone of his base and plinth, respectively. The use of marble in this way has replaced its use for columnar or shaft-like monuments prior to the era of the citizen-soldier. In Lexington's cemetery, the monument (1893) features a Confederate soldier standing on top of a base with the names of

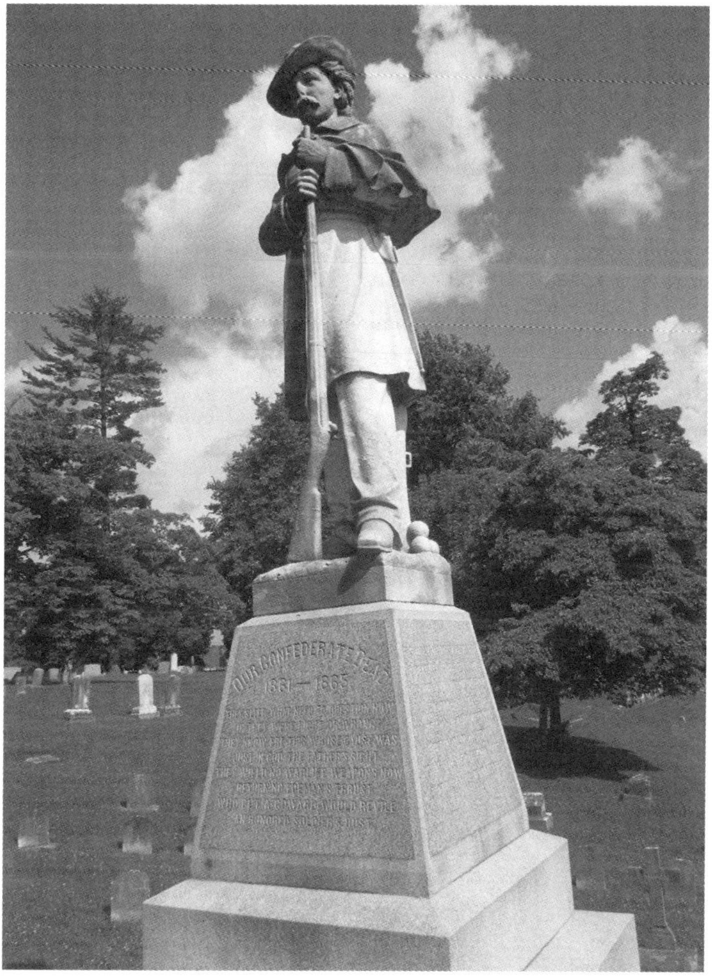

This Confederate monument, erected in 1892 in Frankfort, Kentucky, exhibits the shift in statuary, which began to focus on figurative elements, such as the "citizen-soldier." (Photo taken in June 2013, courtesy of the author.)

160 veterans inscribed in the panels. Finally, at Lawrenceburg (1894), the citizen-soldier had moved away from the cemetery and has entered the civic space of the Lawrenceburg Courthouse lawn. Thus, the representation of the dead became intertwined with the spaces of the living.

The Confederate monument in Louisville was commissioned at this moment, as the style of memorials was shifting. It embraced the citizen-soldier type of statuary. This monument—perhaps unknowingly on the part of the Woman's Confederate Monument Association and the artist—reflected the differing methods of commemoration and representation: the idea for the sculpture was conceived during the first phase of monument building, but the work was erected during the time of the citizen-soldier. Moreover, the monument was commissioned as the geography of representation had shifted; statuary had gained ground and had crept into the spaces of the everyday. The shifting terrain was emboldened by the ambition of the women of Louisville, who wanted to recognize the lives of those who served and who were lost.

In the latter years of the nineteenth century, as Civil War veterans organizations were gathering steam, the notion of the "Lost Cause" became the driving force behind the actions of veteran associations, ladies' memorial associations, and hereditary societies. The Ladies' Memorial Associations were among the earliest of these organizations, established as early as the end of the war, with their stated tasks including burial of the dead. After most of their local work had been accomplished, they organized into a confederation at Louisville in 1900. Local veterans organizations in the South joined forces as the Confederate Veterans (or United Confederate Veterans). The United Daughters of the Confederacy formed as a hereditary society of Southern women in 1894 and assumed leadership over a number of memorial associations. All of these organizations specialized in organizing, remembering, and perpetuating socially constructed representations of the past for the public in word, deed, or artistic form.[7]

The Ladies Memorial Associations had as their mission a trio of duties: care of the Confederate dead through burial; annual decoration; and the erection of monuments. These activities honored the past, the dead, and the Cause. Such efforts were critical, particularly those around Decoration Day and memorial making, because "in the case of the Confederacy there was no nation" to care for and honor its dead and, as such, the "domestic tie between these women and their lost men bore the weight of that political burden."[8] Margaret Cary Green Davis, historian of the Confederated Southern Memorial Association, described in 1904 the Lost Cause and the reasons to perpetuate it as follows: "In the great struggle for a noble and just Cause, for which the men of the South sacrificed their all, the women with a faith and confidence, sublime almost in its intensity, cheered and encouraged Fathers, Sons and Husbands in their gallant defense of their rights, weaved, spun, nursed the sick, and wherever a woman's hand could tend or soothe, there her mission. When defeat came, it passed through the fiery ordeal of ruined hopes; to accept with a brave and dignified resignation, a fate so adverse, its memory can never be effaced."[9]

The resulting desire to bring the memorial beyond the gravesite was palpable. Statuary served as a way to carve out—literally, in many cases—a "third space" for commemoration outside of the home and the graveyard. In so doing, the placement of such monuments lent legitimacy to the claim of representing the will of the community, the importance of commemoration, and the recognition of the role of women as contributing, if not leading, such efforts. Through commemorative statuary, women gained agency in civic space in a way that they had not previously held. They were bound in community with their sisters in mourning throughout the South as members of each memorial association "work[ed] on in its own plan of Memorial, emulated and encouraged by the efforts of their sisters in other States, all with the single idea and purpose of perpetuating the memory and deeds of their valiant dead." These women asserted their agency and, in turn, shared power with these markers, emblems that Gaines Foster has called "the ghosts of the Confederacy."[10]

Louisville's Monument to the Confederate Dead

In Louisville, the intent to memorialize seemed tied to a concurrent plea for the writing of history, allowing for the possibility of commemoration through both word and image. At Cave Hill Cemetery in Louisville, an address was delivered at the decoration of Confederate graves on May 26, 1879. Here, the politician William Campbell Preston Breckinridge (1837–1904), who had served in the Confederate cavalry of John Hunt Morgan, called for memory to be served and for history to be written as a monument to the fallen. Breckinridge further called for memorialization by women, commanding: "Mothers of Kentucky, these are your son's widows, your husbands; daughters, your fathers. Above us and around us these spirits sanctify this day's work. As you bend over to place the flowers on these graves, loved spirits bend over you and hallow the work." Breckinridge implored young women to learn of the sacrifices and history, further noting that visits to the cemetery and memorialization and ritual practice allow for the honoring of life, death, and memory. The burden fell to them to commemorate their dead.[11]

In 1887, Louisville resident Susan Preston Hepburn answered Breckinridge's call by leading the efforts to organize women and to commission the city's monument, in honor of the state's Confederate dead. She suggested that the women of the South might accomplish great good if only they were organized. The idea met with a ready response, and steps were immediately taken that resulted in the organization of the Kentucky Woman's Confederate Monument Association, with Hepburn as president. The association was organized in 1888 with a membership of fewer than 20; by 1894, the year their monument was commissioned, the group boasted 238 members.[12]

Hepburn planned and led the campaign for funds, entering into the work with the greatest enthusiasm. She forged interest among the city's women, many of whom were ardent Southern sympathizers. Funds were raised through appeal as well as through social events and entertainments such as oyster suppers, lawn fetes, and pageants—all in aid of the monument. The process, at times, seemed arduous, as noted by Enid's mother, who contributed to some of the affairs. Louise wrote to warn her daughter that some of her other projects might be completed "long before the Confederate people have their money." Even so, over this eight-year period (1887–1894), the monument came to be associated with the Civil War and the state's fallen Confederates, but also with Hepburn and her crew.[13]

Through organization, subscription, and supplication, Hepburn championed the monument above her other efforts. She spent "three fortunes" and many years of her life "making brighter the pathway of those less fortunate . . . the one dream and ambition of her life was realized only when the giant monument . . . rose in all its splendor, a memorial not only to the heroic dead of the Confederacy, but to Mrs. Hepburn's great service as well."[14]

In addition to her fund-raising prowess, Hepburn also had a hand in the land allocation, which was given by the mayor and the Board of Public Works at the suggestion of the park commissioners. The site for the monument was away from Cave Hill Cemetery and south of the city center, at Third Street and Shipp Avenue. Anticipation for the monument was so great that the intersection came to be known as the monument site even before it had been erected. Advertisements for real estate and notice of events mentioned their proximity to the monument.[15]

With donations coming in and a site identified, it seemed the only task left was to commission the monument. A call for participation was announced, but it gave little instruction to the proposers. Stone seemed to be of utmost importance: the call for submissions stated, "Material to be used to be of first-class standard granite, or granite and pure bronze, and cost when erected, including foundation not exceeding twelve thousand dollars. The Association reserves the right to reject any or all designs or to accept any one of same but the one furnishing such as is accepted will be awarded the contract and work." Other than the use of granite and the restriction of a budget, no guidance as to form or subject was provided.[16]

The expectation for form was not expressly articulated in advance perhaps because the form had been prescribed, according to precedent, to follow one of two motifs: the symbolic, shaft monument; or the common soldier. Even so, quite a bit of variation on those themes could occur. To make the selection from the submissions, an Executive Committee would review the designs submitted by artists and architects. The committee would then make a recommendation to the Woman's Confederate Monument Association, which would seek approval from its membership. What seemed like a fairly straightforward process in fact required several occasions for feedback and discussion. Thus, it could be some time before the monument would be carved in stone.

With funding and a location set, the monument commission moved forward. The deadline for submissions was set for September 15, 1894, and it seemed as though the erection of the monument was imminent. Unfortunately, however, the awarding of the commission turned out to be more complicated than this straightforward outline of the process would suggest. (For a detailed timeline of the submission and selection process for the Louisville Confederate monument, see the Appendix.)

Enid's Design

In contemplating her submission for the Louisville competition, Enid turned to classical sculpture—the grandiose constructions from the spectacle of 1893 Chicago—to develop her idea for a monument to the Confederate dead. She also turned to an architect with whom she had previously worked, William J. Dodd. Although the ultimate design was submitted as "Yandell-Dodd," the details of the pair's collaboration are unknown because sketches of their work and documents detailing just how they worked together do not exist. Newspaper accounts indeed identify the work as a collaboration; one article states, "Two of the contestants are Mr. Will Dodd, the architect, and Miss Enid Yandell: They, however, have entered their drawings together," with Enid in charge of the figure and Will in charge of the pedestal. Thus, we may assume that Enid held the primary role in terms of the form, content, and intended meaning of the piece.[17]

The monument's location, as noted above, would be at the intersection of Third Street and Shipp Avenue, a short distance from the streetscapes of Broadway, where Enid had grown up and where she was fashioning a studio. Given Enid's experiences as a site-based sculptor who had, in Chicago, created monumental works that could be viewed from afar, she would doubtless have considered the location, its sightlines, and its visibility when she fashioned her design, in consultation with Dodd.

In her design, Enid proposed an allegorical female figure of Fame holding a wreath in one hand and a Confederate flag in the other. Fame stood triumphantly, appearing to have just alighted atop the Corinthian capital shaft. Two bands of decoration divided the shaft into thirds; and, at the base, a series of panels would display inscriptions, such as the names of donors or soldiers. The column and figure were situated on a base of radiating steps; and on the furthest of these, five bronze candelabra, each fifteen feet tall, were to be installed.

To put Enid's design into context, it is useful to consider her body of work up to this point alongside the generation of commemorative sculpture of which this monument was a part. Enid's education had trained her to sketch from a model and draw from the antique—tasks that would have positioned her to create either a figurative or an allegorical subject. In addition, she had experience creating work on both small and large scale, in the form of busts and tabletop sculptures (including bas-relief), as well as monumental subjects, such as the Daniel Boone she had created for the Kentucky Building in Chicago. Her designs for decorative and architectural motifs, including desk panels and capitals of buildings as well as the caryatids at Chicago, demonstrated that she might add decorative elements to balance her compositions and to evoke appropriate images

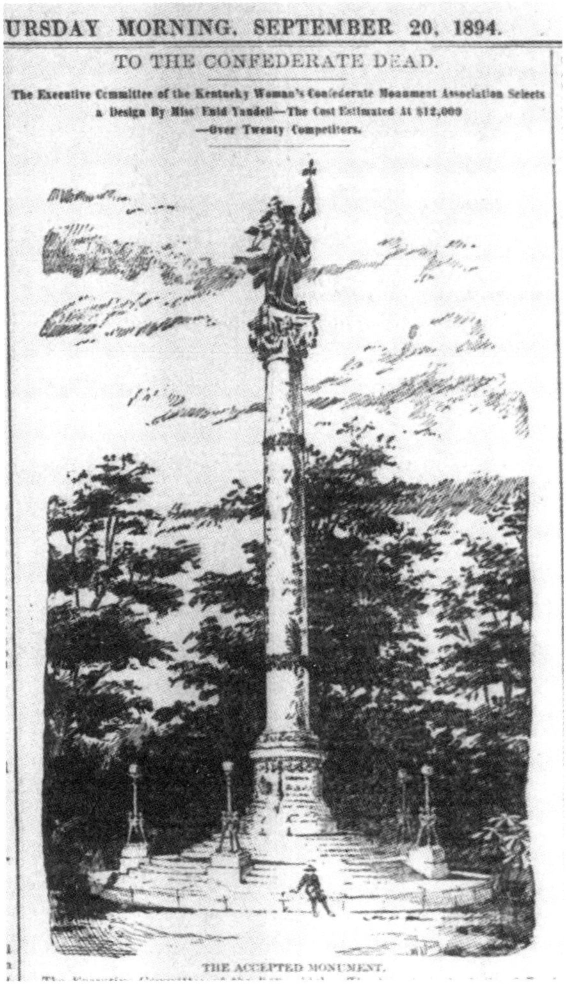
URSDAY MORNING, SEPTEMBER 20, 1894.

TO THE CONFEDERATE DEAD.

The Executive Committee of the Kentucky Woman's Confederate Monument Association Selects a Design By Miss Enid Yandell—The Cost Estimated At $12,000 —Over Twenty Competitors.

THE ACCEPTED MONUMENT.

Announcing the selection of the Yandell-Dodd design for the Confederate memorial, this illustration appeared in the *Louisville Courier-Journal* on September 20, 1894, with the headline "To the Confederate Dead" and the caption "The Accepted Monument."

of commemoration. In addition, Enid's experience working with clay—and lots of it—meant that she could handle the physical labor of creating a mold for a large enough work to be seen from the ground. Finally, Enid could meet expectations. As a professional artist in the service of the

Board of Lady Managers as well as the Art Department at the Columbian Exposition, she had experience navigating the bureaucracies of large-scale projects. Further, her experience working as an independent artist meant that she had developed a reputation for being able to meet the needs of patrons.

Professional factors aside, Enid's monument would serve as the exemplar of Louisville's commemorative spirit. In other works, it would function as a physical embodiment of the sorrow and grief of those who laid flowers and greenery on graves in the cemetery. The stakes could not have been higher for any other work up to this point in Enid's career: submitting a design for this project, in her hometown, entwined her identity, as well as her family's. And her design was awarded the commission.

Enid's design was unique: no other Confederate monument, in Kentucky or anywhere in the former states of the Confederacy at that point, had elected to employ a classically dressed woman as the instantiation of commemoration. Perhaps, the emblem was inspired by the actions, if not the taste, of Kentucky women in nearby Lexington.

Two decades earlier, on May 19, 1869, the Ladies Memorial and Monument Association was created in Fayette County. The women began raising money for the monument that was erected six years later in Lexington on May 26, 1875. Known as the Ladies' Confederate Memorial, it depicts a cross draped with a Confederate flag, onto which a broken shaft is leaning. Beneath the cross, on the base of the monument, is a broken sword and flowers. The choice of emblem is understood, given the monument's construction as part of the earliest days of monument building in Kentucky. Yet the theme of this monument conveys loss and sorrow rather than glory and honor of the deceased, as all other Confederate monuments in Kentucky from the previous two decades had. Thus, while the image conveyed the sorrow of the women of the Ladies Memorial and Monument Association, the actual building of a monument to their work recognized their contribution to the work of commemoration. It gave them a material presence in what was, at the time, the only space of commemoration—the cemetery—and reminded others of the important role they played in perpetuating the Lost Cause.[18]

In crafting a design for the monument to the Confederate dead in Louisville, Enid invoked the body as a vessel of meaning and developed a symbolic as well as a conceptual design for the memorial. Her design had a figure at the top of the column draped, as if in classical attire, holding a laurel wreath in her right hand as an emblem of victory and honor. In her left hand, she holds a shaft with cloth and a cross at the top. A column topped by a draped, almost goddess-like figure, Enid's Confederate monument thus suggested a different meaning than those of the traditional monuments, which had focused on grief, loss, and sorrow. The figure took on the identity of a Greek goddess, familiar subject matter for Enid, given her classical training. It appears to resemble Nike, the victory figure who was often depicted with a laurel wreath and a flag or similar attribute; more specifically, the placement of the figure on top of a column called to mind victory columns that had been used since classical times and for which there were contemporary examples. In adopting this form and content, Enid's design for the Confederate monument had the capacity not only to commemorate, but also to change the narrative from one of loss to one of honor and victory.

By employing a woman in the figurative role, Enid gave her the burden of dual representation. On the one hand, Fame, which can be interpreted as fame for the Confederate dead, signified the men who had earned prominence due to their individual and collective achievements as Louisville's sons. The second meaning, which is evident only through reading the iconography that Enid employed along with the context of the commission, signifies victory. For while the South had lost the war and Kentucky and Louisville had lost so many men, the representation of victory was a necessary element to fertilize the myth of the Lost Cause. Moreover, the inclusion of a woman holding a flag and wreath enabled Enid to foreground the women of the monument effort as leading the charge for extolling the victory and honor of their husbands, brothers, sons, and fathers. It erased, according to social historian Lawrence Goodwyn, the "patterns of deference" that permeated women's social order. After all, in Enid's view, the women were victorious in achieving their aim of commemorating their dead.[19]

The Decision

Commissioning a Confederate monument was an action that had been normalized in communities across the South by the time Louisville commissioned its monument in 1894. Lineage and heritage societies led the efforts, and contributed to the knowledge building, of the community of (largely) women who were spearheading these activities. Elements of sculpture could be mass-produced and entire monuments could be ordered from catalogues, with purchasers identifying what attributes they desired and whether the soldier should be Union or Confederate. Monument building was clearly an industry.

And yet every commission was unique. The Louisville Confederate monument project was anything but an ordinary undertaking in the hands of the Woman's Confederate Monument Association. From the call for submissions to the celebratory dedication, newspapers gave accounts of every stage of the process, including the selection of Enid's design, which was a result of the voting of the expert architect panel, along with the ensuing controversy over the decision, followed by the laying of the cornerstone and the eventual dedication in July 1895.[20]

Just as the move to erect a Confederate monument was a long time brewing, Enid also had a long time to prepare for this commission. Her training at the Chicago fair positioned her well to take up a project steeped in emblematic purpose. Her training in Cincinnati and subsequent work and study in Chicago prepared her for what social anthropologist Burton Benedict, in his analysis of world's fairs, has termed the "mammoth rituals" that employed visual communication to "manufacture tradition" and "impose legitimacy." Arguably, such a trio of purposes was replicated in the memorial work that Enid intended to undertake.[21]

On September 19, 1894, while staying with family in Tennessee, Enid received a telegram that read: "Letter 'K' [K(1) was the designation of the Yandell-Dodd submission] unanimously selected by the Committee. Accept our hearty congratulations. Alice B. Castleman." The author of the note, was Alice Castleman, was a longtime family friend (one who knew the tropes of commemoration, as evidenced by her ritual gathering of roses and cherries recounted at the beginning of this chapter). News of Enid's victory came from others, as well. Her aunt Fanny reported, "Let your mind rest, yours unanimous vote" while a friend reported, "Hoorah lady [? indecipherable] they can't beat us artists."[22]

Immediately following the September 1894 announcement of the winner of the competition, newspaper accounts published the sketch of the winning submission and described the work's specifications, noting that it was to be 75 feet high and 42 feet in diameter, made of Bowling Green white limestone with North Carolina gray granite, with the figure, candelabra, and flag described earlier. Among these, the *Louisville Courier-Journal* reported the selection, included an image of it, and identified it as "The Accepted Monument" on September 20, at which time Susan Preston Hepburn called a meeting for the purpose of "getting an expression from the members as to the recent action of the Advisory and Executive Committees in selecting Miss Yandell's design for a monument."[23] The selection of the winning design, which was made by the Woman's Confederate Monument Association's Executive Committee, was to be confirmed by the membership at large.

Newspapers far and wide made account of the decision, as well as the controversy that followed. The *Louisville Times* reported what happened next: "The ladies of the Confederate Monument Association were enthusiastic in their indorsement [*sic*] of the proposition to transfer to a committee of architects the responsibility of selecting from the number of designs offered in competition the one best suited for the monument. This committee, which was an excellent one, unanimously recommended the design that had already been accepted by the Executive Committee. Thereupon the ladies rejected the report of the architects, who had been called in as experts, and voted two to one for a monument 'with a soldier on it.'"[24]

The *Louisville Courier-Journal* reported that when Hepburn saw that matters were becoming complicated, she said that she had hoped that by selecting architects to review the Executive Committee's selection, the members of the association would abide by the decision. According to the *Courier-Journal*'s account, several women in the association shouted in response, "We won't! We won't, though! We want a soldier on the monument!" Put simply, the women wanted a man on their monument, not a woman; they wanted a man, not a woman, to be part of a lasting memorial to their men.[25]

A member of the Executive Committee of the association, Basil Duke, intervened to ask that ballots be cast to secure the winning selection; all of this, of course, took place more than a week after Enid's design had been selected and printed in the newspapers. The resulting vote among the membership revealed support for a monument other than Enid's by a ratio of two to one (24 votes for another design; 12 for Enid's). The "new" winning design had been submitted by Michael Muldoon, the owner of a local monument company, who had submitted a design based upon one that was already erected at Richmond, Virginia. In other words, the winning design would be a copy of one installed nearly 600 miles away! It seemed unreasonable that Louisville had gone through all of this trouble to run a competition only to commemorate their dead with the representation created for another city. The Richmond monument did indeed share some characteristics with Muldoon's proposal for Louisville (both featured a figure atop a Corinthian capital); however, the design for Louisville more closely resembled the Confederate monument at Raleigh, North Carolina's capitol building. That monument, with its trio of figures, Corinthian capital, and inscription to the Confederate dead, was commissioned in May 1894, although it was not dedicated until a year later. It was also engineered by Muldoon.[26]

Crisis erupted for a second time when the women realized that the Muldoon submission so closely resembled the Richmond monument. According to the *Louisville Courier-Journal,* "some of them expressed disappointment, and said if they had to vote over they would vote differently." Enid's design proposal was again read, "and its fine points and originality dawned on many." After this, the women charged that the earlier vote was fraudulent, with only 32 women present for an election that had 36 votes cast (even if this were so, however, a difference of four votes would not have given Enid the win). As the meeting concluded, to be resumed on October 5, the *Courier-Journal* pointed out that the issue with gender came from Enid's own: "It is deeply regretted by all Miss Yandell's friends that her design should be rejected by a body of her own sex, and in direct opposition to the decisions of those asked to judge such matters." The consummate professional, Enid reported back to the association, via a friend, that she would abide by their decision, whatever it might be.[27]

Re-Viewing Enid's Design

Although both the Executive Committee and the architect's committee had selected Enid's design, the Woman's Confederate Monument Association had rejected it. In comparing the two designs and their contexts, it is easy to see the differences between what Enid had offered and what the women of the Woman's Confederate Monument Association had wanted for their monument. Whereas Enid offered an iconic figure, a symbol of Fame, the women wanted a soldier. Whereas Enid had designed an entirely new monument built upon classical precedent to endow the sculpture with heroic meaning, the women were content to have a reproduction of another work that would be sited in front of the courthouse in Raleigh, North Carolina. Whereas Enid had presented emblems that were aspirational, the women selected a work that was commemorative but ordinary, the figure of an Everyman. Finally, whereas Enid was a woman, the women of the Association wanted a man to design their sculpture.

The search for a Confederate monument for Louisville, a commission under the aegis of the Kentucky Woman's Confederate Monument Association, discloses a conflict between the gains women in the South had made and the strictures of Southern monument culture. The public roles that women took in these memorial activities contributed to the broader efforts at valorizing the men. As historian LeeAnn Whites has noted, "The problem was how to provide a means for the reconstruction of their men's self-image without reconstructing themselves in the process—or at least without appearing to do so. They gave over conventionally 'male' aspects of public organizational activities . . . to prominent men." In their commitment to male representation, the Woman's Confederate Monument Association held to tightly constructed gender roles that predated the war. Put simply, Enid didn't fit the mold of a woman who stood by her man.[28]

Because Enid had won the votes of the Executive Committee and the panel of architects, the stumbling blocks came from the membership of the association and appeared to be twofold: her gender and the figure on top of the column. Of primary concern was the identity of the monument's creator. Although the submissions were blindly reviewed, published reports announcing the winning submission focused on Enid's gender and her family name. One of the members of the association was reported to have remarked that the Woman's Confederate Monument Association "did not desire to perpetuate Miss Yandell, but the Confederate dead." For at least some members of the association, selecting a memorial design from Enid's hand meant privileging her over Confederate men.[29]

Contrary to the assertion that Enid's commission was revoked because she was a woman, we should consider how gender simultaneously supported and subverted Enid's work relative to her alignment with Southern gender performativity, as noted above. While perhaps part of the controversy revolved around gender, in actuality the bias reflected the dissolution of ideals of the Southern woman. Enid was no longer one to "beat biscuit," but was one who could manage 2,000 pounds of clay. She was no longer content to pick flowers to lay upon a grave, she was an active agent determining how to catalyze commemoration in civic space. Enid was a testament to the contrast between the women of her mother's generation and those of her own. She was indicative of the shifting definition of what it meant to be a Kentucky woman, part of a long history and diverse cross-section that led historian Margaret Ripley Wolfe to claim that "a composite of the Kentucky woman would require an unusual chameleon-like character."[30]

Thus, the story of the Confederate Monument was enmeshed in the chameleon-like character of the women involved as well as the oscillation between positions of agency and lack thereof. As historians have noted, women were marginalized, if present at all, in the writing of history; their stories were "the fallen leaves, the missing pages, in works that chronicle and interpret the state's past." As historian LeeAnn Whites has eloquently stated, "it is, however, precisely because gender has apparently mattered so little in the nineteenth-century South that it does matter so much." In the case of Enid's entry in the design competition, gender was an essential part of this project, from the patron and the artist originally commissioned to create the memorial to the depiction of a female allegorical figure in the memorial's design.[31]

Women of the South have been characterized variously by historians; of particular note, however, is their trajectory following the war. Scholar Mary Elizabeth Massey has noted that "the Civil War provided a springboard from which they leaped beyond the circumscribed 'woman's sphere' into that heretofore reserved for men." Likewise, historian Anne Firor Scott has argued that after the Civil War "door after door" was "flung open" for elite white Southern women as a result of women's independent activities during the war and the dissolution of patriarchal power from the war and emancipation. The significant loss of life served as a pragmatic reminder of this blurring of distinctions; but the crossing over into other arenas intentionally and long-term, as in the choice of occupation, was a significant step in the change. Moreover, during a period Massey defines as the end of the Civil War and the outbreak of World War I—many years of Enid's life—the women "outran and outdistanced their predecessors."[32]

Such generational differences might have prevented Enid from creating a lasting monument of durable material in her home city. Such a commission, while it might have pigeonholed Enid into being a Civil War monument maker, would have given her the opportunity to make a name for herself in her home city and in support of a burgeoning business: commemorative statuary at the turn of the century. Seeing what was at stake and how events were unfolding, Enid undertook a revision of the original Yandell-Dodd design, hoping that such an aesthetic compromise would win over the women of the association.

After hearing the membership's criticisms of their earlier design, before the October 5, 1894 meeting Enid and her collaborator submitted a revision of their original design to the Woman's Association, making minor adjustments to the material, the shaft, and the landscaping. They changed the figure on top from a standing figure holding a wreath and a Confederate flag to a seated figure of grief and sorrow—a change that they felt women of the association would have related to, given that the design most frequently chosen for early Confederate monuments evoked death and grief.[33]

Enid and her collaborator offered the following rationale for their changes:

> This shaft is surmounted by a bronze figure sympolic [*sic*] of "Fame," martial fame, as denoted by the sandals, corselet and breastplate covering the upper part of the body. Instead of a standing aggressive attitude, suggesting the brilliant triumphs of a victor, a sitting posture has been deemed more appropriate, as expressing deep grief for a "Lost Cause," which the years have sublimated into a glorified sorrow. As the figure stoops forward she holds in her right hand a wreath of olives, gentle emblem of peace, seeing to summon the sleeping heroes, now that the hush of peace has succeeded the noise of strife, to lift their eyes and

> behold the true measure of values, for in the light of fame the crown is not alone to the victor, but to all noble souls who have lost self in a sublime devotion to duty—a duty whose call reaches them through the voices of loving wives, little ones and the land irradiated by the sacred fires of "home." As she holds the wreath in her right hand, from her left there floats backward to the wind the partially furled Confederate flag. As a crown of glory awaits the heroes whose valor and bravery have transformed defeat into victory, so their banner has been lifted from the dust, and untarnished by shame or dishonor, its bedimmed fact thrilling the memory to thoughts of those immortal souls "who live again in deeds sublime that pierce night like stars."[34]

The emblem of Fame was reinvented into a seated figure so as to express grief rather than (perceived) aggression. She was to more closely resemble the women who were commissioning her creation—paying homage, laying evergreens before the men. The new form also connected intentionally to the women themselves, who also deserved recognition. Yet Enid's revisions did not meet the prescriptive interests of Hepburn and the membership of the Monument Association. They had an idea of what they had wanted based upon what they were familiar with, as evidenced by the visual language used in Kentucky monuments to the Confederate dead over the previous fifteen years.

The Chosen Monument

Ultimately, the decision was made by the association to award the commission to Muldoon, whose firm completed the work the following year. Newspapers reported on the loss felt by some women who were denied the opportunity to see the work of another woman. One account stated regret "that this talented young artist should have lost the opportunity of giving to her people this piece of monumental work, in which she would have embodied much of that patriotic sentiment found in the women of the south, and which would also have been an encouragement to young artists of both sexes."[35]

Some published commentary made very clear the issue at hand. The credentials by which Enid was initially chosen to create the monument (her lineage, her father's war service, and her professional accomplishment) were ultimately not the contributing factors to the commission being revoked. As the *Memphis Commercial-Appeal* reported:

> Miss Yandell is a Louisville girl. . . . It may be remarked, in passing, that Miss Yandell is a member of the family of Dr. David Yandell, the famous surgeon, who staunched the wounds of Albert Sidney Johnston at Shiloh. . . . But the deplorable phase of the matter is seen in the failure of the women of the association to rejoice in the fact that a Southern woman of genius, after submitting to all the conditions of the proposals, had gained the verdict of the judges. It is hoped the association will reconsider its vote and apologize to Miss Yandell in the only proper way—by accepting her de-design [*sic*] upon the reconsideration of the vote, she may enjoy the satisfaction of knowing that she deserved it, and, with the report of the proceedings before us, we are convinced that she did deserve it. The women of the association have lost a rare opportunity to exploit the genius of their own sex, and if they can endure the effect of their action, Miss Yandell can well afford to be indifferent.[36]

While mentioning Enid's connection to Dr. Yandell, Enid's uncle and the tragic outcome for Johnston at Shiloh, the article focused instead on the inability of the women of the association to support another woman.

Other criticisms were leveled at the trio of architects charged with the task of reviewing the submissions after the Executive Committee's recommendation had failed the association. The poem below, which appeared in the *Louisville Times,* poked fun at the process of including an outside jury of experts that in the end was overruled by the women of the association, who had a preconceived notion of what they wanted in their monument.

> Three pleasant architects, all in a line,
> Were chosen by the chosen to choose a design.
> Three pleasant architects, telling what they knew,
> One had prostration, and then there were two.
> Two luckless architects, scared enough to run.
> Shied at the monuments, and then there was one.

One luckless architect, ready to go mad,
They shot him with a ballot-box; now, wasn't that too bad?[37]

After much controversy, on Saturday, May 25, 1895, the cornerstone for the memorial was finally laid in the presence of several thousand. Susan Preston Hepburn officiated at the exercises and placed in the cornerstone a box containing souvenirs of the eight-year campaign for monument funds, along with relevant items, to create a time capsule of sorts. Among these were a picture of Hepburn herself; a photograph of Jefferson Davis, president of the Confederacy; a cigar that Davis had touched when he visited Louisville years earlier; and personal effects related to the war dead, such as a mourning scarf. The dedication of the finished monument was held on July 30, 1895, at which commemorative ribbons were distributed to attendees.[38]

With its commission and subsequent dedication, the Confederate monument was the first piece of public art erected in Louisville. As such, protocols did not exist in terms of communicating information about the work to its audiences. In the short term, as long as Decoration Day was marked on the calendar, attention would be paid to this, and the continuing, memorial activity of Southern women. Awaiting the fresh blossoms and ripened greens that coincided with the full bloom of spring, young girls and women tending to Decoration Day performed the sole public ritualized task in postbellum Louisville. The pilgrimage to Cave Hill was an annual ritual now that the Confederate war dead had been buried and memorialized. Sharing stories along the way to visit their dead, someone in the family could recall and share what they knew about the Confederate monument, Louisville's very own ghost of the Confederacy.

Enid's Memorial

Over the years, errors slipped into the monument's history a generation later, shortly after Enid's death in 1934. A specific example of misinformation occurred within the context of documenting the state of Kentucky and the city of Louisville during the interwar years for a series of guidebooks aimed at the general public. In these, Enid was associated with the Confederate monument, a commission that was in fact, as we have seen, given to her and then taken away. Pinpointing the moment when the attribution shifted from Michael Muldoon to Enid Yandell is a difficult task; however, it seems to have occurred between 1934 and 1939. The incorrect information persisted for a decade, until a University of Louisville student, Mary Phyllis Schaefer, corrected the error.

As part of the Works Progress Administration (WPA) activities in the 1930s, a guidebook for every state in the United States was authorized, covering each state's archaeology, topography, history, and culture. The guidebooks for Kentucky and a subsequent version issued by an automobile club that focused on the city of Louisville incorrectly named Enid as the artist of the Confederate monument. The entry in the Louisville guidebook read: "*Confederate Memorial.* . . . was designed by Enid Yandell (1870–1934), Louisville-born sculptress." Kentucky's guidebook from 1942, the third printing of the initial run from 1939, likewise mistook Enid as the creator: "*Confederate Memorial* . . . This memorial, unveiled in in 1895, was designed by the Louisville-born sculptress, Enid Yandell." That state guidebook, however, correctly attributes other works to Enid: "Enid Yandell (1870–1934), whose work in sculpture is well known, was a native of Louisville. Her *Daniel Boone,* a character study, first exhibited at the Chicago Fair in 1893, stands in Cherokee Park in Louisville. Near by [*sic*] is Hogan Fountain also designed by her."[39]

The error in attribution for the Confederate monument was pointed out by art historian Justus Bier, a scholar of German sculpture at the University of Louisville, who had supervised Schaefer's undergraduate thesis, "Enid Yandell, 1870–1934." For her thesis Schaefer had consulted these guidebooks. Although perhaps not "scholarly" resources, such works were the only published materials outside of memory and newspaper clippings that referenced Enid's work and her role in the broader field of public art at the time. In writing about Enid, Schaefer was careful not to include the monument in her list of Enid's works. Her research then led Bier to pursue further scholarship focused on the monument, which revealed information that was known at the time of the monument's commission but had been forgotten over the years.[40]

After her experience with the Louisville Confederate monument, Enid's trajectory as an artist took her work to many locations in the United States as well as to Paris. She went on to secure work for the 1897 Tennessee Centennial Exposition in Nashville, where her colossal Minerva/Athena drew great attention. Enid submitted work to a number of world's fairs, all the while maintaining a studio in New York or Paris. She also pursued other commissions, including a memorial fountain to be placed in Providence, Rhode Island—a competition that she won over eighteen other competitors, all of whom were male. She successfully navigated both worlds—that of the monumental and the male as well as the figurine and the female. But she also had to withstand scrutiny. Those outside of the art world questioned, as Julia Grant had, Enid's authority to work, particularly within the field of sculpture. In response, Enid's mother had grown used to answering such questions with a quip, as she related in a letter to Enid in 1899: "People ask me so often how you happened to be a sculptor & I always make the same reply you were just born that way."[41]

A more jubilant tone was taken by Enid's paternal grandmother, Eliza B. Yandell, wife of the family namesake, Dr. Lunsford Pitts Yandell I. Grandma Yandell moved to Louisville in 1867, just two years before Enid was born, and was a part of her life until the elder Dr. Yandell passed away in 1878, at which time Eliza returned to her Tennessee home. Away from her "Sunshine," Eliza saved everything that her granddaughter sent to her, whether pencils, photographs, pieces in wood, or watercolors. Such a collection of Enid's from ages ten to thirty, her formative years, constituted a memorial of sorts, in the words of her mother—though hardly one worthy of being saved. After receiving the crated materials in Louisville, Louise wrote to Enid in August 1898, after the passing of her paternal grandmother:

> This morning a box came to you from Mason-Tenn—I opened it & found they had sent you all of your letters which for years Grannie had kept—really from the number I imagine she must have kept every one you ever wrote her—Some are in the childish hand of eight-years old—& in the box they sent all the pictures of yourself you had given her—the queen picture [Queen of the Satellites] & those taken when your father died—& then they sent you the woodcarvings you had given her—& the drawings—it was very sweet—& pathetic to see how she valued the "sunshine" you had put into her life. . . . I have packed all the thing[s] back in the box & nailed it up & put it in the 3rd story—When you come

> home you can look over them & destroy them—They are a memorial & one of the sweetest things in your nature.[42]

Fortunately, a number of these items were not discarded; instead, they functioned as a living memorial to Enid during her lifetime, and their remains continue to do so today. They commemorate her beginnings as an artist and how she managed to overcome the controversy surrounding the Louisville memorial to the Confederate dead.

Looking back on her career thirty years later, after the death of the strong-willed Yandell and Elliston women, Enid considered the worlds in which she had navigated, how she negotiated her ambitious path of hard work that yielded a successful career and philanthropic work at what was perhaps the world's greatest time of need. When asked in 1924 about the role of women in the arts, Enid saw promise in what lay ahead for future generations of women sculptors. "Yes, I think it is a lovely occupation for women, if they have love for form. It requires much study and is wonderful for developing the mentality. It requires a great deal of physical strength and, of course, one must have talent before entering the field. The field is not overcrowded for art is still much unappreciated in this country, but every year I see it advance."[43]

Right she was. In 2004, the Kentucky Historical Society and the Kentucky Department of Highways offered a form of commemoration of a different sort than what Enid had turned her attention to throughout her career. Near the enduring bronze that Enid had designed of Daniel Boone, a historical marker was erected in Louisville's Cherokee Park in recognition of her efforts in challenging women's roles in the visual arts while also recognizing her monumental contributions to the national and local sculptural scene. Acts such as this, the placement of a historical marker, have enabled us to commemorate Enid today. In so doing, they have contributed to the sculpting of her legacy.[44]

4

Fairs and Figureens

Even though she had worn a tiara in a pageant in 1890, by the latter part of the decade, Enid outwardly eschewed such ostentatious frivolity and femininity and preferred pronouncements of her occupational success. She stated this preference when commenting on the colossal sculpture of Athena that she had designed for the Tennessee Centennial Exposition (1897): "It brought me into such prominence . . . that I was represented in the newspapers with a tiara on my head. The tiara and the photograph, however, belonged to Mrs. Van Leer Kirkman, president of the Nashville Centennial Woman's Board." To correct any perception that she might be privileged, or even feminized, with the crown jewels of a queen, Enid remarked candidly, "I assure you I do not own a tiara." Such crafting of her image distanced her present bachelor-maid days from earlier events in her life, particularly when she did wear a crown, as Queen of the Satellites in 1890. Thus, the characterization of Enid that emerged during this decade was tied to her accomplishments in the field of public statuary, resulting in a self-image of independence and agency. Such skillful crafting, backed by evidence of work, enabled Enid to achieve recognition within her peer group, culminating in her election in 1898 to the National Sculpture Society, the first organization of professional sculptors formed in the United States.[1]

Enid's studio output from New York and Paris—the capitals of the art world at the time—resulted in a thread of public works, including her colossal Athena for the Centennial Exposition in Nashville in 1897, which was the largest work ever created by a woman artist at the time, and pieces exhibited at subsequent fairs at Buffalo (1901) and St. Louis (1904). Consisting of mythological as well as realistic portraits and ethereal, expressive works, the sculptures Enid created over this decade-plus, as described in this chapter, are placed within the context of Enid's broader body of work, and connections are made between these works and their permanent installations elsewhere. Attention is also paid to Enid's busts of individuals, works she affectionately called "figureens," which were on a smaller scale, in contrast to her monumental sculptures. To set the stage for this examination, an overview of trends in American sculpture and a consideration of some of Enid's contemporaries would be helpful.

Trends in American Sculpture, 1890s–1900s

Enid Yandell's career mirrors the trends in American sculpture, including the influence of the École des Beaux Arts, the Académie Julian, and other art schools that bore witness to expanding definitions of form and audience. Like her contemporaries, Enid developed a practice of oscillating between commissions for public sculpture and statuary in parks, squares, and open areas such as the fairs, on the one hand, and tabletop portraiture and embellishments for wealthy, or at least noteworthy, patrons and their indoor retreats, on the other.

Moreover, Enid's private and public commissions show that, given the trajectory of her career, none would have been possible without the influence of Paris and the decade's world's fairs. Through her continuing education as well as sustained engagement with male sculptors in her field, Enid gained attention as a capable sculptor at a time when sculpture was still an emerging field for women. During the 1890s, Enid worked in a manner that was in keeping with the practices of her male contemporaries. She was not tethered to the strictures of "female sculpture"; in other words, she worked like a man.

Also, as mentioned in Chapter 2, Enid's use of language in describing her work and labor set her apart from her peers. To illustrate this point, it is useful to consider Enid's career alongside that of a fellow White Rabbit as well as one of the male teachers with whom she worked in Chicago. This allows us not only to see differences between the careers of Enid and her peers, but also to understand more fully how they navigated their sculptural worlds and how their professional activities affected their production from the 1890s through the end of their careers.

Bessie Potter Vonnoh and Auguste Rodin

A native of St. Louis, Bessie Potter Vonnoh (1872–1955) attended the Art

Institute of Chicago, where she engaged in the studio practice of Lorado Taft. She continued her work with Taft in the development of the Horticulture Building at Chicago's Columbian Exposition. She also sought an independent commission for the state of Illinois, which resulted in the creation of her work entitled *Personification of Art*. Vonnoh traveled to Paris in 1895, where she met the noted French sculptor Auguste Rodin (1840–1917). She also sent work to subsequent world's fairs in 1901 and 1904. Vonnoh's primary focus, however, was on smaller-scale works and with domestic interiors rather than large-scale, monumental, and outdoor pieces. Vonnoh even developed "potterine," a term she coined for her lightly tinted, plaster, tabletop portrait sculpture. Likewise, in the arena of smaller domestic works, Enid developed a term for her own small-scale sculpture, "figureen," intending to differentiate these works from traditional "figurines," which were considered decorative arts objects, not fine art. Also, in creating this term, Enid found a way to distinguish her work from Bessie Vonnoh's, if even in name only.[2]

Beyond these small-format works, where both women excelled, Enid also secured a competitive commission for a major public monument, Louisville's Confederate monument, even though the work ended up an unrealized vision, as described in Chapter 3. With the Louisville award coming on the heels of her work in Chicago, Enid demonstrated that she could negotiate large-scale monuments and smaller, domestic portrait work. Enid's pursuit of sculpture led her to take the initiative and (boldly) serve as host to some of the leading sculptors of the day.

Around the time that Vonnoh sought training from Rodin and introduced small-scale works to an American public in 1895, Enid had shifted attention to Paris, the art capital of the nineteenth century, and Rodin as well. By January 1895, Enid had taken a studio in Paris and had begun to seek advice from Rodin, as Vonnoh did. By establishing a connection to such a prominent sculptor of merit, Enid and numerous other artists working in Paris in the late 1890s desired to learn from the master and also to be in his orbit.[3]

However, Enid took it upon herself to go a step further. Rather than limiting her discourse with the famous sculptor to his studio and the academies, she invited Rodin to her own studio at least once, as noted in letters between the elder Frenchman and Enid, who was nearly thirty years his junior.

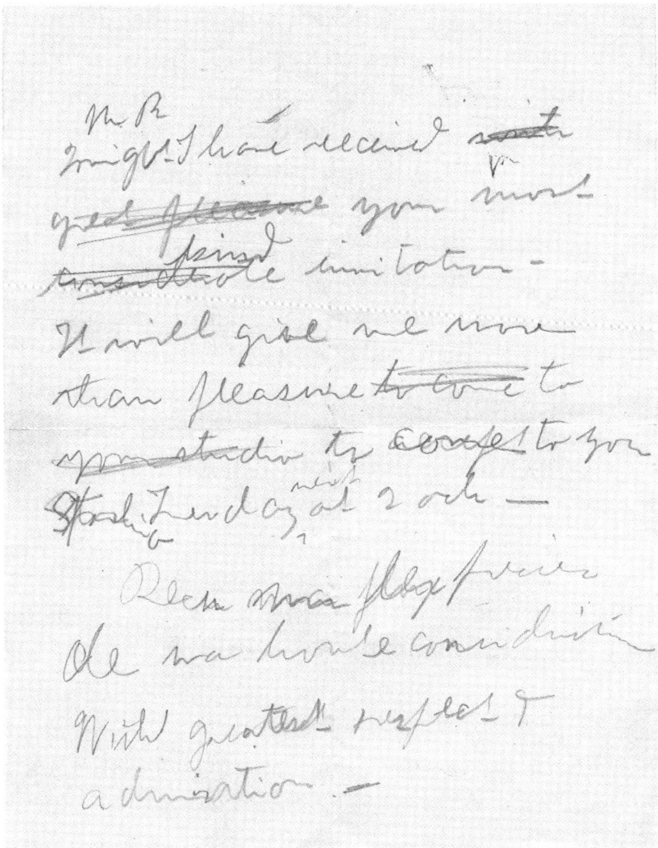

This document is a handwritten draft of a response from Enid to noted French sculptor Auguste Rodin (1840–1917). In this note, Enid thanks Rodin for his "kind invitation" and explains that it will give Enid "more than pleasure to come to your studio Tuesday next at 2 oclock." Enid signs the letter "With greatest respect & admiration." (Enid Yandell Papers, Mss A/Y21b, Folder 33. The Filson Historical Society, Louisville, KY.)

On July 12, 1895, while Enid was at work on a number of busts, Rodin wrote to Enid requesting her presence at his studio for a drawing session. The next month, on the back of an envelope she had received from Rodin with another letter, Enid wrote a guest list, presumably for a dinner, that included at least seven names, among them Geysa, Enid's mother, Rodin, and Frederick William MacMonnies. (Note the mix of family, a close female companion, and sculpture colleagues in the list.) Enid's ties with MacMonnies (1863–1937) stemmed from their shared time in Chicago earlier in the decade. There he had achieved notoriety for his work *Columbian Fountain* in the Court of Honor, featuring the Barge of State accompanied by Columbia, Fame, Father Time, and the personifications of Arts and Industries. Enid's connection with Rodin was likely to have some through MacMonnies, though it could have come through any of her colleagues who were part of the sculptural program at Chicago and who were then engaged in the Parisian studio practice.[4]

Over these years, Rodin was engaged in a monumental undertaking, a memorial to city burghers from the medieval town of Calais who had given their lives in exchange for those of their town. The size and scale of this, and other works by Rodin, as well as that of MacMonnies were in alignment with Enid's recent work —realized or not—and future aspirations. Importantly, Enid was making a name for herself as a colleague who could help to realize someone else's vision, just as she had in the earlier part of the decade while she was at work in Chicago. In an interview (1898), Enid reported on her education and training after Chicago, which included professional work for Karl Bitter: "*not studying with him*, you know, but *helping* to execute his designs. He had a lot of work on hand for the Vanderbilts and Astors: and I got a good deal more experience, and found the year a profitable one." Enid's assertion that she was working, "not studying," with Bitter, is important in the context of her becoming an independent sculptor. Rather than continuing her education, at this point she was executing work-for-hire for high-profile clients.[5]

In this same article, Enid noted her ties to Chicago and her associated sculptural lineage through Philip Martiny— a French-American sculptor who worked in clay and handled decorative work for the allegorical and classical figures at Chicago—and Lorado Taft—in whose studio Enid was employed. Enid also acknowledged sister sculptors, including Vonnoh, whom she refers to as "Miss Potter"—though she found occupational identity through the men who employed her. Enid stated that she "worked there under Martiny. Though Martiny was my master, I worked in Mr. Taft's studio. Those were good old days, and we had a jolly time. Miss Scudder, Miss Potter, Miss Gaft [Taft], Miss Brooks were in the studio, too; and all those girls have done splendid work." Enid went on

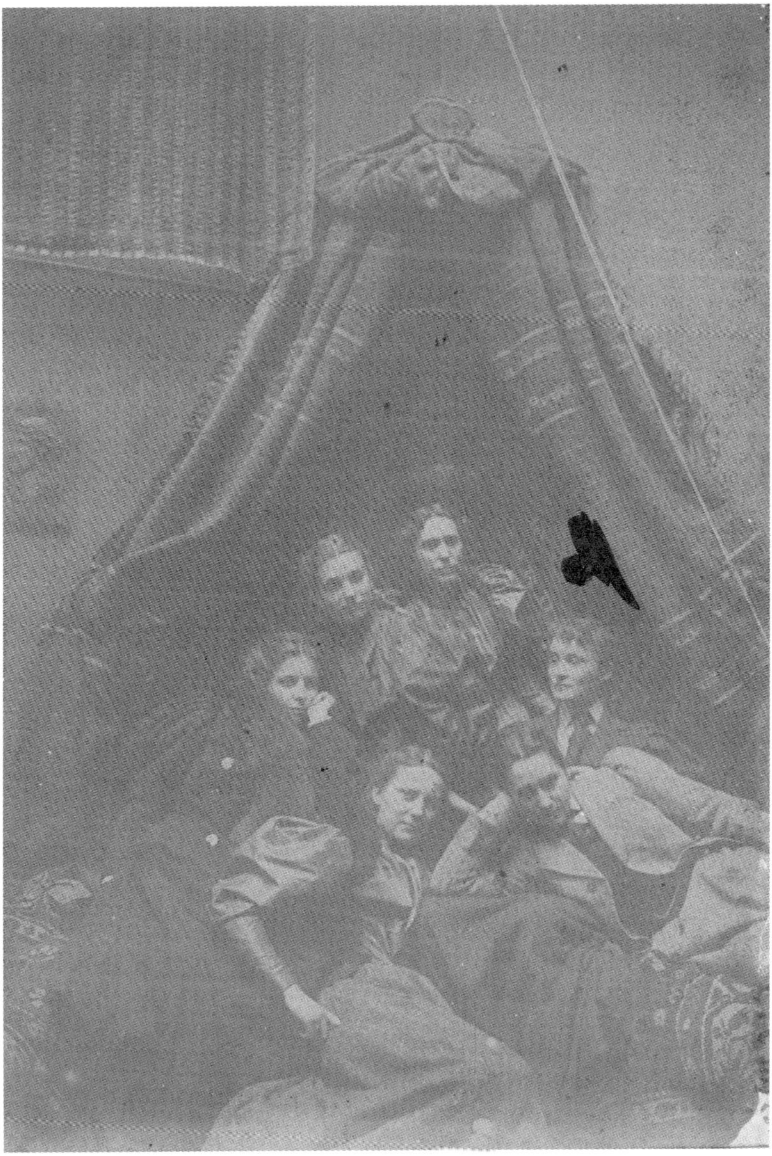

The group of women who came together in the studio of MacMonnies came to be called Atelier des Anges (Studio of Angels). In this image of the group, Enid is seated at the lower right, in a light-colored blazer; Janet Scudder is directly behind her on the right. (Enid Bland Yandell Photograph Collection, 987PC52X.167, Box 1, Folder 6. The Filson Historical Society, Louisville, KY.)

to say that her association with artists in France rounded out her education and situated her as an artist who could settle down to work: "After that I went to Paris and studied with Macmonnies and Rodin; and last fall I settled down here [in New York] to stay." Over these years, her work attracted so much attention that she hired a clipping service to gather and forward her reviews.[6]

Chicago Teachers and Rodin

Through exhibition, personal acquaintance, and association with a cohort of Chicago sculptors, Enid and her peers developed a body of work that bears witness to Rodin's influence. Karl Bitter (1867–1915), who was educated in Austria and emigrated to the United States in 1889, did not study in Paris, but set up a studio in New York, where he came into contact with architect Richard Morris Hunt, who put Bitter's decorative talent to good use. Bitter contributed to Chicago's World's Fair efforts, where he came into contact with Enid. Philip Martiny (1858–1927) worked in a Paris studio before coming to the United States in 1878, where he gained employment under the tutelage of Augustus Saint-Gaudens and met fellow sculptor Frederick MacMonnies. Martiny gained success through his contributions to the Chicago and subsequent fairs, including those in Buffalo (1901) and St. Louis (1904).

Enid's occupational trajectory and intersection with Rodin most closely resembles that of Lorado Taft (1860–1936), who studied in Paris beginning in 1880. While a decade separates their introduction to the city and its allure, they seemed to share a sentiment about the field and their place within it. They appear to have grown to see each other as colleagues, as demonstrated by an anecdote relayed by Enid's mother in a letter from September 15, 1898. While Enid was at work on a bust of Frances Willard (1839–1898), a social reformer and an advocate for woman suffrage, Enid's mother and sister Maude traveled to Chicago. In Chicago, they met Lorado Taft, to whom Louise mentioned Enid and her current project. Taft told Louise that he had created a death mask of Frances Willard. Because of its use of the human body as the model from which the form is created, such a mold could, in the hands of a skilled sculptor, guarantee lifelikeness. Enid's mother asked to see it, went to Taft's studio to measure it, and sent the measurements and notes to Enid. The sharing of information through a third party suggests a shift in the relationship between Taft and Enid, moving away from teacher-pupil to a more equivocal one.[7]

The hallmarks of Taft's path demonstrate the ways in which Enid followed his lead in some ways and yet how each ran their course alongside Rodin. Taft may have come into contact with Rodin at some point at the École des Beaux Arts or through exhibition at the Salon de Paris, beginning in 1882 (when Rodin also exhibited two sculptures) or the following year, when Taft began attending the Petite École, the site of Rodin's training. Surely, though, Taft's intersection with Rodin's work would have come the previous decade, when Taft submitted work to, and attended, the Centennial Exhibition in Philadelphia (1876). Although Taft's works were, unfortunately, lost or damaged and were not displayed, Rodin's works were shown in Philadelphia, although they went largely unnoticed.[8]

After a brief stint in the United States (1883), Taft sought to flesh out his training and connection to contemporary American sculptors by returning to Paris in 1884, where he made contact with Frederick MacMonnies, who also attended the École. Returning to the United States in 1886, Taft established a studio in Chicago and taught at the School of the Art Institute while managing commissions for memorials. This work and teaching prepared Taft for the Chicago World's Fair, where he juried the American sculpture exhibition and executed sculptural decoration for the Horticulture Building (designed by William Le Baron Jenney)—one of the structures to which Enid and several woman sculptors contributed, as noted earlier. There Taft also rubbed elbows with MacMonnies, Daniel Chester French, and Augustus Saint-Gaudens, the leading figurative sculptors of the day.

The back-and-forth transatlantic passage, continued education in Paris, and fascination with spectacle—even before his participation in the World's Fair at Chicago—are hallmarks of Taft's education that mirror Enid's own occupational path, which was running parallel to the introduction of Rodin to American audience. In contrast to his lackluster reception by American audiences in 1876, Rodin's work, along with that of many other sculptors, dominated the Columbian Exposition of 1893, as American sculptors showcased their Beaux arts training in the White City. After this, Rodin's work was featured in public and private collections in Chicago, Boston, and New York. Part of the attraction to Rodin was the novelty of his style, particularly the expressive qualities shown in, for example, his *Burghers of Calais*, as well as his finished and unfinished surfaces, which many sculptors adopted.[9]

With myriad opportunities for exhibiting works of sculpture, as well as architectural sculpture, artists sought opportunities on the grand scale, including the international expositions in Nashville, Buffalo, Paris, and St. Louis. Such "fair work" also enabled artists to work on multiple projects and keep their work in front of audiences.

Tennessee's Centennial Exposition

Just as the Chicago World's Fair gave artists an opportunity to make names for themselves, so too did the Tennessee Centennial Exposition, held from May through October 1897 in an area west of Nashville proper and in the environs of Vanderbilt University. All professions and trades took part in the preparations, with the intention of bringing as much of the nation as possible to the city. Herman Justi, head of publicity for the exposition, compiled the official guidebook, which stated: "The clamor for space makes sure a vast and interesting exhibition of the industries and resources of the United States, and as Nashville is in the center of a rich, fertile and well settled territory, a large attendance is assured. In fact, Nashville is within a night's ride of a population of between ten and eleven millions." He called upon the nation's railroads to cooperate in providing amenable travel for those interested in attending. Transportation companies heeded the call, among them the Nashville, Chattanooga, and St. Louis Railroad in the person of John W. Thomas, the railway's president, who also served as president of the Tennessee Exposition.[10]

The appearance of the Centennial in Tennessee was similar to Chicago's exposition four years earlier, where the City Beautiful movement situated grand classical buildings in a park-like setting highlighted with walkways and water features. At Nashville the centerpiece of the midway was the Giant See-Saw, an attraction that was meant to stand up to signature attractions of Chicago with its Ferris Wheel (1893) and Paris with its Eiffel Tower (1889), both of which drew tremendous visitorship. In addition, new technologies debuted at Nashville, including Thomas Edison's "Mirage," an early form of cinema.

Beyond these individual endeavors, the overall theme of the fair, which adopted mythological and classical subjects, was part of the spectacle. Among these, the Fine Arts Building offered a full-scale reproduction of the Parthenon atop the acropolis at Athens. The selection of this emblem was intentional: Nashville was referred to as the "Athens of the South," making the selection of such a building apropos. In keeping with this theme, Enid created a colossal sculpture of the goddess Athena (also known by her Roman name, Minerva).[11]

Enid's *Athena*

For the fair in Nashville, Enid created a colossal figure of Athena, a forty-foot-tall staff figure that took between nine and ten months to create. As Enid worked on her designs for *Athena* while she was living in Paris, it was a way of connecting to home. The site of the fair was converted farmland, a portion of which had belonged to Enid's family, through her mother's line. Enid had spent a great deal of time there, as evidenced by a handful of photographs taken of her there. As such, Enid could envision her work as it might appear just past Burlington, the family's home. Moreover, she could enlist the help of her mother. For just as Reuben Durrett had assisted Enid during her creation process while Enid was in Chicago and the relics of Daniel Boone lay in Louisville, Enid's mother served as a studio assistant of sorts to Enid as she worked in Paris on *Athena*. Correspondence between the two detailed Louise's maneuvers. A letter of March 1, 1896, from Enid's mother, who was then staying at Burlington, recounted Louise's insight and service as go-between for Enid and her client, the Fair Board. On February 1, 1897, Louise wrote to Enid: "I wrote to the Nashville people about the Minerva—They say they will pay you just as soon as it reaches Nashville, but it has never gotten there. . . . I will remit the Minerva money just as soon as I can get it. I am going to Nashville the middle of this month to try to get some money. Every body sends love—Give my love to Geyza." A week later, Louise wrote again to Enid, indicating that she had learned that "your Minerva had reached New Orleans, so I may possibly get your check for you this week."[12]

Enid's mother's also served as an informal agent for Enid. The type of attention Louise paid to Enid's commissions for the Tennessee Centennial, which may be interpreted as helping her daughter while the younger

Yandell was abroad, continued after Nashville. Louise asked Enid if she could retain some of her work, as well as photographs, to keep at her home in Louisville so that as requests came in for potential patrons to see or to exhibit Enid's work, Louise could better oblige. "Do send me something—Geyza's bust photo—& a Boone & a Hermes & any thing else you have—I have the Minerva but that is about all—I really ought to have a set of your things just for this purpose—I am so constantly asked for the loan of them." In addition, Louise kept Enid abreast of the press: "There have been nice notices in C[ourie]r Journal & Post—of the Minerva."[13]

In considering the Tennessee Centennial in Enid's body of work, the status of Enid's family should not be overlooked. This is not to suggest that her familial connection is why she obtained the commission, but rather that her family connection through the Elliston line allowed, for instance, her mother to intercede on her behalf. And intercede she did, in terms of work in process as well as future commissions. To the latter point, consider that in 1896, a year before the fair, Louise wrote to Enid regarding the sculpture she had been contracted to complete. "He wants the Minerva so soon you can finish it because he thinks it will have an influence in securing you the fountain . . . I want you to be patient about the fountain order. . . . Minerva is to be the central idea of the whole thing . . . prominently forward even if it be but a reproduction." The detail about "securing you the fountain" is vague, particularly at a fair where "the number of fountains was large enough to relieve the landscape without making them common." Such a commission would have been in keeping with Enid's previous work; she had carved columnar supports for the Woman's Building in Chicago. At Nashville, however, this particular commission was not to be hers, as no fountain has Enid's name associated with it.[14]

However, for Enid, the execution of *Athena* was a measure of pride and happiness, so much so that she threw a celebration inside the belly of the goddess on the eve of the colossal deity's voyage to the Athens of the South. A farewell dinner was held in Enid's studio, with guests assembling in the interior of the sculpture: "The night before it left Paris, Miss Yandell gave a farewell supper in her studio, the guests assembling in the interior of the statue, which measured twelve feet at the broadest point. The banquet was laid out on platforms fixed inside, and the hollow figure, from which the upper portion had been removed, was lit from above."[15]

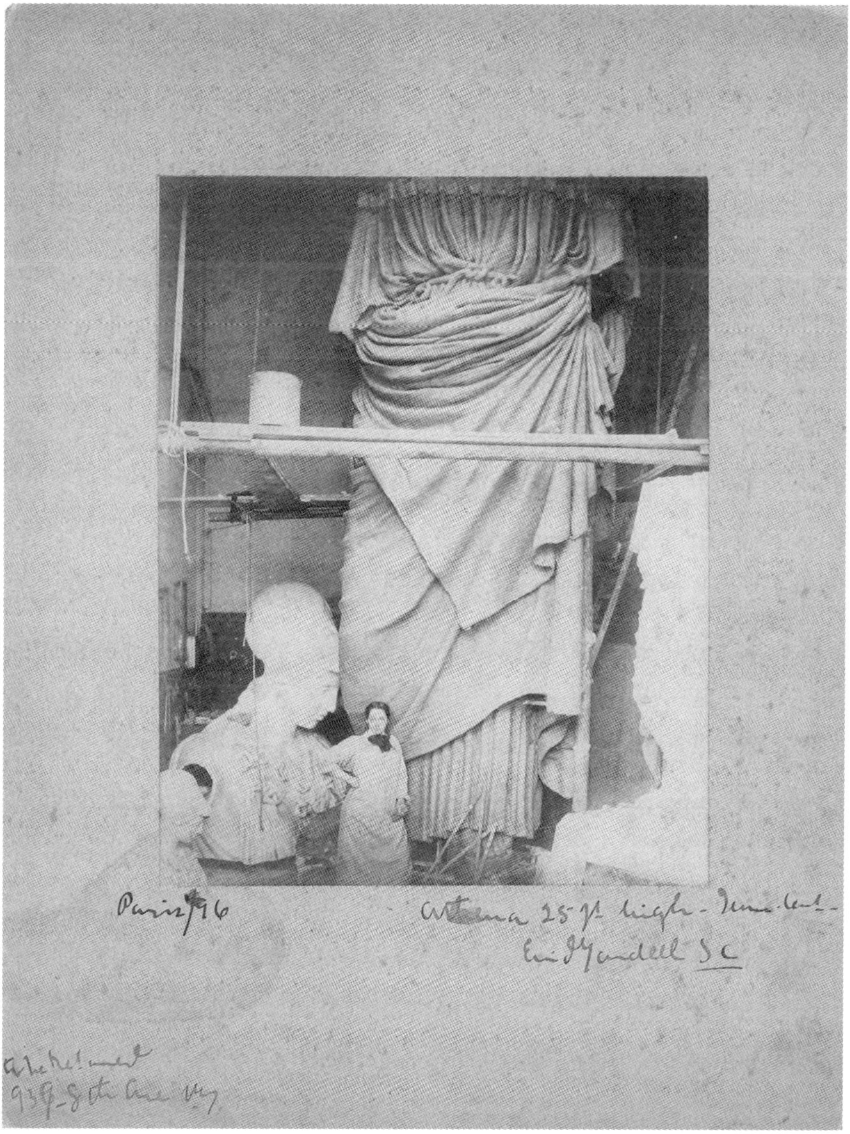

Enid in her Paris studio with the statue of Athena (also known as Minerva). Enid has annotated the matboard with location and date of creation, the height of the statue, its purpose and location, and a request that the image be returned to her in New York. (Enid Bland Yandell Photograph Collection, 987PC52X.230, Box 3. The Filson Historical Society, Louisville, KY.)

Athena had to be cast in three pieces so that it could travel from Paris, where Enid was living and working at the time, to Nashville. The tripartite *Athena* was transported by "three good sized wagons, each drawn by three horses," and quite a crowd assembled to see it off. The sculpture then traveled by rail to Antwerp, where its size caused a problem, as Enid recounted several years later: "When Athena arrived at Antwerp, she was found too bulky to go through the gang-way, and the biggest portion of her head had to be left on deck, so that she lay for two months exposed to the weather and the sea-air. However, she was none the worse for it, except that portions of her drapery were covered with moss and fungus, which had to be scraped off before she could be exhibited." *Athena* then went by boat from Antwerp to New Orleans and then by rail to Nashville.[16]

Upon the sculpture's arrival, Louise trekked from the family home at Burlington down to see it and reported on the progress of its installation atop a fifteen-foot base. She wrote to Enid: "The Minerva is up but the base isn't finished yet. It is a superb figure & gives an air of dignity to all the grounds." Given the issues with the work's exposure in Antwerp, care had to be taken with the installation. Louise reported that the installation was being tended to by the superintendent of the fair: "I went in to see Major Lewis yesterday & he told me that the day the Minerva was unpacked he staid [*sic*] all day at the grounds & superintended setting it up & that so soon as it was finished he went back to town & sent you a cablegram." The superintendent of the entire fair was in communication with Enid about her work and even oversaw the installation of it. While it is unclear if work of other sculptors commanded the same treatment, the attention paid by Lewis gives credence to the quality of Enid's work, as well as her rise in stature as an artist in comparison to just four years earlier, when she was referred to as a "White Rabbit" by the head of Chicago's fair, Daniel Burnham.[17]

Measuring forty feet, *Athena* was treated as a sightline and architectural wonder at the Nashville fair, in both visual and verbal terms. Narratives about the fair included its placement as a point of reference: "The dome of the Commerce Building, the ridge line of the Parthenon, the statue of Pallas Athena, and the dome of the State Capitol were in a straight line."

Athena's size also affirmed her responsibility as "protectress of the intellectual, as mistress of the home where her treasures are conserved."

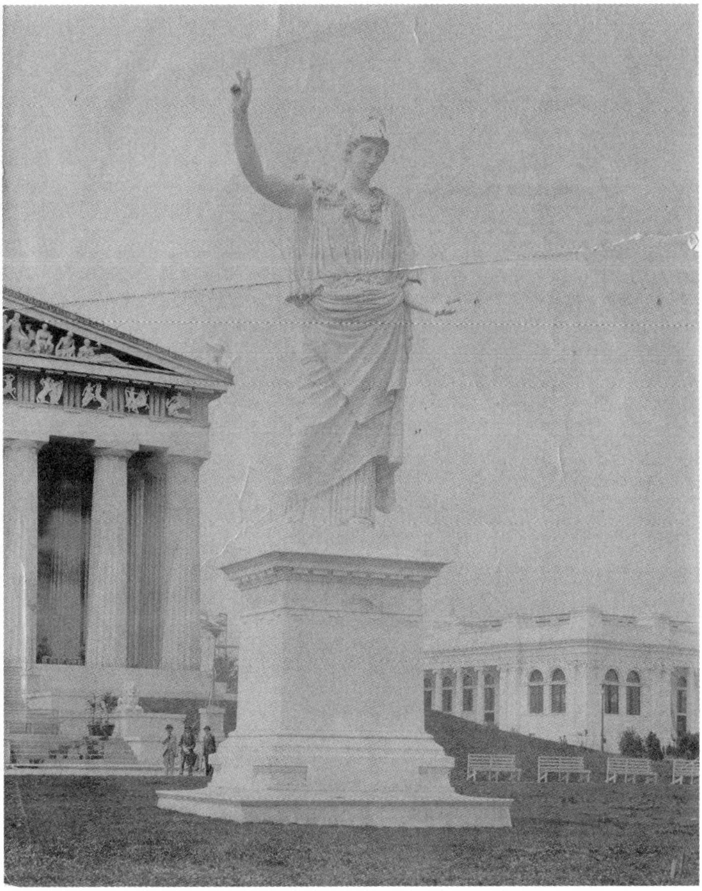

At more than forty feet high, Enid's colossal *Athena* stood like an architectural feat of wonder on the grounds of the 1897 Tennessee Centennial Exposition in Nashville. (Enid Bland Yandell Photograph Collection, 987PC52X.069, Box 3. The Filson Historical Society, Louisville, KY.)

These attributes were viewed less favorably on occasion, however, as Justi wrote:

> At the other end of the Parthenon was the gigantic statue of Pallas Athena, which was made in Paris under the direction of Miss Enid Yandell, and sent to this country. It is an exact copy of the Pallas Velatrix in Paris, and was an accomplishment that

> was remarkable for any one— much more for a woman. There was a smaller copy of this statue over the main entrance, which made really a better impression on the visitor, from the fact that the gigantic statue was on a base thought by many to be much too low, and the eye could not properly adjust itself to the huge figure.[18]

Programs, souvenirs, and fair ephemera also pictured *Athena*. In some ways, Enid's creation became the emblem of the fair.

In addition to Enid's work being sited on property that belonged to Enid's maternal family, and the fact that images of the sculpture and the artist called both Enid and the sculpture she made "Pallas Athena," Enid's work for the Tennessee Centennial was personal in a third way. Enid's mother reported that it was "a source of pride and gratification to Ma [Enid's maternal grandmother]. She can stand in the yard at Burlington & look at it and I think rarely a day passes that she does not make a pilgrimage down to the back gate just to see the sun setting behind the Minerva."[19]

Praise for Enid's work was swift and abundant: "In front of the Parthenon, facing the State House on Capitol Hill, stands Miss Enid Yandell's colossal statue of Minerva, forty feet in height, including pedestal, modeled after Frohner's Pallas de Velletri, which is in the Louvre, Paris. This model, while not so well known in America, is regarded by critics abroad having a high and just conception of art as the most beautiful and most justly celebrated of all. Miss Yandell has been most fortunate in preserving in her huge copy all the grace and beauty of the original; and in this connection, it may be proper to say that this is perhaps the largest statue ever executed by a woman." Attention was drawn to the size in advertisements for the fair as well. A large poster (approximately 10 x 30 inches) calling attention to the Exposition read: "Opening Day May 1st TENNESSEE CENTENNIAL EXPOSITION-AT-NASHVILLE STATUE OF MINERVA, FORTY FEET HIGH, ON EXPOSITION GROUNDS. VERY LOW RATES." Indeed, this was the largest stand-alone sculpture ever created by a woman at the time.[20]

Perhaps such significant recognition melted away the hardships Enid had endured over the previous four years. Despite a number of commissions and the promise of fair work, from 1893 to 1897 Enid had struggled as an artist. She had artistic, emotional, and social support through her companionship with Geysa de Braunecker and a number of women and men in her artistic circles. This network included her family her mentor, Reuben T. Durrett (who sent Enid crates of cider while she was in Paris). Nevertheless, Enid was on her own financially in Paris. She occasionally received assistance from her mother; but given the needs of the younger Yandell children, funds were short. As Louise wrote to Enid in January 1897, "I am sorrier than I can say that you are so poor, but indeed money is very scarce with me. . . . I have not spent a single cent on myself since I bought my dress etc. in Paris fifteen months ago—not even a pair of shoes." Enid's sister Maude tried to assist her by sending money that she had earned doing housekeeping and caring for the boarder that Louise had taken in. Repeatedly, Louise reminded Enid of her contractual obligations to supply remaining items for the Nashville fair, as they were a pipeline to funds. It seemed as though Enid's work was a family affair.[21]

Also at the Fair, 1897

Enid's work for the Tennessee Centennial Exhibition was not confined to the landscaped grounds near Athena. She contributed at least several other figures to the fair, including her Daniel Boone, a smaller, male figure, and several busts. The placement of these works in various buildings and out-of-doors meant that visitors could encounter Enid's works in several locations. Boone was outside; one work was on view in the Woman's Building; and the others were inside the Parthenon.[22]

The request for Enid's Boone came from the chairman of the Centennial Exposition, Major Eugene C. Lewis (1845–1917), who wanted to position it near the train terminal of the fair. (To meet this demand for a work that was widely viewed only four years earlier, Enid needed to act quickly. To facilitate the work's timely delivery, Enid's mother served as go-between.) The placement was intentional, as Lewis had a vested interest in attracting tourists to the city. He was on the board of directors of the Nashville, Chattanooga, and St. Louis Railroad. Having Daniel Boone greet fair visitors upon their arrival, he felt, would create a memorable experience for them. Boone was sure to be a hit, given Tennessee's shared history of the pioneer spirit with Kentucky, even if the character was occasionally misidentified. Some reports referred to Boone as Davy Crockett (1786–1836), the Tennessee frontiersman and pioneer![23]

An article from the *Nashville American* reported: "In the Parthenon and in the Woman's building Miss Yandell has a number of pieces, and has the splendid statue of Davy Crockett near the railway exhibit building." While the identity of the subject was mistaken, many of the details in this article were accurate, including the location. Boone stood near the Terminal Building, where it was "the object of much commendation and attention" due to both its appearance and its location. In terms of aesthetics, "the pose of the figure was perfect, and the poetic idea of the great hunter was well conveyed." Enid's reproduction of Boone was situated amidst a pile of rocks, twigs, and remnant greenery so as to give the appearance of the wilderness and was situated near the facsimile of a tree from Boone's (and Tennessee's) wilderness days. Moreover, "the workmanship was of the best, and the artistic finish and grace such as characterized all the work of this clever artist, much of which was found in the displays in the Parthenon and in the Woman's Building."[24]

The other figures that Enid contributed, beyond the large Athena and the recognizable (or perhaps not) Daniel Boone, included three other, smaller works. One of these, *Allah-il-Allah*, was awarded a silver medal for the skill of the artist, who fashioned a lifelike depiction of a figure at prayer. Justi characterized it as "a serious and most excellent piece of work," so much so that it might ordinarily receive a higher mark had there not been such excellence at this fair. However, Enid's bust of the president of the Woman's Department, Mrs. Katherine (Kate) Kirkman (referred to as Mrs. Van Leer Kirkman) fared less well; it was called "sketchy and not equal to other statuettes on exhibition in the Woman's Building." In contrast, other busts of Enid's were better received, including her depiction of her sister Elsie, which had the "sketchy" quality of the Kirkman but was said to be "one of the most graceful" works. Enid's bust of Landon Cabell Garland, a fully finished marble exhibited as a loan from the alumni of Vanderbilt University, was "greatly praised by all who see it." The Garland bust deserves a bit more attention as a means of teasing out threads of Enid's connection to the Volunteer State.[25]

Landon Cabell Garland (1810–1895) served as Vanderbilt University's first chancellor. Enid created a bust of him twice, once in 1896–1897 and then again in 1909, from money collected by alumni to replace her earlier work, which was destroyed when a fire destroyed a large portion of Kirkland Hall in 1905. Ties between Enid's family and Garland extended back to the university's earliest days, when tracts of land were acquired in 1873, of which two parcels came from women—one of them being Enid's grandmother, Elizabeth Boddie Elliston, who sold a first parcel for $5 as a means of supporting Vanderbilt University. Elliston repeated this gesture four more times over the next twelve years—during Garland's tenure as chancellor—peeling away parcels from her plantation at Burlington at very modest prices for the university.[26]

Enid's work in Tennessee extended beyond the fairgrounds temporally and spatially. In the decade following the fair, she also created a large public monument to John W. Thomas, a railroad magnate who had served as president of the Exposition. The memorial was commissioned by employees of the Nashville, Chattanooga, and St. Louis Railroad in honor of their late president. In this work, Enid used bronze, granite, and limestone in the two parts of the work, the platform and the statue proper. Cast by the Henry-Bonnard Bronze Company, the sculpture features a bronze figure atop a base with three relief panels (allegorical depictions of railroading, citizenship, and philanthropy). The fourth panel, on the back side of the pedestal, carries a plaque recounting the subject and commission. Thomas stands in his suit and knee-length jacket with his right hand extended down to the viewer. His left hand holds a cape. The platform is composed of concrete and granite, and has four columns topped with bronze and glass lanterns. Eight benches form the balustrade. Dedicated on November 24, 1907, the monument is located in Centennial Park, near Nashville's Parthenon and not far from the original site of Enid's *Athena*.[27]

Given Enid's family ties to Tennessee, it is not surprising that she completed a number of important works for that state. By the time the monument to Thomas had been erected, her *Athena*, sadly, was long gone, although the Parthenon remained on site, even if in a deteriorated state. Publications paid tribute to this work as well as Enid's connection to the state. In 1902, an article in *The Outlook* called Enid a "Tennessee girl" due to her parents' lineage. "Have we not the right to claim the daughter?" it asked. Her association to the state went even further, in 1916, with Enid's inclusion in the volume *Women's Work in Tennessee*. She was identified there as one of the sixteen "Women Artists of Tennessee." Her description read: "Sculptor—Studied in New York and abroad; Rodin in Paris. Has executed many important commissions, including the John W. Thomas statue in Centennial Park, Nashville, Tenn."[28]

Other Fairs

Enid's work extended beyond fairs where she may have felt, literally, on familiar ground, such as Chicago and Nashville. Following her pursuits at these venues, she sought opportunities for public exhibition at fairs in Paris (1900), Buffalo (1901), and St. Louis (1904), at all of which she offered a range of works to showcase her abilities in large-scale statuary alongside smaller works, including plasters and bronzes, and garden statuary illustrating genteel domestic or literary subjects. In some ways, Enid's transition as a sculptor fit the aim of the fairs, which President William McKinley articulated in his address to the public at Buffalo in September 1901: "Expositions are the timekeepers of progress. They record the world's advancement. They stimulate the energy, enterprise, and intellect of the people and quicken human genius. . . . The Pan-American Exposition has done its work thoroughly, presenting in its exhibits evidences of the highest skill and illustrating the progress of the human family in the Western Hemisphere. . . . The wisdom and energy of all the nations are none too great for the world's work. The success of art, science, industry, and invention is an international asset and a common glory." Such ties between the fairs and human progress raised the stakes for sculpture.[29]

Great acclaim was given to Enid's new, smaller portrait bust sculptures, which she called "figureens." Even as they aimed at likeness, they were also often imbued with an expressive quality, in keeping with the emergent Art Nouveau style, as well as the emotive qualities found in the work of contemporary French sculptors. Certain elements in Enid's sculptures possess the flowing lines, curved forms from nature, ivy, leaf-inspired rinceau, and the celebration of design and craft that were hallmarks of Art Nouveau. Such approaches were in congruence with the contemporary interests, in England as well as in the United States, of the Arts and Crafts movement, which sought to unite arts within decoration. Therefore, among some communities of sculptors during the late 1890s, expressive qualities were dictating outcomes as form was becoming divorced from function; aesthetic choices were informed by the feeling to be evoked in the viewer. Given that Enid was spending studio time in New York and Paris from the 1890s onward, her absorption of contemporary practices in sculpture was keen, as was her development of her own take on these innovations.

The notion of creating a new format for portraiture, in sculptural form, was not new, of course. Consider the contributions by Enid's contemporary, Bessie Potter Vonnoh, who, as mentioned earlier, introduced "potterines." For Enid, the emphasis was on likeness, even if the treatment varied. Besides the commentary by Herman Justi (the Nashville fair's chief of promotion and publicity), which remarked on the poor appearance (in his opinion) of Enid's bust of Mrs. Van Leer Kirkman, others found the work admirable. An article in the *New York World* from September 1897 reported, "The work [Kirkman] is not only charming from an artistic point of view, but also an excellent likeness." The article went further to note Enid's contributions to the field: "It has remained for a woman to accomplish something wholly new in the line of sculpture. Miss Ella [*sic*] Yandell, of Louisville, a young woman of twenty-seven, who has for some years been known as a sculptor, has lately invented the 'figureen,' which represents in sculpture what miniature does in portraiture. The popularity of the 'figureen' has been wide and immediate. . . . The centennial exhibits will include a large number of figureens, all the work of Miss Yandell."[30]

Clearly the figureens had achieved the goal that Enid had set for them. She pursued this genre of statuary for a number of years, even going so far as to translate it into a new medium of profile reliefs. All the while, Enid kept riding the wave of Boone by exhibiting versions of him in the United States whenever possible.

Paris, 1900

Paris had held several expositions prior to 1900, having been host to world's fairs in 1855, 1867, 1878, and 1889. The first of these to which Enid could contribute was the one in 1900. As we have seen, Enid had fully engaged in the work of Chicago, where she lived from 1891 to 1893, then worked as a studio artist, and contributed to the Tennessee Centennial in Nashville in 1897. For the Paris fair, Enid was on familiar soil in the sense that she had been living part of the time in Paris. The draw of the fair as spectacle was no less in the City of Lights than it had been in earlier expositions where Enid had exhibited her work.

Extant correspondence by or to Enid provides little information as to Enid's fair experience. What is known, from a survey of the catalogue for the exhibition, is that at Paris, Enid exhibited *Kiss Tankard.* The work (identified in the catalogue by its literary name, *Mermaid and Fisher Boy*) was listed as a pewter tankard. She had intended to exhibit her Daniel Boone at Paris; however, she could not secure the Boone from Reuben Durrett. She had negotiated the details a year earlier, when she wrote to Durrett and explained that because she was in Paris she would rely upon him to be the liaison such that "When the Paris Committee wants the 'Daniel Boone' I'll give them an order on you for it. We will pay all expense of packing and shipping and will have it returned after the exposition to you." Enid had even made the point in her request to Durrett that the French "are much interested in our American pioneers."[31]

When Enid had stated an interest in pioneers, she was referring to the frontiersmen, not herself. Yet she was coming into her own as a pioneer sculptor. Consider the difficulty in placing Enid's work among the sculptural production of women in Paris during the nineteenth century. Put simply, there was no peer for Enid among women sculptors. Legendary figures such as MacMonnies and Rodin loom large in terms of production as well as dominance in the field of training. Enid held her own in this company, unlike most, if not all, of the women working in the field of sculpture at the time.[32]

Buffalo, 1901

The Pan-American Exposition, held in Buffalo, New York, was an expansionist visioning of the United States abroad, particularly in Latin America. For this display, however, Enid contributed three works that were not directly related to the theme of the fair. They were a figureen featuring her companion, Geysa (*Baroness de Braunecker*); the pewter *Kiss Tankard,* which had been shown at the Paris exposition; and a bust of John G. Carlisle, a former Kentucky senator from Kenton County.[33]

It was in the category of monumental sculpture, however, that Enid found her niche. Paying heed to the importance of the waterway to the history of this western New York town (situated on Lake Erie, on the western point of the Erie Canal, and near Niagara Falls), Buffalo's fair exhibited a series of interconnecting canals and lagoons that served as the backdrop for large-scale sculpture. Curated by established sculptors and members of the National Sculpture Society, Karl Bitter and Charles Y. Turner, the fair sculpture was intended to be "a decorative feature forming a part of the entire artistic scheme of the composition." Rather than isolated works of art, the sculptures were meant to cohere with the architecture as well as the landscape. Thus, location mattered.[34]

Enid's contribution was a plaster entitled *Struggle of Existence,* which was located in the Rose Garden and near the lake system of the fair and offered a naturalistic setting for the writhing classical figures. The garden was situated between the Woman's Building and a forecourt and triumphal bridge festooned with four architectural forms with a crowning emblematic sculpture designed by Enid's mentor Karl Bitter, who served also as Director of Sculpture for the fair. Between the electric lighting and a manicured garden designed and installed by Vaughan's Seed Store, the sculpture emerged, just as tall as the nearest tree specimen, situated to draw one's eyes upward toward the pylons of the triumphal bridge. Statuary designed by Bitter adorned the bridge from every angle and addressed such themes as courage, liberty, tolerance, truth, benevolence, hospitality, justice, and patriotism. Bearing the inscription "To love one's country above all others is not to despise all others," patriotism offered moral guidance to those who read its charge and in its show of masculinist power, in its mighty charioteer towering over Enid's *Struggle of Existence.*

Like contemporary works from other sculptors of the late nineteenth century who emphasized naturalistic forms, Enid's work required explanation. In response, and perhaps as a measure of pride in proclaiming how the field had expanded over the decade since a world's fair was last held in the United States, sculptors and the public more generally in Buffalo were treated to an entire volume focusing on art at the fair. For this, Bitter prepared a full description of each work, which was paired with maps and other locational details. For Enid's *Struggle,* Bitter wrote: "The five figures which comprise the group represent the effort of the soul to free itself from earthly tendencies and the infirmities of the body. The struggle is symbolized by an angel with outstretched wings in the grasp of the Human Passion, represented by a male figure. Duty hinders the flight of the Soul, clinging to it, and holding the figure of Life with the left hand. Avarice is represented by an old man, seated and holding the robes of the angel, while he clasps a bag of gold." The entry concluded with a reminder

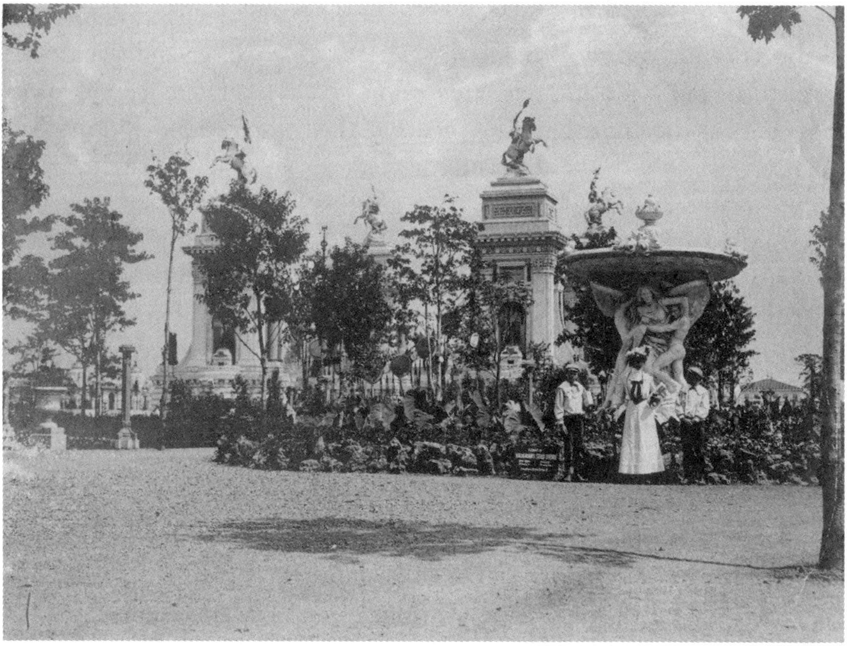

This photograph was taken at the 1901 Pan-American Exposition in Buffalo, where Enid's *Struggle of Existence,* a plaster model of the Carrie Brown Memorial Fountain for the city of Providence, Rhode Island, may be seen at right. The display surrounding the fountain was presented by Vaughan's Seed Store. The identities of the individuals depicted, as well as the photographer, are unknown; however, this photograph was among Enid's collection of photographs and memorabilia. (Enid Bland Yandell Photograph Collection, 987PC52X.083, Box 2, Folder 19. The Filson Historical Society, Louisville, KY.)

to audiences of Enid's earlier presentations at fairs: "Miss Yandell was the author of the heroic statue of Daniel Boone at the World's Fair."[35]

The title of this work, *Struggle of Existence,* was only used for its exhibition at the Pan-Am fair in Buffalo. Its more common names include *The Struggle of Life,* which references its subject generally, as well as the names of the honoree and the donor, the Carrie Brown Memorial Fountain, or the Bajnotti Fountain.[36]

St. Louis, 1904

Just a few years later, in celebration of the 1803 Louisiana Purchase, the

St. Louis World's Fair (also known as the Louisiana Purchase Exposition) highlighted themes of race and empire while introducing fairgoers to a number of foods that made their debut at the fair (including peanut butter, iced tea, and cotton candy). This emphasis on leisure stood in stark contrast to the many exhibits where people were on display. While this type of subject was not apparent in work submitted by Enid, her Daniel Boone was in keeping with the ethos of westward expansion. This sculpture and other portrait statues were exhibited on the hillside of statuary and fountains near Festival Hall. For this installation of Enid's Boone, a slightly different approach was taken than that of the previous installations at Chicago in 1893 and in Nashville for the Tennessee Centennial. Here, Boone was situated on top of a pedestal, a traditional presentation that would call to mind national heroes, statesmen, and political figures. On the pedestal, in the only image of the work in situ, a text has been carved out of the stone. It reads: "Daniel Boone 1734–1820 Kentucky Pioneer . . ." (the rest is indecipherable). While the sculpture was erected in front of a large shrub, suggesting the figure's appearance from the wilderness, the pedestal was not covered with wood, rock, or brush, as was the case with earlier installations. Bennitt's historical guide to the fair, which included the only published photograph of this work on site, did not restate the plaque information, but instead offered a lengthy biographical paragraph about Boone and his wife, including his death and initial burial in Missouri before reinternment at the cemetery in Frankfort, Kentucky. The statue of Boone, said the volume, was one of a number of "portrait statues representing some of the most important historic characters that have bearing upon our subject."[37]

In addition, Enid created another statue, entitled *Victory*, for two restaurants in Cascade Gardens, an area near the center of the fair nestled between the fine art pavilions to the south and the manufacturing, electricity, and machinery pavilions to the north. A single woman figure, draped in a flowing garment that barely covers her upper torso, Victory extends an arm with a wreath and sounds her trumpet, which forms a strong vertical from her left arm across the body and extending to the right leg, which extends to the back body. While the subject is classical, its treatment is expressive, with a lesser degree of finished qualities found in Boone.

Cast in staff or plaster, these two figures (Victories) were called

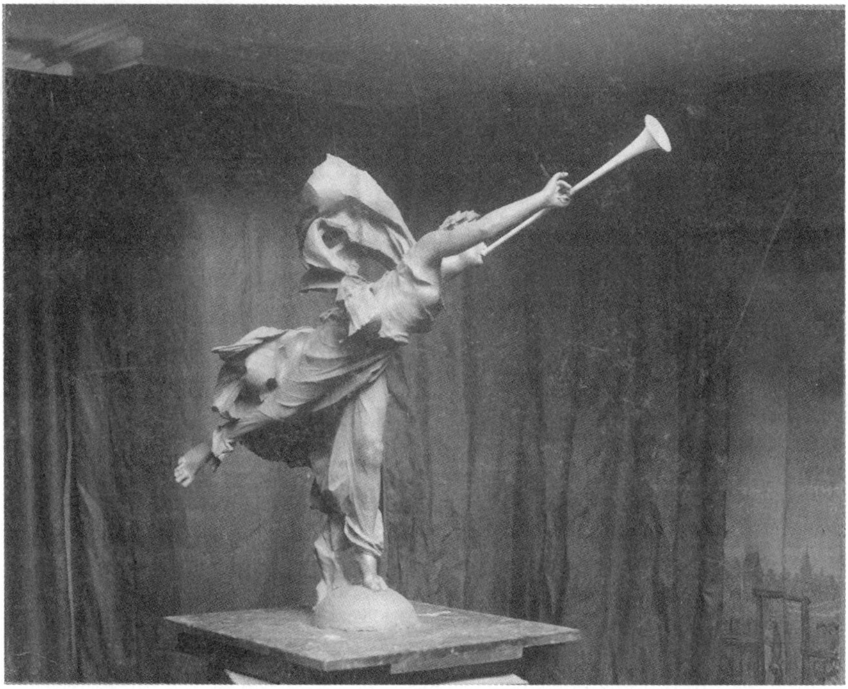

This photograph of Enid's model of *Victory* for the Louisiana Purchase Exposition, also known as the St. Louis Exposition, (1904) was taken in Enid's studio, as evident by the painting on the right, which is an original or copy of David Teniers's *Peasant Wedding*. This painting appears in whole or in part in a handful of photographs showing Enid's studio. (Enid Bland Yandell Photograph Collection, 987PC52X.232, Box 5. The Filson Historical Society, Louisville, KY.)

"exquisite" decorations for the restaurants, which were situated on each end of the Colonnades of States, an area of the fair formed by pillars that enshrined allegorical and symbolic female figures of the fourteen states that resulted from the Louisiana Purchase.[38]

While we have very little documentation about these sculptures, and only one photograph, some evidence of Enid's process exists. A drawing on lined paper, which Enid retained, shows a classically draped figure on top of an orb. Her arms are extended in a left-right position, as she stands on one foot with the right leg extended to her right. In her hand, instead of a wreath and trumpet, which the finished work is holding, she holds a palm frond. On the top of the sheet, in Karl Bitter's handwriting, the drawing is addressed to "Miss Enid Yandell," and notes at the bottom of the page offer the context: "Suggestions for crowning figure Restaurant for St. Louis Worlds fair April 1, 1903 Karl Bitter, Chief Dept. Sc." It is unclear if these suggestions were coming as an initial suggestion to Enid, to offer a guide for how the work might be approached initially. It seems more likely that the drawing is a response to an idea that Enid had generated, submitted to Bitter, and to which he replied. The drawing contains suggestions from Bitter that Enid clearly rejected, given the different axis, attributes, and pose of the finished *Victory*.

While the notion of embellishing a restaurant with a figure of victory may seem odd, truly the connection to theming is apparent when viewed within the context of the entirety of the fair, where many other emblems of victory appeared. Such theming served as a reminder of the reason for the Fair: the celebration of the expansion of the nation.[39]

Following the Fairs

After St. Louis, Enid did not submit work to world's fairs again. She did continue to exhibit work extensively in the United States, however. In examining her work over the first decade of the twentieth century, it is clear that Enid's final entries to world's fairs bookend her entrance to the fairs ten years earlier in both their approach to classical subjects and their reliance upon the pioneer Daniel Boone. After her work for the St. Louis fair, she detached from these spectacles and instead focused on developing sculpture that would be made of enduring materials and long-lasting.

Over the years that Enid exhibited at the world's fairs and the Tennessee Centennial, she found herself working alongside her contemporaries. In fact, a number of sculptors found themselves making a similar circuit between Chicago and the subsequent US fairs, including Buffalo and St. Louis; these included Karl Bitter, Philip Martiny, Gutzon Borglum (1867–1941), and F. Edwin Elwell (1858–1922).

From the time of the Chicago fair (1891–1893) through the latter days of St. Louis's fair (1904), sculptors in their thirties and forties were the generation with whom Enid would grow as a professional, even as she was slightly their junior, being twenty-three to thirty-five years old over these years. While more attention is paid in this volume to the other men just mentioned, Elwell is worth at least brief consideration here because his career bears witness to the synergy among the sculptors. Elwell began his professional career, as Enid did, in Chicago and went on, after submission to Buffalo, to serve as curator of ancient and modern sculpture at the Metropolitan Museum of Art in New York in the years 1903–1905. He and Enid were acquaintances, if not colleagues, who corresponded in the early part of the twentieth century, thus affirming the connections that artists made in a sculptor community through exhibitions such as world's fairs and their studies abroad. Theirs was a network of sorts, and Enid's orbit was in the realm of these men.[40]

And yet attention was drawn to women sculptors as a group apart from men. A 1904 article in *Woman's Work* drew attention to the field of women sculptors, citing approximately 100 women as professional sculptors, thus evidencing a breakthrough in contrast to women of the previous generation. The article stated, "Today the woman sculptor finds a comradeship among her sisters that has meant much for her work." Enid was mentioned among this young group of artists, along with Julia Hecht (a musician), Elsie Ward (a sculptor), and Grace Wishaar (a painter). But even as women wanted to claim her, Enid's trajectory was traced in the article through male lines: that of her father (and Durrett, although he is not mentioned in the article), the pipeline of professors at Cincinnati, the tutelage of Taft in Chicago and Rodin and MacMonnies in Paris. Attention was also drawn to the choices she made that gave her more opportunities than she would have had otherwise. The article mentions Enid's work in Chicago before citing a work of Enid's "more remarkable in point of design": the *Kiss Tankard.* Works such as the tankard and other works of a domestic stature called attention to the fact that Enid oscillated between the two worlds: the large-scale, public, and monumental, and the small-scale, private, and life-sized. She easily navigated between the world of fairs and memorial fountains and that of garden sculpture, bronze decorative objects, and tabletop items. She also navigated styles, from the classical, academic, and prescribed to the modern, avant-garde, and expressive. Although never making a definitive break in tradition, Enid moved freely between these worlds. This ability was remarked upon in an article "A Southern Sculptress and Some of Her Work." Appearing in 1898 in the

New York Journal, the article offered a comprehensive list of Enid's recent work from the fairs, along with commentary and photographs. One of the these showed Enid with a crown of flowers accompanied by a proclamation of her "exceptional talent," thereby proving that some efforts did prompt Enid to wear a crown—though only on her own terms.[41]

5

Passions and Pursuits

Enid's decision to become a sculptor was a passion as well as a pursuit of an occupation that brought her the independence through which she could forge her identity. Her mother realized early on that her eldest daughter was determined to build a name for herself through sculpture, regardless of any disappointment family members may have felt about her taking on an occupation. In a letter to Enid of 1896, Louise remarked how she knew that Enid was "an original in many things" and that Enid's "life had gone out of my moulding and into your own." Through her work, Louise's daughter would sculpt her legacy.[1]

By the start of the twentieth century, Enid had become known through her work. For instance, she had been associated with the Chicago World's Fair, where her classical figures served as architectural support for the Woman's Building. In Louisville, her proposal for a Confederate monument evoked allegorical representations of fame and victory. In Nashville, she produced a monumental figure of the Greek goddess Athena for the Tennessee Centennial. Shifting from classical exemplars in her public statuary of monuments and architectural elements of the fairs, Enid's work became more expressive after the 1890s. Strikingly different from the classical statuary of her works for public spectacle and her traditionally posed busts, in this new body of work, Enid garnered praise alongside a developing public for her art. By late in the decade, she had already developed some interest in busts, usually commemorative, and figureens. Living in Paris, she came into contact with cutting-edge works of sculpture by artists such as Auguste Rodin (1840–1917), with whom Enid grew acquainted on her subsequent stays in Europe as a professional artist from the late 1890s onward. Rodin's *The Kiss* (1892), a carved block of marble revealing two figures entwined in each other's arms, was shown at the Paris Salon in 1898. About this time, Enid began to develop a body of work that took a dramatic turn in terms of form and in its emphasis of expressive qualities and sensuality, emphasizing themes of love, loss, and companionship on a scale both small and large.

By the turn of the century, sculptors were taking notice of the shifting terrain of sculptural form. In any one exhibit, for instance, works embodying classical form, realism, idealism, and fantasy might be represented. A case in point is the International Exhibition of Modern Art organized in 1913 by the Association of American Painters and Sculptors, an event known colloquially as the "Armory Show" in New York. Here Enid exhibited both realistic and expressive works, the former tending toward the treatment of form she had used for large-scale public commissions (such as the world's fairs) and the latter tending toward the abstract and expressive qualities championed by Rodin and others. She developed an intentional practice of choosing an exposition of form that conveyed meaning. And in 1899, amidst the swirl of activity in her studios in Paris and New York, Enid was clearly in pursuit of passion. To examine this theme, this chapter will discuss two Yandell works of the period: a small-scale decorative piece (a silver loving cup and another related work, *Kiss Tankard*) created in 1899 and a large-scale, outdoor memorial fountain featuring several sculptural groups and two basins commissioned the same year and installed in Providence, Rhode Island, in 1901. The chapter concludes by considering a work that was given to Enid by a fellow sculptor as way of furthering the theme presented here.[2]

Before moving into a discussion of the first of these works, we should note an issue regarding Enid's work from 1895 to 1899 and, in particular, the *Kiss Tankard*, which is also known by the title *Mermaid and Fisherboy* as well as *The Kiss.* Historians, art historians, and museum professionals have repeatedly associated the work(s) known as the *Kiss Tankard,* a yachting trophy, with the loving cup that Enid created for her sister Elsie's wedding in November 1899. There is not enough evidence to state definitively that these vessels are one in the same. No written description of the silver loving cup given by Enid to Elsie exists. Moreover, the date of Enid's gift to her sister—November 1899—is several months after the debut of the yachting trophy cup's design in January 1899 on the pages of a jewelers' magazine. The announcement of Enid's design for the trophy appeared alongside two images of the work that we now call *Kiss Tankard,* or *Mermaid and Fisherboy.* Therefore, there is certainty that *Kiss Tankard* was conceived as a yachting trophy, made its pictorial debut in January 1899, and was intended to be cast in bronze and silver. A second certainty is that Enid created a silver loving cup that was admired by all who had attended her sister's wedding reception at Enid's family's home in Louisville in November 1899. No mention of this silver cup's relation to a preexisting work was made by anyone in Enid's family, nor in the press. Moreover, it is difficult to accept the idea that the silver loving cup (given to Enid's sister as a wedding present in November) was based upon a design that appeared in a professional publication the preceding January, as this seems to be at odds with the propriety of gift giving. It would have been peculiar for Enid to have given Elsie a cast in silver of an already existing work and to have no mention of this connection in any of the documentation from the period.[3]

Further complicating the biographies of these works are issues related to the interpretation of the multitude of versions of the *Kiss Tankard* that exist. At the present time, at least three versions exist— "version," here referring to the medium in which the work was made. Only one plaster is known, presumably the earliest of these, since Enid used that medium as preliminary material. This work is in the collection of the Speed Museum, where it came through the descendants of Elsie Barber, Enid's sister.

A bronze is extant as well, dated to around 1899, in the collection of the Museum of Art at the Rhode Island School of Design (RISD). This version was a gift from one of Enid's students and a RISD alumna, Elizabeth Hazard. In internal documentation and external correspondence as well as publications, this tankard has been described by the museum as being cast by Rudier (although no mark is found) and is said to be the version given to Elsie: "*Kiss Tankard* was created as a yachting trophy. The RISD version is believed to have been cast by Yandell to give to her sister as a wedding gift. There are ten other tankards known to have been cast by Gorham for the 1898 Christmas season." One or more silver versions are extant. A silver version, called simply *Kiss*, was cast by the Henry Bonnard Bronze Company and was sold at Bonhams in 2017. A (possible) second silver cast called *The Kiss* sold at Sotheby's in 1996.[4]

Enid's working method was to create a plaster model before using more durable materials. Therefore, the earliest of these tankards is the plaster version. Moreover, this plaster, in the collection of the Speed Museum, is

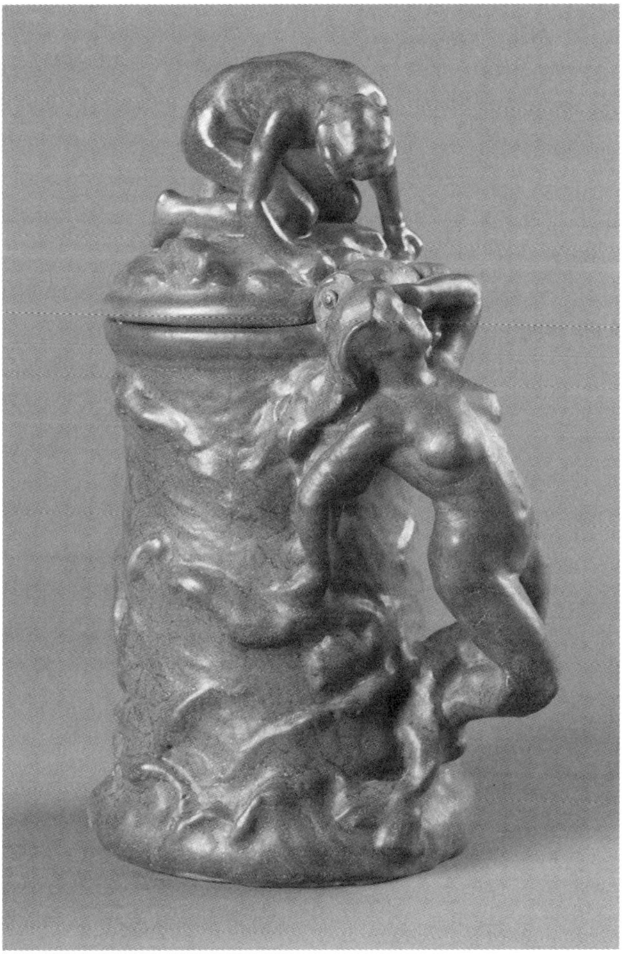

The earliest of Enid's renderings of a cup decorated with an embracing couple, *Mermaid and Fisherboy* dates to around 1897. (Painted plaster, 11 × 6 3/4 × 5 1/4 in. (27.9 × 17.1 × 13.3 cm.), Gift of Mrs. J. J. Trask, 1941.14.7. Collection of the Speed Art Museum, Louisville, Kentucky.)

very likely the work from which the publicity images that appeared in January 1899 were taken, thereby positioning the date of the tankard to ca. 1897–1899. The bronze at RISD is slightly later than the plaster, by virtue of its medium (bronze), which would have necessitated an earlier model, such as the Speed's plaster. The silvers date from around the same time as

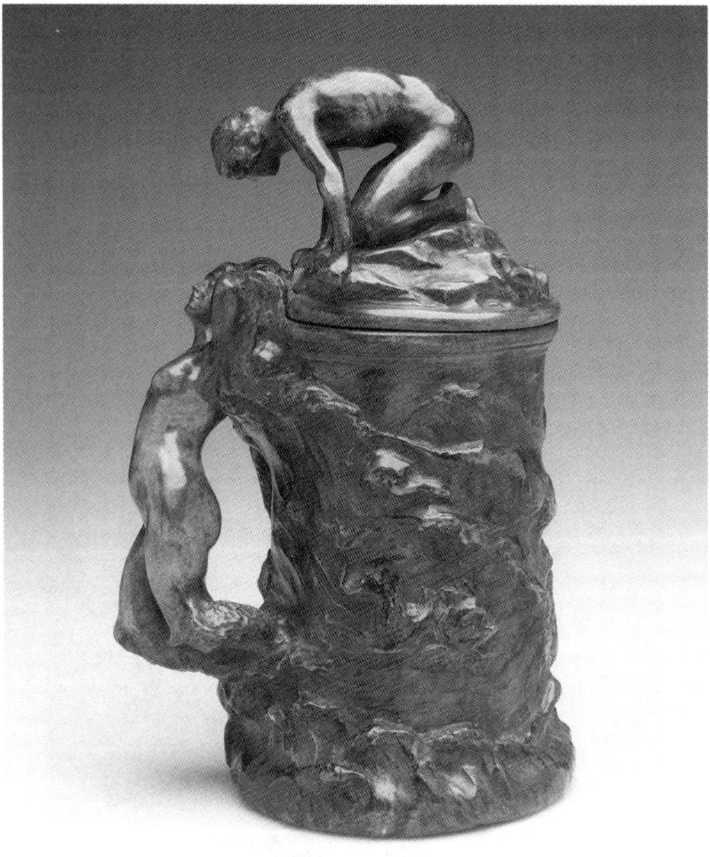

Unlike *Mermaid and Fisherboy,* which was painted plaster, this 1899 *Kiss Tankard* is bronze and is slightly larger: 29.2 x 17.8 cm (11 1/2 x 7 inches) at its widest point; diameter: 14 cm (5 1/2 inches). (Gift of Elizabeth Hazard. 76.190. RISD Museum, Providence, RI.)

the bronze, 1899, since they were marketed to allow purchasers to secure a tankard in their medium of choice. If any of the 1899 works were given by Enid to Elsie, it would have been a silver version of the *Kiss Tankard,* not the bronze at RISD, since every account of the Yandell-Barber wedding in November 1899 referred to the loving cup from Enid as being silver.

Regardless of the medium, Enid's use of this form at this particular point in her career serves to underscore the importance of her Paris experiences and her professional connections in her development as an artist.

Kiss Tankard: Precedents, Form, and Function

In considering the place of the *Kiss Tankard* in Enid's life and career, attention must be paid to the subject matter and its precedent, as well as antecedents of similar works—that is, yachting trophies. Each of these considerations must also take into account style.[5]

Amorous subjects have been a common theme in art since the classical era; the particularities of Enid's approach may be linked to literature as well as the visual arts, and not just Rodin. For example, on the vast grounds of the Tennessee Centennial, just as in Chicago, decorative statuary abounded. There was Enid's *Athena*, of course, as well as the fountain designed by Giuseppe Moretti, which showcased the marvel of electricity. Sculpture also formed part of the landscaped elements, as in the case of the constructed grottos, which were enhanced with statuary. These included the *Purity Grotto*, a fern-covered cave amidst flowers and vines, which was the site of the eponymous female figure with her hand serving as a fountain, a conduit for a trickling stream of water. A second grotto on Lily Lake, on the west side of the Rialto near the Transportation Building, was titled *Fisherman and the Mermaid.* The figure group nearest the Transportation Building includes a man lying on rocks and leaning over to kiss a woman who is rising up to meet him, a sort of alternative Narcissus. Enid would have seen this piece firsthand if she visited the fair (it is unclear if she made the trip to Tennessee, although she did return to the United States to settle her New York studio later that year). If Enid had not actually seen the sculpture in the Lily Lake, she would have learned of it from reports or published proceedings. Given its timing, 1897, this work seems a possible influence in the creation of her *Kiss Tankard.* A number of other pieces in the Nashville fair, although unillustrated in the printed material, may have had a bearing on Enid's subject, if not her treatment. These included Moretti's *Mermaid* (item 980 in the sculpture listing) and a number of works by Italian artists, including the Lapini Brothers of Florence, who exhibited a number of classically inspired works, including women and amorous figures, in the foreign section of the exhibits (artistic marble statuary).[6]

Enid's *Kiss Tankard* represented a blending of the vitality, liveliness, and realism of sculptures that depicted classical and contemporary subjects and the emotive and evocative forms of Rodin and Enid's Art Nouveau contemporaries. In her rendering of her fisher boy (or man) and mermaid, the two figures are engaged with each other, not through touch, but through emotion. The man, crouching, and casts his glance over the rim to a woman, whose back is arched off of the side of the tankard. The hair, arms, leg, and fins of the mermaid torso melt into her setting, including the sea and gulls surrounding her. Waves surround the body of the tankard. When the tankard is closed, the eyes of the two figures do not meet, nor do their bodies touch; however, when the lid is up, the man's lips touch the woman's lips as they kiss. Enid signed the work with "E. Yandell" on the rock below the kneeling boy's right leg.

The tankard features characteristic elements of yachting trophies and loving cups, a genre that had blossomed from modest items into larger and more spectacular wares from the 1870s on. Their design and purpose were described in detail and often illustrated in newspapers and magazines of the day and were treated seriously as works of art. Announcement of the availability of Enid's trophy design was made in January 1899 and described the tankard as having "two figures . . . very beautifully and carefully modeled, and the ensemble is most attractive and artistic from a decorative standpoint. The tankard was designed for a yachting trophy, and has been cast in a limited number, some in sterling silver and some in bronze." In May 1899, mention of the tankard was made in the *Jewelers Review*, calling attention to the exhibition of the tankard, its subject, and its sculptor, even though Enid's name was misspelled: "There has been on exhibition the past week in the window of Doring Andrews one of the unique tankards designed by Enid Yaudell [*sic*], now in New York and a former Cincinnati girl who has attained fame as a sculptor. The tankard is a sea design, being a representation of the fisher boy and the mermaid of Goethe." After defining the appearance and subject, the article noted, "When the lid is thrown back, the face of the boy approaches *and touches* the face of the mermaid, *their lips touching in* a kiss. A comparatively small number of the tankards have been made and it is understood they are held at $250." When the casts by Tiffany & Co. were completed, notice was made in the *Illustrated Kentuckian: A Journal of Art, Literature, Education, Religion, Society, Sports and General Information*. The June 1899 issue noted: "Miss Yandell writes that she has just completed the marine tankard ordered some time ago by Tiffany & Co. This is a beautiful conception. The subject was suggested by Goethe's poem, *The Fisher Boy and*

Mermaid. Boy and girl, below them are the sea symbols, over which hovers a flight of gulls." Part of Enid's approach with the tankard, then, was to market to her audience.[7]

Kiss Tankard and Loving Cup

Either simultaneous to or following her work on this tankard, Enid pursued another cup design. While living in Paris in November 1899, Enid sent a silver loving cup to her sister, Elsie, who was betrothed to Donn Barber, an architect in New York. As the *Interior Journal* of Stanford, Kentucky, reported: "Miss Enid Yandell, the noted sculptor . . . gave the bride a silver loving cup of her own design, from which the health of the bridal party was drunk prior to their departure."[8]

Family reports made note of the cup, its impression on all who saw it, and the family's praise of Enid. Her sister Maude reported many of the wedding day's details to Enid in a four-page letter: "Your cup made as formed of you & made you seem near to us it has tremendously admired & looked pefectly [*sic*] stunning as the center of attraction I will send clipping for descriptions—There was rain outside but never did I see so much Sunshine inside I never saw Louisville people so pleased & appreciative." Enid's mother sent a letter also to Enid, written from Burlington on December 3, 1899: "We missed you so much & all talked of you, & next to the bride your cup was the center of admiration[.] The Bishop drank to the health of the gifted girl far away & your mothers [*sic*] eyes were filled with tears & her heart with loving thoughts. . . . All send love to you & we are so proud of your successes."[9]

At the same time that Enid was celebrating the love that her sister had found in marriage to Donn Barber and marketing her *Kiss Tankard* to a wide audience, she was at work on her largest commission to date, the Carrie Brown Memorial Fountain (Providence, Rhode Island). The contrast between the domestic piece and this large-scale public work is remarkable, when considering just the intent and the genesis of each work. However, another distinction between the two has to do with the records for each. Those for the tankard are sporadic at best; to construct the history of the tankard requires sifting through materials that may or may not have relevance to this particular work and to situate these bits of detail within the broader narrative of Enid's practice as well as sculpture in the late nineteenth century. By contrast, the Carrie Brown Memorial Fountain was a private commission, the completed work gifted to a city; the entire endeavor, from selecting the artist to designing the work and negotiating details of its construction and installation, was well documented. Newspapers recounted these details regularly, and the city's own record of meetings and transactions is also available. The information gleaned from these sources can be combined with materials that Enid herself produced and retained, as well as correspondence and records from the donor and family members, who deposited materials at Brown University. Thus, the study of the Carrie Brown Memorial Fountain is useful not only in its own right, but also in terms of helping us to construct a narrative as to Enid's process. Such details, when corroborated and interpreted, offer an overview of how Enid may have approached other works and how scholars might begin to understand her process more fully.

The Carrie Brown Memorial Fountain

In Enid's hand, the Carrie Brown Memorial Fountain became an exercise in form to the service of content. Put simply, it visualized the impact of losing one's companion. It was a gift to the city of Providence, Rhode Island, from Paul Bajnotti (1842–1919), a diplomat who wished to honor the memory of his late wife, Caroline "Carrie" Mathilde Brown (1842–1892). Brown, who died after contracting pneumonia, had long ties to the city of Providence and came from a prominent family there (the namesakes of Brown University). In recognition of this, Bajnotti also commissioned a second memorial to her on the campus of Brown University, Carrie Tower, a clock tower inscribed with a passage from the book of Solomon in the Old Testament of the Bible: "Love is Strong as Death."[10]

The memorial fountain has various names, including the Bajnotti Fountain, the Carrie Brown Memorial Fountain, and *The Struggle of Life*. The first of these refers to the person who commissioned the work, Paul Bajnotti. The second recognizes the person being memorialized and is the more common name in use today. *The Struggle of Life* is the symbolic title that was used to refer to the work during Enid's time, particularly when she shared earlier designs for the work or referred to it in interviews, perhaps because this title is the most apt in conveying an interpretation of its form. For the purposes of this discussion, the title Carrie Brown Memo-

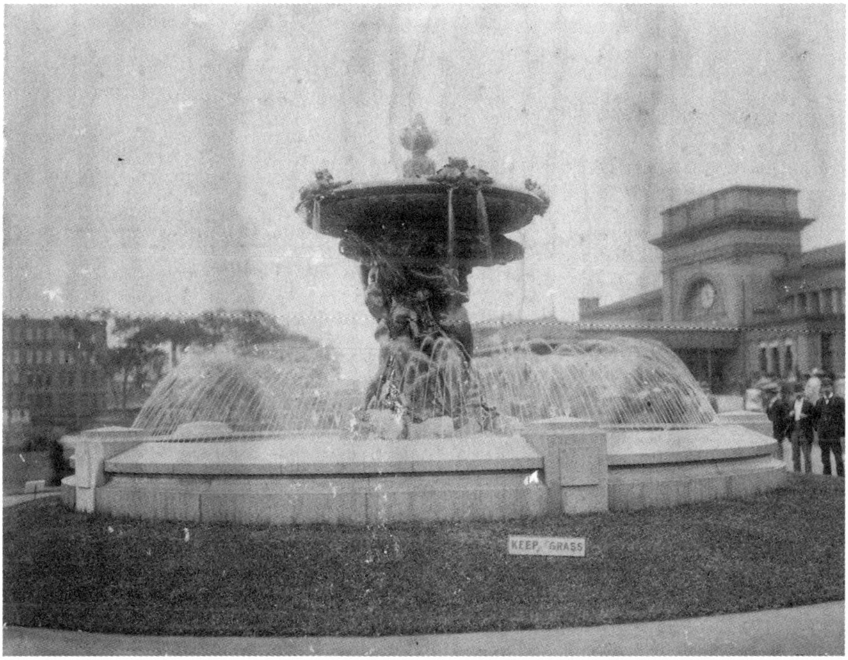

The Carrie Brown Memorial Fountain, installed near the train station in Providence, Rhode Island. (Enid Bland Yandell Photograph Collection, 987PC52X.081, Box 2, Folder 19. The Filson Historical Society, Louisville, KY.)

rial Fountain (shortened as Brown Memorial Fountain) will be used, as it was the name expressly intended by the donor.

Beginning in 1899, the office of the mayor of Providence managed the affairs related to the implementation of the donor's memorial gesture. A resolution accepting the $10,000 gift from Bajnotti, and enacting the deadline, was passed and approved on January 25, 1899. Bajnotti's donation came with certain expectations attached: first, that the fountain would be erected within twenty months of the acceptance of the funds (a condition Bajnotti later extended to two years); second, that fine materials, "such as bronze and granite, or granite and stone," be used (so as not to allow soot to decay marble, as much as he preferred that medium); and that the design have "merit well corresponding with the importance of the outlay." Bajnotti left the design, location, material, preparation, and execution in the city's hands. He directed that the name of the fountain be "the Carrie Brown Memorial Fountain," and an inscription was to bear this intent for the work. He also sought confidentiality in the process and requested that Carrie's brother be involved in it. Once the gift, with its stipulations, was accepted, Mayor William C. Baker appointed a committee of individuals to preside and to invite submissions from eighteen artists of various statures. In response, both leading and lesser-known sculptors of the day submitted their concepts for the fountain.[11]

After receiving an invitation to submit, Enid replied to Daniel F. George, secretary of the Carrie Brown Memorial Fountain Commission, on March 13, 1899, noting that she was grateful for the committee's asking her to compete and adding, "altho it is not my habit to enter any competition, as this is to be limited to artists asked to submit designs, I shall be glad to make you a sketch for the Fountain." Enid asked for more information about the overall process—such as the prize, the number of artists who would be asked to compete—as well as more specific information, including a request for a map showing the size and shape of the area where the fountain was intended to reside, along with the elevation and location of nearby buildings. In May 1899, Enid wrote to the commission secretary again, asking how many competitors there might be and the desires of the committee with regard to commemoration on the fountain. Specifically, she asked, "Is it the desire of the committee to have a portrait of Carrie Brown Badjnotti [*sic*] or anything she has done commemorated in the fountain? If so will you kindly send me a photograph and tell me of her accomplishments?" While we do not have correspondence that indicates how Secretary George responded, the letter from Enid containing this series of questions enables us to piece together Enid's ideation. They helped to guide Enid's work, although her choice of style was certainly connected to her move toward a less resolved, less classical finish. In addition to her queries of content, she outlined her expectation to "have an architect colaborate [*sic*] with me in executing my design." This demonstrates Enid's growth in terms of her ability and comportment as a professional artist at this time. She also asked the secretary how the model should appear for the deliberations, asking in two separate letters, that the work be sited as high as possible, at least four feet from the ground, and that George "pay attention to get them straight and level." Enid also submitted a text that explained her central group of figures, which she intended would accompany the display of her model.[12]

In terms of prizes, the commission named finalists in addition to the winner of the competition. From the eighteen artists selected to compete, fourteen designs and models were ultimately exhibited in City Hall, and four awards were given: first, second, and third prizes, in addition to the commission, which was awarded to Enid.[13]

The submissions appeared in the *Providence Journal* as rough sketches, identified with the artist's name and accompanied by text that addressed the artist's conception, qualifications, and/or body of work that might inform this commission. For instance, Robert Kraus, a Boston-based artist, developed a model for a work he called *Scene of the Deluge,* which showed the struggle of a man "against the elements in an effort to save himself and his kind. The man, a father, is represented as bearing the prostrate form of his wife and her suckling child out of harm's way." The accompanying passage in the newspaper noted that the strengths of the design included its harkening back to Renaissance style through the decoration on the cone-shaped pedestal (which appear to be animal faces used as spouts through which water could pour into the basin below). Another model, submitted by T. J. Pairpoint of Providence, took a different approach through its representation of a seated ideal figure of womanhood "holding with uplifted arms a medallion portrait of Carrie Brown Bajnotti, entwined with ribbons." The surrounding plinth included high relief frieze of symbolic motifs, such as "the lily for purity, the oak for strength, the laurel for victory and success, the poppy for sleep, and the ivy for eternal life." The words "Faith," "Hope," and "Charity" would be included on the frieze as well.[14]

In surveying the handful of designs, it is apparent that Enid's work differed from the other submissions in both form and content. Aspects of some of the designs (for instance, Kraus's man bearing the body of another) invoked an expressive form, which stood in contrast to the stoic, iconic imagery of many a memorial at the time. Aspects of other designs invoked a classical past, perhaps through the use of iconography, allegorical figures, and decorative elements (for instance, Pairpoint's single figure with decorative and emblematic elements in a frieze). But Enid's design captured both expressive qualities and allegorical content. Moreover, her design approached the subject of a memorial fountain to a woman in a way that differed from her contemporaries, particularly in her use of allegorical figures and her approach to subject. Finally, in review of Enid's visual and verbal renderings about this very project (as documented in the correspondence to Secretary George, as well as scribblings in extant notes and scrapbook pages), it appeared that her work was intended to function more as an installation consisting of several components viewed from multiple angles, unlike much (if not all) of her previous body of work, which saw the creation of singular works taking on the forms of a bust, a life-sized figure, or a colossal statue, monuments with one focal point.

Apparently, the commission from the mayor's office that was overseeing the creation of the fountain saw merit in Enid's efforts. On July 22, 1899, the *Providence Journal* reported that Enid's design was accepted by the commission. Her design featured a multipiece stone fountain consisting of a central group of figures surmounted by the basin and a central spray. Enid reported her award of the commission to Reuben Durrett and noted its significance: "I have won the Providence Fountain. It is a great chance for me and I shall do a beautiful thing. This order will mean more honor than money but it is sure to bring me much work. . . . It is a great pleasure for me to be able to do this work for them. The winning of this fountain over 18 of the best men sculptors is a great feather in my cap." She also noted that she would seek advice on her drawings and sketches from Rodin: "I shall complete it with the criticism of the greatest French sculptor Rodin who is my teacher." The term "teacher" in this case refers to Rodin's status among sculptors at this time rather than Enid's abilities. Relative to the greatest sculptor of the day, any sculptor would have considered themselves a pupil.[15]

Following the announcement of Enid's selection to create the Carrie Brown Memorial Fountain, responses varied. On the one hand, Enid's friends, family, and circle of Louisville friends expressed joy and affirmation. The context for such an achievement was not lost on the news outlets, with the *Boston Globe* reporting that the commission was "the first time a woman's hand was ever in evidence in Rhode Island statuary, and she may well be proud of the fact." However, some backlash came from the sculpture community, particularly the male sculptors.[16]

Robert Kraus, whose design was rejected in favor of Enid's design for the Brown Memorial Fountain, wrote a letter to the *Boston Evening Record:* "To the Editor of the Record: You had in today's Record an article on Miss Enid Yandell, the sculptress, in which she 'over many of the leading sculptors of America,' received an award. Now, I, as one of the competitors who saw all the designs and models submitted for the fountain, must say in truth that a commission consisting of better judges would have decided very different as they did." Never criticizing Enid or her work directly, Kraus went on: "That Miss Yandell is a member of the National Sculptors' Society does not amount to so very much. We have in Boston half a dozen sculptresses which, if they like, can join that society just as well as she."[17]

Modeling behaviors and proprieties she had learned in the South, and even perhaps recollecting the controversy over the Confederate Monument for Louisville, Enid kept her comments to herself. Her scrapbook contains a clipping from the *Providence Evening Bulletin* with summaries of each sculptor's submission. Over the top of each page from the paper that has been pasted into Enid's scrapbook, handwritten assessments were appended over the description of each memorial. Although it is unclear if Enid wrote these or dictated them, the comments on the submissions include the following assessments: "Awfull [*sic*], Useless . . . Too Fussy, N. G. [No Good], Funereal." Others noted the inappropriateness of the submission for its stated purpose, for example, "good for interior memorial." Of Kraus's submission, the annotator wrote, "Tame." Enid was obviously keenly aware of her competition.[18]

Perhaps what mattered most was the fact that the patron, Paul Bajnotti, was quite pleased with Enid's design. He wrote an appreciative letter to Mayor William C. Baker, who oversaw the submissions from the invited artists, stating his "sincere gratitude and . . . cordial thanks for the very valuable co-operation in a project deeply cherished by me, the development of which could not be more satisfactory and satisfying." Of Enid's design, Bajnotii wrote to Mayor Baker: "I gather the impression, from the design sent to me, that the model presented by her is very fine indeed and gives promise of an artistical [*sic*] and impressive structure."[19]

Designing the Fountain

Enid called upon all of her training to date in the design and execution of the Brown Memorial Fountain. For it, she built upon her abilities in creating large-scale, architecturally focused works, such as the caryatids at Chicago and *Athena* at Nashville. She also began to settle into the expressive, Art Nouveau, Rodinesque approach to form witnessed with her figureens. Her fluid, gestural handling of the surface with such tabletop works grew into an overall treatment compositionally, as in the case of *Kiss Tankard,* where the figures as well as the background convey a less academic, formulaic approach and rely instead upon the intertwining of form in the creation of an aesthetic entirety. In other words, form followed feeling. Third, Enid was again pushing her expectations. In this case, the complicated engineering and mechanical aspects of the fountain had to be integrated into the design. This is in stark contrast to Enid's earlier fountain design, completed just two years earlier in Louisville. *Wheelman's Bench* (also known as the Ruff Memorial Fountain, 1897) was a slender fountain situated at the center of a landscaped area with an arched bench as part of the design. For the Brown Memorial Fountain, the water was an integral part of the design, even though it was the aspect of the design over which Enid had no control. Put simply, she wasn't an engineer. She had to rely upon such specialists to carry out the work to her expectations—to assure that the granite basin with more than two hundred spray outlets functioned and cohered with the overall plan for this memorial fountain.[20]

There was great consternation over the amount of time it took Enid to create the work. Given the parameters of the initial bequest, it is fair to state that time constraints, as well as the particularities of siting and medium, were placed on the artist. None of these should have presented a serious obstacle. Yet the clock was ticking, and the patron wanted to see his memorial to his wife realized.

In a letter of April 27, 1901, beyond the twenty-month deadline instituted by Paul Bajnotti's commission, J. W. Bishop (the granite supplier) wrote to Secretary George regarding these issues, as well as the delay in contract. He noted: "The delays on this contract have been very disappointing to us. . . . We cannot place the blame with Messrs. Morris, Butler & Rodman [the architects], because they have certainly done all in their power to help us out in this matter, but we do think that Miss Yandell has been very lax in prosecuting this work and put us to a good deal of unnecessary expense on account of these many delays." Enid, in her reply of April 29, retorted that Bishop's blaming her for delays was "absurd." In an in-person meeting on May 10, 1901, Enid assured the commission that she had seen the contractors and "explained to them in detail everything required of them by her and the commission and that the work would probably be done in about two weeks. . . . [and] authorized . . . the placing of the rough granite stones under the bronze work, having explained to him just how she would like to have them arranged and accompanying her explanation with a photograph of her model showing their exact position."[21]

Secretary George tried to mediate among all parties to carry the work through to completion. Throughout the process, from 1899 to 1901, several issues arose, not the least of which was a disagreement about how to support the basin of the fountain between the granite company, J. W. Bishop, Gorham Manufacturing, and Enid, with the city acting as liaison. When it became apparent that the deadline to install the fountain would not be met, Secretary George reported the news to the patron, who agreed that an extension could be made, which may be seen as affirmation of Enid as a professional sculptor whose body of work and promise were valued. The Secretary reported this news to Enid in a letter of October 30, 1900:

> The Commission has received a communication from Mr. Bajnotti in which he very willingly extends, by three additional months, the terms within which the Fountain is to be erected and completed. This extension of time is very gratifying to the Commission, for they agree with you in all you say concerning the time required for the proper execution of a work of art of the importance of this Memorial. They are really much pleased with the progress you have made, and they desire me to assure you that they never for a moment had any doubts about your purpose and ability to furnish them with a Fountain within a reasonable period which will be artistic and entirely satisfactory. Do not let the tone of my last letter lead you to think the Commission does not fully appreciate your faithful endeavors.[22]

Despite the back-and-forth of the commission—the numerous letters, telegrams, and conversations—Enid remained committed to following through on this project, as well as keeping up with her other work at this time and the pursuit of future commissions, into the twentieth century. The latter part of the 1890s was a period of robustness for Enid, a period that saw her transition from fair work to her own, unique pursuits.

Like many successful sculptors, Enid found herself juggling commissions for large-scale work, such as this memorial fountain, alongside smaller projects and more fair work. In addition, each work was in different stages of planning or execution: she had modeled clay of some statues while tending to the plaster or polishing of others. In between, she entered competitions, such as the one in Providence; answered queries from a variety of sources (including her loving mother, who was her greatest booster); negotiated contracts; and attended dedications and unveilings.

The Carrie Brown Memorial Fountain is a multipiece fountain that measures twenty feet tall and thirty feet wide. Three elements comprise the sculptural group: the central group of figures, which serves as columnar support; the basin on top of the figures, which features a central spray; and the basin beneath the figures, which includes an inscription and a dedication along its beveled rim. The arrangement's central group of five intertwined bronze figures supports a stone basin above and suppresses a basin beneath, also of stone. The figure grouping includes a draped, winged female figure with flowing hair and a serene gaze moving forward and resisting the clutches of a male on either side of her. The back side of the grouping features a second woman, whose nude body faces forward as she turns to resist the male to her right (who is also involved with the other woman) and a third male, an emaciated older figure, who crouches at her feet. All of the figures take shelter beneath the wings of the primary figure, the partially clad woman. The primary figure is the Angel of Life, who wears wings that may be viewed as the Mantle of Truth; the males may be seen as three earthly concerns: duty, passion, and avarice. This group represents the allegory of the soul's departure from the body, showing two nude female figures and two nude males. Each of these figures is approximately twelve feet high, making an impressive statement both on the part of the sculptor and in light of the narrative of love and loss. When the fountain is operational, the attraction is the water coming from the bowl on the ground in upward streams that bathe the figures in a thin, misty veil of water from 234 nozzles. A smaller stream of water emerges from the top of the fountain and gently falls into the basin above the figures. The engraving on the fountain reads: "Erected AD MDCCCC a gift to honor the memory of Carrie Mathilde daughter of the late Nicholas Brown of Providence from her husband Paul Bajnotti of Turin, Italy."[23]

The completed fountain was the result of two years' labor. Enid was commissioned to undertake the work in July 1899; it was unveiled on June

26, 1901. On that day, the Commission and Enid met at the site of the fountain, rather than the Commission's usual chamber in City Hall, and undertook the inspection with one of the architects (Mr. Rodman). The water was turned on, and "the fountain was accepted by the Commission, subject to a few minor corrections to be made in the lining of the upper basin and small outlets for water in some of the bronze figures."[24]

The completion of the fountain, which was such a monumental undertaking, demonstrated successful managing through the most ambitious period of her career. Enid managed a suite of private commissions over these years and participated in both the Paris Exposition in 1900 and the Pan-American Exposition in Buffalo in 1901. She left no time for rest, as she went to Paris after the design for the Providence fountain had been accepted, "to prepare the plaster cast," which was then sent to the United States so that it could be entered into contract with Gorham for the purpose of carrying out Enid's design in bronze. Details of the process from model submission to selection and then subsequent casting in bronze are a bit murky. It is known that the models received as part of the competition were documented (by list) and annotated with an indication that the submission from Enid was to be "Del[ivered] to Gorham Co." Enid would have to return to Paris to begin working on her cast so that she could "point up" her own design. This was an aspect of work that she knew well, given her training in Chicago, but also in her own sculptural practice.[25]

Photographs taken in Enid's studio shed light on her process a decade into her professional work as a sculptor. She combined methods that she took up as part of her earlier work in Chicago, where she had crafted award-winning caryatids in addition to pointing up works for male sculptors. She also had shown expertise in rendering a freestanding, larger-than-life figure two years earlier, with her colossal Athena at Nashville. In rendering the life-sized winged figures for the fountain, Enid modeled, carved, cut, scraped, chipped, brushed, and smoothed the clay into its next iteration: a loving memorial.

In fulfilling commissions such as these, Enid worked without a network of assistants to bring pencil sketches to reality. While she, like many a White Rabbit in Chicago, served as a studio assistant in her early years, her middle years saw independence and autonomous execution. Prior to securing the Providence memorial fountain commission, Enid had only sized up in staff, an impermanent material. For the Brown memorial,

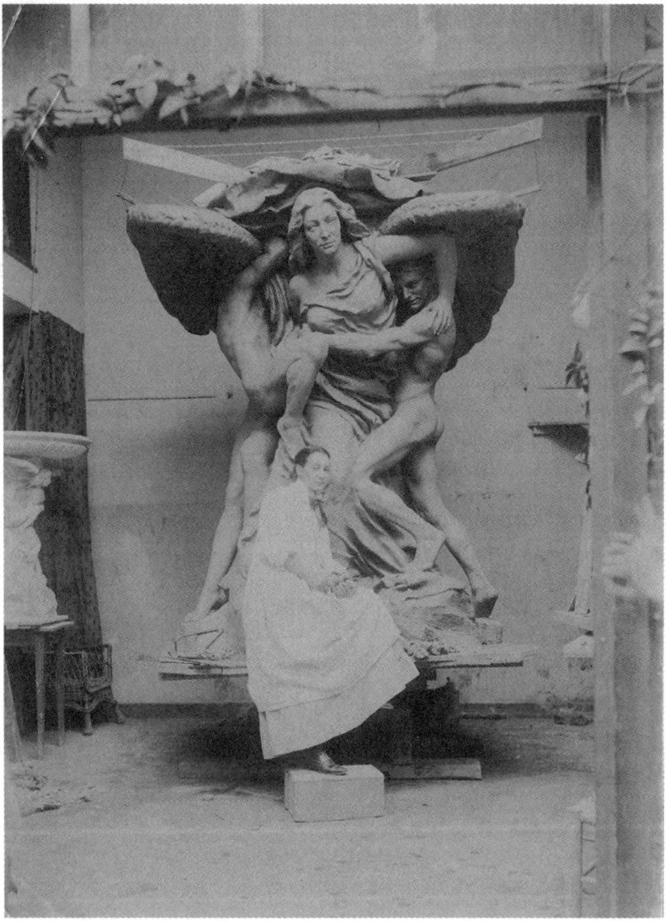

Enid in her Paris studio, ca. 1899–1901, with the Carrie Brown Memorial Fountain. Behind her is a smaller version, which she would have made in order to work out some of the mechanics of the composition before enlarging it. (Enid Bland Yandell Photograph Collection, 987PC52X.086, Box 2, Folder 19. The Filson Historical Society, Louisville, KY.)

however, Enid drew a sketch that she then enlarged and adapted into 3-D plaster before sizing up. Previously, this would have marked the end of her process. Here, though, the plaster had to be sized up again and converted into clay so that a mold could be made in order to cast the full-size rendering in plaster and, eventually, bronze. Most of this work was done by Enid herself, a practice that both contributed to the length of time from commission to delivery and gave the artist ultimate control over the finished work. In addition, for this fountain, Enid employed a model to aid her in creating lifelike qualities in the draped and undraped figures that bore witness to the sculpture's purpose.[26]

A timetable, from start to finish, for the creation of the Carrie Brown Memorial Fountain is possible to reconstruct from Enid's letters. Having completed smaller formats of the finished work by January 1900, Enid took eight months to create the final, full-sized clay model (calling it "about finished" on August 10, 1900). A cast in plaster would then be manicured and finished before being disassembled and shipped across the Atlantic in order to be cast in bronze stateside. Two months later, however, by October 12, 1900, Enid had not yet resolved the form of the plaster, but reported that it was nearly completed, and she estimated the timing of the subsequent steps. The plaster, which was the basis upon which the bronze was cast, was not completed until November of that year. Enid sent it via Antwerp on November 17 to the United States and exclaimed her satisfaction: "The cast is excellent!" Although Enid had estimated that it would take three weeks for the plaster cast to be shipped from Paris to Providence (including additional, interstitial modes of transport), delays occurred in transport "on account of its size."[27]

Just as Enid's sculptural work traveled the ocean, so did she. Enid arrived stateside in December 1900 and remained for several months. Meanwhile, the plaster was cast in bronze at Providence-based Gorham Manufacturing Company over three months. Though Enid had suggested that the work be completed by March 1, 1901, the work was not completed until June 1901. All the while, in her timetable and its necessary adjustments, Enid referred to the importance of durability, permanence, and the lasting legacy of a memorial—attributes of the Carrie Brown Memorial Fountain that were part of memorial culture of the late nineteenth century but were lacking in the large-scale works in Enid's oeuvre up to that point. Working on a grand scale and in materials of permanence required a different, if not stronger, skill set from Enid and by this point in her career. As a thirty-year-old sculptor living in Paris, her first documented entry into a large-scale, spirited competition had proven a time-consuming affair that simultaneously offered her the opportunity to make a name for herself as an independent artist who could execute an elaborate work that required equally elaborate coordination.

In addition to the labor involved while engaged in other work, Enid negotiated a multifaceted collaboration. In July 1899, for instance, Enid requested information about the water and sewer lines at the fountain, as well as about the pavement. She left no detail unconsidered. Later, she negotiated with other companies and their representatives as a wholly new form of collaboration involving multiple partners who might help Enid to realize her vision.

For the fountain, for instance, Enid managed the work with Gorham Manufacturing to bring her plaster design into durable metal form, so that the bronze could weather the Providence winters. The basin work was completed by J. W. Bishop and Company. She also worked with the architectural firm Morris, Butler & Rodman, although we can assume she called upon her earlier experiences working with architects to help her navigate these waters. In Louisville, Enid had worked under Mason Maury and William J. Dodd in developing decorative renderings for Louisville Trust. She had also worked with Karl Bitter in the service of architect Richard M. Hunt to execute figural ornaments for the Breakers at Newport and caryatids for the Astor mansion in New York. She had started making efforts toward collaborating with architects in her design for Louisville's Confederate Monument in 1894, although that commission never came to be.[28]

The firm Morris, Butler & Rodman sent designs for the final fountain, complete with measurements, to Enid's Paris studio in August 1899, which led to letters and back and forth about concreting the foundation in lieu of piling (discussed in October 1899). From her Paris studio in January 1900, Enid wrote to Secretary George and remarked that the 1/3 size model was complete (as of December 1899) and that it had been seen several times and praised by fellow sculptors including Auguste Rodin. Enid reported that they "were most complimentary and are satisfied with my work so far." Six months later, she reported that American sculptor Daniel Chester French had visited and viewed the full-size model: "Mr. Daniel C. French was here a few days ago and saw my group about which he was exceedingly complimentary."[29]

Enid converted the 1/3 size to a full-scale clay version according to a letter dated January 6, 1900, and was resolving its form so that it could be cast into plaster by August 1. Remarking on its size and complicated nature, Enid wrote, "It is a very large piece of work to accomplish properly in so short a time." In this same letter, she asked about the dedication, which was planned for December 1900, and expressed concern about turning on the fountain in the cold Providence air. Further updates followed, including written affirmation by the donor, Paul Bajnotti, about the inscription and other elements that had been decided while the work was in process. Enid also entertained studio visits by Bajnotti, which she in turn relayed to Secretary George as additional affirmation of her work. On May 24, 1900, she wrote that she had "had the honor and pleasure of several visits from Mr. Bajnotti. He was in Paris for a few days; and expressed his entire satisfaction with every thing that has been done so far in regard to the Fountain. . . . For my group and the basin in bronze on which I am now engaged he was more than complimentary. I will not repeat what he said, but he was greatly [?] satisfied a fact of which I feel most proud."[30]

Throughout the correspondence among Enid, Secretary George, and Paul Bajnotti, the artist affirms her abilities and asserts her artistic vision. For instance, when deciding upon the memorial's location, Enid wrote Secretary George, "My preference would be that the Fountain should be placed in Exchange Place as you had decided: but if the Commissioners are willing to change the location 'to the site originally selected in the Park in front of the Railroad Station', of course it will be agreeable to me. I have entire confidence in their judgement." In the end, the fountain was installed in front of the railroad station.[31]

In one important matter, Enid had to correct the work of the architects. On the designs they had drawn up for the competition, they had written "marble" rather than "granite." Immediately after learning of the mistake, Enid wrote to Secretary George: "The marble is a mistake of the architects and should read 'granite' same as main outside wall of basin or standard bronze. I will make the main group upper basin and finial of bronze if preferred by the Committee and outside wall of basin of light colored granite." She also sent notice by telegram. From this series of correspondence between Enid and George, it is clear that Enid had assumed a great deal of responsibility regarding both the work and the Commission, often asking multiple questions and communicating via various means. Such expansive information gathering, follow-up questions, and throughput in decision making demonstrate her capacity to manage her own affairs successfully and go toe-to-toe with sculptors of her day.[32]

Newspapers called attention to Enid's abilities. For instance, the *Providence Journal,* in its article on the fountain's debut, reported that she was the "only woman member of the National Sculpture Society" and pointed to her lineage through her father's skill as a surgeon "noted for his manual skill," which the writer felt may "to a certain extent account find a measure for Miss Yandell's dexterity in using the materials with which she works."[33]

Following the unveiling of the fountain in June 1901, the Commission in October of that year voted to provide additional monies to Enid for her outstanding expenses. While Enid had brought the need for additional funds to the commission's attention, as well as Bajnotti's, earlier in the year, it was only after the dust had settled that the issue was taken up. They voted that, "in view of the excellence of Miss Yandell's work, and in consideration of her statement that she had sustained a large pecuniary loss in the execution of her contract, the unexpended balance [in the Commission's fund] of $351.91 be transmitted to her as an extra compensation on account of her contract with the City of Providence." This was not to be the final decision, however. Bajnotti recognized the labor and concern that Enid had expressed to him nine months earlier and went so far as to suggest that some circumstances, though unspecified, "had been unfavorable to the artist." Thus, he provided an additional sum of $1,000 to be paid to Enid if the Commission so wished. And they did.[34]

In an interview, Enid remarked that Rodin, "her master," critiqued her work on the fountain throughout the creative process; and she reported that he had mixed feelings about the work. Her former mentor and employer at Chicago, Lorado Taft, considered the plaster cast of the fountain, which Enid showed at the Pan-American Exposition in 1901, to be an "important work" (it is unclear if he means generally, or within Enid's oeuvre) and recognized that Enid was attempting difficult combinations of scale. He called the result "confusing," while finding some of the figures in the struggling group "very fine indeed"; he noted that it was "the product of a considerable stay in Paris." Saint-Gaudens, however, called it "awful" and Enid "incompetent." Perhaps these differences in assessment are due to the form that Enid employed.[35]

In the Brown Memorial Fountain, Yandell's figures are not fully separate from their columnar supports; the forms emerge from their solidity, just as Rodin's sculptures appear unfinished, as did Michelangelo's sixteenth-century statues, the non finito. This fountain marks the first time that Enid had approached figures on a large scale in this manner. Because of this, some areas of the work may have been less resolved than others. However, this departure in form matched the spirit of the content—in short, form and subject were aligned for good purpose, even if the result was less superior than her critics may have envisioned.

Moreover, in the case of Saint-Gaudens, his critique may be a reflection of his own memorial making rather than an autonomous assessment of Enid's work. Specifically, Saint-Gaudens' own earlier memorial to a woman differs considerably from the innovative approach Enid took with her Brown Memorial Fountain. Like the Brown fountain, the Adams Memorial in Rock Creek Cemetery (1891, Washington, DC) was commissioned as a memorial to the subject's wife, Marian Clover Hooper Adams. In his work, Saint-Gaudens presented a shrouded figure seated against a block of stone and situated as part of a granite plaza. The seated, solo figure—perhaps a reference to the subject, who committed suicide—is a stark contrast to Enid's writhing forms shrouded under the Mantle of Truth. As she had done with her design of the Confederate Monument for Louisville, Enid depicted women in active roles. She gave them agency as bearers of the legacy of the Confederate dead, in the case of Louisville, and likewise in Providence as an embodiment of truth and light triumphant over the vices of life.[36]

Enid's active, message-laden sculpture found a welcome home in Providence's Burnside Park, which was known as City Hall Park in Enid's day. The park was dedicated in 1892 and landscaped upon the completion of the train station in 1898, which offered a prominent setting for the memorial Enid created. It was situated near the monument to General Ambrose Burnside of the Rhode Island Regiment in the Civil War. Designed by Launt Thompson and erected in 1887, the equestrian sculpture to Burnside is a memorial to the local soldier who became a general in the Union army and had significant losses of men under his command. As an equestrian, military monument, Burnside's memorial offers a contrast to Enid's monument to Carrie Brown Bajnotti, which is a private visualization of the struggle of life.[37]

Beyond these contrasts in approaches, it is worth noting how the memorial's location near the train station meant that it welcomed (and continues to welcome) visitors when they arrived and sent them off on their departure, just as Enid's Daniel Boone welcomed visitors to Nashville. Before its completion, the Carrie Brown Memorial Fountain sought to be "a work that cannot fail to attract the attention of visitors to Providence, as well as residents of the city." In fact, Enid wanted more for the fountain, declaring, "It must be so fine that its fame will make persons stop over a train to look at it." Perhaps she succeeded in this, for in writing about the fountain in 1924, George D. Laswell noted that the public admired the fountain even if they knew little about the circumstances of its commission. He also called the work the "culmination of an international romance" between Bajnotti and Brown. It was well known that Paul Bajnotti was pleased with the fountain. When he visited Providence for several weeks during 1913–1914, for instance, he came to the memorial frequently.[38]

When she visited the site of the memorial fountain just before the unveiling of the sculpture and for the inspection, a photograph was taken of Enid. In it, we see the accomplishment and pride of a thirty-year-old sculptor who had built a name for herself in cities such as Louisville, Cincinnati, Chicago, and now Providence. Trading in her sculptor's smock and tools for a shirtwaist, purse, and feathered hat, Enid stood inside the lower fountain basin before the water has been turned on. She cast a glance upon the figure grouping, which she had only exhibited in plaster previously (it was currently on view at the World's Fair in Buffalo). Behind her were three men engaged in their own conversation. Perhaps Enid was reflecting on all that she had accomplished with this memorial, which was unlike any she had created to date. For this, she was gaining recognition among sculptors and being called upon to lend support to the work of others, as evidenced in her relationship with American sculptor Gutzon Borglum.

Centaur and Centauress

Though little known as a sculptor prior to 1901, in some ways, Gutzon Borglum (John Gutzon de la Mothe Borglum, 1867–1941) was the father of American sculpture in American museums. His *Mares of Diomedes* (1904) was the first piece of sculpture by an American artist purchased for the Metropolitan Museum of Art. Unlike other artists of his generation, including Enid, who participated in the Columbian Exposition and then matriculated to Paris, Gutzon studied in San Francisco before moving to Paris in 1890, England in 1896, and New York in 1901. Their paths may have crossed in Paris during the late 1890s, when Enid was traveling back and forth between Paris and New York, among other cities. At this time, one could trace the lineage of sculptors by their degrees of separation from Rodin's studio, an association that both Enid and Gutzon could make.

It is more likely, however, that their acquaintance was made in New York, given the proximity of their studios and the community of male sculptors engaged at work in the area. It is very possible that Enid and Gutzon met in New York in 1901, while Enid was completing the Carrie Brown Memorial Fountain. Her studio, at Fifty-Sixth Street and Eighth Avenue in the Van Dyck Studio Building, was just over a mile and a half from his at 166 East Thirty-Eighth Street. The city was brimming with activity among sculptors and other visual artists at this time. There was also a pecking order. Enid went toe-to-toe with them as she entertained submissions to fairs and worked alongside these artists on decorative programs for new or renovated architecture. The city had a captive audience for new architecture, both public and private. New buildings, such as the New Amsterdam Theatre, required decoration to suit. Enter the skilled sculptor.[39]

If Enid and Gutzon had not met earlier, initial contact may have come through their connections in New York museum circles; recall that Enid had befriended F. Edwin Elwell, who became curator of sculpture at the Metropolitan Museum of Art. He and Enid were in communication about this time. Elwell may have introduced the two, given his connection through the museum to Borglum. Regardless of how they had met, the friendship of Enid and Gutzon lasted until at least 1915–1916, as evidenced by three letters and a sculpture between them.

To put the relationship of Enid Yandell and Gutzon Borglum into context, we should consider the life and work of each. By 1915, Enid had been living and working in New York and Edgartown on Martha's Vineyard, as well as in Paris. Her work had reached a period of robust growth; she had completed several large-scale commissions, including the Carrie Brown Memorial Fountain, Hogan's Fountain (1905, Louisville), Daniel Boone (1906, Louisville), and a monument to John W. Thomas (1907,

Nashville). She also began to develop themes for her decorative works, including literary sources. Later, between her travels for World War I relief efforts (discussed in Chapter 7), Enid used Gutzon's studio, which he offered to her because he was engaged in work elsewhere.[40]

In October 1915, Borglum corresponded with Enid about this new project, a memorial to Confederate Army leadership carved in bas relief out of the north façade of Stone Mountain in Georgia. Jefferson Davis, Robert E. Lee, and Stonewall Jackson were envisioned as a fitting memorial by the United Daughters of the Confederacy, an American lineage society, which commissioned Borglum. He was contracted to begin work on Robert E. Lee in 1916.[41]

Given the significant size and scale of this commission, Gutzon knew he needed help. On at least one occasion, in a letter of October 7, 1915, he asked for Enid's assistance in carrying out this work. In a follow-up letter, sent to his own studio address, thus indicating that Enid had moved to that space by the end of 1915, Gutzon sent Enid wishes for the new year and "for a happy and prosperous life." In a third letter, he asked for her help in a plan to bring Rodin to the United States, suggesting to Enid that she help him obtain a commission from the Metropolitan Museum of Art or some other place for about $5,000. He asked Enid to write to Rodin with the invitation. Thus, in word and deed, Gutzon considered Enid a trusted colleague and friend. He sought her advice as well as her help.[42]

In the end, the invitations Gutzon extended to Enid, as well as the requests for assistance, did not materialize. Enid helped neither with Stone Mountain nor Borglum's later project, Mount Rushmore; Rodin did not travel to the United States; and Gutzon and Enid maintained their own studio practices independent of each other.[43]

As their careers continued, Enid appears to have kept track of Gutzon's work as a sculptor. She retained clippings about him, among her many sculptor friends, in her scrapbook. For instance, she kept one clipping about Borglum's monumental depiction of Lee on Stone Mountain (from 1925, as the project was delayed due to the Great War) and biographical information about him. In addition to these items (which she may have clipped as part of her sculptural practice), Enid held on to something much more personal, a gift from the artist.

The tabletop plaster *Centaur and Centauress* shows two creatures in a passionate embrace. The two fluidly modeled figures emerge from the

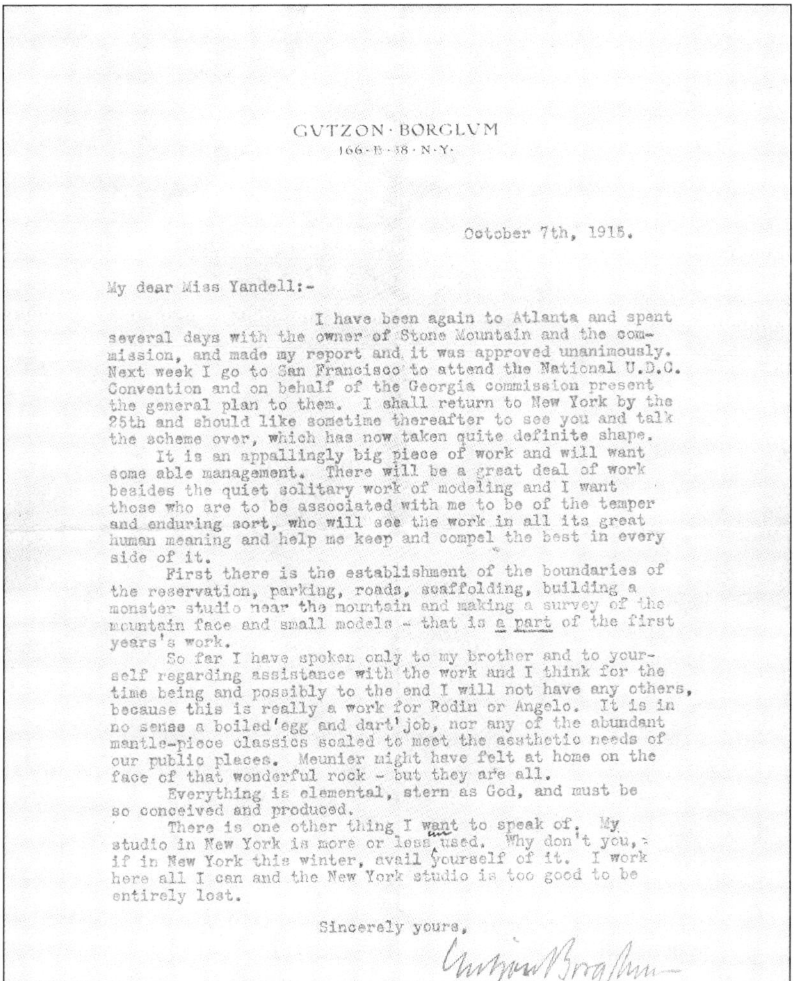

GVTZON · BORGLVM
166 · E · 38 · N · Y ·

October 7th, 1915.

My dear Miss Yandell:-

I have been again to Atlanta and spent several days with the owner of Stone Mountain and the commission, and made my report and it was approved unanimously. Next week I go to San Francisco to attend the National U.D.C. Convention and on behalf of the Georgia commission present the general plan to them. I shall return to New York by the 25th and should like sometime thereafter to see you and talk the scheme over, which has now taken quite definite shape.

It is an appallingly big piece of work and will want some able management. There will be a great deal of work besides the quiet solitary work of modeling and I want those who are to be associated with me to be of the temper and enduring sort, who will see the work in all its great human meaning and help me keep and compel the best in every side of it.

First there is the establishment of the boundaries of the reservation, parking, roads, scaffolding, building a monster studio near the mountain and making a survey of the mountain face and small models - that is a part of the first years's work.

So far I have spoken only to my brother and to yourself regarding assistance with the work and I think for the time being and possibly to the end I will not have any others, because this is really a work for Rodin or Angelo. It is in no sense a boiled'egg and dart'job, nor any of the abundant mantle-piece classics scaled to meet the aesthetic needs of our public places. Meunier might have felt at home on the face of that wonderful rock - but they are all.

Everything is elemental, stern as God, and must be so conceived and produced.

There is one other thing I want to speak of. My studio in New York is more or less unused. Why don't you, if in New York this winter, avail yourself of it. I work here all I can and the New York studio is too good to be entirely lost.

Sincerely yours,

Gutzon Borglum

83x57

Letter dated October 7, 1915, from Gutzon Borglum to Enid. (Enid Yandell Papers, Mss A/Y21b, Folder 36. The Filson Historical Society, Louisville, KY.)

mass of the base. Each has the upper body (head, arms, and chest) of a man or woman, while the body and legs have equine characteristics. The male centaur, which is larger than the other figure, has wild hair and a beard, with a lower torso that is equally large, muscular, and compact. The

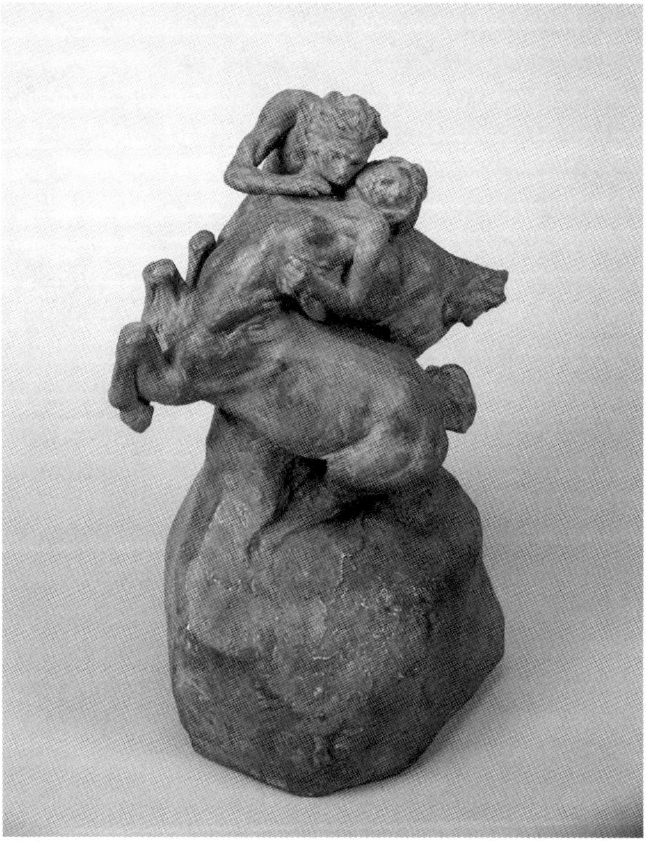

Gutzon Borglum, *Centaur and Centauress*, 1916–1917, Plaster, 20 5/8 in. (52.4 cm.). (Gift of Mrs. J. J. Trask, 1941.14.6. Collection of the Speed Art Museum, Louisville, Kentucky.)

female centauress appears to turn from the male and thrusts her bare chest upward as she rears up.[44]

Centaur and Centauress may appear at first to convey a sense of fright or aggression. However, upon closer review, the work and its inscription convey, in visual and verbal terms, a radically different meaning. First, in terms of the posture, the centauress's position could be read as one of excitement instead of fear or aggression. Second, the encircling of the male centaur's hands around the woman's torso conveys a sense of resolve more than restraint, as no other contact is made between the two beings. Third, the inscription proves useful: "To my confrère Enid Yandell/Gutzon Borglum 1916–17." In interpreting this, we must reject any romantic reading, given that Borglum was married when the work was created and no record of any romantic interest between him and Enid exists in the manuscript material. Thus, the sculpture must speak to the professional relationship between the two. Through the use of the term "confrère," it is apparent that Borglum considered Enid a colleague, a fellow professional, an associate. It seems, then, that *Centaur and Centauress* is a reinvention of Rodin's *The Kiss,* the large-scale, marble, floor sculpture showing two lovers in a passionate embrace—the artist's signature work, which Borglum and Enid would have seen in Rodin's studio some twenty-five years earlier. In Borglum's hands, chisel and plaster became the tools through which to demonstrate his sense of camaraderie, fellowship, and companionship with his fellow sculptor and "confrère," Enid Yandell.[45]

Love, loss, and companionship: like many American sculptors who trained in Paris in the 1890s, Enid gained access to and embraced the expressive possibilities of the figure. Her fluidly modeled figures emerge from their bases in *Kiss Tankard* and bear the burden of classical allegory in the Carrie Brown Memorial Fountain. Her exploration of the aesthetic qualities of finished and unfinished surfaces, partially formed figures, and themes based on personal expression, physical and spiritual sensations, and narrative sources persisted as she continued her work in the early part of the twentieth century.

In addition to pursuing her own work, Enid cultivated artistic education by establishing an art academy at Edgartown, Massachusetts, on Martha's Vineyard (1908). At Branstock, Enid taught summer classes to aspiring artists, akin to the schools that were becoming popular among American modernists. She also reevaluated her subject matter, techniques, materials, and styles following World War I. Having been raised in a tradition of philanthropy as domestic enterprise and having witnessed the effects of war firsthand, Enid engaged in activism and advocacy that pointed toward woman suffrage and war relief work. In addition, she searched for an appropriate language to express the chaos and carnage that emerged from this period of crisis—the era of industrial warfare.

6

Edgartown and Education

Enid first visited Edgartown, Massachusetts in 1907, as she was entering her late thirties and engaged with a number of commissions. After this visit she decided to summer there annually even as she remained connected to her Kentucky home. Establishing her own roots in Edgartown meant that family had a place to visit her, unlike her studio years up to that point, where she had eked out a more peripatetic existence. Some of the most touching recollections from family visits come from Enid's niece, Elsie Barber Trask, who recounted later in life all of those summers with her Aunt Enid, who shared the world she had come to love: sailing around the island in her catboat, picnicking at Gay's Head cliffs, and exploring rustic jaunts. Elsie could also "run freely" and enjoy the island, provided she had a "note pinned to her clothing that she belonged to Miss Yandell."[1]

In establishing a physical place to take root, Enid also immersed herself into the community by building a network of friends. She became involved with the local history scene as a member of the Dukes County Historical Society and the Martha's Vineyard Chapter of the Daughters of the American Revolution (DAR), which is apropos given Enid's longstanding interest in history. She even lectured on topics in art and history. For the DAR chapter, in 1908, she gave a talk on American Art, which was supplemented by an exhibit of photographs of sculpture. She also secured a position as a lecturer for the Women's program "What Art Means to Us" in 1916, where she contributed to the three-hour program of lecture, music, and figures from art. While away from the Vineyard, engaged in work for the war effort, Enid called her friends in Edgartown "my dear friends." She also reconnected with an aspect of her upbringing that informed her mother's philanthropy, as well as aspects of her own life, by becoming a member of a church community. At Edgartown, Enid found a home at St. Andrew's Episcopal Church and also pursued inter-

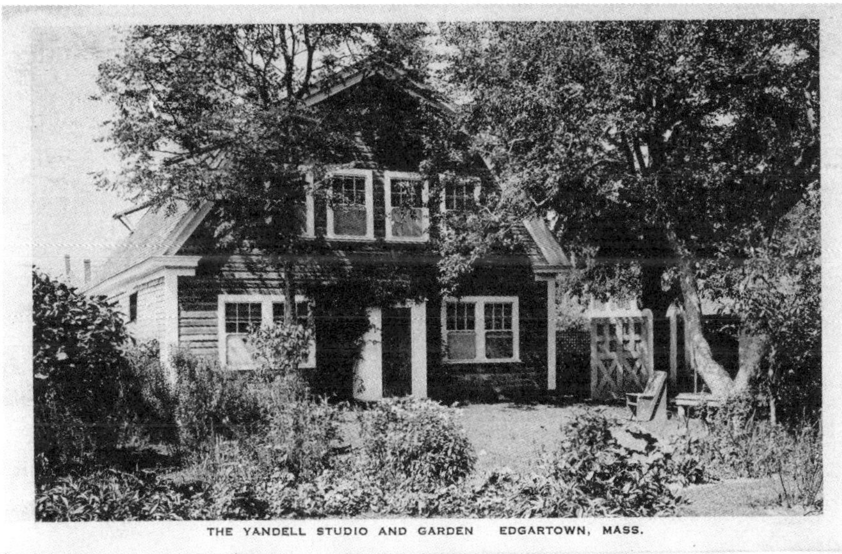

Enid worked in the winter in New York and in the summer at Edgartown. While on Martha's Vineyard, she resided in this building, shown in this undated postcard of "The Yandell Studio and Garden," which was the site of the old Thaxter Academy. The silhouette of the studio informed Enid's design for her art school, the Branstock. (Courtesy Martha's Vineyard Museum.)

ests in sport and the outdoors, with the hills of Boone County replaced by the coves nestling the beaches and marshes of Martha's Vineyard. Clearly, Edgartown was more than just a *summer* home on Martha's Vineyard for Enid; it was *home*.[2]

Enid spent her winters at her studio in New York and summers at her Edgartown studio. She also continued to visit Paris. Being in the larger cities enabled her to visit foundries, meet with other artists, and build her portfolio for potential commissions. While in Edgartown, Enid exhibited her work often, opened her studio to the community, and for some time operated a tearoom, where guests could take in nourishment for the mind as well as the body. She built a portfolio of works for sale. She also spent a good deal of time devoted to important causes, such as women's rights and relief work. During this period, Enid continued to be mentioned in the periodical press in Kentucky, and particularly in her hometown of Louisville.[3]

On Martha's Vineyard, Enid's social and artistic worlds became intertwined. Because her life and her art were tightly interwoven, the work she created over these years in one location informed her practice at the other. Therefore, although this chapter focuses on Edgartown, it also considers, briefly, a work that Enid created in New York and one she developed while in Paris during the early part of her Edgartown years, as well as a series of works that she chiefly designed in Edgartown. The chapter concludes with recollections about Enid by her Edgartown friends.[4]

The Branstock

By her mid-thirties, established as a sculptor, notably by her successful commission for the Carrie Brown Memorial Fountain, Enid had grown adept at managing her business, negotiating contracts, and working with foundries and suppliers as well as collaborators. Her years in Edgartown brought on a new opportunity: to acquire business acumen as an operator of a school, a landlord, a real estate investor, and a community resident. In the course of her stay on Martha's Vineyard, Enid purchased and managed three Edgartown properties: one that functioned as an art school; a tea garden; and a residence on Davis Lane (then called simply "the Lane") and School Street. As a result of her taking ownership of these properties and expanding her output beyond sculptural practice to include connections with visual arts more broadly, Enid developed skills in operations and management by taking tenants, organizing a summer school, and shuttling between Massachusetts and New York. She developed a keen business sense. Reviewing extant contracts and documents in conjunction with business directories from these years provides insight into Enid's aspirations and accomplishments in Edgartown, her newest frontier.[5]

In 1907, Enid purchased property in Edgartown with the hope of transitioning to a life on the island, a place that was entirely new to her, perhaps as a respite from city life in New York. With her mother's death the following year, Enid's hope of summering on the island came into sharper focus. The purchase of a building known as Thaxter Academy on Davis Lane afforded Enid the opportunity to open a modern-day academy of sorts. Her choice of this property for this purpose seemed intentional, as the building was known as the former home of a fine academy. In taking ownership of this 1825 structure, Enid may have intended it to be

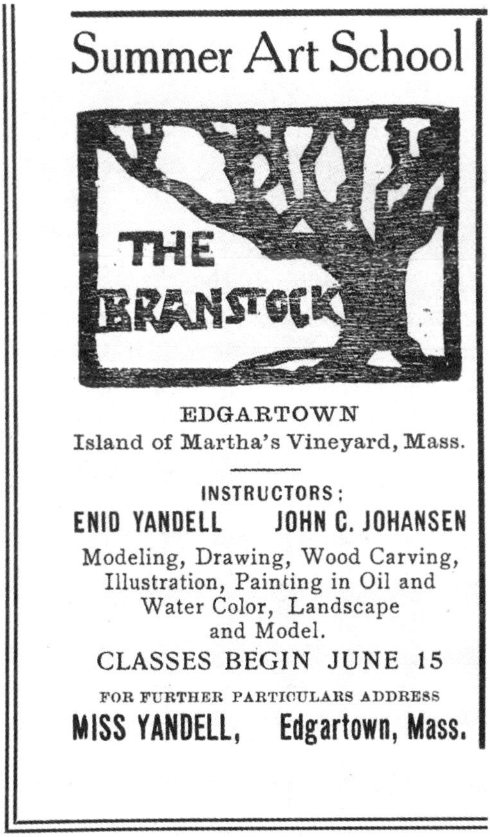

Advertisement for the Branstock. Enid established the Branstock in 1908 as an art school and, with John C. Johansen (1876–1964), ran a program of courses for several years. (Courtesy Martha's Vineyard Museum.)

used for art instruction. In any case, in 1908, at the former Thaxter Academy, Enid established The Branstock Studio as an art school and, with John C. Johansen (1876–1964), ran a program of courses for several years.[6]

The rationale for the name Branstock is not explained in any extant documentation. However, throughout her life Enid showed an interest in theatre and, to a lesser extent, opera throughout her entire life—whether at Louisville's Macauley's Theatre, performances of her sister or her friend Geysa, memorabilia and clippings related to these art forms, and the various forms of street theatre she had encountered to date. One particular intersection with opera may have occurred in 1889, when she traveled to Europe. A letter to Enid from her mother announces the plan to travel to Beyreuth to hear "three of Wagner's operas about the 25th of July." While it is uncertain if Enid attended these performances, the intent to attend indicates interest and suggests that the name "Branstock" may have come from German composer Richard Wagner's *The Ring of the Nibelung,* or the Ring Cycle. In Wagner's musical drama, Branstock was a sacred tree that had healing and magical powers. Perhaps Enid was channeling that capacity for her arts colony, which was, incidentally, established under the bough of a large tree.[7]

The academy's location in Edgartown, and Martha's Vineyard generally, situated the school in an ideal location for teaching students of all ages and for showcasing art through the exhibition of small paintings, works on paper, and sculpture. Beyond this broad aim, the primary focus of Branstock was to offer summer classes to aspiring artists, akin to the summer schools that were becoming popular among American modernists. The early twentieth century was a golden age of artist colonies, a phenomenon built out of European academic tradition and transplanted to the often-inspiring beauty of nature as one source of inspiration amid creatively fertile communities of artists.[8]

Similar establishments included the Martha's Vineyard School of Art, established at Vineyard Haven in 1904. A community of artists was also forged at Chilmark, on the west end of the Vineyard, spurred by Thomas Hart Benton (1889–1975), a regionalist painter and Jackson Pollock's art teacher, who first visited in 1920. At Cape Cod, on the mainland, the Provincetown Art Association was organized in 1914 for juried exhibitions and was established as an artist enclave by 1916, serving as a refuge for artists and expatriates after World War I.[9]

Perhaps the closest example to what Enid aspired was Augustus Saint-Gaudens' retreat in Cornish, New Hampshire. The Cornish Art Colony was first established by Saint-Gaudens in 1885. It emerged from his interest in cultivating a retreat away from the studios of New York and by extending the network of students from the Art Students League (where he was an instructor). In Cornish he created a circle of professionals from all fields, beyond visual art. Colonists included painters, sculptors, and decorative artists as well as architects, novelists, musicians, composers, and playwrights. With Saint-Gaudens' death in 1907, the colony began to lose steam until World War I, after which there was minimal community activity.[10]

As Saint-Gaudens' colony began to falter around 1907, seasonal offerings to foster fellowship alongside teaching and exhibition were taking hold on Martha's Vineyard and Cape Cod. In some ways, Enid was the inheritor of Saint-Gaudens' legacy; the Branstock served as her reinvention of his concept. Beyond simplistic connections between the two artists (both were sculptors, were educated in Paris, and exhibited at World's Fairs), each had repertoires of significant public works by the time they forged arts communities. However, Saint-Gaudens' résumé was much more impressive than Enid's at this point due to his stature as *the* American sculptor. When he moved to Cornish, he had just been awarded the commission for the Civil War memorial to Robert Gould Shaw and the Massachusetts 54th Regiment.[11] Similarly, by 1908, when the Branstock was established, Enid had just completed her a major work of her own, the installation to John W. Thomas (Nashville, 1907). One difference between the two artists, however, was their ability to attract an audience for their colony. Saint-Gaudens had a legacy of instruction at the Art Students League on which to depend for attendance. A number of his students eventually purchased property in the region of Cornish, thus extending the colony. Enid had not taught professionally and therefore did not have a circle of artists ready to travel by train from New York (or otherwise) to Massachusetts and then to ferry out from the mainland every season. However, she was intent on settling in Edgartown and cultivating arts instruction there, in her new home.

To attract students, Enid capitalized on distinguishing her school from other artist communities nearby. Like her competition, Enid advertised the school, the application process, and its offerings. Because courses began in June, Enid had inquires sent to her studio in New York, affording her the time to review the applications and establish the curriculum for that year. However, there may have also been a bit of professional strategy involved in advertising her home base as New York: the city was, after all, the capital of the art world and, after the Armory Show in 1913, the center of the modern art movement.

One major point of distinction between Enid's endeavor and any of its predecessors or competitors is the fact that this was a serious art school with a woman at the helm. In other words, Enid served as the contact person for Branstock, whereas with many (if not all) of the other schools, a man was listed as the director or superintendent. In other cases where a woman was listed as the head of a school of art, the focus was on the dilettante arts of Enid's mother's generation—sketching, pottery, design, porcelain—not serious art, such as sculpture.

Curriculum

An ad in *Craftsman* magazine drew attention to Branstock's "fourth season," announcing that the school would offer courses in modeling, portraits, drawing, wood carving, painting in oil, and watercolor. Besides the courses offered, the instructors were listed, making note of Enid as the head of sculpture and John C. Johnansen as the head of painting. Another instructor, Albert Sterner (1863–1946), taught painting and drawing. The three artists were contemporaries and had developed following similar paths, navigating the academy system in Cincinnati (Johansen and Yandell) and advanced training in Paris (all three) while also contributing to expositions and exhibitions over their careers. Such training and professional practice were fashioned for the students in their tutelage.

Another advertisement, which appeared in 1911, highlighted Branstock's location and how that informed the school's practice: "The school has an unusual place in the quaint old whaling town, yet unspoiled by visitors and offering every advantage for the student seeking the picturesque. Studio facilities are the best, so that no time is lost to the student in inclement weather. The studio itself is 30- by 50 feet, by 25 feet high, with movable partitions to accommodate various classes working indoors."[12]

In fact, Martha's Vineyard's twenty-mile stretch of land made it the largest island off the New England coast, known as the "Gem of the Atlantic." The air quality—an important need for sculptors, like Enid, who inhaled their share of clay dust over the years—was valued for its purity and was accompanied by abundant fresh water. Beyond these attributes, Edgartown offered historical relevance accompanied by picturesque views, all of which provided a healthful climate that Enid called "life-giving and nerve-soothing." An environment that was nature-focused and place-based differed vastly from Enid's earlier experiences in Miss Bartlett's classes in the studio above the gymnasium at Hampton College and Louis Rebisso and Benn Pitman's studios in the historic arcade of the Art Academy in Cincinnati.[13]

In terms of curriculum, Branstock mirrored Enid's own background in modeling, portraits, and wood carving with courses in painting and landscape. In addition, courses aligned with decorative arts were added, and faculty artists taught these areas of expertise. As the *New York Times* noted in 1909: "It is the intention of the Branstock School management to develop an arts and crafts movement in the school, and this year the ceramic department is in [the] charge of Mrs. Anna B. Leonard, Vice President of the New York Keramic Society. Miss Canfield is in charge of the brass and leather work." In creating a comprehensive program, Enid selected the finest faculty with the hopes of providing high-quality educational instruction under the bough of the large oak tree.[14]

A portfolio of materials located among Enid's studio belongings upon her death and now in the Filson Historical Society, apparently either used in instruction or created by students, provides an understanding of the classroom experience. Sample compositions and printed, preexisting imagery serve as reference material that may have been used in teaching or studio prep. These include photographs, examples of ornament, poetry, drawings, pages from *Country Life,* and individual sheets pulled from magazines, such as the December 1921 issue of *Keramic Studio,* a publication focused on pottery, decoration, and ornament. It is unclear how Enid and her staff used these materials, but their dates suggest that they were intentionally building a library of resources for use by instructors at Branstock.[15]

A portfolio of drawings and notes in Enid's handwriting provides some insight into Enid's working method with her students. They emphasize drawing as a foundational skill. For instance, paintings and watercolors that have applied instructions ("paste down like this & let the cut reverse") may have been used as a pattern for executions in woodcutting or wood carving. Some drawings are clearly documentary in terms of practice, including a drawing of a crab that has been traced over many times, perhaps as practice of replicating a form.[16]

In addition, color studies appear to be teaching tools, as do drawings with annotations. One such sketch includes a citation off to the right "Modern Impressionist Dodge McKnight" [*sic*], which may have indicated that MacKnight created the sketch for teaching purposes. A drawing of a black-and-white vase as well as a green ball includes the notation "when black fails . . ." Multiple drawings of the same subject (two on board from the same vantage point using reds and blues and one on paper using green and yellows) have marks at the edges of the paper to indicate their placement on a wall for critique or for instruction, indicating that they may have been hung on a wall, either as inspiration or for education.[17]

Perhaps most interesting from a processual standpoint is the list headed "Different possible ways of expression in drawing & painting," which includes a number of modes, as if lessons, for instruction. This list appears to serve as a syllabus for a series of courses and perhaps informed the instruction in drawing and painting at Branstock. In addition, a series of sketches of trees from March 16, 20, and 26 (although without a year), appear to be timed drawings from three to three-and-a-half hours. Such sketches and documentation indicated how drawing was emphasized as part of the curriculum at Branstock, as it had been when Enid was a student thirty years earlier in Louisville and Cincinnati.[18]

It is difficult to say how successful the Branstock was. It opened in 1908 as a school of sculpture and then, in 1909, added the other media, as well as a space for refreshment. An examination of one such exhibition gives insight into the purpose of the settlement and its place in the community. On July 22, 1909, an advertisement in the *Vineyard Gazette* announced the forthcoming exhibition on the weekend of July 24 and described its focus: Enid's work alongside that of two fellow instructors. Days later, in its review of the exhibition on July 29, the *Vineyard Gazette* situated the location and noted that the school was developing into an "artist colony," where forty to fifty persons were enrolled. The article went on to describe the "colony of artists who have become associated with her in art instruction." Clearly, even in the very early days of the school's existence, it had made a mark and had become associated with Enid alone. The notice went on to praise Enid for her efforts: "This successful exhibition affords us the opportunity to voice the appreciation of the town and its summer visitors of the work of Miss Yandell and her associates and our pleasure in having these genial artists numbered among our summer guests, bringing in their train[ed?] pupils of ambition and culture. They are all most cordially welcome." The review also reported on the attraction of "the entire community" to the art exhibition at Enid's "spacious residence and studio." Such an assertion was affirmed with attendance over 350, thereby demonstrating the interest of Edgartown in what Enid had devised at Branstock.[19]

Related Endeavors

In 1909, the year following the opening of Branstock, Enid opened a small space for exhibition and outdoor refreshment called the "Arts & Crafts Cottage in the Lane" and "The Tea Garden." The cottage, across from the Thaxter Academy building, offered displays of fine arts and crafts, while the garden was reserved for daily tea from three to six o'clock, with the exception of Sundays. The cottage also offered catered lunches for summer tourists to take "tramping" on rough island hikes or offshore. Clearly, this venture (for which Enid was proprietor) combined elements of food and art in order to bring art into the everyday tourist experience, much like the outdoor exhibitions and displays that had democratized art and spectacle through the world's fairs and expositions of Enid's younger days.[20]

A notice appeared in the *Vineyard Gazette* announcing the opening of the tearoom, which was said to fill a "long felt want in our summer life." The article remarked on the uniqueness of this venture, a venue for refreshments to sustain the body and the mind, for which credit was given to Enid alone: "The cottage is the latest acquisition to the Art Colony in the lane [on Davis Lane], being opposite the Branstock Art School, and indeed, quite under Miss Yandell's glorious, big tree, so that one might really feel the protection of the *pioneer* enterprise, as well as the superb protection of its giant arms." Clearly, Enid had found her niche through pioneering efforts such as the Tea Garden in Edgartown.[21]

Art from the Edgartown Years

In the years leading up to her transition to Edgartown, Enid's professional status grew and her body of work expanded. She continued to create a number of works for private and public audiences, including Hogan's Fountain (1905, Louisville), a life-sized, bronze replica of Enid's 1893 Daniel Boone funded by C. C. Bickel (1906, Louisville), and a monument to John W. Thomas (1907, Nashville). She also continued to create works in many media and for many purposes. She also continued to seek larger commissions, which resulted in her *Chief Ninigret* (1912) and the Pioneer Monument (1924). Enid, however, rejected offers to contribute to more significant undertakings, such as Stone Mountain, because such work would have removed her from her own practice and would require her reporting to another sculptor, something she had not done for many years.[22]

During the time that Enid summered at Martha's Vineyard, she also maintained studios in New York and, on occasion, Paris. In addressing the art that she created over these years, it is unclear what portions of the work were done in any one location, unless documentation from Enid, or more likely the patron, gives some indication. For instance, in 1920, when Enid created a bas-relief of Julia Dinsmore, her longtime friend from Kentucky, she designed the work in Julia's hotel room, not her own studio in New York. Even with such a straightforward format as a profile bas-relief, which Enid had already intended to be a tabletop or hanging portrait, the subject matter was unique. Therefore, over a period of a few weeks that spring, Enid carried out the drawing from life, plaster cast, and eventual bronze reproduction in New York.[23]

Documentation about Enid's transatlantic travel over her Edgartown years comes primarily from newspaper accounts. Based upon these, we can piece together factual bits of information to understand how Enid moved between her locational bases. For instance, between 1912 and 1914, Enid conceptualized her Chief Ninigret, a figurative work that doubles as a fountain in the tourist cove of Watch Hill, Rhode Island. Enid designed this work while she was in Paris, based upon her studies of a person from Buffalo Bill's Wild West Show who joined Enid in her studio in Paris so that she could draft a design from life, rather than her having to rely on a photograph or sketch. From this study, Enid created a plaster model, which was brought back to the United States and exhibited at the Armory Show in 1913. The full-size sculpture was cast in 1914 in Paris and dedicated in Watch Hill that same year. It is unclear what role, if any, Edgartown played in this sculpture's creation; however, it was one of the works that Enid created during her earliest years in Edgartown.

Working with a home base of Edgartown, Enid built upon an earlier methodology of creating one form that could be reproduced by a manufacturer and sold to customers directly. Enid was somewhat familiar with this method from the distribution of the *Kiss Tankard,* which was available for order in 1899 and could be purchased in bronze or silver. After moving to Edgartown, Enid further developed this practice of selling a work that she designed and reproduced: she offered sales and distribution of ready-made works that stemmed from uniquely commissioned pieces.

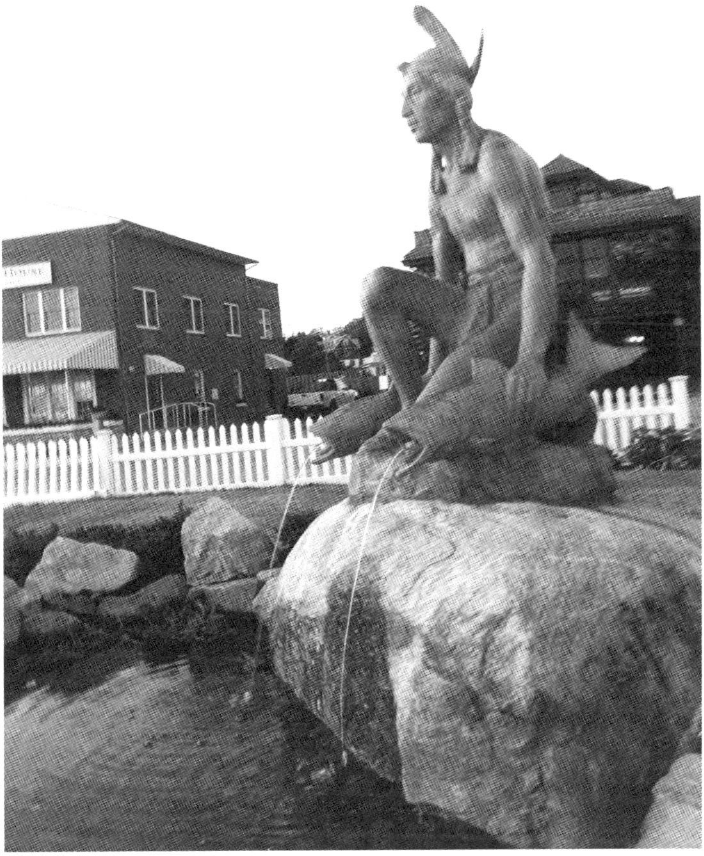

Enid's *Chief Ninigret*, bronze, 1914, Watch Hill, Rhode Island. Enid designed this work while she was in Paris, based upon her studies of a figure from Buffalo Bill's Wild West Show, who joined Enid in her studio so that she could draft a design from life, rather than from a photograph or sketch. Photograph taken in 2017 by Ardi Schneider. (Courtesy of Ardi Schneider.)

In other words, she took an idea for a piece, produced it to order, and then mass-produced it. In addition, she also began to develop themes for her decorative works, such as nature and the senses, as subjects appropriate for fountains and sundials. By developing a practice that allowed for variation on themes that she had already created, Enid could meet the needs of an already existing market and could communicate with her customers directly. Whereas before, purchasers would have perhaps appealed to Tiffany to purchase a silver *Kiss Tankard,* buyers came directly to Enid during her Edgartown years. She catalyzed her self-promotion skills and business acumen and ultimately exploited the perspective that came with fifteen years of experience in the field of sculpture, from her first employment at Chicago in 1891 until her move to Edgartown in 1908.[24]

One work of this sort, *Five Senses,* made its debut at the Armory Show in 1913 and was developed as part of the series "Enid Yandell Bronzes for Gardens, Edgartown, Mass." This "Bronzes for Gardens" series included six works, ranging from the aesthetic in single or double-figure compositions to the functional, with sundials and fountains: *Boy Blowing Shell; Narcissus; Sundial, Four Seasons; The Five Senses; Faun Emptying Shell;* and *The Water and the Flowers.* The works were photographed and featured in a price list that Enid distributed. Given its format on green paper that folded in half and was placed in an envelope, there probably were myriad distribution methods for this price list, including mail, delivery at someone's door, or as a handout, perhaps at the Tea Garden. At the bottom of the price list, a note indicated Enid's desire to meet the needs and interests of customers: "If none of these is exactly what you wish for your garden, let me design one for you specially."[25]

Enid's apparent shift in sculptural form to garden works was not really so much of a shift at all. The existence of sculptural forms amid verdant spaces harkened back to Enid's exposure to statuary among manicured spaces, even at such early locations as the garden displays at the Southern Exposition. Gardens also became more of a priority as men came to dominate the field of architecture while women moved increasingly into the field of garden design. Bearing witness to the nineteenth-century cult of domesticity that positioned women as tastemakers and guardians of the home, female landscape designers took cues from the Arts and Crafts moment, which elevated carving, embroidery, and other art forms—such as those Enid would have taken up through courses with Louis Rebisso and Benn Pitman at the Art Academy of Cincinnati—even as their migration to the out-of-doors threatened the status quo of the woman in the home and the man out-of-doors. Enid turned to nature just as Beatrix Farrand (the first female landscape architect in the United States, though she preferred to call herself a "landscape gardener") took to the field pioneered by Frederick Law Olmsted. As journalist Mary Bronson Hartt observed this small group of emerging professionals invading the closed world of architecture in 1908, she referred to them as "a gallant little group of women" who "have forged for themselves National reputations. It is a very little group, it is true, scarce half a dozen all told," and yet they could hold their own with the men. They were, as historian Judith B. Tankard has observed, "pioneer women."[26]

Like these other pioneering women, Enid created a niche for herself in the field of large-scale sculpture, and she was expanding that reach to include garden statuary. Like her women landscape designer counterparts, Enid demonstrated aesthetic abilities and strong artistic abilities as well as business acumen and skills of collaboration necessitated by large-scale projects, such as her fair work and her memorial to Carrie Brown in Providence. Her focus oscillated between large-scale fabrications for public settings, which required collaboration with architects and engineers, and smaller, though equally site-dependent, garden statuary, where attention to detail was required amid the borders, blooms, and bricks. (In fact, Guy Lowell, an advocate for women in the field of landscape architecture, commended women for an attention to detail that outshone men's abilities, particularly insofar as domestic landscape architecture was concerned.) In 1914, Enid's memorial to Clement Griscom at Watch Hill in Westerly, Rhode Island, reflected this marriage of site, nature, and sculpture. Her bronze fountain depicting Chief Ninigret holding a fish in either hand as he crouched on top of a granite boulder served as the focal point of a garden designed by rising landscape architect Marion Coffin, who later designed Winterthur. Enid relayed such attention to nature as site to her student, Betty Hazard, who later created a decorative bronze for Ambassador Frederic Sackett's estate, Edgecombe, in Louisville. Hazard's sculpture *Boy with a Snail* was sited alongside an Olmsted-designed reflecting pool.[27]

Nature served as a site for Enid's creations, although she rarely employed nature as a subject. Two exceptions include a carved mahogany panel and an embroidered linen. Though both works are undated, their medium and subject harken back to Enid's days at the Art Academy of Cincinnati, where she studied wood carving and where she would have

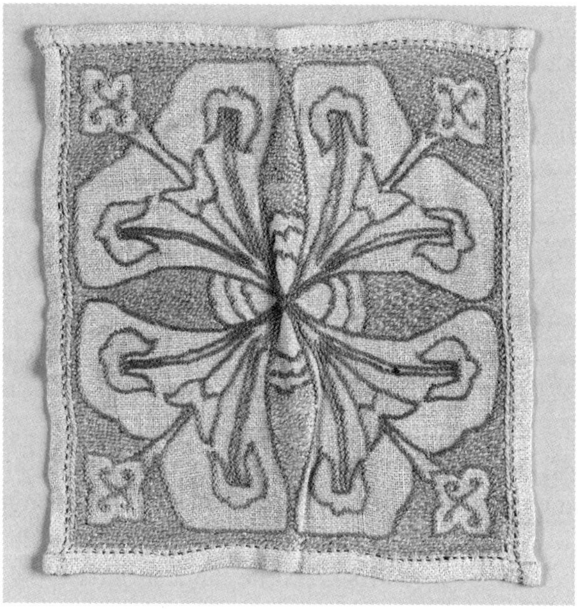

This embroidered linen was one of three in Enid's possession at the time of her death. This one is believed to have been created by her. Such works speak to Enid's training in decorative arts much earlier in her career. Enid Yandell, textile, linen, 22.7 x 20.6 cm (8 15/16 x 8 1/8 inches) square. (Gift of Mrs. John J. Trask. 83.215.1. RISD Museum, Providence, RI.)

been exposed to textile work. The panel features a single stem of milk thistle with nine leaves and five berries. The pattern repeats, with an identical specimen beside the first, suggesting the repeated practice required of an academy student or its eventual service as a wooden border, such as on a headboard or footboard. The forms are carved in variable reliefs so as to give depth, with the stems resting upon a matrix of dots, which serves as the background. The equally small linen is adorned with moss-green thread, couch-stitched to fill in the background, while brown thread in a spiral stem stitch defines the silhouette of a pressed iris.[28]

Even without an abundance of subjects taken from nature, Enid did adopt the growing trend in Paris toward the naturalistic, sinewy, vinelike forms of Art Nouveau that she had encountered during her time in Paris.

Her evocation of naturalistic form began with *Kiss Tankard* around 1897 and continued over the following decade, even as she continued to design figurative sculpture and busts. These nature-derived shapes and forms adapted well to garden statuary and related formats. Such subjects were becoming popular. In the essay "A Word or Two on Sculpture," Charles de Kay, managing director of the National Arts Club, noted that even as sculpture "is the masculine art and painting the feminine," demand was rising for other kinds of sculpture that extended beyond portraiture. He claimed that "as to sculpture for the house and home, it is growing again, and from a much sounder stock than ever before, trusting less to foreign examples and more to the demands for decoration in our daily lives." Enid's commissioned pieces and sales from about 1910 revolved around such small-scale works. For instance, she carved figureheads and trail boards for sailboats that represented the Edgartown Yacht Club in area competition. One body of work, duplicated in series, that she developed a bit later was inspired by a work of children's literature, *The Wind in the Willows*. Even as Enid operated in this market economy, she was negotiating the world of fine art galleries through her participation in exhibitions near and far.[29]

Birthday Beasts

The *Birthday Beasts* series was Enid's interpretation of the anthropomorphic characters from Kenneth Grahame's children's book *The Wind in the Willows* (1908). The series dates from about 1921, and it appears that Enid continued reproducing the figures until at least 1924. There are at least eight figures in the set, with an additional version of a toad and several rose candle holders. Each figure related to one of the primary characters in the book (Mole, Rat or Ratty, Badger, Mr. Toad) or the supporting cast of Otter, Rabbit, Owl, and "an errant May-fly." The entire set is depicted in an undated photograph of the beasts on a dressed table, with a cake and candles, simulating the impending celebration.[30]

The production of *Birthday Beasts* is tied to Enid's years in Edgartown (1907 and later) and her association with politician William M. Butler (1861–1937), through whom Enid secured permission to use the characters from Grahame's book as source material. In a letter of February 1921

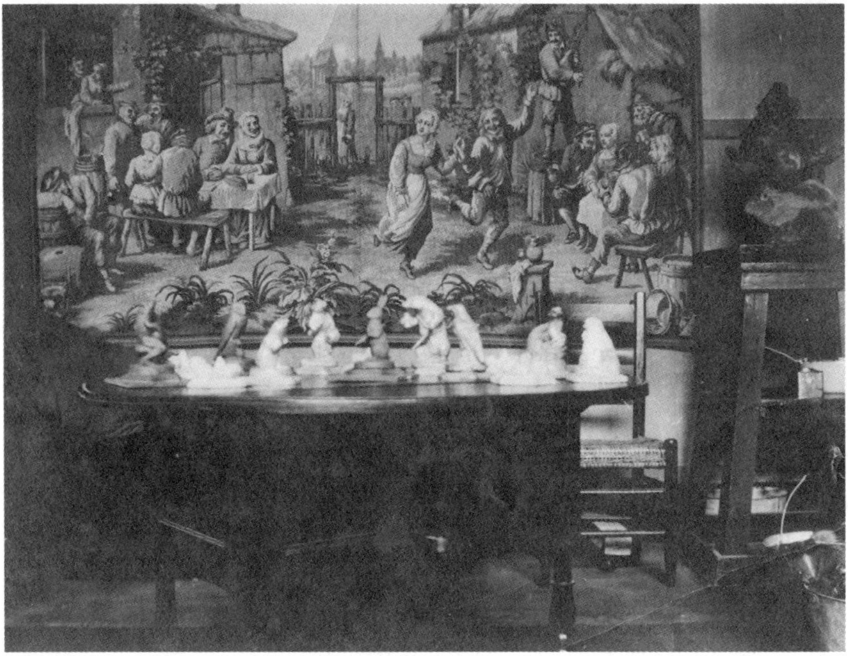

Table in Enid's studio with an assortment of Enid's *Birthday Beasts*. In the background is a version of David Teniers's *Peasant Wedding*, which appears in whole or in part in a handful of photographs of Enid's studio. At the far right, Gutzon Borglum's *Centaur and Centauress* is visible on a square table. (Enid Bland Yandell Photograph Collection, 987PC52X.134, Box 2, Folder 40. The Filson Historical Society, Louisville, KY.)

from Italy to Butler, the author wrote in response to Butler's query "on the subject of Miss Yandell's little animals, which she is very welcome, so far as I am concerned, to name after the book," adding that "a photograph of the group, which you are so kind as to suggest sending, would indeed give me much pleasure."[31]

Enid called these items "Branstock Birthday Beasts" and named "E. Yandell" as the creator with the date of 1921. A paper label with this name, along with the word "copyrighted" and "Edgartown, Mass." indicated the authority of the miniatures. Drawing inspiration from a work of children's literature, the *Birthday Beasts* were intimately tied to Enid's identity as a sculptor, business owner, and Islander and served as miniature works of art as Enid sought to engage new audiences for her work.

Exhibits outside of Edgartown

While migrating between her artistic centers of Edgartown and New York (with occasional stays in Paris), Enid submitted her work to exhibitions far and wide. One of these exhibitions proved to be a landmark: the International Exhibition of Modern Art organized by the Association of American Painters and Sculptors, which opened in New York City's 69th Regiment Armory, colloquially referred to as the "Armory Show." This was the first large show of modern art in America and an early example of a multicity tour. It began at the New York City armory, where it was on view from February 17 to March 15, 1913, before moving on to the Art Institute of Chicago and the Copley Society of Art in Boston, where it received a frenzied reaction.[32]

This exhibit has been recognized as a watershed in the history of American art, introducing astonished New Yorkers to modern art. Some would argue that "modern" art did not exist in America before the Armory Show; indeed, the show served as a catalyst for American artists, who became more independent and created their own "artistic language," as apart, though springing, from their European roots. The exhibition contained approximately 1,300 works by 300 artists. Many of the original works have been lost, and some of the artists have been forgotten, Enid among them. Her works on view included one of unknown medium (probably plaster or staff) entitled *Indian and Fisher,* which was exhibited in Gallery A, American Sculpture and Decorative Art. Moving from documentation to allegory, Enid's other contribution, a bronze vase sculpture entitled *The Five Senses,* bore witness to classical subject through its representation of the five senses, with allegorical figures holding a ball, flowers, a conch shell, a mirror, and grapes (for touch, smell, hearing, sight, and taste). Word of the show was shared widely, including notice in the *Chicago Evening Post* and *Outlook,* where Theodore Roosevelt wrote both in favor of and against the works from the perspective of a "layman." No individual mention was made of Enid's work in any of these publications; however, simply being associated with the Armory Show was a mark of distinction.[33]

During these years of high-profile exhibitions, Enid continued to exhibit regionally as well. Very much in contrast to the context of the Armory Show, Enid participated in the Indiana Circuit Exhibition (1910), which was marketed as a pioneering exhibition for its intent to bring art to the people. It was announced that the aim of the exhibit was for the general public to use art as a means to an end. Using art as a guide, it was possible "to learn from the great artist and catch his inspiration"—tasks that are "difficult anywhere in America when the subject is painting and sculpture, and especially difficult in a State remote from art collections." Note the gendered representation of the artist as male, even as a number of women contributed to the exhibition, including Enid. She contributed at least one work, although it is unclear which of her works was on view. A discussion and analysis of the exhibition situated the state of art among the American public, noting that the public might know historical figures but was unaware of American artists. The article "Art and the Nation," appearing in the journal *Art and Progress* (1911), called for American works to be brought to children in schools, with sculpture as well as paintings: "All over the country, within the past few years, organizations whose chief, if not sole, object is to decorate the public schools, have come into existence. These societies would gladly make use of American works if they could be obtained, but as yet no one with the power to supply the demand has apparently realized this opportunity." Such were the competing aims facing sculptors—art for the public or art for the museum. Enid worked in both arenas.[34]

Edgartown after Enid

Enid's life and work were inseparable. Obituaries reflecting on her life always invoked her career. In fact, the tagline for the notice of her death in the *Vineyard Gazette* simply stated "Career Ends." Enid was sixty-four when she died in 1934 and had been hospitalized for several months prior. According to a lengthy article in her hometown paper on Martha's Vineyard, her "death was apparently due to a heart attack following a nervous breakdown." Put simply, Enid died of exhaustion.[35]

While much of this volume takes a multifaceted approach to build out a narrative of Enid's life and art through the examination of primary accounts in newspapers, exhibition work, documents, and photographs, Enid's impact on Edgartown, and its impact on her, are best served through memory. Some residents knew of Enid due to the proximity of Branstock to their own houses: the school and her studio were in a residential area. Youngsters such as Alexia Brown took art lessons from Enid. She recalled later that Enid was known to have "a world of patience with children/students." Three of Enid's students over the span of the Edgartown years (1908–1934) became sculptors and thus trace their lineage to Enid. Betty Hazard, Mary Tarleton Knollenberg, and Helen Sahler can both connect us to Enid's profession and offer recollections of her.[36]

Elizabeth "Betty" Hazard (1908–1994) studied at the Rhode Island School of Design before studying with Enid for two years in Boston, where Enid also spent some time later in life (probably after 1930). Like her teacher, Betty went to Paris, where she worked and opened her own studio, in the company of Enid. Like her teacher, Betty favored family and Louisville in her early work. In 1930, Betty created a small statue for Edgecombe, the country estate of her uncle, Frederic Moseley Sackett Jr., and his wife, Olive Speed Sackett. The three-foot-tall, bronze garden work *Boy with a Snail* was sited for the formal garden to the south of the English Arts and Crafts–style estate designed by John Bacon Hutchings. Amid the manicured spaces designed by the Olmsted Brothers firm, the leaning torso of the nymph boy contemplating a small snail as he gazes at the pool of water beneath him found a home among the boxwoods, wildflowers, walkways, and turf of the walled enclosure.[37]

Such garden statuary was fashionable and was a popular way for artists to build a repertoire. Betty's *Boy with a Snail* calls to mind Enid's garden statuary of her Edgartown years in form and function. Connections between Betty and Enid were drawn by the *Louisville Courier-Journal* in its announcement of the arrival of Betty's sculpture in the city with the headline "Miss Yandell's Pupil Sends Statue Here." The newspaper noted Enid's fame, some thirty years after leaving her home city and her status as "a famous woman sculptor" who, in her childhood, "patted out her first mudpies." Her artistic ambition was realized, through her student's work, as another form of a legacy in Enid's hometown, where "a statue in bronze, modeled by the sculptor's student," had been commissioned. In return, part of Enid's legacy is owed to Betty, who provided recollections about Enid and artifacts for loan in preparation for the exhibit that focused on Enid and the Branstock School held at RISD Museum in 1982. Moreover, the location of Betty's first Louisville commission, on the outskirts of Cherokee Park, was near the location of two of Enid's works—her Daniel Boone of exposition fame and Hogan's Fountain (1905). Known also as *Pan,* this fanciful work was commissioned by William H. Hogan as a public fountain for dogs and horses in the park, and its siting amid the Olmsted-designed undulations occurred prior to the arrival of Enid's Boone there in 1906.[38]

Unlike the association between Enid and Betty Hazard, the connection between Mary Tarleton Knollenberg (1904–1992) and Enid is less clear, as biographical narratives and archival materials related to Knollenberg's life do not reference this connection, nor does her obituary, thereby making the tie between the two difficult to ascertain. Their paths may have crossed in one or more of the following ways. First, Mary studied in New York in the sculpture circles of which Enid was a part. These include artist circles as well as business networks. Second, Mary's studies took her from New York to Paris in 1933 as a result of a Guggenheim Fellowship. Enid was in Paris at that time. Given the cadre of expatriates and sculptors as well as their frequenting local museums, it seems likely that the two women would have met and/or associated with one another in Paris. Third, secondary sources point to a connection between Mary and Enid.[39]

A third student of Enid's, Helen G. Sahler (1877–1950), took the education she gained from Enid in Edgartown, Boston, or New York and built a career for herself through similar channels as Enid had—the world's fairs. Sahler exhibited *Head of a Boy* in the Panama-Pacific Exposition in 1915, a fair that Enid missed on account of her war work. Attention was drawn to Sahler's lineage as an artist through Enid in articles mentioning that she had undertaken study at the Art Students League of New York and with Enid Yandell.[40]

The importance of these connections is that Enid's students had direct access to Enid through both their art and hers. In addition, their stories helped to provide context for the first museum exhibition devoted to Enid, which was held at the RISD Museum in Providence, Rhode Island, in 1982. Recollections by these three women helped paint a picture of Enid. According to scholar Nancy Baird, who interviewed Betty Hazard and Mary Knollenberg, they remembered Enid in great detail. Baird noted, "they remembered that she was muscular and stout, and usually wore mauve smocks over her somber clothes; her voice was deep and soft." They also recounted specific behaviors related to sculpture and others that were not: "I only remember that her hands always held bits of clay that she continually kneaded and molded"; "She was the first woman I knew who smoked." Such recollections convey a bit more about who Enid was. They capture bits and pieces not mentioned in newspaper clippings, and they bring Enid's personality traits and behaviors to the fore for us today. Yet these characteristics surely would have been witnessed by those who came into contact with her on the Lane for the twenty-six years she called Edgartown home.[41]

Citizenship, Edgartown School

Another form of recollection comes through the viewing of Enid's work as part of everyday experience. Here again, the context is students; however, in this instance the pupils were from the Edgartown School, just a few blocks from Enid's home. The "Old School" was built in 1925 as a single unit structure to accommodate grades one through twelve. In 2003, an entirely new two-story building was completed, putting the "Old School" to rest. A decade later, in 2013, the "Old School" was torn down. Before its demolition, however, a fixture of the school—a plaster relief created by Enid in 1906—was rescued.

The plaster, *Citizenship,* was one of the preparatory works that Enid had created for the monument to John W. Thomas in Nashville. It was one of three such panels that adorned the pedestal of the monument, beneath the monumental sculpture of Major Thomas. The rectangular plaster framed in wood shows a classical female figure wearing a crown and textured peplos, a tunic-like garment worn over the top of a gown. She kneels beside fasces, offering a torch to the visitor. The imagery connects visitors to a classical past—even if the exact subject of citizenship may be less clear. Such an image seemed relevant in a school where civics or Latin lessons were part of the everyday experience of the students.[42]

It is unclear when the relief came to reside in the school, but for at least one generation (from the 1950s through the 1990s), it was a mainstay. It hung in the interior, near the staircase, which made it an eye-catching attraction for all passersby. According to one of these children, who remembered the artwork from her years as a student from 1959 to 1967, it was the only work of fine art in the entire school. It was not referred to by any particular name. It was simply the work of art that "everyone knew."[43]

When the Old School was torn down, the relief was in very poor

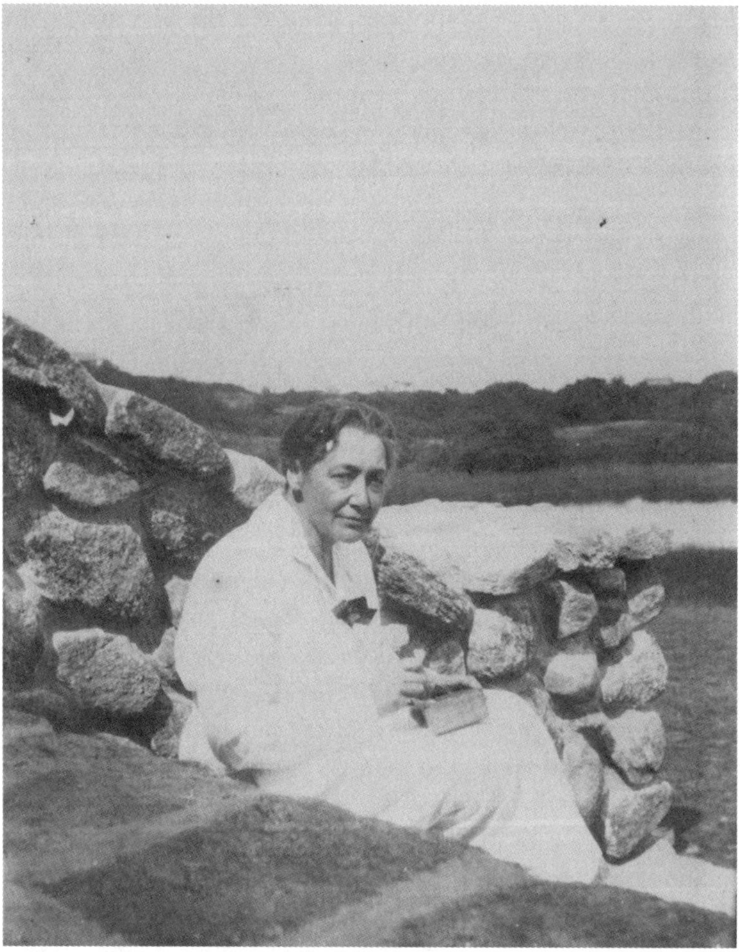

Enid at Mohu, the estate of William Butler, ca. 1928. Inscribed on back: "At 'Mohu'—Martha's Vineyard. Enid Yandell at Senator Butler's Place in Lambert's Cove." Enid often rubbed clay between her fingers; perhaps this is what she holds in her box. (RISD Museum, Providence, RI.)

condition and in need of preservation. The Edgartown Historic District Commission deemed it to be "historically significant to the Town of Edgartown," and this enabled the commission to seek funding to restore it, with the goal of displaying it in the town hall. The designation "historically significant" was important: it authorized Enid's art and its legacy in a way that heretofore had not been done in Edgartown, her second home.[44]

When visiting Edgartown today, there is no indication of the role that Enid had in the community nor the important role the community and the village played in Enid's life and art. Only one of her works is on view in all of Edgartown. Enid's tabletop sculpture of Frank Worthing (1866–1910), the American stage actor, can be found in the Public Library, though it is tucked in an upstairs meeting room. A handful of works are in the collections of the Martha's Vineyard Museum, although they are not on permanent view. They include two animals, one of which is from the *Birthday Beasts* series that Enid conceived in Edgartown; a pair of rose candle holders; and a small plaster of Daniel Boone, Enid's signature work. None of Enid's old haunts are recognized as having any connection to her; these include Enid's home, the Branstock, the Tea Garden, or one of her favorite spots, Mohu, which was William Butler's place at Lambert's Cove.[45]

In the absence of any legacy, perhaps the Edgartown Historic District Commission and the community of organizations with which Enid was associated—the Dukes County Historical Society (now the Martha's Vineyard Museum), the Martha's Vineyard Chapter of the DAR, St. Andrews Episcopal Church—might begin to acknowledge Enid Yandell's life and legacy publicly through the repair and proper display of works by her. In addition, the Martha's Vineyard Museum might reexamine Enid's legacy through the works in their collection, which could be put on view as her one hundred fiftieth birthday approaches.

7

Advocacy and Activism

Enid's pathway to advocacy and activism may be traced through her interest, largely at the encouragement of her mother, in benevolent work outside the home. As a "clubwoman feminist," Louise Yandell was engaged in social welfare and humanitarian reform—for instance, through support of the orphans and infirmed, an extension of her commitment to the Episcopal Church. Having been shown the way, Enid sought to memorialize those whose efforts in the nineteenth century begat the broader strokes of women's reform in the twentieth, namely woman suffrage. In short, the women who commissioned Enid to create memorials in honor of J. J. Rucker and Emma Willard were of Enid's mother's generation, whose activities outside the home cohered with religious and educational work. They shared the interests and aims of Louise Elliston Yandell and Elizabeth Boddie Elliston, chief among them women's education—a right to which Enid had already been the beneficiary.[1]

Enid benefited from the broader aims and initiatives of others who also intentionally fostered the careers of women artists. In at least two instances, Enid was awarded a commission *because* she was a woman artist. Still, the commissions she received for her busts of J. J. Rucker and Emma Willard, although related to the fostering of the careers of women artists, had as much to do with the fact that Enid was a sculptor of merit by the late 1890s and had earned the accolades she received. Consider that she also had won competitions for the Confederate Monument in Louisville (earned in 1894, though rescinded) to the Carrie Brown Memorial Fountain (won in 1899, completed in 1901). She also fulfilled significant commissions that were not the result of competitions. Moreover, Enid contributed to large-scale projects, such as the embellishment for the New Amsterdam Theatre in 1903, putting her work alongside that of her colleague and former mentor, Karl Bitter. When mentioning this project to

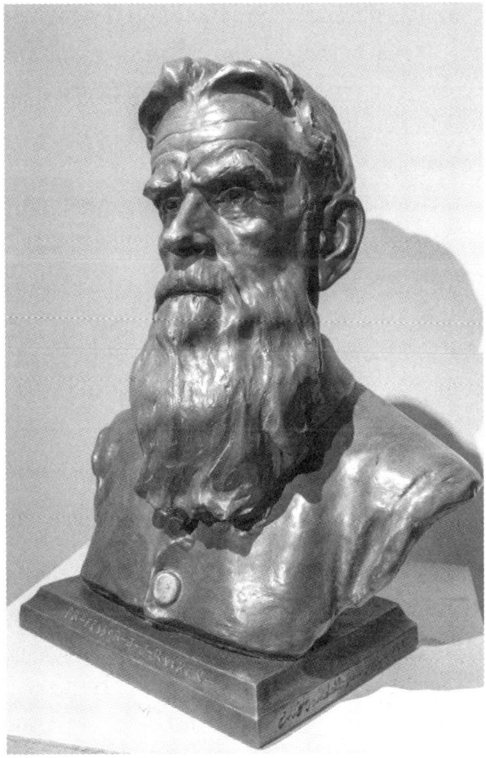

This bust was created by Enid in honor of Professor J. J. Rucker, who led the efforts to enable women to be educated alongside men at Georgetown College. Its inscription reads: "Presented by Mrs. Fannie Tucker Summers to Rucker Hall MDCCCXCVII. Professor—J—J—Rucker—Enid Yandell—Sculp—KY." (Enid Yandell, J. J. Rucker, 1897, bronze. Photograph by Boone Clark. Courtesy of The Galleries at Georgetown College.)

others, Enid pointed out that she was *working*, rather than *studying*, with Bitter. This distinction revealed her clarity of purpose toward a larger goal—of becoming an independent sculptor.[2]

Enid's own experiences and her drive to make a name for herself as a working professional did not overshadow her advocacy and activism. Parallel to her own accomplishments, Enid engaged in social reform movements through her work on the campaign for universal suffrage as well as through relief efforts for French artists, soldiers, and families during World War I. In each of these humanitarian endeavors, Enid showed time and again how she was a pioneer, even outside of her professional pursuits in sculpture.

J. J. Rucker

Cast in bronze in 1897, the bust of J. J. Rucker was commissioned by Fannie Tucker Summers (1855–1943) as the jewel in the crown of a dormitory that was named after educational reformer James Jefferson Rucker, professor of mathematics and administrator from 1855 to 1910 at Georgetown College, a small, liberal arts institution in Kentucky. Rucker's long tenure was befitting of a monument by Enid, as he was truly a pioneer of women's education.

Rucker believed that young women were just as entitled to a higher education as the young men who already were attending the college. With the help of Rucker, Georgetown College became one of the first co-ed schools in Kentucky through the introduction of the college's female seminary program, where female students were able to take part in the same courses as their male peers. Women from the Female Seminary began attending classes with men in 1884, and by 1892 women were admitted as regular students of the College. They first received degrees in 1893.

A campaign for funds to build a women's dormitory to house this population was subsequently spearheaded by Rucker, who had been appointed to this charge by the trustees of the college on June 6, 1894. After successfully raising the requisite funds, the college built the women's dormitory, Rucker Hall, in 1895. The three-story structure became home to thousands of women over the years. Besides recognizing the faculty member who had led the charge for Georgetown to become co-ed, the bronze bust Enid cast in Rucker's honor became part of the social fabric of the dorm community.[3]

Perhaps Enid saw something of herself in this commission. The assignment simultaneously recognized pioneering women's education (attributes that she herself subscribed to), a Kentucky connection, and an association with Enid's confidant and father figure, Reuben Durrett, who had attended Georgetown College. An examination of Durrett's speech to the alumni at Commencement in 1894 pays heed to the impact his life and vision may have had on Enid. In the address given to the college on June 13—just one week after Rucker's charge for funding began—Durrett mentioned his personal connection to the institution while also affirming women's right to equal education. He reflected upon his own matriculation fifty years earlier, when there were just forty-eight students who joined the college's ranks in 1844. After mentioning the changes on the campus, Durrett commented on the faculty and composition of the student body: "The enlarged faculty have laid aside the prejudices which followed colleges from their origin in the dark ages, and adapted the course of study to the wants of modern students. More than this, they have done that justice to woman which presumptuous man had denied her for thousands of years, by admitting female students to the college upon an equality with males."[4] Acknowledging the power of education to liberate women, Durrett reflected on the earlier iterations of the female seminary and its turbulent history. In closing, he commended the institution for its growth in size, faculty, and status apart from its admission of women.[5]

The following year, in 1895, the woman's dormitory was created, after which the Young Ladies' Dormitory had been named Rucker Hall by the college trustees "in recognition of Professor Rucker's life-long work for co-education." Two years later, in 1897, Enid was called upon to create a bust in Rucker's honor. The tabletop, life-sized bust was presented by Summers at a ceremony on January 10, 1898; Rucker's grandson, J. J. Rucker Bristow, "unveiled the bust and disclosed an almost breathing likeness."[6]

A series of speeches followed that paid heed to the donor and the namesake, including one from Professor J. C. Metcalf, who said:

> All these objects are tributes to that honored gentleman whom we love and respect, and the crowning glory of whose life is his triumphant work for woman. It is very fitting, therefore, that this statue should be the gift of a woman—an old pupil bound to her instructor by the firmest ties of admiration and affection. It is very fitting also that this bust should be the work of a woman—an enduring monument not only to her own genius, but to the memory of the man who for many years has fought for woman's advancement through broader culture.

Metcalf continued,

> Kentucky is proud of Miss Enid Yandell. Her artistic genius is recognized far beyond the limits of her native state as having already accomplished much that is enduring, and as promising even greater things. In this work of hers which we unveil this evening she has shown the spirit of a true artist; she has made out of the lifeless bronze a speaking image. . . . For the lessons which such works of art suggest are in the end of deep spiritual signifi-

> cance. Especially is this true of the bronze bust at my side: it is the abiding monument to the memory of a noble life.

Following Metcalf's remarks, Dr. John A. Lewis, President of the Board of Trustees, officially received the bust on behalf of the College and commented that after Rucker, Summers, and all present had passed, "this bronze will speak to and inspire those who shall come in and go out from this place."[7]

Enid's bust of J. J. Rucker found a home in the Fannie Tucker Summers Parlor of Rucker Hall, a fitting tribute to the man who led the efforts to introduce women as full-fledged undergraduate students at the college and to the woman who wanted to memorialize his efforts. More than 6,000 women students passed through the doors of Rucker Hall from 1895 through 1970, after which the dormitory was torn down to make way for the south campus residential complex, a newer style of lower-capacity living around landscaped green spaces that were better suited to the college environment. During that seventy-five-year period, women residents would rub or tap Professor Rucker's nose on their way out of the door of the hall, when the bust was positioned close to the main entrance. On the way to an exam or an afternoon out with friends, a friendly tap assured J. J. that you would return. In the mid-twentieth century, the tradition gained momentum and became the talk of the campus, as no other hall had a bust of its benefactor. In addition, as the only women's dorm, Rucker Hall and its eponymous bust became the object of prankery. For several years, if not decades, the bust was "stolen" by one or another fraternity on campus, holding the bronze likeness captive until it could be rescued by the women. Every year, the bust by Enid was returned and left unharmed, until the next antic.

While it is unknown if Enid ever saw her work on the campus of Georgetown College, it is likely that she never envisioned its role in the everyday life of students and the campus community. Such a work stands in sharp contrast to another work Enid created just two years later that was more broadly known, not only because of the fame of the sitter, but also because of its placement in the State Library within the State Capitol in Albany, New York—a public, civic space where it was charged with the task of serving as a monument to female achievement entirely.

Emma Willard

Emma Hart Willard (1787–1870) gained recognition through word and deed, first with her publication, *Plan for Improving Female Education* (1819), and subsequently with her advocacy for public funds for women's education, of which the Troy Female Seminary (founded at Troy, New York, in 1821) was a model. Educator, writer, and activist, Willard was a pioneer for the advancement of education for women and recognized by a number of memorials, including a bust created by Enid and dedicated at the State Library at Albany in June 1899, "making a space in New York's civic culture for this monument to female achievement."[8]

Awareness of Willard was widespread during this time. The effort to commission Enid to create the bust of Emma Willard was led by the president of the Emma Willard School Alumnae Association, Mrs. Russell Sage. Born in 1828, Olivia Sage was seventy-eight years old when she became a widow (in 1906) and won control of the family fortune built by her husband, a financier who dabbled in Wall Street and railroads. The memorial effort spoke to Sage's philanthropic side, a product of her Presbyterian heritage.[9]

Willard's granddaughter, Sarah Willard, expressed to the commission her hope that "to a woman might be committed this work of delineating a woman." The request was granted. "A woman was found, an artist whose work had found a place in the Woman's Building at the World's Fair, and who had earned for herself a meritorious place as the first woman to be made a member of the National Sculptors' Society, Miss Enid Yandell. To her was committed this almost sacred trust, to embody in marble all that is represented to our minds, the grand woman who led and fashioned the minds of so many American women and whose record is still with us." The responsibilities of likeness, as well as embodiment of an ideal, were bestowed upon Enid.[10]

Enid followed through on this commission with a marble bust depicting Emma with a lace bonnet and a serene look, recalling photographs taken of her. The bust offered a likeness visually and seemed to resonate within its context, a library, which of course was a cornerstone for education.

Further details of the work's history and its introduction to the Wil-

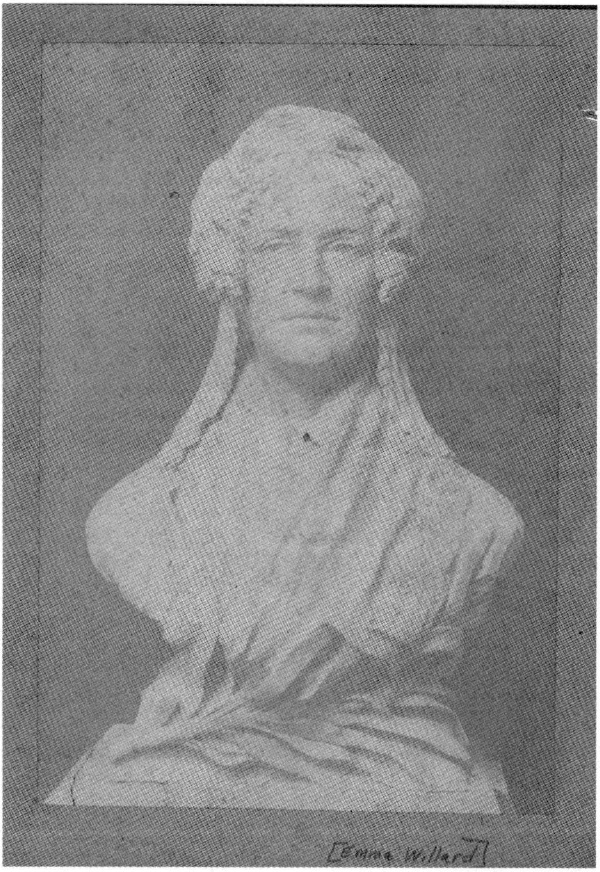

Enid depicted women's education reformer Emma Willard with a bonnet and a serene look, recalling photographs taken of her. The whereabouts of this plaster are unknown; it was the precursor to the creation of the final work in marble. That bust, which was on view for just over a decade in the New York State Library's Reading Room, was unfortunately destroyed in a fire that engulfed the New York State Capitol at Albany on March 29, 1911. Publications about the blaze recounted the loss of numerous manuscripts and books, as well as works of art, including Enid's bust of Willard. (Enid Bland Yandell Photograph Collection, 987PC52X.077, Box 5. The Filson Historical Society, Louisville, KY.)

lard alumni are documented in the *New Orleans Daily Picayune,* in a feature column on women. The newspaper pointed to Enid's fame—marking her "among the talented young women of whom the earth may be justly proud"—while also commenting on the group's impression of seeing the bust of Willard, several weeks before its installation at the library. The bust was on view at Tiffany's in New York City in the weeks leading up to its placement in its permanent home, in the reading room of the library in Albany. One account noted, "Last week [early May] in New York city one of the prominent social events was a tea given by Mrs. Charles Huntington Gardiner to Mrs. Russell Sage and the other members of the Emma Willard Association to view for the first time the bust of Mrs. Willard, which is to be placed in the state capitol at Albany, and which has just been completed by Miss Yandell. The bust was placed against a background of white and pink, the association colors, and after referring to the fact that it was to be put in the capitol, in the gallery of educators, in recognition of Mrs. Willard's work as the pioneer of the higher education for women."[11]

The Willard bust was formally unveiled during an educational convention at Albany on June 26, 1899, where it rested upon a white pedestal, covered with a piece of Duchess lace belonging to Mrs. Sage. The lace was cast off, the marble was revealed, and exclamations of satisfaction from the attendees were heard. Accounts of the event drew attention to these details, as well as the reception of sandwiches, wafers, and lemonade.[12]

Beyond the immediate circle of those involved in its commission, publicly the sculpture was recognized as the work of Enid Yandell from Louisville, and offered "a very fine example of this young artist's best work." While Enid did not attend the ceremony, a fellow Louisvillan did, and told of the event: "Miss Yandell was the recipient of the most enthusiastic encomiums on her work. . . . All Miss Yandell's friends in Kentucky may feel proud of her success in this piece of work. It seemed peculiarly fitting that the bust of 'a pioneer in the higher education of women'—which is the lettering on the base of the bust—should have been made by the woman who first went to work in Jackson Park—truly a pioneer in woman's work in sculpture."[13]

A similarly astute observation between Willard and Yandell—pioneers in their fields—was made in an article from earlier that year that commented on the role of sculpture at this time. Writing for *Harper's*

Bazaar, Pauline King described women sculptors—Enid, Bessie Potter Vonnoh, and others: "Until very recent years the fact was tacitly accepted by even the warmest admirers of the artistic work being done by women that they never had been and never would be sculptors. Common-sense was against it: the mechanical ability for setting up large figures or groups must be considerable, the strength to handle large masses of clay was denied to most of the sex, and the close application required to accomplish even the most ordinary results was felt to be far beyond a woman's endurance."

So, the reasons given earlier for preventing women to pursue a career in sculpture were physical: mechanical ability; strength to handle clay; lack of endurance. King went on to mention the importance of organizations such as the (New York) Art Students' League, which had leading male artists on the faculty, including Daniel Chester French and Augustus Saint-Gaudens, both of whom Enid knew. She also made note of women artists who went abroad "to study under the French sculptors, and in more than one instance celebrated artists who never admitted women to their studios, broke through the rule after seeing sketches and studies brought for their inspection." King pointed out that these male sculptors were concerned with talent, not gender, as they "were willing to give their criticism and encouragement as freely as they would have given it to young men of equal talents." King asserted that the time had come to judge the results of this educational endeavor, the labor of the woman artist to study in the same manner as men. King points out that Enid is among these pioneers, and uses the Willard bust as one of her hallmarks.[14]

King's account served as an important contemporary articulation of women sculptors, how they were perceived and marketed after the Columbian Exposition, where women artists established themselves as capable craftsmen and sculptors. She began her article with an account that women "never had been and never would be sculptors." King then disclosed accounts from the Art Students' League, where women, under the tutelage of noted artists, could "come forward as sculptors," with their "demand for place and opportunity to study under the best advantages no longer to be repressed." Another support for women in the profession was study abroad under French sculptors. These areas were the foundation upon which women sculptors of the day could build their practice and their careers as well as associate their careers with males, something that would have been expected in order for them to establish credibility at this time. King also claimed that the women were "as errant as [James Abbott McNeill] Whistler" (1834–1903), an expatriate artist who established his own avant-garde school, which fostered the development of a community of artists.[15]

Even as fame was proclaimed and projected for Enid through the Willard bust, its fate was not to be long-lived. Sited in the New York State Library's Reading Room, a space or aisle ten feet wide on one side of the general library, the delicate marble did not survive a devastating fire suffered by the capitol building on March 29, 1911. Reports of the blaze recounted the loss of numerous manuscripts, volumes, and works of art, including Enid's bust of Emma Willard. Perhaps Enid took solace in the words of one of her earlier mentors, Frederick MacMonnies, who spoke of the benefit of having one's work destroyed. In retrospect, Enid's bust of Willard could be referred to as a masterpiece, whether it truly was—or not.[16]

While Enid's work evidenced support of women's rights, education, and social reform, a closer look at her familial ties and a return to Louisville aids our understanding of Enid's own civic engagement.

The Work of Women

Enid's maternal grandmother, Elizabeth Boddie Elliston (1820–1904), and mother, Louise Elliston Yandell (1844–1908), were community leaders and philanthropists, but Enid herself seemed not to engage in broad reform movements—at least as far as can be determined from her correspondence with these two role models and mentors. She also rarely engaged in the language of advocacy with her sister Maude, who preferred to discuss dilettante arts, candy making, and travel. Enid's sister Elsie was committed to her family, with four children under the age of ten by the first decade of the twentieth century. Enid's brother, Lunsford Pitts Yandell III, started his working life in a plow factory before taking part in the Spanish-American War and later finding a career in industry.[17]

Louise tried to get Enid to support her own advocacy. For instance, in 1895, Enid's mother sought her daughter-sculptor's involvement in Louisville philanthropy by asking Enid to write a piece for the "Woman's

Edition" of the *Courier-Journal* in 1895 in support of the Children's Free Hospital. As part of a broader movement in the 1890s, women's editions were a form of newsroom philanthropy that generated interest among women to direct the contents of an issue of the paper and to encourage purchase of it. Various organizations worked on such editions, including women's groups as well as established charities, such as the YMCA and the Woman's Christian Temperance Union.[18]

Even as a twenty-five-year-old artist living in Paris in 1895, Enid was asked by her mother to participate in the woman's edition effort by writing for the *Courier-Journal* and the *Southern* "if you have time to write but don't undertake it if it will burden you." While that qualifier of time relative to Enid's work seemed understanding, Louise's follow-up statement expressed a full measure of devotion: "The one for the Woman's paper of the 27th I do want tho." Enid did not comply with her mother's request, because of lack of time, lack of interest, or perhaps both reasons.[19]

Even as Enid chose not to engage fully with the efforts of her mother and grandmother, she had the benefit of an independent education—an effort that Rucker and Willard fought for and that clearly Enid's mother and grandmother supported. Put simply, she may have viewed her occupational field very differently than her female mentors. Nevertheless, at least one reform effort caught her interest. Enid was a suffragist.[20]

Woman Suffrage and the Political Climate of the 1910s

The campaign for universal woman suffrage in the United States grew out of the Second Great Awakening of the 1820s and 1830s, which encouraged action against perceived moral failings. Part of a triumvirate of reform movements (including temperance, abolition, and women's rights more broadly), the suffrage campaign in the United States began in Seneca Falls, New York, in 1848 and climaxed in 1920, when the Nineteenth Amendment was passed. Over this period of social, political, and economic upheaval brought on as a result of changes wrought by the industrial revolution and its ripple effects, grassroots organization fomented unrest and spawned action. In the South, for instance, as historian Anne Firor Scott has noted, "a generation of women born since the war was arriving at maturity, the number of working women was steadily increasing, and communication with the world outside the South was ever more active."[21]

On the national and local level, women (and a few men) organized meetings and lectures, carried petitions door to door, and served as the "boots on the ground" to gain support for the cause and to deflect antagonism. While the full extent of Enid's involvement in these efforts is unknown, we do know that she supported the cause through her art as well as her actions. She participated in one exhibition and one parade in support of the enfranchisement of women. The dearth of material, however, should not suggest that these were isolated efforts. It seems appropriate that as a pioneer in her field, Enid would have been interested in efforts to foster women's equality through their right to vote.[22]

Debates about woman suffrage and economic parity were often made public through parades. Using parades for civic activism had been ongoing in New York City since 1908, when the first unofficial woman suffrage parade brought a march down Broadway with 400 women and several thousand spectators. Even as suffrage and parity were important reform issues, World War I created a new urgency and presented a case for women to participate, activate, and agitate. Enid was among these women.

Suffrage Parade

A previously unpublished photograph of a suffrage parade on a street, presumably in New York City, shows Enid in a suit and hat donning a "Votes for Women" sash and holding one tassel of a banner bearing the identifier "Sculptors." To her left are two other women: the middle figure (next to Enid) appears to be Janet Scudder, while the third person on Enid's far left is unknown. The three have traded in their sculptors' smocks for the uniform of the New Woman, one who shed undergarment bondage and could move out and about, even perhaps running to and from work. Darker in color than the garments of the women behind them, the attire of this trio of figures seem to exude the purple and yellow of the suffrage movement, even if the black-and-white film fails to show the colors. Behind this triumvirate is a handful of women, mostly wearing white, marching in support of the cause.[23]

An examination of the photograph's paper mat board reveals information about the identity of the photographer, Jessie Tarbox Beals (1870–1942). Beals was one of the first female photojournalists to have her work published and, by this time, she had already taken her first photograph

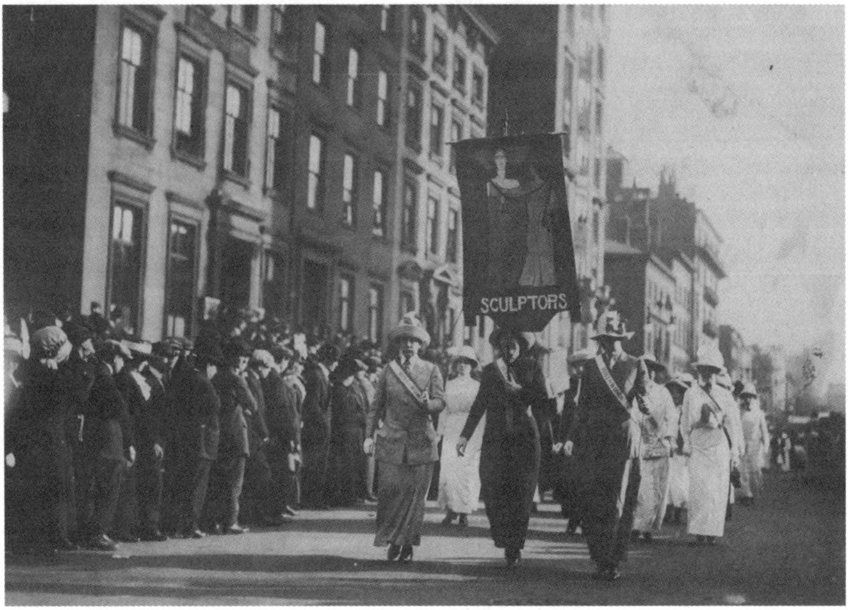

Photograph of Enid participating in a suffrage parade in New York City around 1915, marching alongside two other women. Leading a group of women dressed in white, the trio wear "Votes for Women" sashes and together carry a banner identifying their profession as "Sculptors." Enid is on the left, alongside fellow sculptor Janet Scudder, in the middle of the group. This photograph was taken by Jessie Tarbox Beals (1870–1942), who is among the first female photojournalists to have their work published. (RISD Museum, Providence, RI.)

for a newspaper. Beals shared a studio with her husband on Twenty-Third Street around 1912–1918, and given the address printed on the mat board, it is likely that the photo dates from this period, too.[24]

Given this photograph's recent discovery and the lack of information about the number of times this "Sculptors" suffrage banner was employed, it is impossible to say just when the photograph was taken. One of the largest parades was on May 6, 1911, when 3,000 people marched from Fifty-Ninth Street and Central Park South to Union Square, where they met up with a crowd of 10,000 others. Enid, however, was not identified as a suffragist in 1914, in that year's edition of *Woman's Who's Who of America*, thus pointing more toward her years of involvement being 1915–1917. Given the fact that the women of New York state won the right to vote on November 6, 1917, we can surmise that, even though the need for activism was still present nationally after that time, as a New Yorker Enid likely would have been less motivated to engage politically in the movement, especially as she was by then committed to other causes.[25]

Enid's activism may have come when it was needed most. Several states had granted women the right to vote prior to 1912, though to gain agency in principal, populated areas suffragists targeted New Jersey, Pennsylvania, New York, and Massachusetts in 1915 to add these four states to the movement. This push would have been front and center in Enid's mind, as two of these states—New York and Massachusetts—were her home base after 1908, when she spent winters in New York and summers in Edgartown (aside from her trips to France). We may also assume that Enid's political engagement conjoined with advocacy and activism upon her witnessing the horrors of war firsthand after 1914. In short, this photograph, and Enid's participation in at least one suffrage parade, likely dates from between 1915 and November 1917; the specific date may well have been October 23, 1915, when a parade for woman suffrage took place down Fifth Avenue with more than 45,000 supporters.[26]

Consider the last time Enid was known to have participated in a parade of any kind. In 1890, she reigned as queen of a festival intended to promote Louisville's growing material prosperity. At that point she had completed her formal education in art school and had traveled abroad. She had begun exhibiting her work and had gained some experience decorating a number of buildings in Louisville but had not yet left home to gain employment as an artist. Now, twenty-five years later, she could exploit the perspective that she had gained professionally and personally as a result of her work. She had established work practice on site in Chicago, Paris, New York, and Edgartown and fulfilled commissions that saw to her legacy in visual form in large, public sites in Nashville, Buffalo, St. Louis, and Providence, in addition to numerous smaller cities, their interiors decorated with busts of famous and not-so-famous men and women. Comparing her professional output to Enid's participation in parades bears witness to an exercise in contrasts, as Enid exchanged one form of spectacle for another. The suffrage parade seemed to eschew the claim that Enid was one of a gender who was called, in her home city of Louisville in 1890, "beautiful, cultured, traveled, wealthy," and instead recognized her as one of a vigorous procession of sculptors among the many marchers who were part of a national movement actively protesting the exclusion of women from political organization. In addition to being a part of this spectacle, Enid contributed to the work of suffrage by putting her work on exhibit to support the cause, as did many artists of the era.[27]

Suffrage Exhibition

On September 9, 1915, the *New York Times* made notice of artists being involved in the suffrage movement. The article "Art Sale to Aid Suffrage: Prominent Women Offer Works for an Exhibition Here" detailed the benefit, with half of the proceeds going to support the suffrage campaign. The exhibit at Macbeth Galleries ran from September 27 to October 16, 1915. Sculptors, including Enid, were mentioned by name as contributing toward the 20 bronzes, 10 sculptures, and 7 other works of varying media and finish, for a total of 37 works, along with 63 paintings and works on paper. For this exhibition, Enid contributed two bronzes, although we do not know what works these were. By the time the reviews for the exhibit started pouring in, the number of contributors had grown from seventy-five to close to one hundred. In addition to bringing work to exhibit and sell, many artists offered to create new work for donors, and agreed to remit 50 percent to the suffrage campaign. The article closes with the assertion that "all the contributors are enthusiastic suffragists." While the statement may be perceived as journalistic flair, its appearance in print made clear Enid's association with the movement. As art historian Mariea Caudill Dennison points out, "Many of the artists seized the exhibition opportunity to contest antisuffrage claims to the powerful tropes of motherhood and feminine virtue."[28]

This movement among artists to develop exhibits for auxiliary purposes seems to have emerged during the Panama-Pacific International Exposition, which was held in San Francisco from February through December 1915. Although Enid did not participate in that fair, perhaps due to her work abroad over this period, her student Helen Sahler did, along with a number of woman artists whose circles Enid would have shared.[29]

Enid engaged in suffrage work as well as broader political activity through her home base in Edgartown, Massachusetts, where she connected with William M. Butler (1861–1937) and Calvin Coolidge, who was then governor of the state. The political lives of Butler and Coolidge were intertwined, as Butler served as a legislator for the state of Massachusetts in the 1890s before turning his attention to the national political scene, as manager of Calvin Coolidge's 1924 campaign for the presidency. Butler's Republican politics were aligned with Enid's, particularly in relation to women's reform, including suffrage. And he served as a conduit for Enid's support of candidate Coolidge. Coolidge served as vice president in the dawn of universal national suffrage, succeeded to the presidency upon the death of Warren G. Harding in 1923, and served as president from 1923 to 1929. During these years, Enid attended events, such as a dinner at the home of Senator and Mrs. William M. Butler, in support of the National Republican Committee (which was reported in the *Washington Post* of March 6, 1925). In support and celebration of her political activity, Enid received an invitation to Coolidge's inauguration as president in 1925. She had clearly crossed over into the realm of advocacy and activism at home as well as abroad, supporting the causes of her generation rather than those of her mother's.[30]

World War I

Shifting from national to international matters of concern, Enid was engaged with war relief from 1914 to 1919, actions that may well have affirmed her commitment to woman suffrage. When World War I began many Americans were in Europe, especially Paris. Most left; however, some did not. Among them were artists who felt a debt to their adopted country. Seeing the millions of Europeans who were on the move as their own armies shifted ground, Edith Wharton drew attention to the effects of war by reporting in *Scribner's Magazine* and offered aid to refugees. She also published *The Book of the Homeless* (1916), reflections on the war from artists, composers, and writers of the day—many of whom were friends of hers or tapped to contribute by friends of friends. This curated presentation was much like the exhibition work to which Enid contributed. American painter Elizabeth Nourse also worked to assist refugees and solicited friends in the United States to contribute funds to aid in relief.[31]

For Enid, support meant boots on the ground—literally. She supported the war effort by lending aid to the French at home who contributed to the efforts of the Allied Powers. Enid gave this support in France as well as stateside from 1914 through 1919; for even before the United States joined forces in 1917 with Britain, France, and Russia and

US troops began arriving on the Western front in 1918, the war had made an impact on Enid.

At the outbreak of hostilities in late summer 1914, Enid was in Paris and remained in the city to aid artists and orphaned children. She was among the founding members of Appui aux Artistes (Aid for Artists), which provided meals for those involved in the arts and their families. She also served a French organization for the care of war orphans, La Société des Orphelins de la Guerre (Society for Orphans of the War), and was involved in work with the Red Cross. After returning to the United States in May 1915, Enid served as director of the Bureau of Communications for the American Red Cross in New York and as chair of the Women's Committee for the Council of National Defense. She spent time promoting the causes she was involved in abroad and established a national indexing system for hospitalized soldiers. Enid's activism resulted from witnessing the impact of war on a culture, profession, and people whom she had come to know, from whom she had learned much, and who greatly needed her support.[32]

Appui aux Artistes

Choosing to stay in France at the outbreak of war, Enid helped establish the organization Appui aux Artistes (Aid for Artists) in August 1914. Engaged as a quartet, the artist-founders who worked with Enid included Mme. E. van Saanan-Algi (Marie Louise Gibson), Mme. la Vicomtesse de Rancougne, and Malvina Hoffman. They also enlisted the support of a number of other artists, artist societies (including those who called themselves Independents, Futuristes, and Humoristes), and patrons of the arts.[33]

The main purpose of this organization was to provide meals for artists and their families. The need was essential, both due to the economic conditions that diminished investment in art during wartime (thus causing artists to see significant decreases in funding) as well as to the overall economic downturn in general brought on by the situation in Paris. Relief was needed to aid the artists' impoverishment caused by the war. Rather than relying on government assistance, the artists sought help from within. Their grassroots approach, described for American audiences in detail through a *New York Times* interview given by Enid and recounted in the papers on May 30 of the year following the organization's founding, explained the enterprise.

The article explained that the origins of the group dated to the week immediately following the declaration of war in France: "The American sculptor, Miss Yandell, who has just returned from Paris, gives a vivid account. . . . During the week following Aug. 1, 1914, four women . . . formed themselves into a committee and inserted an announcement in the papers stating that if the various factions of the art institutions in Paris would send representatives to meet . . . this committee would arrange to procure funds for relief and would work out with them a system of distribution." The committee had 100 francs in hand and had raised a bit more before the meeting, which was held at the home of one of the organizers. Fully aware of the inadequacy of the funds, they knew they needed more money.

They sent a cable immediately to Mary Williamson Averell Harriman, an art collector and philanthropist. Harriman had supported Enid's art directly through purchase, or by extension through her support of exhibitions, including the famed Armory Show, which brought European avant-garde art to the United States. Harriman committed $1,000 to the cause. The committee then chose officers, naming as honorary president Auguste Rodin, who had lent advice and his name to the operation's founders, two of whom were sculptors, Enid and Malvina Hoffman (1885–1966).[34]

The group was founded to take care of many, including those "who are unable to go to the front, the older men who could not be mobilized and the wives and children of the men who had gone. Also the studio assistants and the models. . . . We give them one meal for nothing, and those who are able pay 5 cents for a second if they wish." The organizers established dining quarters in convenient studios of the most crowded art quarter of Paris. The fees for food were subsidized such that if one could pay, one should; otherwise, individuals could eat for free. Artists who were "deprived of their work by the War can have a good dinner in congenial surroundings. All the cantines are directed by artists." Tasks of the organizers varied from cooking, managing, and supervising the cantines (or canteens) to furnishing them. By 1915, the organization was feeding 900 to 1,000 people per day; May was a record month that year, with the group supplying 100,000 meals.[35]

The work required extensive coordination, support, and space. The system was structured and yet it allowed for ease of aid if needed over the long term. Each canteen also had its own ethos depending upon who organized it and how it was facilitated. Enid worked in at least one canteen over her 1914–1915 service (cantine number 1); details as to the spirit of the canteen, its decorum, or its interior workings are, unfortunately, unknown. Support was given in the form of space by landlords, furniture by shop owners, and labor by models who were suddenly out of work.[36]

The French government saw to providing storage space for the group in one of the pavilions of the Louvre. French art and patrimony were at stake, but even more so were the lives of thousands of artists, their families, and their networks. Relief work to aid artists meant more than philanthropy to Enid; it meant life.

Given that the United States did not enter the war until 1917, pleas could be made stateside to support French war relief. Appui aux Artistes made its appeal to every rank of individual stateside, though focusing on American philanthropists with funds to spare and art students with a sympathetic ear. The case was made that artists who had learned skills or honed their abilities in Paris over the past generation owed it to the French artists to support them as their artistic ancestors, as the academy had supported American artists. An appeal for aid noted that the cost of 10 cents per meal might be seen as repayment for the welcome given American artists who studied in Paris: "You, who studied in Paris and remember the warm greeting given you, can you not help your unfortunate comrades there—the men who extended to you, in those days, the hand of friendship and good fellowship?"[37]

Enid and other artists served both inside the cantines and outside of them by seeking funds from individuals as well as organizations, through a variety of means (newspaper publicity in the *New York Times,* public appeal through lectureship or other group organization, and individual outreach). Once appeals were made, artists would gather donations, offer lectures as a way to attract groups interested in the effort who might donate after the talk, and organize art sales along the lines of the aforementioned suffrage exhibit of which Enid was a part. One effort that Enid spearheaded was a doll and toy sale. For this, Enid brought from Europe a number of Polish dolls and other toys and showcased them for sale, taking orders for their purchase. An American-based committee, the American

Polish Relief Committee, placed a large order for the dolls and other toys designed by the Polish artists in Paris and sold these at an event held in November 1915.[38]

The French ambassador and others praised the efforts of the Appui aux Artistes, heralding its tight organization, focused effort, and ability to collect and manage across its units. The press also recognized the group's efforts and their collaboration with other French societies.

La Société des Orphelins de la Guerre

In addition to supporting the daily needs of hungry artists and their families and associated staff through Appui aux Artistes, Enid was among those who cared for orphaned and abandoned children through the organization La Société des Orphelins de la Guerre (Society for Orphans of the War), a group for which Enid served as the American representative. Enid and other artists, including Janet Scudder and Malvina Hoffman, raised thousands of dollars for children in France by organizing relief work, speaking at organized events, and taking up donations.

Even though it was an international enterprise, war-orphan work is one of the less studied aspects of this era's cultural history. The source may be found in a speech Enid delivered on November 11, 1915, in Chicago at the home of Mrs. Robert McGann, who was herself an artist specializing in portraits and landscapes. Enid began her lecture by linking her two worlds: that of sculpture and that of stewardship on behalf of others. "It is a great pleasure to be back in Chicago again," she said; "it is a great pleasure to see how Chicago has realized her dream, and dreams, since the World's Fair, how beautiful it is and how it has developed, and it is a great joy to me to see that her heart is keen with sympathy and her people still realize the highest and best there is in the world. That is why you are here to listen to me."[39]

She talked of how she felt called to service: "I wanted to do something too, so I joined the Red Cross and applied for service among the women, children and old people." She went on to explain how she became responsible for children during the mobilization, when a father of two children who had been mobilized was obliged to leave his children (a boy age six, and a girl age nine), as their mother had died. He came to Enid asking for help, to which she replied, "I will take care of them." She felt responsible for these and many other children, feeding and caring for as many as 800 of them, "not knowing whether or not their fathers would come back. They were not orphans and could not be put into asylums, a great many of the schools had been closed and those which were open were expensive and my funds would not admit of paying for them."[40]

Enid continued her speech, explaining how the care for these children shifted from artist studios to the Université Populaire, an institution similar to Chicago's own Hull House. The system required a great degree of organization, with the children being divided into "families" of ten to twenty children, with a house mother and an assistant. The children "went to school and dined in the hotel which had been engaged for the purpose, and the house mother was responsible for their bringing up, manners and character." Enid remarked on her attachment to the children whose care she oversaw, saying that "that was the beginning of my special family." Enid documented the work and explained why the work was done, as voluntary service: "Every child is of value to France and we wanted to do all we could to save them, and we had a wonderful record." In remarking on the sickness in the units, Enid said that such occurrences were rare, apart from the illnesses of "trench babies," children without parents who had befriended soldiers.[41]

Enid commented on the value of her work and how she found great satisfaction in watching the children grow and develop mentally and physically. She also remarked on the treatment of soldiers, and that caring for the wounded was also a form of service. She pointed out the horror of the trenches and the psychological torment these conditions caused by mentioning the case of a sculptor she knew, who oscillated between times of solitude and insanity as a result of seeing the devastating losses among humans and animals (particularly dogs and horses). Finally, Enid turned to her reason for addressing this group of women in Chicago: a plea for funds.[42]

Enid made several such speeches and requests for funds, as noted in a *Chicago Evening Post* article from November 1915, which mentioned "Miss Enid Yandell, the American sculptress, who has been speaking in a number of homes in behalf of the sufferers." Enid's accounts of the orphans and of the "trench babies" carried a poignant appeal and resulted in subscriptions amounting to nearly $3,000. Although Enid never stated how she felt about this accomplishment, or if she even considered it as such, it is fair to say that this kind of work is in line with the reform work that her mother and grandmother espoused. For Enid, though, the call to action was on her own terms—activated through her agency as a sculptor and through her abilities to lead others to participate through financial stewardship.[43]

Clearly, Enid had developed her own personal investment in humanitarian work, rather than merely following the interests of her mother. Instead of writing for newspapers to support the charities of her mother's day in Louisville, Enid endeavored to be covered *in* the newspapers, through her philanthropic work with Appui aux Artistes and La Société des Orphelins de la Guerre.

Red Cross

The third avenue by which Enid contributed to the war effort was in support of returning soldiers through a position she held at the Red Cross Debarkation office in Hoboken, New Jersey. In this role, Enid established an indexing system for the Red Cross's Debarkation Records Department in Hoboken and managed a staff of women to locate soldiers returned from the War. Before engaging in this work, however, Enid had to prove her loyalties to the United States. For this, she relied upon a Louisville connection, Colonel Henry Watterson, editor of the *Courier-Journal.* Writing on behalf of Enid, Watterson stated: "My Dear Sir: I understand that Miss Enid Yandell has taken Red Cross service under your management, and I write to commend her to your particular consideration. She is not only an artist of distinguished merit, but an American of 'purest ray serene,' sprung from a family of eminent surgeons, and socially of the very highest standing in Kentucky. There is nothing she undertakes to do which she will not do well."[44]

Enid's work in this office began in November 1917 and over the next year plus, she made quite an impression with the Red Cross administrators. In a reply to Watterson, the administrators wrote, "You particularly mentioned Miss Yandell, I remember, and you may be sure that you touched a very tender spot, here, for I can say that no one in our organization is regarded with greater appreciation or more affection. The young women in her department—among whom is a daughter of mine—address her as 'Aunt Enid' and quite glory in their service under her!"[45]

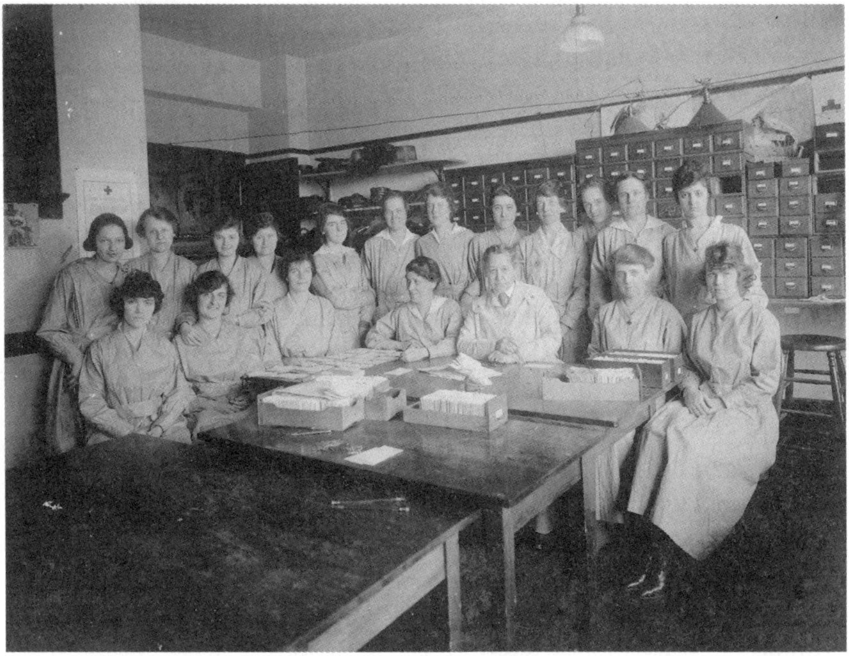

Enid established an indexing system for the Red Cross's Debarkation Records Department in Hoboken, New Jersey. She is shown here in her office with her team, who aspired to locate the index card corresponding to a given soldier's location within five minutes. In the photograph, Enid is seated in the front row, third from right. (Enid Bland Yandell Photograph Collection, 987PC52X.023, Box 7. The Filson Historical Society, Louisville, KY.)

Gainfully at her country's service, Enid created the most complete file of American sick and wounded, spread among forty-two general hospitals, sixteen base hospitals, seven camp hospitals, and eight debarkation hospitals. The system had 200,000 cards on file representing all the men brought back to America. Enid noted the accuracy of their system, her workers' attention to detail in their tasks (as file clerk or typist), and their understanding of the human side of the system, that each card represented a soldier: "If one of the clerks drops a card, she feels as badly as though the card were the wounded soldier himself." Boasting of her team's ability to locate a wounded soldier within five minutes of a request, she added, "There's no magic in it at all. It's just my filing system, and a very simple one at that." Enid took over the position in this office in January 1919, and through her transfer of organization and people skills "brought fame to the department" due to her management of the facility rather than her fame as a sculptor. Under her authority, the office claimed never to have lost or misplaced a single name among all those listed.[46]

After this four-year period of intense activism and advocacy, Enid wrapped up her Red Cross service. In support of the organization, and perhaps as a reminder of her accomplishments in the service of others, she continued to wear her Red Cross lapel pin for years. She kept it among her decorations and badges from a lifetime of artistic and philanthropic awards and achievements. Among other tokens of appreciation Enid received for her war efforts was a bronze medallion with a palm branch around one side of the circle and a partially draped, winged female figure reaching her right arm so as to extend her olive branch toward her left palm. The inscription reads: "A Enid Yandell pour ce qu'elle est et ce qu'elle a fait '*l'Appui aux Artistes*' 1914–15." While the iconography speaks to the solemnity of the loss of life while honoring the peace of victory, the inscription "for who she is and for what she did" recognized Enid's commitment to helping others. Enid's service as secretary of this relief organization in 1914 and 1915 was part of several efforts she undertook to contribute to causes and to activate an American public far from the site of war and its effects, which she witnessed firsthand.[47]

It is unclear if Enid created art while serving the war effort. Given the economic depression, and the poor reception for artists during this time, her attentions shifted away from art and toward her significant charitable efforts until the war concluded. Yet some scholars have claimed that Enid was so affected by her humanitarian work that she subsequently withdrew from her profession. For example, Stephanie Darst, art historian and curator of the 1993 exhibition that focused on Enid, wrote that "her humanitarian efforts profoundly affected her outlook and physical health" and that "she would never again be totally devoted to her career in sculpture, beginning a sort of semi-retirement at the age of forty-five." While indeed the war had an indelible impact on Enid—as it did on so many others—her work after the mid-1910s, upon her reaching middle age, shifted to an interest in smaller sculpture and regular work from Branstock and New York.[48]

Enid's work continued, but on a smaller scale as she moved between her worlds in Edgartown (in the summer) and New York (in the winter).

She also continued her engagement with professionals upon whom she relied, perhaps including a network in industry, such as foundries. Enid continued to lead a productive, busy career in tabletop sculptures, garden and decorative statuary, fountains and sundials, and relief portraits, as evidenced by her business materials, including advertisement records and some reference to, and correspondence with, foundries. Thus, rather than enter semi-retirement and shun working in art, Enid continued after World War I to create work, to manage and teach at Branstock, and to promote her work. She prepared catalogues for sales and new ventures, such as the Branstock Birthday Beasts. She also continued to design works on a much larger, public scale, including her submission to the Pioneer Monument project for Harrodsburg, which will be discussed in the following chapter.

8

Pioneer and Promoter

Some of the earliest accounts of Enid's abilities and accomplishments in sculpture drew comparisons between her and her subjects, at least in appearance. An undated clipping that Enid kept in a scrapbook described this phenomenon, connecting her with the image of the caryatid, the columnar support she designed as a draped female figure for the Woman's Building at the World's Columbian Exposition in Chicago: "She sits aloft on a scaffolding in Martini's [Martiny's] studio, clad in a corduroy gown and muddy apron, and deftly puts life and emotion into brown lumps of clay. Miss Yandell is a beauty of the black-eyed, black-haired, fine-figured K[entuck]y type. She has ridden and driven, and rowed and skated, and used tools, until every muscle is fully developed, and she looks as though she might be a model for one of the statues. But she isn't content with this variety of accomplishments."[1] The article thus bore witness to her musculature as well as her active lifestyle; she was involved in sport throughout her life. Moreover, the sculptor's garb did resemble classical drapery. The connection between ideation and creation was made; it was as if she breathed life into her subjects.

Verism was highly praised, particularly in reference to reliefs, busts, and "figureens" of known subjects. Beyond physical appearance, other characteristics of Enid's subjects have been attributed to her. For instance, the connection between Daniel Boone and Enid in terms of the pioneer spirit was heralded in headline after headline, beginning with Boone's entry to the world's fair stage. While the meaning of pioneer relative to Boone is clear, for Enid the association was anchored in several key points of reference: her adoption of Boone as a subject for art; her imaginative likeness of Boone, which became the signature likeness of him adopted for use by others; her election as one of the first women to be granted membership in the National Sculpture Society in 1898; and her innovative approach to bronze statuary.

By being a pioneer, then, Enid was forever tied to Kentucky. Such tethering also manifested itself in the subjects that Enid chose to work on. This chapter examines subjects that Enid undertook with explicit reference to Kentucky and pioneerism. These include subjects from, about, and in Kentucky: the plaster and bronze relief of Julia Dinsmore, Enid's longtime friend who managed a homestead in northern Kentucky; a plaster model for a silver cup that celebrates Kentucky's agricultural bounty; and a memorial fountain in honor of a pioneering cyclist who made Kentucky his home. Enid's ties to Kentucky are also evident in her treatment of Daniel Boone: smaller-scale, domestic works depicting Boone are contrasted with Enid's conception for what would have been her final large-scale public commission, a monument in celebration of pioneers and Kentucky (1924). For this, she returned to Kentucky—literally and figuratively—by making visits to the sculpture site at Harrodsburg and reviving the subject with which her occupational identity was first cast, that of Daniel Boone. The chapter concludes with Enid's reflections on her career and the field of women sculptors in her lecture "The Pioneer." The confidence emanating from Enid in the lecture bears witness to her hard-fought victories over her past decades and her self-actualization as pioneer.

From Kentucky: Julia Dinsmore

Enid and Julia Dinsmore had been friends since the late 1880s. The earliest seeds of this connection between the two were rooted at the Dinsmore homestead in northern Kentucky and served as a means of fostering Enid's growing independence from her family and the social mores of the South. Dinsmore visited New York City during the spring of 1920 while Enid was wintering in New York. The purpose of the visit, among other things, was for her to have Enid make a bas-relief of her profile. After drawing a sketch and making a mold of Dinsmore's face, Enid took her to the Roman Bronze Works foundry whose task it was to convert the plaster model into the enduring medium. We know details about their visits that spring, including the foundry visit, thanks to comments that Dinsmore

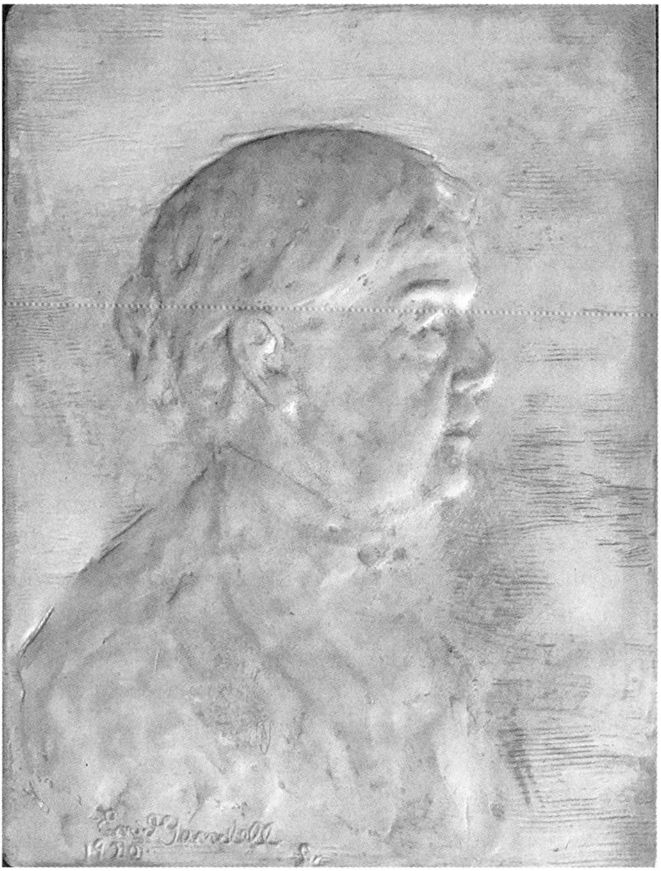

Enid's relief of Julia Dinsmore, plaster, 1920. This work, like many of Enid's low-relief works, was eventually produced in bronze. In this case, the artist gave the plaster to the sitter as well as the bronze. Photograph taken by the author. (Courtesy of Dinsmore Homestead, Burlington, KY.)

recorded in her journal, which offer insight into how Enid worked and how her practice was evidenced in the final work.[2]

Enid continued her friendship of thirty-some years with Dinsmore ever since she, the "girl sculptor" from Kentucky, began her professional education. By 1920, it was Enid's turn to share her world by connecting those from the Bluegrass State to a world outside of it. When Dinsmore visited Enid, it was not enough for Enid to draw a sketch, create a plaster, and seek the patron's approval before sending her on her way. Enid extended the experience by taking Julia to the foundry, allowing her to learn about the methods of casting a bronze mold and about the coloring applied to bronze, referred to as patination. In this way, Enid shared her world with her lifelong Kentucky friend, Julia Dinsmore, a pioneering woman and kindred spirit with whom Enid found camaraderie and companionship.

About Kentucky: Design for a Silver Cup

A second connection to Enid's Kentucky home may be found in a cup, or stein, that she created in honor of William Edmund Halsey. The only other drinking vessels that Enid was known to have created were the *Kiss Tankard* and the loving cup for Elsie's wedding. Because the appearance of the loving cup is unclear, we can use the *Kiss Tankard* as a comparison to the Halsey stein. The tankard took inspiration from literature in its amorous subject of a mermaid and boy who cannot reach each other when the tankard is closed but connect when the lid is lifted. The treatment of these figures situates *Kiss Tankard* in the Rodinesque phase of Enid's work: the figures and their background appear unfinished, expressive, and evocative. The cup honoring Halsey takes some visual cues from *Kiss Tankard,* most notably the less-than-realistic treatment of the subject matter and the unconventional rendering of the handle. Whereas *Kiss Tankard* presented the mermaid's body as the handle, the Halsey cup offers long stalks of corn for this purpose. Their forms undulate and fold over one another so as not to be reduced to mere representation of agriculture. The treatment of this cup may be tied to the *Kiss Tankard,* Enid's time in Paris, and her evocation of Rodinesque tendencies, given that Enid conceived of and designed this work while she was living in Paris. And, like the *Kiss Tankard,* a plaster was created before its translation into silver.[3]

In terms of subject, the cup is not rooted in literature, as *Kiss Tankard* was, but is tied to Kentucky's agricultural bounty. Designed in 1904, the same year that Enid presented Daniel Boone and two figures of *Victory* for the two pagodas at the World's Fair in St. Louis, the Halsey cup provides a snapshot of Kentucky's agricultural past as well as its promise. It presents a trio of crops: corn along the handle, with the top third of the bowl showcasing tobacco at its peak moment of flowering before the harvest

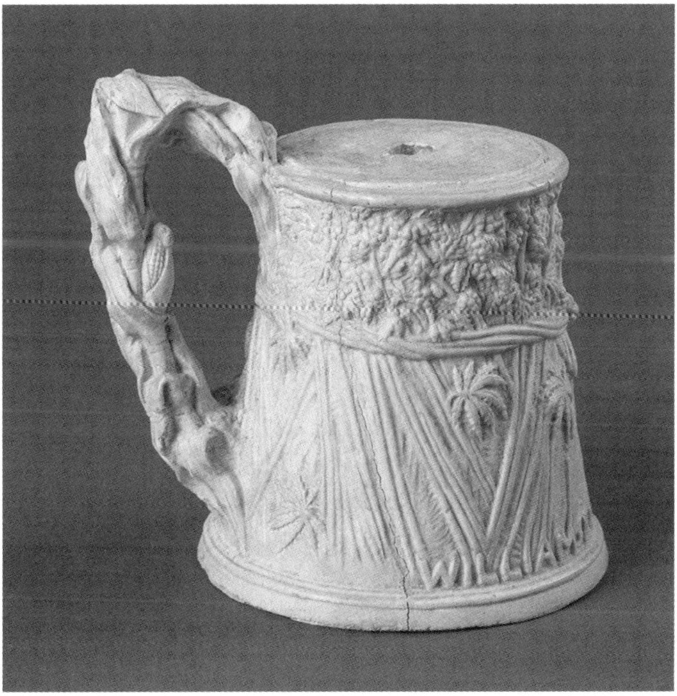

Enid Yandell, *Design for a Silver Cup,* 1904, Plaster, 5 3/8 × 5 5/8 × 4 1/2 in. (13.7 × 14.3 × 11.4 cm.). (Gift of Mrs. M. L. Halsey, 1927.19.1. Collection of the Speed Art Museum, Louisville, Kentucky.)

and the lower two-thirds displaying long, slender, fibrous stalks of hemp. All three loomed large in the Kentucky imaginary. According to historian Thomas D. Clark, by 1802, flour from ground corn and small grains had become the "most important processed Kentucky agricultural commodity sold on the western market" by virtue of the grist being shipped down the Ohio and Mississippi Rivers to market. By the beginning of the twentieth century the commodities trade positioned Kentuckians as "restless and aggressive participants in western politics and economics."[4]

This trio of emblems characterized Kentucky's agricultural strength in growing crops for varied purposes: human and animal consumption, luxury, and manufacture. The cup's handle served as the perfect means of conveying the long stalks of corn for people and livestock. The tobacco, a crop of luxury and vice, is shown at the ripe point of "topping," when the tobacco flower is removed before the leaves are taken and the crop harvested. The cup's bowl also shows a third crop in Kentucky's agricultural repertoire: hemp.

Hemp was a major crop in the early to mid-nineteenth century in the commonwealth, a fact that was highlighted at the St. Louis World's Fair in 1904—the same year that Enid created the Halsey cup. Despite its origins in Asia and its nonnative status in the United States, hemp was first grown in Kentucky for manufacture as early as 1790; its fiber was used for manufacture into cordage and rope that was used in the boat trade, as well as coarse cloth. During the age of cotton, hemp found a new purpose when it was woven into bagging for bales of processed seed cotton. Despite its ties to the Bluegrass State as a major cash crop for nearly half a century (from around 1840 through the century's end), hemp was marketed as a new product by the early twentieth century. On this international stage at the world's fair, hemp was all the rage, and accounts in the *Louisville Courier-Journal* touted its promise. Hemp's role declined, however, as tobacco became the cash crop of the commonwealth. From 1865 to 1928, Kentucky produced more tobacco than any other state in the United States.[5]

It is clear that Enid had Kentucky on her mind when she made the cup, and her selection and inclusion of this trio of sister crops gave it a Kentucky connection as well as a history of her state's agricultural roots. In short, Kentucky's heritage was agriculture, such that "the pattern of Kentucky political, social, and economic life was cut to the lay of the land." The Halsey cup embodied this heritage.[6]

In Kentucky: The Ruff Memorial Fountain

Unlike the bas-relief of Julia Dinsmore and the Halsey cup, both of which were private commissions, the Ruff Memorial Fountain was a large, public work in Louisville that Enid designed in 1897. Created at a time when she maintained studios in New York and Paris, the work demonstrates how Enid retained ties to her home city. Also known as the Wheelman's Bench, the memorial features a curved limestone seat in memory of A. D. "Pap" Ruff (1827–1896), an English expatriate who had been born aboard a ship en route to Canada. Given his entry into the world, Ruff was born to travel, it seems, having crossed national and state borders before settling in Owingsville, Kentucky, for the latter half of his life. Ruff was one of the state's oldest cyclists at a time when cycling was all the rage. Full of enthusiasm and a zest for travel, he made a trip on a bicycle from Louisville to Yellowstone National Park in 1893, thus raising his athletic profile locally and nationally. He died in January 1896 without heirs and left a fortune, a small portion of which was dedicated to the Kentucky Division of the League of American Wheelmen for the purpose of providing water and shade for cyclists in pursuit of their journeys.

Enid was commissioned to design a bench and fountain as a memorial to Ruff. Details as to the commission are hazy, but Enid mentioned the work on more than one occasion. Enid designed other comparable fountains (such as Hogan's Fountain in Cherokee Park, Louisville, and Brown Memorial Fountain in Providence, Rhode Island) as well as large-scale works for world's fairs. The Ruff Memorial Fountain is her only work that incorporates seating as a primary feature, the water being secondary. The bench's original design included a cusped, marble slab fountain at the center of the semicircle as its focal point. Over time, the original fountain was removed, and a modern, slender, metal version replaced it. On each end of the bench, metal light posts provided illumination. These have been removed as well, although the holes where the posts were affixed to the limestone remain.

The Ruff Memorial Fountain meant a lot to Enid. In fact, when she spoke of the bench and fountain, she remarked that with it she wanted to make the people of her city proud. In some ways, her unusual approach guaranteed this. For here she aimed to reinvent the notion of a memorial, both in terms of her own body of work and memorials generally. Ruff Memorial Fountain is unique because it is a nonfigurative memorial—a unique contribution by Enid to a genre that saw in this period other, more historical memorials, such as Civil War monuments. Unlike those other commemorations, the Ruff memorial offered respite and solitude in a location Enid knew well—not far from the site of the Confederate Monument and the Speed Museum not that distant from her family's home on Broadway.[7]

For Kentucky: Daniel Boone

Daniel Boone, as has been recounted throughout this volume, was a calling card of Enid's. She showed plaster or staff versions of the same Daniel

Boone that had been commissioned by the Filson in 1891 at several world's fairs and centennials over a ten-year period (1893–1904) and continued to build her career off this early work of hers in the twentieth century. The various casts were identical, and ultimately the life-sized Boone was cast in bronze in 1906. Enid's depiction of Boone was ubiquitous, having been at fairs, reproduced in publications, and permanently installed in her home city.

Because neither the sitter nor representations of him were extant, Enid created a sculpture for the Chicago World's Fair in 1893, that became his visage. In other words, she actualized an idea of what people *believed* Daniel Boone looked like. Her career was, in large part, built upon this act and its legacy. In short, because Enid was amazingly talented at creating a likeness by weaving together various threads of representation, she was responsible for crafting a likeness of Daniel Boone that still looms large in the Kentucky imaginary today.

Clearly, Enid's work was associated with the pioneer, and her depiction of Daniel Boone became a representation of the frontier more broadly. For instance, the work was used as to illustrate an article on expansion that appeared in *The Outlook* on January 25, 1908. At the head of the article, journalist H. Addington Bruce presented a full-page image of Enid's Boone—cap, fringed jacket, and rifle in tow—to set the tone for the article "The Romance of American Expansion: Daniel Boone and the Opening Up of the West." In addition to the full-page photographic reproduction of Enid's Boone, the article was supplemented with engraved images of source material that Enid had used to model her sculpture: the rifle, hunting shirt, powder horn, tomahawk, and hunting knife from Reuben Durrett's collection described earlier. Thus, the Boone legacy followed Enid into the middle phase of her artistic career.[8]

Looking back at her career, it is apparent that Enid wanted control over that singular accomplishment. The earliest evidence of this came from the Tennessee Centennial celebration. At the time, Enid was abroad, at work on Athena, the largest figure at the fair, and she enlisted help from her mother to facilitate Boone's arrival in Nashville, as recounted in Chapter 4. Following the fair, the Boone statue was supposed to remain on the fairgrounds or, at the very least, in Nashville. A series of letters from Enid to Major John W. Thomas, who facilitated project management at the fair, indicated her interest in parting with the Boone, which had been cast in staff (the plaster mixture used at the fairs) expressly for the purpose of exhibiting at Nashville. The Tennessee Boone, while modeled from the Boone at Chicago, was a unique cast expressly for this purpose.

In the discussion with Thomas, Enid explained the arrangements for having "multiple" Boones: "When the Filson Club ordered it [Boone] they allowed me to make three casts for one of which they paid me $1,750—I have the privilege of selling the other two or reproducing them in bronze. The cast in staff which is in Nashville actually cost me $150 to mould." Enid then went on to address the issue of cost. Between this letter and the subsequent one Enid wrote to Thomas, on February 22, 1898, the staff Boone was damaged severely. Enid took issue with this and reported her frustration to Thomas: "I am exceedingly annoyed and regret deeply that my statue of Boone should have met with so serious an accident—I consider the figure fully worth $500. However I will accept your proposition to pay me $250 in full of the damage." While this correspondence demonstrates Enid's understanding of the value of her work, it also signifies her wish to maintain control over her work, and in this case also suggests her dual identity with Boone. In addition to being paid for the broken statue, Enid requested that it, even in its broken state, be returned to her mother's home in Louisville. Enid recognized that the Boone was not only a work of art, it was also part of her identity as a sculptor. She was not about to let anyone gain agency in that arena.[9]

The following year, in a letter to Reuben Durrett, Enid expressed concern over any other artist encroaching upon her domain—the likeness of Boone—and her research materials. In explaining a potential commission for silver service on the battleship *Kentucky,* Enid wrote to Durrett: "I have been asked by several of the firms to model the indian [*sic*] and Boone figures if their designs are accepted. I write to ask that you will remember your promise to me *not* to give any of the Boone relics or portraits to any other artist but myself to copy. As you have the only authentic likeness and I have made for you the only portrait statue." Clearly, Enid wanted to maintain control over the likeness of Boone that she had created, and, moreover, over who else might have access to the resources she had used to create her Boone. In short, she was sculpting her legacy as *the* creator of Boone's likeness.[10]

Enid even attempted to cement the image of Boone in her home city. She wrote to Durrett in 1903 seeking a loan of the Boone for the St. Louis fair and explained that acquiring the statue of Daniel Boone from Louisville might thus secure its permanent commission in bronze. She wrote: "The St. Louis Exposition have asked me to send them a copy of my Daniel Boone. Will the Filson Club give me or lend me the cast that is now at Mr. Bickels? I will pay all expenses of boxing and shipping and returning if they do not give me the cast. You have one copy, the first and best. It would be a very good thing for me to exhibit this figure and perhaps when Mr. Bickel learns someone else wants the cast he will decide to have it done in Bronze at once." Enid's letter here was attempting to do double duty. First, she was negotiating the loan of a work of hers that was, at the time, on loan to another individual (the Filson's Boone from Chicago had been lent to C. C. Bickel, presumably as part of a marketing campaign for his "Daniel Boone" cigar). Second, she was attempting to negotiate her legacy in Louisville, by having the statue cast in bronze. Enid followed up with another letter a few weeks later, again requesting that the Boone be sent to her and that the bronze be cast in perpetuity for her city and the Bluegrass State.[11]

That day finally came in June 1906, as part of the week-long statewide celebration known as "homecoming," which issued a welcome home to "men, women, and children who possess the priceless heritage of having a drop of Kentucky blood in their veins," through a number of events to honor Kentucky's forefathers. Daniel Boone was celebrated on June 16 for his "vital citizenship" and as "the pioneer of our early days," for which Enid's monument was "Kentucky's loving tribute to all that he was and all that he did." The sculpture was seen as more than the sum of its parts. It was more than a memorial; in fact, it represented the embodiment of all art. Enid's depiction of Boone was testament "to that love of Art which is one of the first fruits of a civilized society." Further, Enid was praised as a daughter of Kentucky. In his presentation of the sculpture to the city, General John B. Castleman (1841–1918), president of the Board of Park Commissioners, praised Enid: "We pay tribute to the genius of one who was born and reared upon the soil we love so well, and who among the great company of Home Comers, is one specially marked and set apart for honor and acclaim. We ask her to accept this humble acknowledgement in the sure knowledge and belief that her fellow countrymen are least of all unmindful of her prowess and most of all her well-wishes for that which the coming years may bring."[12]

Following Castleman's remarks, Reuben Durrett addressed the crowd who had gathered at the sculpture. Durrett said that "a gifted artist and a progressive citizen combined in this instance to make an imperishable representation of a distinguished pioneer." After commenting on each of their merits—Enid's and C. C. Bickel's—Durrett noted a way forward through art: "it is hoped that this gift . . . will be followed by others until these charming grounds become a kind of rural art gallery in which will be preserved the statues and busts of Kentuckians who leave imperishable names at their departure from this world."[13]

The sculpture's unveiling was perhaps the most compelling moment of the day. As the band played "Dixie" in the pouring rain, Miss Helen Bickel Stewart, granddaughter of the benefactor, C. C. Bickel, pulled on the ribbon surrounding the red mantle that covered the sculpture. When the ribbon was tugged, cheers went out for several minutes by the crowd gathered around. It was raining so hard that day, however, that the mantle over the statue released its dye over the ground, coloring it red and reminding those present of the figure of the "Dark and Bloody Ground" by which Kentucky was known during its pioneer days. Enid could never have foreseen such a series of actions and remarks when she had begun work on the bronze, of course; but the scene at the sculpture that day functioned as a visual metaphor for the path that Enid had taken, her pioneering spirit, and the ground she had covered as a female sculptor, from her first representation of Boone at Chicago to this one—which would not be her last.

The Pioneer

Building upon her interest in pioneer and Kentucky-related themes, Enid turned to Daniel Boone again in 1924. *The Pioneer*, a smaller work fashioned as a bust of Daniel Boone that year, was among the possessions she retained until her death. Clearly, the figure of Boone was compelling for Enid throughout her life.

The Pioneer functioned like a résumé, if you will, by offering a glance to the past and Enid's first professional commission as a sculptor, the Daniel Boone she created for the Kentucky Building at the World's Fair in Chicago. Likewise, this later tabletop plaster functioned as a stand-in for Boone, an abbreviation of her previous efforts in its simplicity of face,

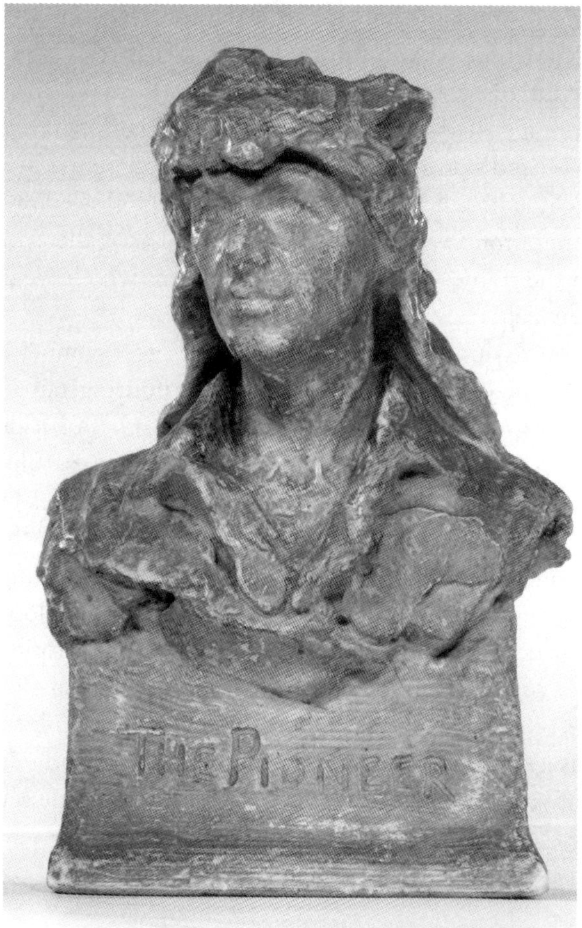

Enid Yandell, *The Pioneer*, plaster, 1924. (Courtesy of Warren and Julie Payne.)

coonskin cap, and lapel. Gone are the trappings of the large-scale Boone that Enid first undertook thirty years earlier.

Given its date, 1924, we can assume that this sculpture was not a finished work but rather a model, or maquette, for the project that she would begin in Harrodsburg that year. It is, however, important to note that Enid included this work in a professional photograph of herself that she had taken in her studio. In that photo, she has replaced her flowy smock of her art academy days with a fitted weskit and her Red Cross insignia pin, calling to mind her service to her country in the previous decade.

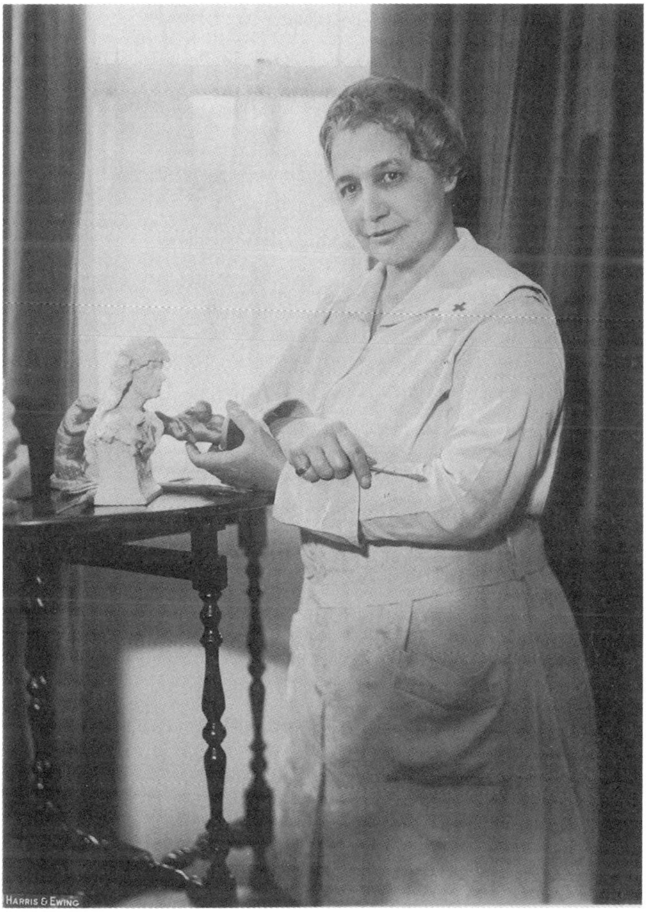

Enid in her Edgartown studio with several *Birthday Beasts* on the table and in her hand, as well as a sculptor's scraping tool. On her weskit she wears a Red Cross pin, thus calling to mind her patriotic duty. Given the dates of Enid's works shown, including the miniature bust of Daniel Boone, we may assume that this photograph was taken around 1924. (Enid Bland Yandell Photograph Collection, 987PC52X.008, Box 1, Folder 6, The Filson Historical Society, Louisville, KY.)

She presents herself as being engaged in her work, holding an identifiable plaster animal figurine in her left hand and a swab for applying tint or smoothing plaster in her right hand. With a carving chisel on her table between a number of the small pieces by Enid—which have been staged on a clean, shiny wooden table as opposed to sprawled on a sculptor's work table—Enid stares at the viewer, at us, as if we are catching her in the midst of work. The photograph is an invitation for the viewer to commission Enid to create her next sculpture.

Enid's bust of Daniel Boone functioned as a substitute for Enid herself: she gave versions of it to close friends, among them First Lady Grace Coolidge, whom Enid knew through political circles and through neighboring Islander William Butler and the Republican Party. She also sent one to other staff at the White House. It is unknown how many copies of the bust were made, but the whereabouts of two are known; one of them was found in Enid's Edgartown studio upon her death.[14]

The Pioneer Monument

As noted previously, in 1908 Enid settled on Martha's Vineyard, Massachusetts, where she ran the Branstock School of Art in Edgartown for nearly thirty years. She taught mainly summer classes to aspiring and established artists, akin to the summer schools that were becoming popular among American modernists. In addition to classes, Branstock offered exhibitions of small paintings, works on paper, and sculpture. The environment proved to be a crucible of artistic activity for Enid. Here she completed smaller works that were derived from literary and historical subjects, including sundials as well as public and private fountains.[15]

While her prewar years were dominated by the creation of sculptures for world's fairs and monuments to individuals, her postwar production diminished, as it had for many artists, due to the economic depression and the poor reception for artists at the time. During and after the war, Enid was committed to improving the lives of others by undertaking significant humanitarian work, both at home and in France. It is unclear, however, if she created art while serving the war effort.

Following the war, given her age and her interests in teaching, exhibition, and small-scale commissions, Enid pursued only one significant large-scale composition after World War I: the Pioneer Memorial Park Monument, a 1924 effort of the Kentucky Pioneer Association, a local group of citizens, to construct a memorial to the early settlers of the state. The competition for this commission drew the most prized American sculptors of the day. Enid submitted her design and was awarded a contract for the Harrodsburg, Kentucky, project, beating out sixteen male competitors. Her selection was noted in the press, which mentioned her fame without explicitly stating her position as a pioneer sculptor: "ENID YANDELL, a woman famous in the art of sculpture, has been selected to design the monument of the Kentucky pioneer which will overlook the grounds dedicated to the memory of the early settlers of this 'back door of the nation.'"[16]

It is no wonder that Enid was selected to design the monument at Harrodsburg. She could draw not only on her abilities as an artist, but also on her association with her home state. Leading the praise was her native city, whose newspaper proclaimed her victory in securing the commission. The *Louisville Herald* announced, "A Woman Three Times a Pioneer in Art Is Chosen to Do a Pioneer Monument at Harrodsburg, Kentucky." Enid was proclaimed as a pioneer in Chicago; as being among the first women elected for membership to the National Sculpture Society, "therefore a pioneer for the second time"; and as a pioneer for the third time with her design of the gnoman and sundial *The Four Seasons* using a wing of a bird "held in the hands of summer," a commissioned piece that Enid had completed in 1900.[17]

For the Pioneer Memorial Park Monument, Enid returned to Kentucky, literally and figuratively. Unfortunately, her design for this site was not executed, although photographs annotated by her detail her plans and, when coupled with her typed description of the monument design, offer an understanding of her authority as Kentucky's frontier sculptor and bachelor maid. Enid's monument was intended to embody much more than a personal likeness—a milestone she had achieved with the Boone on display for the Kentucky Building at Chicago's fair. Here, back in her native state, her work could convey the pioneer spirit of Boone, who first encountered the wilderness in 1767 and led to its establishment as a settlement in 1775. Daniel Boone, frontier military leader George Rogers Clark (1752–1818), and many other unnamed individuals who served as pathfinders and trailblazers were to be heralded for their expansion into the wilderness of Kentucky and points westward. They were the early settlers of the state who, a century and a half later, still merited celebration.[18]

For this project, Enid attempted to branch out from her earlier pioneer depiction of Boone. According to the artist's visual and verbal renderings, the work would be an installation consisting of several components. On

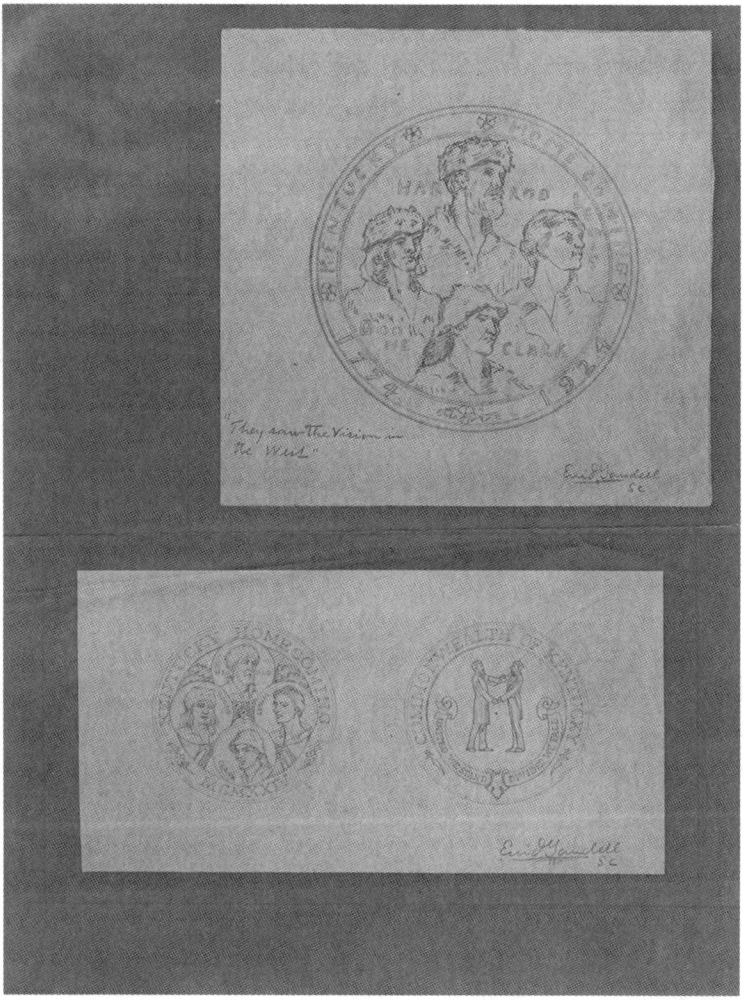

Sketches by Enid for the proposed Harrodsburg memorial. (Enid Bland Yandell Photograph Collection, 987PC52X.276, Box 6. The Filson Historical Society, Louisville, KY.)

that measure alone, it was a departure from her previous projects. These included singular works in the form of a bust, life-sized, or colossal figure; a monument conceived with one focal point—such as the Carrie Brown Memorial Fountain in Providence, Rhode Island, which contains allegorical figures representing "The Struggle of Life" amidst a granite basin of more than 200 spray outlets; or the monument and relief sculpture to

John W. Thomas in Nashville, consisting of a bronze, full-length portrait atop a stone base with four rectangular bronze reliefs.

At Harrodsburg, Enid intended to exhibit reliefs of Meriwether Lewis and William Clark (who formed their famous partnership in Louisville in 1803), James Harrod (who settled the first site in the state in 1774), and Daniel Boone. These were to have been supplemented with the phrase "Kentucky Homecoming 1924." But Enid's ambition extended beyond likeness in order to expand the conception of the pioneer and to create what she referred to as the "Pioneer Unit" or the "Pioneer Shrine." She intended to include a pioneer man in typical Boone fashion—wearing a hunting shirt—though he was not conceived of as Boone specifically, but rather *as* Everyman. According to Enid's notes, "the Pioneer will be typical but not a portrait." Women would also play a role in this commemoration: "The woman Pioneers, who had equal hardships and more uninteresting labor than the men, have never before been recognized." She further acknowledged women's work in tanning the buffalo and elk skins that created the garment, the very hunting shirt of Boone's fame.[19]

Such a vast array of figures and perspectives required more than a series of medallions or even a cluster of relevant figures. Enid rose to the challenge and accordingly conceived of her most ambitious work to date: a platform, set amid a landscaped park area, with several figures: a pioneer man, a pioneer woman holding a baby in her arms, and a youth carrying a flintlock rifle. She claimed that through this work she could immortalize the woman who served also as a pioneer: "The Pioneer Man went to the trackless forest primeval [*sic*], his woman followed her mate. It shall be my joy to sing in bronze the epic of these women and children."[20]

Upon receiving the commission for this project, Enid also received critical acclaim. As Lawrence F. Abbott wrote in his January 1925 article "The Gate of the West," the celebration of the 150th anniversary of the westward expansion of Boone through the Cumberland Gap in 1775 into Kentucky, which opened up a Wilderness Road and Euro-American settlement in this region even before statehood in 1792, presented opportunities to commemorate both the known and the lesser known of the region: "Kentucky is celebrating, therefore, the prowess, not of one man, but of a dauntless host whose names we do not know. The statue by Enid Yandell which will be unveiled at Harrodsburg will stand as a monument not only to Boone, but also to those who, by the wilderness and the

Natchez of all other westward-running trails, fared on into the unknown wilds to lay the stepping-stones for civilization across a continent." The *New York Sun* acknowledged Enid's "gaining for her sex recognition in the field" of sculpture: "It was not many years ago that any statement concerning the work of a woman in sculpture was made with apologies, which, however unnecessary, were rather expected by a public unused to the sight of women laboring in this distinguished field"—a public that included women from the generation of Julia Dent Grant, the figure with whom Enid's character of the Duke argued thirty years earlier.[21]

On at least one occasion, Enid gave a lecture about the monument and her conception for it. At the annual luncheon of the Society of Kentucky Women of New York, held at the Waldorf-Astoria in May 1924, Enid was featured as the guest of honor. In this role, she gave a speech entitled "The Kentucky Pioneer." While there appears to be no account of the content of her lecture, the fact that she was featured as the guest of honor indicates that her attendance may have been prompted by her having been awarded the commission, which had been announced in the papers just a few days prior. Moreover, a manuscript that appears to have been developed by Enid, though undated, articulates her vision of the monument. In it, she gives a long history of pioneers, Kentuckians, and Americans. She also ties herself to her home state: "It is our privilege as Kentuckians to keep the memory of the Pioneers before the American people, and in the mountains of Kentucky still live the lineal, true descendants of these Pioneers." In her monument, Enid planned to draw particular attention to the women and children. She had been an advocate for women's reform (recall that she was involved in the woman suffrage movement, which had granted most, though not all, women in the United States voting rights in 1920) and could supplement this broader aim with her own experience as a woman in a man's world.[22]

Enid's plan would have transformed the Pioneer Memorial Park from rustic forts, fortifications, and the old spring that was then part of the site into a more landscaped area accentuated by figural and relief sculpture that recognized Lewis and Clark, Boone, and Harrod as well as more unfamiliar citizens, who would be embodied as memorable types bearing witness to the hardships undertaken by, and the unintended consequences of, Manifest Destiny. Sadly, for reasons unknown, Enid's conception was never realized. No known correspondence to or from her, scrapbooks, or newspaper clippings explain why the plan was abandoned, although a few possibilities exist. First, Enid's focus: she did travel to Fort Harrod in 1924 to visit the site for the memorial, but that was one of few visits she made late in life back to her native state. By this time, she had established her school on Martha's Vineyard and was devoting much of her time to its development as well as to her own practice, with smaller, though numerous, commissions. Second, and more likely, the death of her architect brother-in-law, Donn Barber, on May 25, 1925, may have dealt a blow to the project, as he may have been her principal collaborator. Her commitment to the project remained strong, however, in terms of her pronouncements about the project as well as her continued work on it.[23]

With her commitment to the project and her commitment to her home state, Enid appears to have worked on the monument for some years, which stands in contrast to some scholars' suggestions that Enid stopped doing sculpture after World War I—as well as my own earlier statement that Enid concluded her work on this monument by 1925. The date of 1925 was deduced given that at least one newspaper account that year mentioned Enid's work for the monument as part of the Kentucky Pioneer Association's efforts to raise funds for the site.[24]

In fact, however, evidence suggests otherwise. First, Enid's proclamations about work and her profession later in life indicated that she was still engaged in large-scale work. In 1926, writing about Martha's Vineyard, she stated, "The climate of the Island is ideal, cool in summer and warm in winter. The air coming off the great Atlantic is life-giving and nerve-soothing. In the eighteen years that I have been on the Island, it has been to me a constant inspiration and joy. If you are sick, you can get well here; if you are well you can dream great dreams of things to do for your fellowmen." While vague, this reference to "dream great dreams of things" could reference her own work on the Pioneer Monument.[25]

Additional evidence to support Enid's extended engagement with this memorial project includes records found after her death, which indicated that she pursued this project until at least 1929. Four items of interest relate to Enid's collaboration with architects or an architectural firm at this time. The first of these included annotated blueprints for the "Pioneer Monument" drawn by Olmsted Brothers of Brookline, Massachusetts—a firm Enid knew from her earlier work in Cherokee Park. The Olmsted firm was commissioned to shape the landscape around the park's interpretive sites, including the buildings and the monument. Blueprints with designs by the Olmsted Brothers dated June 2, 1927, refer to plan number 6, which leads to the assumption that five additional plans for the park had been undertaken. This blueprint is also stamped on the back with a later date of 1929, thus indicating that the blueprint—even as it was two years old—was still being worked on a full five years after Enid was awarded the commission and four years after her (possible) collaborator, Donn Barber, had died. These blueprints were retained by Enid until her death, thereby indicating that she was working on the project for some years past the 1924 award of the commission. Given that the monument to replace Enid's design was installed in 1934, it remains unclear when Enid "stopped" working on her Pioneer Monument.[26]

In addition, annotated maps and photographs, though undated, further suggest that Enid was engaged for some years with this project. One such item is a map of the settlement and area, pasted to a board, on the back of which Enid wrote: "264 feet East & West; 330 feet North & South; 12 lots of ¼ acre each," indicating that she was taking into account the entire site and plan when designing the monument. This map on board featured the settlement at Harrod's Town, 1775–1776, and was based upon the work of W. W. Stephenson, who created the initial sketch of the site. Reproductions by Stephenson would have been invaluable to Enid, as they informed the reconstruction of buildings on the site. These are supplemented by two photographs annotated by Enid, with her name written in pen in the lower left as "Yandell." Each has ordinal directions, indicating that it may have been used in tandem with the drawing and annotated map. One of the photographs shows a man in the background wearing a hat, while the other shows no people but has sight lines drawn on top of it. While undated, these photographs, appended drawing, and blueprint give an indication of Enid's process, her use of photographs as documentation to inform her work, and perhaps most importantly her continued work on this design long after the commission was granted in 1924.

As a multiyear project, the development of the Pioneer Memorial Park site, and the settlement at Harrodsburg, were intended to establish the site as an engine of economic and heritage tourism, an effort that continued over the next several years in phases, bringing the length of time from commission to dedication to a full decade. On June 16, 1927, the Pioneer Memorial Park (now called Old Fort Harrod State Park) was opened as a reconstructed replica of the first fort on that site. Over the next several years, additional enhancements were made through federal funding that yielded what was dubbed the First Permanent Settlement of the West. This was, in effect, the Pioneer Memorial conceived by Ulric Ellerhusen (1879–1957) and architect Francis Keally (1889–1978) to replace Enid's earlier design. While more commonly known as the George Rogers Clark Federal Monument, the newer design diminished the Boone and Harrod connections that Enid's work had furthered. The Ellerhusen and Keally design shows Clark beside his horse, accompanied by a young and old pioneer—perhaps signifying Boone and Harrod. On the other side of Clark, a soldier bids farewell to his family, a wife and child. An inlay map outlines the routes of the early pioneers. The monument was ultimately dedicated by President Franklin Delano Roosevelt on November 16, 1934, five months after Enid's death.[27]

Although the Pioneer Monument was uncompleted at the time of Enid's death, its commission and framing were significant in terms of content and how this project expanded Enid's body of work. In terms of content, as noted in the lecture that Enid had given in 1924, the pioneer men *and* women were a part of her conceptualization. Moreover, Enid's inclusion of women in the narrative as active participants rather than sorrowful soon-to-be-widows, as others might have depicted them, was in keeping with the broader narrative of those who populated the original settlement: women such as Anne Pogue McGinty, who may have operated the first spinning wheel in the West—an individual whom Enid mentioned in her speech to the women's group in May 1924. Enid's articulation of McGinty as a pioneer is easily understood, as she was an early settler who followed Daniel Boone through the Cumberland Gap. She was a successful businesswoman, proprietor of the region's first "ordinary," a cross between restaurant, tavern, and hotel that was run out of her home. In operating "what appears to have been the first tavern in Harrodsburg," she became "one of the more prosperous women in frontier Kentucky."[28]

Perhaps Enid saw in Anne Pogue McGinty something of herself. McGinty was recognized for her investment in work (and survival) by virtue of her bringing the spinning wheel over the mountains. While she was responsible for every aspect of tending to the chores of the cabin, such as chopping wood, cultivating crops, hunting, and so on, her identity was affirmed through a domestic art, namely weaving. In this arena, she thrived. She developed the "linsey-woolsey" combination cloth that could withstand the rugged pioneer habitat. In addition, she was recognized outside of the home, as she was a businesswoman who managed her own affairs as proprietor of the region's first tavern. In her dual roles in art and business, Enid likewise forged an identity through her work: she was recognized early on for her efforts in sculpture, and it was through her work that her identity was sculpted, literally, as a woman in a world of professional men.

Further, in her inclusion of women and children in her concept and verbal articulation of her ideas, Enid was well ahead of her time. Historical overviews, such as *Collins' Historical Sketches of Kentucky,* which was published in 1847 and subsequently expanded and republished throughout Enid's life, recounted how Daniel Boone and others brought their wives and children to the land, and how Boone's wife and daughter were the "first white women that ever stood upon the banks of Kentucky river," a fact recorded in *Collins' Historical Sketches* in the pioneer annals for September 1776. This perspective was one Enid knew well: she owned a typescript of the long passage on Daniel Boone from the 1874 edition of *Collins' Historical Sketches* (pages 56–65). Moreover, she had grown accustomed to having at her disposal the library of Reuben T. Durrett, founding president of the Filson Club, family friend, and mentor. Among her books and handwritten notes, Enid kept Collins' version of the Boone narrative separate from others by appending a handwritten bibliographic citation on the last page of the excerpt.[29]

Kentucky history was further informed by a thread of pioneer histories, such as those written by American historian Frederick Jackson Turner, who offered his famous "frontier thesis." Turner wrote that the frontier established Americans' sense of liberty and shaped American character, aspects of Kentucky's own narrative, which influenced the research and teaching of history through this lens of pioneerism and the frontier. Turner's theory, which emphasized American exceptionalism as distinct from European origins, was widely received and stood in contrast to Theodore Roosevelt's concept of the "winning of the West" as creating a new, distinctly American, sensibility. Subsequent writings about the West maintained women's peripheral, subordinate, and passive roles in the settlement of the frontier. In cases where women were mentioned, their roles were often written in tandem with men's, often having women following their men rather than leading or even acting on their own. As historian Robert Cotterill wrote in his 1917 history of Kentucky, a trek of six families under Boone's leadership in September 1773 "was not a party of hunters or surveyors: it was a migration of settlers. Women and children were along; the pack of horses were laden heavily with the baggage to be used in their homes." Later on, Cotterill went on to describe the men, their number, and precisely what they did. The women and children were relegated to the nameless, faceless realm of livestock.[30]

Given her penchant for history and her practice of extensively researching a topic, person, or moment in history before taking it on as the subject of a work, Enid was very likely aware of the myopic view that had dominated her state's history. In her speech of 1924, Enid called attention to the neglect of the pioneer in Kentucky history and called upon those in attendance to honor those of the past as their ancestors, the Puritans, had been. Significantly, she identified herself as a Kentuckian. She stated, "It is our privilege as Kentuckians to keep the memory of the Pioneers before the American people, and in the mountains of Kentucky still live the lineal, true descendants of these Pioneers." She further connected the descendants of these pioneers to fellow Kentuckians of her own day who served the country in World War I. She continued, "I saw them go to the great War—in my service for the Red Cross."

In addition to extending the line of pioneers to the present day, Enid's intent with this monument was to celebrate the pioneers, both named and unnamed, and to "sing in bronze the epic of these women and children." Such a promise stood in contrast to historical writing, as well as the pioneer imaginary, up to that point. Not until the 1960s, with the rise of social history and later the predominance of micro narratives—both parts of historiography that occurred long after Enid's death in 1934—did historians aim to rectify this marginalization of women. Decades later, in time for Kentucky's Bicentennial in 1992, historian Margaret Ripley Wolfe asserted a means for women to have full agency as "gentle tamers" of the frontier.[31]

While starkly contrasting with the narrative proffered by historical record, Enid's design for the Pioneer Monument at Harrodsburg was in keeping with the spirit of her commissioned projects related to advocacy and her activism of the previous decades (her busts of J. J. Rucker and Emma Willard, for instance). Moreover, the purpose of this design of

Enid's at that historical moment—the 1920s—was significant in its connection to the early twentieth-century shift into heritage tourism associated with pioneerism and monumental work, which created an economic engine for the small town of Harrodsburg. The former pioneer settlement was seventy-some miles from Enid's home of Louisville and a far cry from the palaces of spectacle she grew up with there and on which she cut her teeth in Chicago, Nashville, Buffalo, and St. Louis.[32]

Throughout her life, from 1869 to 1934, even as Enid navigated varied geographic, educational, occupational, and social, she was—literally—a pioneer. She was the first recognized sculptor to call Kentucky her home. Her long, active career, while dimmed by the tragedies of World War I and the devastation of the human condition, afforded her opportunities as a sculptor and to work on major projects, up to and including the commission for Harrodsburg, demonstrating the extent to which she assumed, and embraced, this identity. Enid was forever tied to Kentucky and promoted her state through the subjects that she chose to undertake. Her ties to Kentucky are especially evident in her treatment of Daniel Boone and a self-confidence that came from hard-fought victories over the decades of her life, culminating in her self-actualization as Kentucky's pioneer sculptor.

Epilogue

Lucretia Giese, professor of art and architectural history at Rhode Island School of Design (RISD), commented in 2003, "I find it quite marvelous that Enid Yandell's work was exhibited in the two exhibitions that bracketed late-nineteenth-century American art—the 1893 Columbian Exposition in Chicago, so very Beaux-Artsian and the 1913 Armory Show in New York, so modernist." Professor Giese's claim served as evidence for a successful grant application to restore the Carrie Brown Memorial Fountain, which was over one hundred years old and showing signs of age. Giese knew this significant public art commission well by virtue of its proximity to her institution: a quarter-mile walk from her campus office brought her to the fountain's location at Burnside Park near City Hall in Providence. Beyond its local importance, the memorial was created at the intersection of these watershed moments for making art and for which later feminist interventions in art history have attempted to give female contributions to these efforts their due. Clearly Enid's work had not been given its due, even among interested academics, begging the question as to how such elisions of the historical record are possible. Why do they occur?[1]

Despite her ambitious production, carefully managed career, and transatlantic reputation during her lifetime, Enid Yandell has been neglected in art history. Yet a casual glance at newspapers from the 1890s through the 1910s reveals Enid's name, from the *Louisville Courier-Journal* and the *New York Times* to the *Tennessean* and the *Chicago Tribune*. Her name was noted within the context of spectacle and pageantry, including the Satellites of Mercury as well as four world's fairs, art and exhibitions, politics and suffrage, and relief work in the United States and France.

Enid's behavior and occupation contradicted the notions of feminine propriety in the American South; she lived the life of a "bachelor maid"—a single woman in the late nineteenth and early twentieth century who operated independently of men and managed her own business affairs. With no offspring, Enid left her work and the keeping of her legacy to her niece, Elsie Barber Trask (1907–2007), who over time dispersed her aunt's art-related materials, including correspondence, documents, photographs, and studio contents, among four collections: the Martha's Vineyard Museum (formerly Duke's County Historical Society), located near Enid's home and studio in Edgartown; the Speed Museum, Kentucky's flagship art institution; the RISD Museum in Providence, Rhode Island, situated on the campus; and the Filson Historical Society (formerly the Filson Club), which seeks to preserve materials related to local and regional history. Each of these institutions has played a role in Enid's legacy through exhibition work and scholarship as well as access to the collections. The value of such collections lies in the network of activities that occurred over a number of years, in multiple institutions, and with the involvement of a handful of individuals—most notably Enid's niece, Elsie Barber Trask, and historian Nancy Baird of Western Kentucky University—who facilitated a number of important moments of legacy building as described below, in consort with a multitude of other activities over the past several decades.

This chapter looks at both past and present in an effort to document Enid Yandell's life and work. Making a transition from Southern dilettante, daughter of a Confederate officer, and mentee of men, Enid became an internationally recognized sculptor of large-scale, award-winning works, an independent woman engaging in art and activism, and a pioneer who sculpted a legacy for herself—and left one for us to continue to sculpt as well.[2]

Martha's Vineyard Museum

The Martha's Vineyard Museum was founded as the Dukes County Historical Society in 1922. While it is unknown what role, if any, Enid played in the museum's early days, her affiliation, and the museum's, with the Daughters of the American Revolution suggests a connection. Moreover, Enid was interested in cultivating the culture and heritage of the area, in keeping with her own long-standing interest in history, as well as her association with a similar society in her hometown. Given her long tenure on the island (spending, at minimum, twenty-seven summers there until her death in 1934) and her financial investment there (three properties, including her home, school, and studio), her investment in the cultural community was assured.[3]

Even though Enid lived and worked in Edgartown for nearly thirty years, there is little that remains of her legacy there today. The Martha's Vineyard Museum has four works in its collection (*Pioneer, Monkey, Snake,* and *Candle Holders*). These are supplemented by photographs and postcards of Enid's studio, which are excellent documentary resources, as well as biographical materials in an artist clipping file. They are enriched by other museum holdings, including photographs, postcards, and documents relating to the community while Enid lived there, such as tourist guides from the 1910s to the 1930s as well as directories, such as the *Martha's Vineyard Directory* and the *Business Directory.* Such materials give context for Enid's life and work on the Vineyard, especially regarding her school, the Branstock.

It is unclear if these plaster works were exhibited after their donation to the museum while it was located just blocks from Enid's home and studio; it is hoped that the museum's recent relocation to Vineyard Haven (2019) can afford a tighter connection between the island and its importance in Enid's life and work and, by extension, her legacy.[4]

While the timeline of the donations to Martha's Vineyard Museum remains murky, we know that an intentional effort toward sculpting Enid's legacy began around 1940, six years after Enid's death. Because she had no direct heirs, Enid left her home and studio and their contents to her niece, who began the process of bringing Enid's work back home to Kentucky, where her career began. To help her in building her aunt's legacy, Elsie Trask reached out to a friend of her mother's, who also happened to be the founding director of the Speed Art Museum, Kentucky's oldest art museum.[5]

Louisville: J. B. Speed Memorial Museum, 1941

Already a collector of Enid's sculpture, Harriet "Hattie" Bishop Speed owned a small fountain, *Lotus Flower,* one of the artist's late decorative works. She knew of Enid's work because of her own association within art circles. In fact, Speed was more than an occasional fan of art; she founded

Kentucky's oldest and largest art museum, the J. B. Speed Memorial Museum, in 1925. In this way, Hattie fulfilled the role of what historian Kathleen D. McCarthy has called "cultural custodians," women who "helped to transform the contours of the American art world in the opening decades of the century." Just as Hattie Speed founded the museum as a memorial to her husband, she conceived of collection-building as a form of memorialization. In addition to being well connected in the arts arena, on a personal level she knew Enid's sister, Elsie Yandell Barber (mother of Elsie Barber Trask). The initial outreach regarding the possibility of bringing Enid's work "home" came from the younger Elsie, who drew an association between her mother and Hattie in a letter to Speed: "Josephine [Elsie's cousin] tells me that you knew mother well. I wish that I could see you and tell you how much it means to me to keep my association with mother's friends."[6]

From that point, over several letters from March 1940 through 1942, Trask and Speed corresponded. Trask noted how appropriate it was that the Yandell works be sent to Louisville: "I think it very fitting that Aunt Enid's sculpture should go to Louisville. She was so proud of having been born there and she was such a remarkable woman with all her talent and charm that I would like to feel that there was a memorial to her and also that the public would have a chance to know and appreciate her." She stated, "I would like very much to give all the work of Aunt Enid's that I have together with all photographs or other things pertaining to her which would be of interest to the public. It is impossible for me to have any idea now of what there is available as I cannot be there [?] until Spring." In response, Speed wrote to Trask that she would be delighted to work with her to have Enid's "beautiful work fully represented in her old Home[town]" by bringing Enid back to Louisville: "it will be a joy for us to co-operate with you in such a Memorial!"[7]

Ongoing correspondence between the museum and Elsie Barber Trask secured the items for shipment and delivery to Louisville. The works were installed and thereby introduced audiences to Enid's work as part of the museum's exhibition of recent acquisitions and loaned pieces from January 12 through January 26, 1941. The accompanying catalogue for the exhibition listed all of the works on view, paying special attention to Enid's by giving them their own heading in the catalogue, "The Sculpture of Enid Yandell."[8]

Beyond these works by Enid, photographs of her work and studio were included as part of the donation, and thus the 1941 exhibition and display. Four of the photographs, a gift of Pauline May, depicted the Carrie Brown Memorial Fountain, while a handful of others, donated by Trask, showed Enid at work in Paris for the Tennessee Centennial as well as images of her studio. Rounding out the exhibition was the book that Enid wrote with two of her friends, *Three Girls in a Flat,* their fictionalized account of life at the Chicago Exposition, the setting for Enid's entry into the world of professional sculpture some fifty years earlier.[9]

Even though these items were exhibited among a treasure trove of works donated to or acquired by the museum during its robust period of collection-building, the display enabled viewers to see Enid's body of work, from tabletop sculpture to small models or full-size renderings of busts as well as large-scale works.[10] The monumental, embodied by the plaster of Enid's Daniel Boone and the plasters of the bronze reliefs from the John W. Thomas monument in Nashville, shared space with the decorative—examples of Enid's figureens (*The Gibson Girl, Elsie Yandell Barber,* 1895, plaster), figures from decorative fountain statuary, and diminutive reliefs. The entire display was anchored by busts of William T. Bull (1907, plaster) and Mme. Deckert de la Meillaie (1905, plaster). The photographs were framed or behind glass and laid flat on the table nearby as accessories to the installation.

Unfortunately, this memorial to Enid was short lived. The works were retired to an annex the following year and placed in storage. The key donor, Elsie Trask, was informed of this change, which was precipitated by the death of the museum's founder, Hattie Speed. What began as a memorial effort was denied an opportunity to fully flower.[11]

In addition, some errors crept into the historical record following this exhibition. For example, the sculpture referenced in the Speed catalogue as *Centaur and Centauress* (item 174) was improperly identified as by Enid Yandell instead of Gutzon Borglum, even though internal museum records indicated that the work was by Borglum. Thus, Enid was credited with a work that she had only owned, not created. Fortunately, this misinformation likely made little impact on Enid's reception: since the catalogue's erroneous mention of Enid's authorship, that work's attribution has been consistently correct.[12]

After the Speed exhibit in 1941, little attention was given to research on Enid and cultivation of her legacy. There were likely many other errors and misattributions over this period, from the initial Trask donation to the Speed until the first significant exhibition and research program devoted to Enid's life and work. That effort began in the late 1970s, as a result of the donation of one of Enid's works to the RISD Museum, which spawned additional scholarly undertakings back in Louisville, at the Filson Historical Society and again the Speed Museum.

Providence, Rhode Island: RISD Museum

The introduction of Enid's work to the collections of the Museum of Art at the Rhode Island School of Design in Providence came through an initial donation to the museum in 1976 by an alumna, Elizabeth Hazard, who gifted a bronze of Enid's *Kiss Tankard.* This act spurred a series of visits and conversations between Elsie Barber Trask, Enid's niece, and Christopher Monkhouse, the museum's Curator of Decorative Arts. In August of 1977, Monkhouse cultivated a relationship with Trask. He set aside time, resources, and space in the museum to bring attention to Trask's collection and promoted the museum as an appropriate context for Enid's work. In a letter to Trask, he wrote, "You had far more material pertaining to your Aunt, Enid Yandell[,] than I had ever imagined, and I agree with you that it would make an excellent project for a student to help you put it in order."[13]

The commitment by Monkhouse on behalf of the museum was an important step toward building Enid's legacy. Enid had contributed a significant work to the cultural landscape of the city of Providence: the Brown Memorial Fountain. Moreover, one of Enid's former students, Elizabeth "Betty" Hazard, was a RISD alumna, thereby forging tighter contemporary connections between the city of Providence and Enid's legacy. These efforts resulted in an exhibition, *Enid Yandell and the Branstock School,* which was on view at the RISD Museum from July 23 through August 29, 1982. As a result of the exhibition, nine items were donated to the museum, along with other relevant materials.[14]

The collection of works by Enid in the RISD Museum offers a breadth and depth of Enid's body of work, from embroidery and decorative arts to preparatory works and finished pieces in plaster and bronze. The media and genres that are familiar—the models for larger pieces and the profile

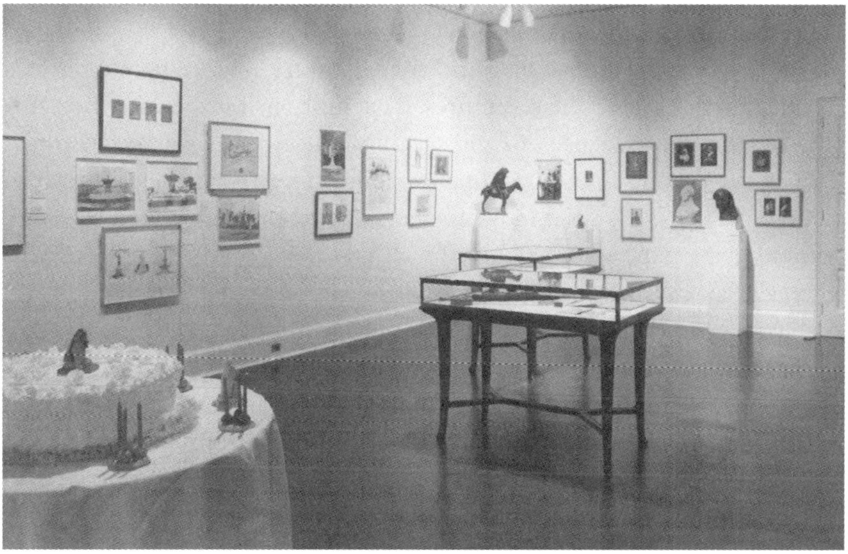

The main room in the 1982 RISD Museum exhibition on Enid and the Branstock School featured a number of sketches, photographs, and small works, including the *Birthday Beasts,* shown here at lower left. (RISD Museum, Providence, RI.)

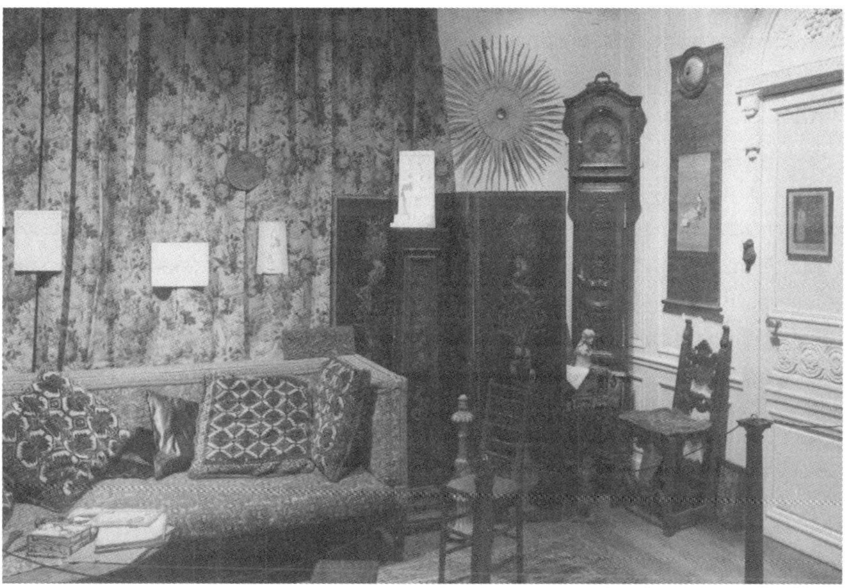

The side room in the 1982 exhibition simulated Enid's studio and home with a number of items that she had owned, including furniture. Her late Daniel Boone, *The Pioneer*, circa 1924, is on the pedestal in front of the grandfather clock at right. (RISD Museum, Providence, RI.)

reliefs that are the figureens reincarnated—were a large part of Enid's artistic practice; they were sculptures, by definition. Yet the collection also offers exemplary evidence of Enid's training in decorative arts and crafts. One of the works, a stunning linen embroidery of Art Nouveau rinceau and foliage forms done in moss and brown flosses, was created by Enid. Although the date is uncertain, it may have been stitched in the 1890s, when she would have encountered such works in Paris. Two hand towels are also part of this collection, identified as works "owned by Enid." One of these small linens has Enid's name in blue; another has her initials in green. Another work, a carved mahogany panel featuring a stylized thistle, identifiable by the urn-shaped flowerheads, transports us back in time—to Enid's earliest mentions of carving to Reuben Durrett and to her brother, Lunsford; and to her decorative work on columns and capitals for numerous buildings, including Louisville Trust in the 1890s. In this carved work in the museum's collection, the background has been roughed out, giving texture that contrasts with the pristine forms of the thistle leaves. The gift to the museum of these early, decorative arts created and/or owned by Enid revealed the importance of arts and crafts in the everyday, an approach that was bestowed upon her by her mother and that she embraced. The gift also reflected the nature of the receiving institution, with its focus on decorative arts and design.[15]

The research and installation of the exhibit was developed by the RISD Museum's Curator of Decorative Arts Christopher Monkhouse, along with Assistant Curator of Decorative Arts Tanya (Boyett) Barter; and Desiree Caldwell, "the student from Brown." The exhibit intended to recreate Enid's Paris studio through the presentation of sculpture and decorative arts by the artist, photographs, and works by contemporaries and students of Enid, including Mary Tarleton Knollenberg. The works were placed in one large room and a second, smaller, adjacent room in the museum. The catalogue accompanying the exhibition served more as a primer on Enid than an exhibition catalogue, offering Enid as "an instructive case study of one artist's interpretation of the conflicting stylistic tenets of the times. Her struggle for self-definition provides added insight into the dilemmas facing an increasingly large number of women who worked as professional sculptors during the pre–World War I period." Caldwell puts forth reasons to study Enid and to exhibit her work, recognizing her importance as a sculptor "in her own right and for her contribution to the advancement of women in sculpture." But she also truncated Enid's career with the war, writing that "this social work totally consumed her time and efforts. Enid's lack of attention to her career continued through the 1920s. By 1925, she apparently had ceased most sculpting. Early in 1934, her health began to fail; six months later she died at age 60." One aim of the present biography is to correct some errors, such as Enid's age at her death (she was sixty-four, not sixty) as well as to examine more closely her life within the context of her work as well as her artistic, cultural, and social milieu. This volume, therefore, moves beyond the preexisting frameworks in order to present a biographical narrative of Enid as self-defined and ambitious, an active agent in her own career. As has been shown throughout this volume, most accounts of the final twenty years of Enid's life fail to show the ways in which the field of sculpture had changed in the aftermath of war and also neglect the shift in Enid's sculptural output to make use of her home, studio, and school at Edgartown as well as the growing interest in decorative sculpture among the buying public.[16]

Louisville: The Filson Historical Society

The Filson Historical Society's role in Enid's legacy began with Enid herself, for she had found a mentor, historical advisor, and patron in Reuben Durrett, one of the key founders of the Filson in 1884 who also served as its first president. Letters between Enid and Durrett as well as initiatives he fostered, discussed in Chapter 1, facilitated Enid's efforts to become Kentucky's sculptor. Given the Filson's mission to collect, preserve, and tell the stories of the region, this institution was the likely home for materials related to Enid's life and work.

Yet the Filson was not among the initial recipients of materials related to Enid's work. Attention had been directed toward tending to Enid's artistic career by donating to art museums. After the initial donation in 1941 to the Speed, no other apparent activity was undertaken to cultivate Enid's legacy, either institutionally or personally, for approximately thirty-five years, when Elizabeth Hazard donated *Kiss Tankard* to RISD. This spurred Elsie Barber Trask to further action. Having found an institution that was interested in cultivating Enid's legacy, Elsie arranged to give some of her own sizable collection of Enid's work to the museum at RISD.[17]

This period—from 1941 to the 1980s—would see two donations to two museums; however, works alone cannot do justice to Enid's story. Despite significant loss of documents and other materials related to Enid's life that were stored at her grandmother's home in Nashville and subsequently lost, perhaps as part of the preparations to divest of material goods in order to sell the family estate in the 1920s, a portion of documents and materials from Enid's studio had been stored in Trask's home in Connecticut. They offered the possibility of building context for Enid's life—for giving a sense of who she was, how she operated, and the ways in which she navigated the nineteenth- and twentieth-century artistic, cultural, and social milieu.[18]

These items would serve two purposes: to benefit the museum at RISD as well as the work of Nancy Baird, historian and librarian at Western Kentucky University (WKU), home to the Kentucky Library. At RISD, the purpose of the efforts regarding Enid was to build out the context for the museum's 1982 exhibition. Meanwhile Baird, who had already completed seminal research on the Yandell family, reached out to the RISD Museum to ascertain the plan for these materials. Would the museum retain them? Could she access them for her article and anticipated full-length biography on Enid?[19]

What followed was a series of triangulated conversations and correspondence over several years (1977–1983) among Trask, Baird, and Monkhouse. Baird told Monkhouse and Trask on many occasions her intent to write a biography of Enid. In a note of February 15, 1982, to Elsie Trask, Baird wrote about a program that she had given about Enid at the Filson. In it, she "stressed Enid's Kentucky years and showed photos, etc. of statuary that is familiar to Kentuckians. Everyone seemed quite interested and encouraged the *immediate* publication of a biography of this Kentucky girl. I wish it was that easy to turn out a book!" In this letter, Baird also advocated for the deposition of Enid's letters to the Filson, an act for which Trask sought counsel from Monkhouse. It was not a question as to whether the letters either would or would not be donated—the question was where.[20]

With the agreement of all parties, most importantly Trask, two scrapbooks of materials were loaned to the RISD Museum and subsequently sent to the Smithsonian's Archives of American Art (AAA) New England Area Center in Boston to be microfilmed. Photographs from the collection were sent from the AAA to Nancy Baird for the Kentucky Library at WKU and for her research on Enid. RISD mounted its exhibition in 1982; and Baird finished her article, the seminal biographical account of Enid Yandell, in 1988. Her essay offered the first attempt to fulfill what historian Barbara Tuchman envisioned when she deemed biography a "prism of history" that engages "the universal in the particular." Baird's article is the starting point for every contemplation of Enid's life. Although she had anticipated completing a book on Enid, Baird ended up not doing so because she felt that "too many questions remained unanswered."[21]

Nevertheless, Baird's advocacy on behalf of the Filson paved the way so that letters, materials, and supplemental texts and source material owned by Enid were donated by Elsie Barber Trask to the Filson Historical Society in Louisville. The bulk of the Enid Yandell papers, totaling 105 folders, including several hundred letters, were mostly written to Enid by her mother and grandmother. They were catalogued and made available for the public in 1989, whereupon they joined two other collections of Yandell family papers at the Filson. These materials are now housed in the society's home in Old Louisville's Ferguson Mansion—a stone's throw from Enid's first studio in the family home on Broadway.[22]

Speed Art Museum, Part 2, 1993

In terms of the presentation of Enid's work and the contribution to scholarship, no single event matched the Speed's 1941 exhibit until 1993, when another exhibition was mounted at the Speed, accompanied by a publication. As was the case with the RISD exhibition of 1982, the Speed project was developed under the aegis of a university and one very devoted researcher, in this case the University of Louisville and Stephanie Darst. Darst's master's thesis from the University of Louisville, "Art's Bachelor Maid: The Sculpture of Enid Yandell," codified Enid's oeuvre by bringing together mentions of sculpture along with works in situ. Darst compiled a substantial, organized list of the works by Enid which, in turn, informed the curation and interpretation of Enid's works for an exhibition mounted at the Speed Museum. This exhibition included works from its collection as well as from the Filson Historical Society, Georgetown College, the Kentucky Historical Society, and the RISD Museum.[23]

Derived from Darst's thesis, *The Sculpture of Enid Yandell* was among the smaller exhibitions in the Speed Museum (with fewer than thirty pieces); however, its scholarly impact was significant. First, the exhibition was accompanied by an exhibition catalogue and catalogue raisonné—the first comprehensive listing of all the known works by the artist. This resource now serves as a starting point for most inquiries into Enid's work, even with its handful of errors and omissions. Second, the catalogue offered a chronological approach to Enid's work and career: the three periods of Enid's career described in the catalogue included her early years, 1869–1894; the peak of her career, including her years in Paris, 1895–1914; and later works and new directions, 1914–1934. The catalogue's introduction offered a rationale for the absence of women in the historical record: "Yandell and her female contemporaries have, until very recently, been 'lost' in the history of American art. Studies are now beginning to recognize the contributions of the women sculptors of the past. . . ." Darst categorized Enid as a "bachelor maid" and noted her ties to the state as a Kentucky sculptor. While little mention is made of Enid's work outside her artistic production, such as her philanthropic work related to World War I, especially her service in France, Darst did acknowledge a bit longer of a career than had Caldwell, stating that "by 1927, she had completely retired from sculpting."[24]

The Speed exhibition and catalogue came at an important moment, both from the perspective of Enid's career and that of the broader field of art history, in that they occurred one hundred years after Enid had made her mark at the Chicago World's Fair. The Speed's show was only the second retrospective exhibition held in celebration of Enid. Moreover, the publication and presentation of *The Sculpture of Enid Yandell* at the Speed and the catalogue "Enid Yandell and the Branstock School" at RISD bear witness to the importance of drawing attention to the work of artists whose names may have been "lost" to history.[25]

Beyond such explicit efforts, the past three decades in the field of art history have fostered the inclusion of works by Enid and other women artists in a number of museum exhibitions and publications. In 1978, three organizations collaborated to create a guide to sculpture in Louisville, and they included Enid among their listings. In *Who's Who of Cut, Cast, Carved: Biographical Sketches of Sculptors Whose Works Are Available for Public Viewing in Louisville, Kentucky,* the Filson Club, the Louisville Free

Public Library, and the Speed Museum offered information about various artists, including Enid, with a biographical listing giving her education, work history, exhibition, commissions, and associations. Enid's work has also been exhibited in several places. For instance, Enid's *The Gibson Girl, Elsie Yandell Barber* (1895, plaster) was shown in the exhibit *Kentucky Expatriates: Natives and Notable Visitors: The Early 1800s to the Present* (Owensboro Museum of Fine Art, Owensboro, Kentucky, 1984). *Kiss Tankard* was included in *Women in Art: Kentucky's Women Artists,* which ran at three venues: the Speed Museum; the Kentucky Museum in Bowling Green, Kentucky; and the Owensboro Museum of Fine Art in Owensboro from December 2001 through March 2002. In December 2001, the Filson Historical Society held a small exhibit that included photographs, personal items, and artwork, during which Nancy Baird presented an overview of Yandell's life in a public lecture. *Kiss Tankard* was also featured in the 2007 publication *The Speed Art Museum: Highlights from the Collection.*

Many other instances exist of such inclusion, and a full exhibition history would foster recognition of Enid's work while also paying heed to the work of scholars and museums in reintroducing the public to her works. But such an exercise would also serve to demonstrate the ways in which Enid's work, which was well known in its day, has suffered from neglect more through institutional and scholarly bias than through records that have been lost.

Feminist Interventions in Art History

In looking back at the recent developments in collection-building as well as scholarship related to Enid Yandell, these seemingly loosely connected episodes just described can be considered, in sum, a network of actions at a particular historical moment (1977–1993) that is in sync with broader interests in the field of art history. Indeed, the interest in organizing materials retained by Enid's niece, Elsie Barber Trask, and the coordination of an exhibit at the RISD Museum reflected professional decisions by a curator and an institution, as did the decisions of those involved with the thesis, exhibition, and catalogue at the University of Louisville and the Speed Museum respectively. It is important, however, to recognize where these contributions fall within the broader strokes of the discipline of art history and, in particular, the field of sculpture. The events described in this chapter may be interpreted as efforts to contribute to feminist knowledge production about Enid Yandell and the broader field of sculpture. Building upon these foundational acts, projects, and publications, this volume aims for the next rung on the ladder. Beyond adding to the existing narrative of male sculptors and inserting Enid into those narratives, this book seeks to reveal the limits and exclusions of art-historical discourse and museum practice in the twentieth and twenty-first centuries.

At about the time when Enid's niece was preparing to dissolve Enid's studio and take materials to RISD, art historian Linda Nochlin had called for a paradigm shift in the field of art history. In 1971, she published an article whose title asked a key question: "Why Have There Been No Great Women Artists?" Nochlin called for a close look at the way art historians had examined artists and their histories. She called for a reexamination, one that acknowledged that institutional frameworks (such as limited educational experiences including early encouragement, access to the nude, and apprenticeship) had prevented women from becoming "great" artists. Nochlin revealed that the elision of women was the result of institutional bias, not gender deficiency. With this framework, a new field of feminist art history was born, and with it the invitation to rediscover and reinstate women artists into the field of art history, a discipline that had neglected them.[26]

Numerous publications answered Nochlin's call for substantive scholarship devoted to women artists. In terms of recognizing the field of the "woman sculptor," a seminal publication, *The Fair Women* by Jeanne Madeline Weimann, scrupulously analyzed the story of the Woman's Building at the Chicago World's Fair in 1893. Published in 1981, Weimann's book opened the door to re-viewing women's contributions in the field of sculpture at the very fair where Enid played a role.[27]

Answering Nochlin's rallying cry and reinscribing women, however, are by themselves not sufficient for writing the history of Enid Yandell, for two reasons. First, Enid did have access to education, and she was encouraged by mentors, including Thomas S. Noble, one of her teachers at Cincinnati, who recommended her for the position at Chicago. She also had access to the nude through the art school there, and she served as an apprentice for Lorado Taft and others. So we might be inclined to respond to Nochlin's question with a simple response: "Oh! There was a great woman artist, and her name was Enid Yandell." In doing so, however, we would have to unravel the threads of a discipline in order to account for a resultant gap in knowledge from Enid's day to our own. Merely inserting Enid into a prescribed narrative would serve a reductive aim that maintains the masculinist narrative and only adds to it. It would yield a cosmetic addition that inevitably falls short. Whereas the aim in this book has been to understand the historical construction of sculpture—rather than "women's sculpture"—and to restore such a construction to the canon. So rather than merely inserting Enid back into the discourse of "women's sculpture," we must tend to history and resituate her within the field of sculpture generally, rather than women's sculpture.

The second reason to go beyond Nochlin's call is to have the opportunity to rethink what art history is and how it operates. Such an approach is in keeping with the work of art historian Griselda Pollock, who called for a reinvention of process in suggesting that merely pointing out discrimination against women and redressing the omission of women becomes a negative enterprise that yields correction and improvement as its only objectives. By inscribing Pollock's vision as the approach taken in this volume, the chapters have aimed to ask how history is written and why it is recorded in that way. Pollock and Rozsika Parker acknowledged that "to discover the history of women and art is in part to account for the way art history is written. To expose its underlying values, its assumptions, its silences and its prejudices is also to understand that the way women artists are recorded is crucial to the definition of art and artist in our society." To write such a narrative is to write the history of women practitioners, such as Enid, and to interrogate the representation of gender difference historically, from Enid's day to our own. Such an approach proffers intersectionality through its making visible what had been invisible as a historical category of analysis, by viewing gender through the lens of work and, in particular, Enid's adoption of an occupational identity as a pioneer. This allows us to go beyond Nochlin's characterization to include institutional frameworks—such as museum collection-building and narrative histories—that have also prevented women from becoming "great" artists.[28]

Around the same time as art historians were constructing narratives of women, the call to construct feminist biography in the academic discipline of history came from historian Gerda Lerner, who redefined the discipline in a number of ways, including the creation of the first doctorate program in US women's history. In a talk to her (majority male) colleagues at the American Historical Association in 1987, Lerner urged scholars to take a "more feminist approach to women's lives, using the new feminist scholarship" in other disciplines so as to enable biographers the room to analyze periods within the context of circles of women, rather than women in tandem with men. She called upon scholars to write broadly—about how one's private and public life intersects and the impact of relationships with women, as well as "familial and female friendship networks that sustained women's public activities," including work, and the "mental product of women's lives, their ideas, their writings, and their discourse." Likewise, Joan Scott and myriad historians and humanists who have since followed Lerner's groundbreaking presentation to the American Historical Association in 1987, positioned gender as a site where lines of thought converged. Such "feminist interventions" have enabled us to reconfigure historical knowledge from within a feminist perspective and to go beyond merely inserting Enid into the narrative of her times.[29]

Enid as Homage, Inspiration, and Brand

To further explicate Enid's legacy, let us turn from collection building and presentation by museums and scholars to the world of makers and the public at large. Here we might consider Enid Yandell as a homage, inspiration, and brand. This brand identity is best exemplified through the formation in 1998 of the eponymous artist collective ENID—Generations of Women Sculptors. Enid has also inspired other creative endeavors, from artwork and creative writing to entrepreneurial foodstuffs.

ENID—Generations of Women Sculptors

The Louisville, Kentucky–based collective of female artists known as ENID—Generations of Women Sculptors was founded in 1998, one hundred years after Enid Yandell was elected to the National Sculpture Society. As a membership group of accomplished sculptors who range in age from thirties to nineties and who are based in the Ohio Valley region (Enid's homeland), ENID organizes exhibits to showcase its members' commitment to the field and to demonstrate what it takes to have an active studio practice and to exhibit as a contemporary artist today. The members

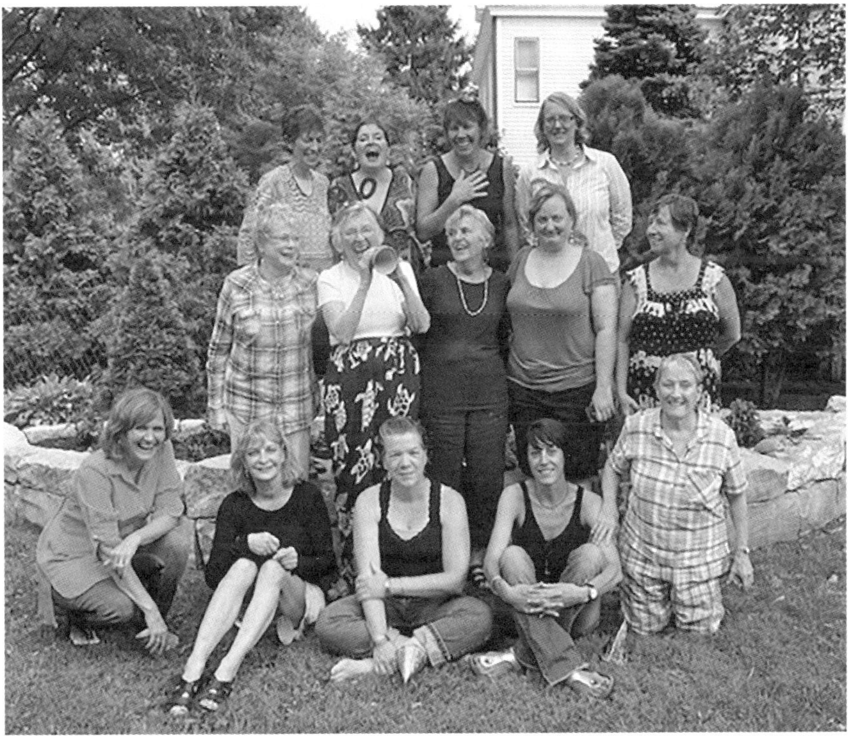

ENID—Generations of Women Sculptors, group photo on Ewing Fahey's ninetieth birthday in 2012. Front row (left to right): Valerie Sullivan Fuchs, Gayle Cerlan, Melinda Walters, Shawn Marshall, Jeanne Deuber; middle row (left to right): Jacque Parsley, Ewing Fahey, Sarah Frederick, Cynthia Reynolds, Suzanne Mitchell; back row (left to right): Gloria Wachtel, Elizabeth Kirkwood, Joyce Ogden, Caren Cunningham. The collective was formed in 1998, one hundred years after Enid joined the National Sculpture Society, as one of the organization's first women. (Photo by Mary Swain. Courtesy of ENID.)

of the collective also range in terms of their introduction and education in sculpture—from self-taught to those with advanced degrees; from artists who choose to work only in sculpture to those who also engage in other art forms. They also approach sculpture variously, in terms of medium, form, and content. In short, their "common thread is their support for one another as artists."[30]

While their selection of Enid's name as their namesake may seem obvious, consider that the group was founded in the middle years of collection building that fostered Enid's legacy. The name for the group came to Ewing Fahey, one of the founding members. Fahey recalls that she was "driving on an expressway one day . . . [when] Enid Yandell sprang to mind—and I went straight to the Filson [Historical Society] to see what they had on her. Got Nancy Baird's excellent bio." This brief explanation speaks to the way in which Enid has become associated with Kentucky and its history through the Filson, and vice versa.[31]

With its name established, the organization was forged with a mission to "encourage, educate, and mentor women artists, students, and each other, as well as to promote the careers of [their] members." In January 1998, ENID was formally established, members were solicited, and the membership began to grow. The group met socially at regular intervals; over time, the meetings became "more purposeful" toward the goal of organizing their first exhibition at the end of 1999. In commenting on that exhibition, curator Albertus Gorman saw a certain symmetry in the span from Enid's day to the establishment of ENID a century later. He noted: "Yandell, and the fifteen women included in this exhibition, can be seen as bookends at the beginning and end of the 20th century. Yandell is the lone female sculptor from Louisville at the beginning of the century. Today, fifteen women from Louisville join together to celebrate their accomplishments in the field." The reception to ENID's first exhibition was noteworthy. According to Ewing Fahey (the resident nonagenarian), it was the "biggest turnout they'd ever had [at the gallery]—they even ran out of wine and food."[32]

The geographical framework, focus on sculpture, and age range of ENID then was similar to its current formulation, although the top age has grown to accommodate the oldest member, who was in her seventies when the group began and is now in her nineties. If, by definition, a brand is a carefully manicured presentation and perception of a person or thing in visual and verbal terms and is used for myriad purposes, the interlocution of past and present with ENID offers an instructive case study of how an artist's life, work, and legacy can foster a new identity.

Having adopted Enid Yandell's name as the name of their group, ENID is a collective born out of Enid. Its members have embraced Enid's art form, work ethic, and commitment to the profession of sculpture. Individually, each member of the group functions like an amoeba that extends itself to the farthest reaches and in time circles back to its anchor. They extend by themselves and come back to the center for learning, insight, and encouragement. In so doing, each of them is a contributing member of the group, equally engaged in her own sphere. Outside of the work of the collective, the group is an integral part of its namesake's legacy. In fact, they identify with Enid by name, calling themselves "Enids."[33]

Other Media: Painting, Quilting, Plays, and Foodways

Enid's reach extends beyond sculpture. In 2011, for example, a contemporary art gallery in Berlin managed an exhibition about women's rules (or, more specifically, rules that women were subjected to) during the Victorian era. An artist by the name of Lady Shove exhibited calling cards of nine women from the era. The card dedicated to Enid was positioned among eight other women of varying professions and levels of fame, including Jane Austen, Emily Dickinson, and Georgia O'Keeffe, among others. While the artist's reason for selecting Enid is unclear, it is important to recognize that Enid's reach extends to gallery work as far away as Berlin—a place where Enid's work was never exhibited.[34]

In the vein of homage, but closer to the Bluegrass State, a quilt in the collection of the Kentucky Historical Society shows how Enid and other women inspire others. The quilt was created in 2001–2002 in a women's studies class at Lincoln County Adult Education. The students wanted to learn about Kentucky women and chose to display their knowledge through the creation of a quilt to which all members of the class contributed. The quilt included twenty-eight biographical portraits presented on fourteen white blocks, each with two computer-generated iron transfers with an image and name for each woman. Among those depicted are women of Enid's day, including herself and Julia Dinsmore, in addition to contemporary women, such as actress Ashley Judd, author Barbara Kingsolver, and others. About this work, the artists stated, "We made the quilt as a class project. We incorporated math, research, computer usage and everyone's creativity to learn about great women of the world and ourselves." While none of the quilters mentioned Enid specifically, the sculptor's legacy seems to continue through the women's working with their hands in a domestic art form that has a long history with women as makers.[35]

In addition, Nancy Gall-Clayton wrote a short play in 2000 inspired by the life of Enid Yandell, as well as fellow Louisvillan Bertha Honoré

Palmer (1849–1918) and Julia Dent Grant (1826–1902). *Yes, I Cut Marble, Mrs. Grant* offers a debate on the "proper role" of women in 1891 by situating three generations—a sculptor in her twenties embarking on a career, a middle-aged activist-philanthropist and organizer of the woman's efforts at the World's Fair, and the aging widow of President Grant. The play is set in Chicago in the two years leading up to the opening of the World's Fair, at the home of Bertha Honoré Palmer, around the time when the memorial to Ulysses S. Grant is unveiled in 1891. This setting parallels Enid's own writing in her 1892 fictionalized account *Three Girls in a Flat.*[36]

The play characterizes generational differences among the three women amidst all of the newness of the fair, from the mundane to the spectacular, including humorous accounts of the Ferris Wheel, which debuted at the Chicago fair. Gall-Clayton presents Enid as an ambitious and energetic artist who announces her abilities in cutting marble (which necessitated muscles that might also be used to beat biscuit). Details about Enid's life are interwoven with an interpretive lens in their handling. For instance, Enid's interest in studying with Rodin is expressed to Bertha and Julia within the fuller context of studying the nude. Such study was inconceivable in Julia's generation but was an accepted part of educational practice by Enid's. The mention of nudes leads Julia to swoon, Bertha to call for a servant, and Enid to wave smelling salts under Julia's nose. After this episode, for which Enid apologizes, Julia acknowledges that times have changed: "The 20th century is just around the corner, and I must catch up, I suppose." The humor turns to advocacy when Enid questions the naming of the exhibition in honor of Christopher Columbus, saying that perhaps it should be cast in honor of Mary Cassatt, whose works were on view in the Woman's Building, or in honor of Mr. Ferris. This conversation then leads to the proposal of a holiday for women. Enid says, "I propose a holiday for all women. Rich or poor. Married or not." By virtue of the fact that Julia Grant insisted that she could only swoon once per day, by the play's end, the three women leave together, mulling over this idea.[37]

In Gall-Clayton's hands, *Yes, I Cut Marble, Mrs. Grant* is richly detailed, with facts that seep through the narrative in an effortless way. We learn, for example, that Enid is the first Yandell woman to earn her own money, and we are given a description of a monumental sculpture, Chicago's memorial to Ulysses S. Grant, in a manner that conveys the aspirations of a younger sculptor looking upon the work of her former Art Academy teacher (Louis T. Rebisso). Such passages skillfully weave together what we know about Enid's life and work with language to illustrate her life experiences, even in areas where little or no letters or correspondence exists. For instance, Enid describes the caryatids as "support[ing] the roof garden of the Woman's Building" and Chicago (as female) welcoming "us all," referring to the artists and writers of important causes. In its weaving together of facts with humor and narrative, *Yes, I Cut Marble, Mrs. Grant* contributes to Enid's legacy by reinterpreting her in a new medium for new audiences.[38]

A third example of Enid's legacy reaching beyond sculpture involves foodways—or, more aptly, foodie culture on an international scale, as developed by a food entrepreneur out of Louisville.

Founded in 2012 by Stanley Chase III, the Louisville Vegan Jerky Company introduced a series of vegan barbequed tofu (coined "jerky"), named after local individuals, mainly famous men. Each individual was the inspiration for a particular flavor of jerky, and the entire enterprise emphasizes "Louisville-centric people," in the words of Chase. For instance, Pete's Bourbon Smoked Black Pepper was inspired by a historic baseball player, Pete Browning of the Louisville Colonels. Tod's Smoked Chipotle was inspired by Tod Browning, director of the original movie *Dracula*. Chase stated that after the company introduced the first flavor, he had to go exploring further into Louisville culture. Fortunately for Chase, he did not have to go much further than his front door. He lived in the shadow of the Daniel Boone statue in Cherokee Park, but he never knew who created it. After seeing it for a decade and passing it without thinking much about it, he suspected that most other people don't know about its history, either. He researched the sculpture and realized it was created by Enid Yandell.

According to Chase, "We tried to imagine the time that she was alive, and from everything I have ever read about her, [she was] amazing." The result of this homage to Enid was the company's Sriracha Maple flavor, which was billed as a staff favorite with that "perfect balance of sugar and spice," made with local maple syrup and organic sriracha. The flavor has recently been reinvented as Perfect Pepperoni, and it still bears Enid's name and likeness. (Other flavors include Reuben's Smokey Carolina BBQ, inspired by Reuben Durrett, and Paulette's Maple Bacon, which was inspired by Chase's mother.) Regardless of the flavor, for Chase, the

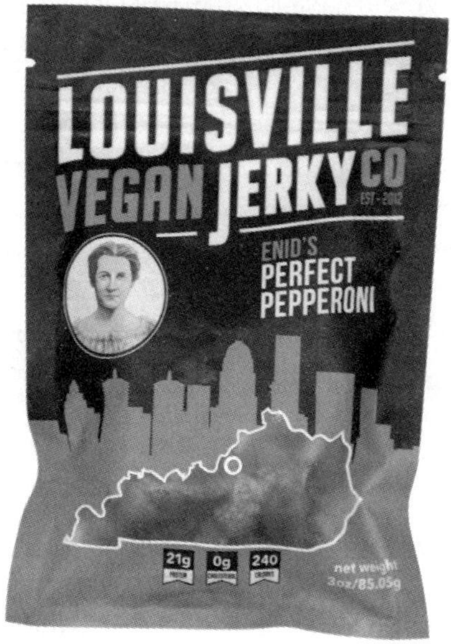

Founded in 2012 by Stanley Chase III, the Louisville Vegan Jerky Company introduced a series of vegan barbequed tofu. One of the flavors is "Enid's Perfect Pepperoni," shown here. This flavor was introduced in 2018 as a follow-up to "Enid's Sriracha Maple." (Artist: Dick Starr. Courtesy of Louisville Vegan Jerky

adoption of Enid as a brand and the entire enterprise is about foodie culture and its intersection with history. Information about each historical person is included on the packaging so that the branding and marketing coalesce. In Enid's case, the flavor pays heed to "the world-famous Louisville sculptor and unstoppable social activist, Enid Yandell. We think this outrageous flavor is way ahead of its time." The image of Enid on the bag of jerky was inspired by history, but is a pioneering effort: it was hand-drawn based on photographs and line drawings of Enid that appeared in the *Louisville Courier-Journal* and elsewhere. While perhaps a niche or even gourmet item, the vegan jerky is widely available in Louisville and beyond, including at Amazon.com, thus connecting Enid's legacy with a much broader audience in an unusual way.[39]

Part of the Everyday Experience: Banners and Boones

The coalescence of past and present seems most apparent in a second cast of Enid's Daniel Boone (cast in 1906 and replicated subsequently), as well as the historical marker about Enid sited in Louisville and the debut of a "Hometown Heroes" banner at Seventh and Main Street in downtown Louisville in the spring of 2019.

From the 1890s to today, much of Enid's identity is tied to her initial world's fair creation, the statue of Daniel Boone. As described earlier, given the scarcity of portraiture of Boone, Enid examined books and materials from Reuben Durrett's collection, where she found clothing, as well as Collins's narrative, particularly useful to her construction of Boone in three dimensions. With her initial sculpture in 1893 and its subsequent casts, as well as its eventual translation into bronze—all of which repeat the form that she first conceived for the World's Fair in Chicago—Enid accomplished a crowd-pleasing portrait for posterity. In contrast to much of the fair work that she and the other "White Rabbits" created, which came down as swiftly as it had risen, Enid's Boone lasted, widened her celebrity, and propelled her to the front ranks of sculpture. Boone, as much as Enid, became platforms for infinite inspirations.

While Fess Parker captured American television viewers' attention with his interpretation of Daniel Boone from 1964–1970, a bronze replica of Enid's Daniel Boone was being planned for the lawn in front of the Keen Johnson Building on the campus of Eastern Kentucky University in Richmond, Kentucky. This initiative was part of a broader initiative of the president of the university, Dr. Robert Martin, who wanted "to emphasize Boone's close ties with the Richmond area," namely its proximity to Boonesboro (the fort Boone built for settlers) and the national forest that also bore his name (formerly the Cumberland National Forest, renamed Boone in 1966).[40]

At the unveiling of the replica of Enid's Boone sculpture on the campus on May 3, 1967, noted historian Dr. Thomas D. Clark noted that Boone's history was intertwined with that of Kentucky: "We should look upon Daniel Boone as a symbol of courage, optimism, and belief in this land." Very shortly after the statue's dedication, a tradition was born: It is said that if a student rubs the statue's toe, the student will have good luck. And after fifty years of wishful rubbings, the tip of one of Daniel's high moccasins reveals a sheen that could never have been imagined by Enid when she created the initial staff version for the Kentucky Building at the Chicago World's Fair in 1892. As alumnus Jerry Miller (class of 1998) stated, "I rubbed that toe every chance I got. Now that we have three children, we've taught them the same tradition when we go back to campus." In addition, remembering Boone has been part of the international social media campaigns of "Throwback Thursday" or "#tbt", an

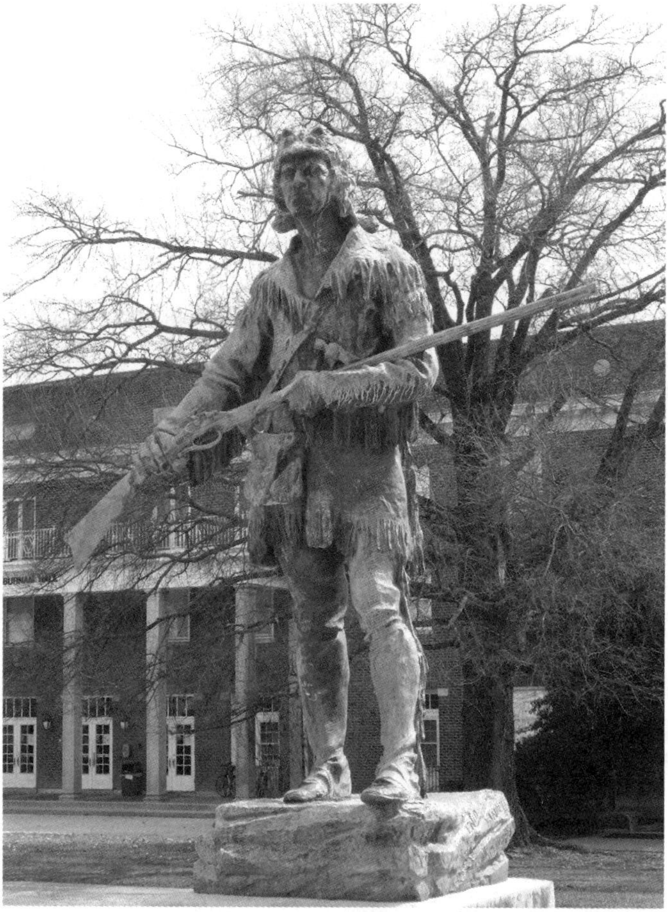

A replica of Enid's sculpture of Daniel Boone was installed in 1967 on the campus of Eastern Kentucky University in Richmond, Kentucky. Soon after its dedication, a tradition was born: if a student rubs the statue's toe, the student will have good luck. (Enid Yandell, Daniel Boone, originally created 1892, cast in 1967, Eastern Kentucky University, Richmond, KY. Photo taken in March 2013 by the author.)

initiative of archives, museums, and libraries, promoting historical collections. At EKU, the sharing of images of Daniel Boone and other campus landmarks and history through platforms such as Instagram brings the heritage of tradition and ritual into twenty-first-century practice, and in doing so connects Enid's works with daily modern life.[41]

Enid herself was memorialized in bronze, a favorite medium of hers, through placement of a historical marker in 2004. The marker is located in Louisville at the intersection of Cherokee Road and Cherokee Park Road, just a few feet away from her bronze of Daniel Boone, cast in 1906 (though based upon her 1892 rendition for the Chicago World's Fair). As one of more than 2,400 markers in the state that recognize people, places, and events, this marker offers an abbreviated biography, meeting the parameters of the program. It was erected as the result of a collaboration among two groups and two descendants of the sculptor. In its succinct rendering of Enid's biography and her importance to the field of sculpture, the marker broadcasts Enid's place in Louisville history, Kentucky history, and art history.[42]

In 2019, Enid was added to the Louisville Hometown Heroes initiative, a campaign begun in 2002 to encourage pride in the city through the unveiling of banners depicting athletes on facades of buildings citywide. Since its inception, with the unveiling of a banner honoring professional boxer and activist Muhammed Ali (1942–2016), twenty-eight vinyl banners have been created, with a handful of others to be added in 2019, the program's final year. The purpose of the project is quite clear, and in keeping with the legacy building that this chapter addresses. According to Rebecca Matheny, the Louisville Hometown Heroes executive director, the initiative "has given us an opportunity to introduce important Louisville figures to the public who otherwise might have remained largely unknown." Enid is on display, figuratively, as part of a slate of professionals, including television journalist Diane Sawyer (b. 1945), actress Jennifer Lawrence (b. 1990), and sculptor Ed Hamilton (b. 1947). She is indeed a part of everyday life in Louisville, just as she is a part of the experience of students on the campus of Eastern Kentucky University (EKU), thanks to the efforts of their university president five decades ago.[43]

This variety of intersections between past and present clearly connects Enid with today's artistic, social, and cultural milieu. Such connections are on the broad scale, such as her sculpture of Daniel Boone (cast in 1906 and replicated subsequently), the historical marker on her in Louisville, and the "Hometown Heroes" banner erected in the city of Louisville in honor of Enid's 150th birthday in 2019. Celebrations of Enid also include new creations, works created in homage to Enid as well as commercial products that bear her name and likeness.

Enid Yandell, Kentucky's Pioneer Artist

This study of Enid Yandell's life and work is the result of the contributions of many artists and scholars. The efforts by the RISD Museum (and a student researcher and faculty at Brown University) and the Speed Museum of Art (as well as students and faculty at the University of Louisville) catalyzed these efforts. Such aligned endeavors between museums and universities signify the symbiotic relationship of university scholarship and museum exhibitions, which in turn feeds further research. Such endeavors are supplemented by generous collection-building efforts that bring awareness about artists such as Enid to the public, who view exhibitions and who learn about these artists through the work on view and the scholarly interpretation presented at museums. Moreover, the stewardship of the Filson Historical Society, the Speed Museum, the RISD Museum, and to a much smaller degree the Martha's Vineyard Museum has made it possible for scholars, the public, and museums to develop interest in, and cultivate scholarship surrounding, the life and work of Enid Yandell. Such activities were made possible by the visionary leadership of Elsie Barber Trask, who realized that her Aunt Enid led an incredible life, managed a successful career, and contributed meaningfully to advocacy and activism, in keeping with her support of women's rights in political affairs and the human condition. In addition to Trask's heroic endeavors, the efforts of scholars such as Christopher Monkhouse and Nancy Baird, as well as staff at institutions such as the RISD Museum, the Speed Museum, and the Filson, deserve credit for seeing the potential in acquiring works by, and materials related to, Enid and for making these available to the public.

These endeavors are supported, continued, and brought into the everyday through the work of legacy builders such as ENID—Generations of Women Sculptors and other contemporary artists, including Lady Shove, the quilt makers from the women's studies class at Lincoln County Adult Education, and playwright Nancy Gall-Clayton. Enid has also served as an inspiration for entrepreneur turned civic booster Stanley Chase III, who has fostered interest in Enid through foodways. In public modes of display—perhaps more akin to Enid's earliest endeavors at world's fairs—Enid's legacy lives on through the large banner in the Seventh and Main Street area of downtown Louisville (at a location not far from where Enid grew up) and the replica of her Daniel Boone sculpture that welcomes visitors to the Eastern Kentucky University campus, and the bronze marker celebrating her in Cherokee Park.

In sum, these collective actions, as well as the present work, have enabled us, on Enid's 150th birthday, to have a greater understanding of her life, work, and legacy by focusing on her contributions to the field, by re-viewing her within the context of the era of which she was a part, and by demonstrating how Enid Yandell was truly a pioneer.

Postscript

In Memory of Enid Yandell

The following verses were found in a strongbox by Elsie Trask after her Aunt Enid's death. They were written by one of Enid's friends a few years earlier after a September gale, and appeared in the *Vineyard Gazette* on October 12, 1934, a few days after what would have been Enid's sixty-fifth birthday. The initials identify the author as Molly W. Butler—Islander, daughter of William Butler, and friend of Enid's.

THE BRANSTOCK

No native knew how many years
The wonderful old tree had lived.
They only knew it had survived,
In sun and rain,
Far, far beyond the memory
Of any man now living
In the town.
And when one night
In a tumultuous gale,
With a groan that sounded
Like the breaking of a gallant heart,
A great branch crashed to the earth,
The hearts of all the village
Seemed broken with it.
For nearly half of the famous tree
Was in that glorious branch;
And it seemed that no one
Could save what was left.
But a tree surgeon came,—

A man, humble but cunning,—
And after painstaking hours
With cement and saws and infinite toil,
The old tree still stood
With crest undaunted tho' robbed
Of much of its beauty.

Some said, "Oh, cut it down!
Its beauty is gone and well nigh
All its shade."
But the gentle owner with a shake
Of her lovely head, made answer,—
"Oh foolish ones, that tree
Has sheltered sleeping babes and laughing children
Beneath its boughs, all silvered by the moonbeams,
Lovers have pledged their vows;
And the old have pressed their withered cheeks
Against the bark and murmured,
'You know, old tree, you know'!
Its head is in the air,
Its roots are in my heart;
And it shall live within my garden
Until I pass beyond.
And it may be that when some day
My form is silently borne
Adown the path and out the gate forever,
When I no more may look on it with love,—
The dear old tree will know,
And all its leaves and twigs will tremble
In an ecstasy of long farewell."

M.W.B.

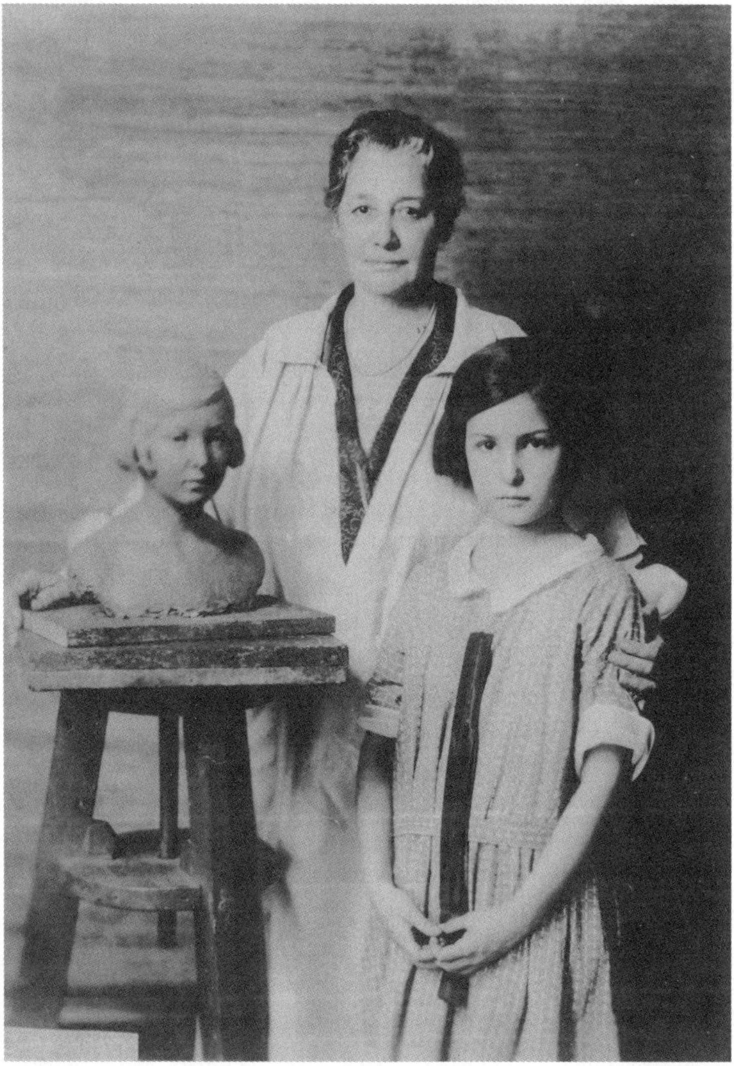

Enid and Molly Butler in Enid's studio around 1924, with a bust of Molly to the left. As the daughter of William Butler, Molly knew Enid from a young age, and the two became friends. She wrote a poem in Enid's honor, and memorialized the aged tree in Enid's yard. The poem takes its cues from the logo Enid used for her eponymous school in Edgartown. (Enid Bland Yandell Photograph Collection, 987PC52X.026, Box 1, Folder 6. The Filson Historical Society, Louisville, KY.)

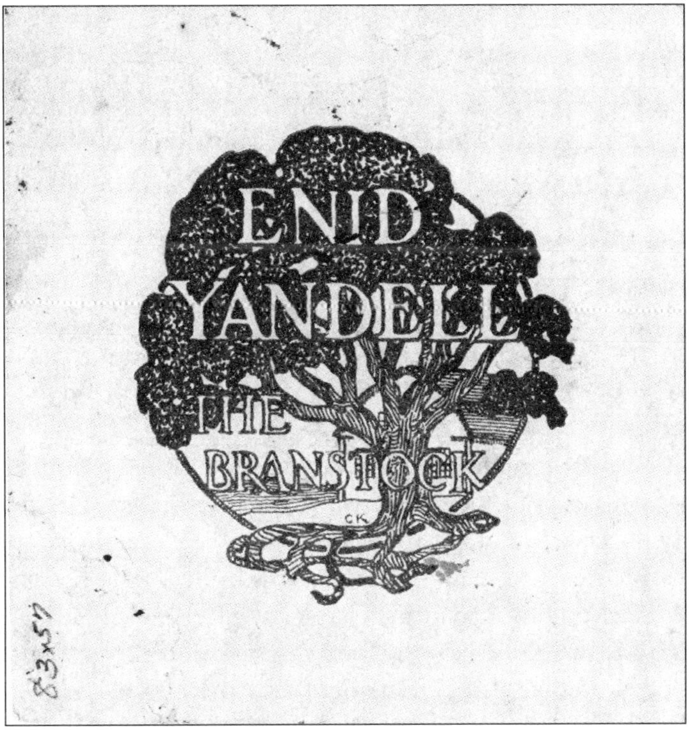

This logo for the Branstock, Enid's art school in Edgartown, draws upon both nature and the built environment in its depiction of the large tree in Enid's yard and (behind it) the silhouette of her studio. Enid's rationale for use of the name "Branstock" is not explained in any extant documentation; however, given Enid's lifelong love of the theatre, including opera, it is likely that the name came from Richard Wagner's *The Ring of the Nibelung*, in which Branstock was a sacred tree that had healing and magical powers. Perhaps Enid was channeling that capacity for her arts colony, which was established under the bough of a large tree. (Enid Yandell Papers, Mss A/Y21b, Folder 74. The Filson Historical Society, Louisville, KY.)

Acknowledgments

Writing this biography of Enid Yandell has truly been a collaborative endeavor. First and foremost, I want to thank the community of Enidophiles, whose admiration, respect, and championing of Enid's life and work have made this journey more enjoyable than I had ever imagined it could be. Chief among these are two of Enid's relatives, David Yandell Wood and Carter Wood Sartor, whom I first met for pimento cheese at Wagner's Pharmacy. Related to Enid through the line of her uncle, Dr. David Wendel Yandell, David and Carter have been incredibly helpful and have reminded me how lovely and close the Yandell family must have been in Enid's day. Thanks also to relatives Wendy Bell, Diana Fisher, Yandell Wood, Pitts Yandell, and Hope Yandell. Beyond the family, numerous individuals who are fans of Enid's works or who admire her persistence and her ambition reminded me on countless occasions that crafting a story about Enid, while an incredibly challenging task, was a worthy one: our understanding of Enid was incomplete because a number of her works were ephemeral, although they were widely proclaimed in accounts of her day. Faced with this challenge and the desire to sculpt a legacy for Enid, I realized that it is through her work, its critical reception, and its presence in museum collections that her story could emerge.

Building Enid's story was made possible through archival and other primary research. I am grateful to the following individuals and institutions for their insight and kind assistance. Foundational research was conducted at the Filson Historical Society in Louisville, Kentucky, which holds the largest repository of documents, materials, and ephemera related to Enid's life and work. This project was greatly facilitated by Jim Holmberg, Heather Potter, and Jennie Cole, each of whom was generous with both time and expertise. In particular, Jim offered generous counsel on the contours—or, rather, the peculiarities—of how to contextualize Louisville and the region. In addition, Heather evidenced Enid's determination as she worked for more than a year alongside a team of individuals from institutions in Louisville to create a series of collaborative events in celebration of Enid's 150th birthday. I am truly grateful for the effort by everyone involved in developing and presenting this series of events, "Enid Yandell: A Life of Art and Activism," which kicked off in March 2019 with the unveiling of a "Hometown Hero" banner of Enid in downtown Louisville on the Harbison Building at the corner of Seventh and Main Streets. I am thrilled to see the events continue throughout 2019 and into early 2020 as a means of celebrating and remembering Kentucky's pioneer sculptor.

Beyond the Filson, my work was made possible by the generosity of library, archive, and museum professionals throughout Kentucky, the South, and further afield. At the Speed Museum, Chuck Pittenger, Lisa Rolfe, and Kim Spence greatly enhanced my understanding of the relationship between Enid's work, its familial legacy, and connections with Hattie Speed. I am grateful to each of them for entertaining my numerous questions, guiding me around museum storage, and facilitating new photography from the museum's collections for this book. Thanks are also due to Erika Holmquist-Wall and Johna Ebling of the Speed Museum for their work and commitment to developing an exhibition focused on Enid.

My understanding of Enid's journeys through northern Kentucky was enriched by conversations with Cathy Collopy of the Dinsmore Homestead. In addition, at the Kentucky Historical Society, thanks are due to Beth Carter, registrar, and Deborah Rose VanHorn (formerly of the society). For information related to Enid's works in the collections of the Kentucky Historical Society that were undergoing treatment, thanks are due to Christina Simms from McKay Lodge Fine Arts Conservation. Sandy Baird, of the Bolton Archives and Special Collections at Georgetown College, provided kind and thorough assistance to contextualize one work by Enid in Georgetown's collection and went a step further in helping me build out the role of that bust in the broader narratives of place. At Vanderbilt University, thanks are due to Teresa Gray and Henry Shipman, who provided information about the bust of Chancellor Landon Cabell Garland.

My understanding of the context for the Chicago World's Fair and Enid's years in that city was aided by the expert staff of the Ryerson &

Burnham Libraries at the Art Institute of Chicago as well as The Newberry. At Martha's Vineyard Museum, I am grateful for the assistance of research librarian Bow van Riper, who kindly oriented me to maps, guidebooks, photographs, postcards, and, of course, Enid's work. At Watch Hill, Ardi Schneider conversed with me under the gazebo so near Enid's sculpture of Chief Ninigret and reminded me of this sculpture's long journey, as well as the way in which it is emblematic of its honoree, Clement Griscom, and the spirit of this seaside town. At Rhode Island School of Design Museum, thanks are due to Joe Leduc and Jac Parker, who gave me unfettered access to curatorial files and collections, and to Sionan Guenther, who fostered the creation of digital surrogates of Enid's works as part of the museum's open-access initiative. Also in Providence, research on the Brown family was aided by Karen Eberhart at Brown University, while the staff of the Providence City Archives and the Rhode Island Historical Society proved delightfully helpful.

Assistance in my research on Enid and in locating related materials was kindly provided by Heather Fox and her colleagues at the University of Louisville Archives and Special Collections; Jim Birchfield, former Special Collections Curator of Rare Books at the University of Kentucky (and a wonderful storyteller); Jonathan Jeffrey, Department of Library Special Collections, Western Kentucky University; Geoff Edwards, Cincinnati Art Museum; Trudy J. Hanmer, Associate Head Emerita, Emma Willard School, Troy, New York; Christine M. Beauregard, Senior Librarian, Manuscripts and Special Collections, New York State Library and Archives, Albany; and the staff of the Archives of American Art, Smithsonian Institution. For insight regarding women sculptors of the day and technical process, thanks to Greg L. Mueller, Mueller Studio, LLC, and Tom Podnar, senior conservator of sculpture, McKay Lodge Art Conservation Laboratory, Oberlin, Ohio.

I am grateful to the staff of the aforementioned and other institutions who kindly provided help to me as I sought particular threads from which to weave together this narrative. A full list of repositories is listed in the bibliography.

Thanks are also due to all those who spoke about Enid with me, including all of the women who are a part of ENID—Generations of Women Sculptors, particularly Caren Cunningham, Valerie Sullivan Fuchs, Joyce Ogden, Mary Dennis Kannapell, and of course Ewing Fahey; Stanley

Chase, founder of Louisville Vegan Jerky Company; playwright Nancy Gall-Clayton; and Mark Weatherington, former director of the Filson Historical Society, who offered feedback on my research early on and continued to express interest in my project. Architect and historian Steve Wiser provided critical insight on a number of topics, including Enid's neighborhood and 1890s Louisville streetscapes. In addition, thoughts on gender, identity, and place were offered by friends Karen Gillenwater, Laura Stewart, and Boris Zakić. Hospitality was kindly offered by my "Kentucky family": Ellen, Barbara and Stewart, Cliff, Kristin, Karyn, and Doug, as well as Glenn and Tracy.

Collectors Warren and Julie Payne were extremely generous with their time and expertise, helping me understand the place of Enid's work in the broader context of tabletop statuary, figurines, and related artwork. They gave me unfettered access to their collections and provided images and information to help build out my narrative. They have also peppered my email in-box with discoveries and observations, which helped make this book project all the more a conversation rather than a work in isolation.

All these conversations and interactions helped me translate my research into book form. Before writing this manuscript, I gave a number of presentations on Enid and her occupational identity, particularly as it related to the commission for Louisville's Confederate monument. I am grateful to have shared my work through conversations at the March 2012 Civil War Symposium at the University of Louisville; a 2012 presentation at the Filson Historical Society following my fellowship there; a 2013 talk at the University of Louisville, in conjunction with the ENID exhibition; a 2013 appearance at the Cressman Center for the Arts; a lecture in 2014 at Transylvania University, Lexington, Kentucky, as part of Transylvania's Gender Awareness Week; and a discussion in 2016 at Seneca Falls, New York, as part of a session at the Seneca Falls Dialogues, "Work as Empowerment."

I have also shared my research on Enid and the broader narratives of Confederate identity construction as part of National Endowment for the Humanities opportunities, including "The Legacy of the Civil War: Changing Memories over Time," held at Virginia Commonwealth University, Richmond (June and July 2016); and "Torn Within, Threatened Without: Kentucky and the Border States in the Civil War," in conjunction with the Kentucky Historical Society (June and July 2013).

In addition, thanks are due to the staff of the Johnson Collection, Spartanburg, South Carolina, who invited me in 2016 to contribute a brief biography of Enid and a longer essay for an exhibition and publication on Southern artists, *Central to Their Lives: Southern Women Artists in the Johnson Collection*. Having the opportunity to write about Enid and to consider her within the context of two other women sculptors (Geneva Mercer and Angela Gregory) helped me bring Enid into sharper focus and encouraged me to consider the notion of what it means to be a Southern sculptor, a topic I hope to pursue in a future project.

That my curiosity about Enid Yandell ever developed into a book is due in large part to the interest and encouragement of many other colleagues, each of whom has played an important role in affirming a reason for my research to pivot from Confederate monuments and statuary toward Enid. Thanks to Peter Morrin, former director of the Speed Museum and the University of Louisville Arts and Culture Partnerships Initiative. His invitation to speak in 2012 started me on this long journey, and I am grateful for our many conversations—and that wonderful journey downriver to Brandenburg in the summer of 2017 to see the relocated monument from Louisville. Realizing that Enid's story could be cast in printed form took some time, however. An earlier version of a sliver of this book appeared in a volume entitled *Kentucky Women*, edited by Melissa A. McEuen and Thomas H. Appleton. Having the opportunity to publish as part of that broader framing was my first opportunity to write about Enid. To Melissa in particular I am grateful for that opportunity, as well as for her patience in guiding me as I turned my brain dump of ideas into a well-formulated chapter, which in turn helped guide my thinking and the creation of the present volume. My fullest thanks are to two icons in the field of Kentucky history. First, to Jim Klotter, Kentucky State Historian and emeritus faculty at Georgetown College, who encouraged me to pursue this book project and offered it a home in the Topics in Kentucky History series. This book's placement in the series makes it clear that, for as far afield as Enid went, she remained tethered to the Bluegrass State. Thanks as well to Nancy Disher Baird, retired Kentucky History Specialist at the Kentucky Library and Museum at Western Kentucky University, whose careful, meticulous research resulted in *the* article on Enid, which laid the foundation for every scholar's meditations on the Kentucky sculptor. I am grateful to Nancy for entertaining questions ever since we met in 2012, and in particular for tending to my inquiries, propositions, and meditations during our lovely research day together in July 2017 and ever since.

Completion of this book was aided by generous financial support from the College of Liberal Arts at the Rochester Institute of Technology (RIT) as well as my former institution, Georgetown College. I am thankful to Dean Jamie Winebrake and Associate Dean LaVerne McQuiller Williams at RIT for research and publication support, and to Dean Rosemary Allen at Georgetown College for funding support that made my initial research possible. In addition, I received a Ballard Breaux Visiting Fellowship at the Filson Historical Society (2012), which served to jumpstart thoughtful research on this topic.

Bringing this book into the broader fold for an eager public has been made possible by the staff of the University Press of Kentucky. Thanks to the two anonymous readers who reviewed the manuscript; your commentary was insightful, thorough, and constructive. I am grateful for the guidance of acquisitions editor Anne Dean Dotson, who eagerly engaged me in conversation about submitting my manuscript and shepherded me through this process. I am thankful for the clarity and attention paid by managing editor David Cobb, as well as the careful consideration, sharp eye, and gift with words of copyeditor Donna Bouvier. Thanks are also due to everyone on the UPK team who has been ready, willing, and able to help celebrate Enid.

In sum, I am grateful to all who have entertained a meditation on Enid with me. And I am astounded by the ways in which each of these interactions has given me an ever deeper love of the archive and a passion to find Margaret Ripley Wolfe's "fallen leaves, the missing pages"—the evidence from which this story about Enid could thoughtfully emerge.

Appendix

Chronology of the Confederate Monument

Thursday, September 13, 1894, was the deadline for submission of designs for the Confederate monument in Louisville, Kentucky. On **Saturday, September 15,** the Executive Committee, consisting of officers of the Woman's Confederate Monument Association (WCMA), received the designs. They met on that day to discuss the designs, but did not finish that day. The Executive Committee met again on **Wednesday, September 19,** reviewed the "more than" twenty submissions, and voted unanimously to choose the design submitted by Enid Yandell and William J. Dodd, one of the architects of the Louisville Trust Building with whom Enid had worked previously. This submission was later occasionally referred to as the "Yandell-Dodd" submission, or "K (1)."

On **Thursday, September 20,** the *Louisville Courier-Journal* announced the Executive Committee's selection on the front page of the newspaper with a notice that the monument will be "erected in this city October 15." On page 6 of the paper, an article detailed the procedure and the decision. It stated that Enid "furnished two designs," of which one was selected. It is unknown what the other designed looked like and whether it was a collaboration with Dodd.

Accompanying the *Louisville Courier-Journal* September 20 article was an image of the design put forth by Enid and Dodd, with the heading "To the Confederate Dead" and, beneath the image, the words "The Accepted Monument." However, although the design had been accepted by the Executive Committee, it had not at that point been accepted by the membership of the association.

On **Friday, September 21,** the WCMA membership met to see the designs and to "pass action," as it was called. This meeting was intended to get a read on the membership to see if they approved the action of the

Executive Committee. No consensus could be reached; the meeting was adjourned, to be continued on Monday, September 24.

On **Monday, September 24,** the WCMA met again and failed to approve the Executive Committee's recommendation of Enid's design. The association then decided to employ three architects to review the designs and to report back to the full body. (The architects, whose identity was kept anonymous until their report was filed the following Monday, were C. J. Clarke, Kenneth McDonald, and Max Drach.)

On **Monday, October 1,** the WCMA met and, after receiving the architects' committee report, overruled that committee, which had, like the Executive Committee, voted in favor of "K (1)," the Yandell-Dodd design. This would be the second time that the association membership overruled a decision regarding the selection of Enid Yandell as the artist of the Confederate monument. The reasons given by the membership included a perception that Enid was "an amateur" and that her young age would prevent her from designing "anything suitable." Moreover, the members wished not to "perpetuate Miss Yandell, but their Confederate dead." (These pronouncements were given by Mrs. John Ferguson in "Rejected the Report: Woman's Confederate Monument Association Refuses Miss Yandell's Design," *Louisville Courier-Journal,* October 2, 1894, 6.)

The association instead accepted the design submitted by a local monument company, M. Muldoon. The association decided to reconvene on Friday, October 5, at which time a regular meeting would be held because, in the eyes of presiding president Susan Preston Hepburn, the issue of the monument commission had been resolved.

Newspaper accounts over the following days (October 1–5, 1894) reported on perceived problems with the membership's voting process, including the fact that 36 ballots were cast, although only 32 women were present at the meeting, and that some women claimed not to understand how parliamentary procedure worked. On October 5, the *Louisville Courier-Journal* printed two notes from the opposing designers. Muldoon presented a defense of his design and criticized the recommendations of the architects and the Yandell-Dodd design. He promised the women of the association "a structure which will be a credit to the city and to the cause." Sharing space on the same page Muldoon's statement, the Yandell-Dodd team responded to the suggestions of the committee of architects.

The next meeting of the WCMA was held on **Friday, October 5,** at which time the association accepted Muldoon's design. In addition, the group adopted a program for the laying of the cornerstone. The laying was scheduled for mid-October, although it would be delayed until the following spring.

All was quiet until the spring. The monument materials arrived in Louisville on **Wednesday, May 15, 1895**. (The twin to the Louisville monument was unveiled on May 20, 1895, in Raleigh, North Carolina.) The cornerstone was laid on **Saturday, May 25,** after which the graves in Cave Hill were decorated. By **Tuesday, July 2,** an immense amount of progress had been made: the three figures were ready to be moved to the monument grounds; the shaft was erected; and the bronze was to be put into position elsewhere on the monument. The monument was completed on **Wednesday, July 10**, in advance of its dedication on **Tuesday, July 30, 1895,** a day that was made a half-holiday by the city government.

Notes

Introduction

1. According to historian Nancy Baird, a family descendant on Enid's mother's side remembered hearing that three generations of correspondence and ephemera were burned in the 1920s as a means of simplifying the process of clearing the family's estate before sale. See Baird, "Enid Yandell: Kentucky Sculptor," *Filson Club Historical Quarterly* 62, no. 1 (January 1988): 6, note 2.

2. The Yandell Collection, now at the Filson Historical Society, has been microfilmed and is available through the Smithsonian's Archives of American Art. For access to this collection, see http://www.aaa.si.edu/collections/enid-yandell-papers-6900.

3. Katharine A. Burnett, "Mold on the Cornbread: The Spore Paradigm of Southern Studies," *Publications of the Modern Language Association (PMLA)* 131, no. 1 (2016): 162–166, especially 163.

4. Ibid., 165.

5. See Henry James, *Life of William Wetmore Story* (New York: Houghton, Mifflin & Co., 1903) as reviewed by Jeannette L. Gilder in *The Critic* 44 (1904): 175–177. In terms of recent scholarship on women sculptors, see Melissa Dabakis, *A Sisterhood of Sculptors: American Artists in Nineteenth-Century Rome* (University Park: Pennsylvania State University Press, 2014), 2–3, with its critiques of novelist Henry James's 1903 categorization. Taking cues from feminist theory, cultural geography, and expatriate and postcolonial studies, Dabakis builds upon the scholarship of Jane Mayo Roos, Nancy Proctor, and others to point out the problematics of the term, not the least of which is its impossibility for flight, movement, and—by extension—agency. Such methods are akin to the approach taken in this volume.

1. Cider and Cigars

1. The Filson Club, now the Filson Historical Society, was founded in 1884 in Louisville, Kentucky, as a historical society aimed at collecting, preserving, and telling the significant stories of Kentucky and the region. See Letter from Enid Yandell to Reuben T. Durrett, April 15, 1892, in Durrett, Reuben T. (Reuben Thomas), 1824–1913, Added Papers, 1883–1910, Mss A/D965c, Folder 97, Filson Historical Society (hereafter FHS). Durrett was also known as "Colonel" Durrett. Enid wrote

to him in 1889 and asked about a book that she had requested he send to her; she also recorded bits about her trip to Europe that year. For instance, she remarks on visiting Blarney Castle, where she "had no ambition to kiss the stone." She mentions that she couldn't attend church but set about to "worship Nature on the water." FHS Mss A D965c/Folder 57.

Enid's birth date is confirmed by several pieces of evidence. First, in a diary entry for 1869–1871 her father noted, "Sunny's child born at 2 a.m." on October 6, 1869. See Lunsford P. Yandell II, Diary, FHS Mss/A/Y21/Folder 53. Second, Enid's grave marker in Louisville's Cave Hill Cemetery has the birth date as October 6, 1869. See Section O, lot 369. Third, in 1899 on Enid's birthday, her mother wrote to her and mentioned that she gave birth to her thirty years ago. Fourth, in 1919, Enid had a nativity chart, a form of spiritualist practice, made by Lida McIntosh. That chart gives her birth year as 1869. See FHS Mss A/Y21b/Folder 94.

As to her siblings, Maud is sometimes spelled Maude; the latter spelling will be used in this volume. Maude lived from 1871 to 1962. Neither Enid nor Maude had children. Next in line was Elsie, who lived from 1876 to 1939. She married an architect named Donn Barber. Enid's youngest sibling was a brother, Lunsford Pitts Yandell III (1878–1927). He married Elizabeth Hosford.

2. Enid attended St. Paul's as a child. Her sister Elsie was married at Christ Church Cathedral in 1899. Enid retained ties to the Episcopal church throughout her life, as evidenced by her continued support of St. Andrews Episcopal in Edgartown, Massachusetts, where she lived from 1908 on. See FHS Mss A/Y21b/Folder 94, p. 73.

3. The office was located on Sixth and Chestnut Streets. Letters from Enid Yandell to Grandmother, June 17, 1878, and undated. FHS Mss A/Y21b/Folder 1.

4. The Breckinridge and Desha families were Lexington political and civic dynasties. Mary Desha (1850–1911) was born in Lexington, was schooled there, and taught before turning attention toward memorialization and lineage as a founder of the Daughters of the American Revolution. A memorial to Desha and three other cofounders was sculpted by fellow DAR member Gertrude Vanderbilt Whitney and dedicated in 1929. Desha was related by marriage to the Breckinridge family through her sister Issa Desha and William Campbell Preston Breckinridge. The Breckinridge family was rooted in law and politics, shifting allegiances between Lincoln, the Confederacy, and, later, racial equality. Although W. C. P. Breckinridge fought for the Confederacy, he became an advocate for racial equality. His and Issa's son, Desha Breckinridge, was editor and publisher of the Lexington Herald from 1897 to 1935. For more on the Breckinridges, see James C. Klotter, *The Breckinridges of Kentucky, 1760–1981* (Lexington: University Press of Kentucky, 1981). When Enid went abroad in 1894 at the age of twenty-five, she was accompanied by her aunt, Mrs. John Lisle, of Lexington. See clipping in FHS Mss A/Y21b/Folder 94, which cites *Critic,* November 18, 1894. Enid began study at Miss Bartlett's art class at the age of fourteen. See "Society," *Louisville Courier-Journal,* July 5, 1891, 10. For Enid's studio account, see Enid's letter to her grandmother, ca. March 23, 1883, FHS Mss A/Y21b/Folder 1.

5. Regarding the fair, see *Louisville Courier-Journal,* August 1 and 2, 1883, as well as the print from William F. Clarke, "Birds-Eye View of Louisville from the River Front and Southern Exposition, 1883." The fair's name firmly associated the city and state with the South, some years after the Civil War had ended. The firm grasp on Southern identity forged a path for Kentucky's cultural meaning during a time when it appeared as though the state had entered as part of the Union and exited as Confederate. As E. Merton Coulter put it, Kentucky "waited until after the war was over to secede from the Union." E. Merton Coulter, *Civil War and Readjustment in Kentucky* (Chapel Hill: University of North Carolina Press, 1926), 27–36; for an updated view, see Anne E. Marshall, *Creating a Confederate Kentucky: The Lost Cause and Civil War Memory in a Border State* (Chapel Hill: University of North Carolina Press, 2010).

6. On September 15, 1885, Grannie also remarked on enjoying a visit with Emma Speed. See FHS Mss A/Y21b/Folder 1. General John Breckinridge Castleman (1841–1918) was referred to as "Uncle Breck." Letter from Louise Yandell to Enid Yandell, August 26, 1887, FHS Mss A/Y21b/Folder 4.

7. CMK, "Art in the South," *Art Union: The Official Journal of the American Art Union* 1, no. 8–9 (August–September 1884): 145. The reference to an art gallery may refer to the Polytechnic Society of Kentucky, which was an educational and cultural institution that operated from 1876 to 1913.

8. Ibid., 146.

9. Letter from Maude Yandell to Enid Yandell, ca. November 6, 1887. See FHS Mss A/Y21b/Folder 6. The name "Little Turner" is in reference to the English landscape painter, J. M. W. Turner (1775-1851), who captured atmospheric effects and, in particular, the color yellow.

10. Robert Crittenden was the first acting governor of the Arkansas Territory; he championed the creation of the capitol in Little Rock. See William F. Pope, *Early Days in Arkansas* (Little Rock: Frederick W. Allsopp, 1895). It was Turner's idea to have a portrait painted of Crittenden after seeing similar works in the State House in Little Rock. See "A Fitting Tribute: The Portrait of Robert Crittenden Hung in the State House," *Little Rock Arkansas Democrat,* December 24, 1887, 4. See letter from Louise Yandell to politician Jesse Turner, September 9, 1887, regarding the portrait of Crittenden. Louise's painting is mentioned in an undated (ca. October 1887) letter from Louise to Enid while Enid is in Cincinnati. See FHS Mss A/Y21b/Folder 5, where Louise mentions having to put the letter in the mail so that she could turn to painting "the Crittenden portrait" and noted that on October 25, 1887, she was at work on the picture. Louise completed the painting in December 1887. It won Louise accolades for not being "a professional artist but a genius in art." See letter from R. J. Menefee to Turner, December 23, 1887, Turner Family Papers, Box 3, David M. Rubenstein Rare Book and Manuscript Library, Duke University, Durham, North Carolina.

11. Joseph Thorpe Elliston (1779–1856) began his career as a silversmith in Nashville in 1798, after having trained in Lexington, Kentucky, from 1795 to 1798, about

a century before Enid took up the tools of her trade. David Yandell quoted in Nancy Disher Baird, "Enid Yandell: Kentucky Sculptor," *Filson Club History Quarterly* 62, no. 1 (January 1988): 23.

Women were expected to be engaged in a different type of work—civic good—as exemplified through the practices of the Woman's Exchange, which was formed in Louisville in 1885 as part of the broader social and civic movement. For its history, see Kathleen Waters Sander, who referred to its members as having "quasi-careers in entrepreneurial philanthropy, offering the lady managers a sense of personal fulfillment and leadership as well as visible public roles as business executives." See Sander, *The Business of Charity: The Woman's Exchange Movement, 1832–1900* (Urbana: University of Illinois Press, 1998), 3. Kathleen D. McCarthy called these organizations a form of "nonprofit entrepreneurship." See McCarthy, *Women's Culture: American Philanthropy and Art, 1830–1930* (Chicago: University of Chicago Press, 1991), 62.

12. Enid continued to carve on occasion, mentioning in a note to her grandmother, "I am going to carve a shield for uncle Breck. It has a design of chestnuts on it." See Letter from Enid to Elizabeth Elliston, June 7, 1885, FHS Mss A/Y21b/Folder 1. Enid was left-handed, according to her niece, Elsie Barber Trask, according to documentation gathered by Nancy Disher Baird, July 31, 1981: see FHS Mss A/Y21b/Folder 71. For information on Hampton College, see, for example, *American College and Public School Directory* (Chicago: C. H. Evans & Co., 1893), 31.

13. Quote from Leo W. Zimmerman, "Sulphurous Oaths, Hammer Clatter and the Great White Arts III Louisville House," *Louisvillian*, November 1957: 7–8.

14. See notice for Hampton College in the *Louisville Courier-Journal,* September 3, 1882, 9; see also "Art at Home: An Interesting Exhibition of the Work of Young Pupils," *Louisville Courier-Journal*, June 1, 1885, 3. In terms of other exhibitions and performance, listings of entertainments of music, reading, and song performed for the public may be found in the *Louisville Courier-Journal*: for instance, January 17, 1882, 6; an announcement of performance of Shakespeare, including the last three acts of *Macbeth,* original poetry, and piano as announced in the *Louisville Courier-Journal,* March 11, 1883, 10; while notice of Mrs. Randall-Diel's elocution classes were remarked in the *Louisville Courier-Journal*, April 18, 1884, 8. *Louisville Times,* May 31, 1885, quoted in Melville Briney, "A Gifted Bachelormaid," *Louisville Times,* July 28, 1949.

15. The article also noticed the distinctiveness of style: "Evidently the pupils have been encouraged to develop individuality of style, as after a slight familiarity with the work one is able to certain hands the sketches that are presented." "Art at Home," *Louisville Courier-Journal,* June 1, 1885, 3.

16. Ninth Annual Catalogue of the Hampton College, Louisville, Kentucky, 1886–1887. Maude, Enid's sister, was a sophomore at this time (1887). Undated clipping [December 4, 1887?] in FHS Mss A/Y21b/Folder 6; undated clipping, FHS Mss A/Y21b/Folder 94, p. 49. I have identified this latter clipping as being from the *Louisville Courier-Journal,* July 5, 1891, 10.

17. The school's original benefactor was Charles McMicken, a real estate baron

who left a bequest for the establishment of a major university in 1858. Funds were used eventually to establish a School of Drawing and Design in 1869 as a department of the university. See *Cincinnati Museum Association Art School Circular* (Cincinnati: Robert Clarke & Co. for the Museum Association, 1884). The academy's roots were tied to the university; here, "university" refers to McMicken, now the University of Cincinnati; as mentioned in the text, the university transferred the School of Design to the Cincinnati Museum Association in 1884. Thomas Satterwhite Noble was the school's first principal in 1869. See James D. Birchfield, "Thomas Satterwhite Noble: 'Made for a Painter,'" parts 1 and 2 in *Kentucky Review* 6, no. 1 (Winter 1986): 35–60 and no. 2 (Summer 1986): 45–73. Such a model of education took its cues from educational institutions such as New York's Cooper Union for the Advancement of Science and Art (colloquially, Cooper Union), founded by industrialist and inventor Peter Cooper, who envisioned an education "equal to the best technology schools [then] established," with education "open and free to all." Cooper Union was established in 1859 and was modeled after French polytechnic education. The school established day classes for women, who could take technical classes in typewriting, photography, and shorthand.

18. Enid's mother's inquiry is recounted in a letter from Louise to Enid dated September 8, 1887. FHS Mss A/Y21b/Folder 4. Janet Scudder, *Modeling My Life* (New York: Harcourt, Brace, & Co., 1925), 25.

19. Description appears in the *Cincinnati Enquirer* October 2, 1887, 12. See also Janet Scudder, *Modeling My Life*, 90–108.

20. "The Art Academy: Pupils' Exhibition of Excellence Opens Tuesday," *Cincinnati Enquirer,* October 2, 1887, 12. Notice was made of securing models for drawing classes in the *Cincinnati Enquirer*; see advertisement for "Model—To pose full length before class in the Art Academy," *Cincinnati Enquirer,* October 9, 1887. "Art Exhibition: Annual Display of the Work of the Students of the School of Design," *Cincinnati Enquirer,* June 7, 1889, 8.

21. Information on courses may be gleaned from circulars from the period. Documents in the Mary R. Schiff Library and Archives, Cincinnati Art Museum, detail the schedule for 1887–1888 with lectures on "artistic anatomy" offered weekly on Fridays at 1:45 p.m. from November 25 through December 23, resuming on Friday, January 6, 1888, and continuing through May 4. Following Enid's attendance, the Academy added photography and etching as part of its coursework in February 1890. See "Art Academy—Lecture on Photography," *Cincinnati Enquirer,* January 26, 1890, 16. From Scudder, *Modeling My Life,* we learn that female students were able to draw from the nude; however, we have no evidence that Enid learned in this way, though Enid does mention, later in life, that she did learn from the nude. As far as early work of Enid's, some very early sketches that Enid sent to her grandmother ("Grannie") in Tennessee were boxed up, along with letters, and returned to Enid's family home in 1897 after Eliza Yandell died (October 4, 1897). Enid's mother retained these, although it's unclear if they are extant. See a letter ca. August 9, 1898, from Louise to Enid, FHS Mss A/Y21b/Folder 25.

22. The Academy student roster indicates that Enid enrolled in two years of carving, one of sculpture, and one of perspective. However, the academy's published list of students indicates that she took two full years of sculpture. See Art Academy of Cincinnati Records, Cincinnati Art Museum. In the catalogue for 1887–1888, Enid is listed as enrolled on page 25. Also in that publication, she is listed as taking the "Second Grade—Day Class" in drawing and perspective, taught by L. H. Meakin (p. 31); the "Fourth Grade—Day Class" and the "Fourth Grade—Night Class" in sculpture, taught by Louis T. Rebisso (p. 37); and the "Third Grade" class in wood carving taught by Benn Pitman (p. 42). Descriptions of the courses are included in the publication.

23. Louis Rebisso settled in Boston prior to taking root in Cincinnati, where he gained a position at the Art Academy. There he taught women and men in three-dimensional form. Signature works include monuments to politician William Henry Harrison (Cincinnati's Piatt Park) as well as Union leaders in the Civil War, including Ulysses S. Grant (Chicago) and General James B. McPherson (Washington, DC). His Grant Memorial, portraying the general seated on top of a horse in full military uniform with a sword at his side, would become familiar to Enid when she worked in Chicago, as the colossal work was created and sited there in 1891. The impact of Rebisso's skill as a monumental sculptor who gained numerous commissions, in addition to his adept teaching, clearly influenced Enid. Her visual (in terms of future work) and textual connections with Rebisso are telling, whether indicative of her ambition, with him as the conduit, or in gratitude for his teaching. In fact, I believe that the Grant memorial described in Enid's literary work *Three Girls in a Flat* (discussed in the following chapter) can be seen as homage to Rebisso.

24. Janet Scudder, *Modeling My Life,* 46.

25. "Society," *Louisville Courier-Journal,* July 5, 1891, 10. This article recounts Enid's trajectory after Cincinnati and gives helpful insight as to her tenure at the Academy. It also extolled Enid's plan to move to New York in the fall of 1891 to study with Augustus Saint-Gaudens. Instead, Enid moved to Chicago to undertake employment at the World's Fair.

26. Pitman lectured at the Cincinnati Art School from 1873 until 1892 on art and wood engraving. He aimed to secure the development of American decorative art and to open up a new profession for women through elaborately carved and decorated cabinets, baseboards and beds, doors, casings, mantels, picture frames, and bookcases. Other instructors include Henry Lindley Fry (1807–1895) and his son, William Henry Fry (1830–1929). The Frys and Pitman promoted wood carving as part of the broader furniture movement in Cincinnati and heralded nature as the essential subject for such works, very much in keeping with the Aesthetic Movement, which, like the expatriate artist-teachers, was imported to the United States from England. Early extant pieces in wood by Enid include a thistle panel in the collection of the museum at Rhode Island School of Design from around 1908.

Even though Enid learned wood carving as a student, it is the extent to which she continued in the medium that deserves further attention. Extant works have no identifiable dates, and the items are not mentioned in letters or correspondence. These include an umbrella handle, a clock case, a mirror, and a large chair that converts into a table. All of these were on view in a 1982 exhibition at Rhode Island School of Design (RISD) Museum in Providence, *Enid Yandell and the Branstock School* (July 23–August 29, 1982), the first of only two exhibits dedicated to Yandell's work. (The other exhibit, mounted at the Speed Museum in Louisville, Kentucky, focused on plaster work, models, and many of the items by Enid that were donated to the Speed in the twentieth century.) Most of the items in the exhibit at RISD were lent by Mrs. John J. Trask, niece of the artist, who retained many of Enid's possessions after the artist's death. Of particular mention, and worthy of further study, is the carved and painted desk chair (referred to as a settee by RISD Museum staff in recent correspondence). The exhibition records from 1982 state that the work currently in the RISD collection is a settee, and further indicate the authorship as by Enid and her longtime companion Geysa de Braunecker, discussed later in this chapter. The RISD curatorial files do not have any further information about the work and only identify it as being created by Enid, thus leaving open to question which portions of the work were created by whom, as well as the date, purpose, and so on. With the exception of the carved mahogany panel (RISD 83.215.4, which does not appear to have been exhibited in the 1982 exhibit), the wood works carved by Enid remain on long-term loan to RISD. As of this writing, then, all of the carved wood pieces that Enid created remain in the family. The Barbee & Castleman desk mentioned later in the text remains unlocated.

27. Academy records indicate that Enid enrolled in 1888–1889 (see p. 26 of that year's circular) and took the "Fourth Grade—Day Class" in sculpture taught by Louis T. Rebisso (p. 38) and the "Third Grade" class in wood carving taught by Benn Pitman (p. 44).

28. Benn Pitman, *A Plea for American Decorative Art with Illustrations and Designs, Showing Examples of Artistic Wood Carving, China and Pottery Painting, Mural Decoration, Etching, Etc., by the Girls and Women of Cincinnati* (Atlanta: Cotton States and International Exposition, 1895), 14.

29. Ibid., 5, 7–8.

30. For the clipping about the wood carving, see FHS Mss A/Y21b/Folder 94. See an ad for the company in the *Louisville Courier-Journal*, September 14, 1898, 8.

31. The students' exhibition notice appeared in the *Cincinnati Enquirer*, June 8, 1888, 5. "Rules and Regulations" in *Circular and Fifth Annual Catalogue of the Art Academy of Cincinnati, 1889–1890* (Cincinnati: Woodrow, Baldwin, and Co., 1889), 9. On the history of teaching art and design in Cincinnati, see Krista Atkins Nutter, "Tracing the Paths of Interior Design Education," master's thesis, University of Cincinnati, 2001, esp. pp. 56–60. Regarding Philippoteaux 's cyclorama, four versions were extant at this time: the first was the Chicago painting, which opened in October 1883 and was shown at the World's Fair a decade later; a second version was displayed in Boston in December 1884; a third version was exhibited in Philadelphia in February 1886, and a fourth (referred to as the "New York" version) debuted

in Brooklyn in October 1886. Discussion of the versions may be found in Chris Brenneman and Sue Boardman, *The Gettysburg Cyclorama: The Turning Point of the Civil War on Canvas* (El Dorado Hills, CA: Savas Beatie, 2015), 69–72. Brenneman and Boardman note that the Cincinnati version was moved from Philadelphia during the summer of 1887, in anticipation of a fall reopening, and was a fixture in Cincinnati for a year, taking part in the state centennial celebration in July 1888 and the Grand Army of the Republic gathering in October of that year (ibid., 40-41). This Philadelphia-turned-Cincinnati-version was referred to as "Philippoteaux's Third and 'BEST' Work." In the *Cincinnati Enquirer* of September 30, 1887, 3, under "Amusements" and near the exhibition announcements offered the "Battle of Gettysburg: America's Greatest Battle-Field" at the corner of Seventh and Elm, noting, "Words fail to describe what you will see, and we won't try to. You will never regret the visit—NEVER!"

32. See FHS Mss A/Y21b/Folder 7. The cousin's full name was likely Elliston Farrell.

33. See FHS Mss A/Y21b/Folder 8; Folder 31 contains Winford's letter; Folder 7 contains the letter from Enid's grandmother that recounts the dream of Enid's mother, as told to Enid's grandmother. See also a letter postmarked September 25, 1893, where Enid's mother, Louise, wrote to Enid regarding her securing the commission for the Louisville Confederate Monument. See FHS Mss A/Y21b/Folder 18.

34. Letter of October 12, 1887, from Louise Yandell to Enid, FHS Mss A/Y21b/Folder 5.

35. Ibid.

36. Letter of October 27, 1888, from Louise Yandell to Enid, FHS Mss A/Y21b/Folder 12.

37. In a letter from Louise to Enid, ca. October 16, 1887, Louise remarked, "I don't understand about the red bed-spread, I never saw one—What is it made of?" FHS Mss A/Y21b/Folder 5.

38. Letter of ca. October 18, 1887, from Louise to Enid. See FHS Mss A/Y21b/Folder 5; Letter of February 21, 1888 from Maude to Enid, Folder 8.

39. An additional concern was noted in Louise's letter to Enid from October 27, 1888: "Your Aunt Sallie has told me of your discomforts at Miss Fosters. I can not bear the idea of your not having enough to eat—and certainly it must be remedied. Forty dollars a month should secure you every comfort. The only advantage in Miss Fosters is the fact that you have some one to go with at night to the school. Surely you can find some other house where there are art students who go at night. I think you had better investigate this subject before you come home at Thanksgiving or sooner if you think best or I will go up and attend to it for you if you wish." FHS Mss A/Y21b/Folder 12. Enid also seemed to have resided, for at least part of 1888, with Amy Campbell, who started a school of phonography (shorthand) in Cincinnati. A letter postmarked November 12, 1888, from Louise to Enid gives the address as "Care Miss A. R. Campbell/College Building/Cincinnati Ohio"; by December 18, the address is still care of Miss A. R. Campbell, but with the street listing as "June

Street": FHS Mss A/Y21b/Folder 13. Around February 8, 1888, Louise wrote to Enid, "We can do your mending for you then. Perhaps, if your cloth[e]s are uncomfortably tight you had best get a skirt such as you spoke when you were at home to work in." FHS Mss A/Y21b/Folder 8.

40. In a letter of January 1888, from Louise to Enid: "I had a hard time getting the plaster from the studio, eventually had to go & root it out of the closet under the steps myself. I hope the tools were all right." FHS Mss A/Y21b/Folder 7. See also an undated letter estimated to be October 19, 1888, FHS Mss A/Y21b/Folder 12.

41. Letter from Eliza B. Yandell to Louise Yandell, November 2, 1888, FHS Mss A/Y21b/Folder 13; Letter from Louise Yandell to Enid, November 7, 1888, FHS Mss A/Y21b/Folder 13.

42. FHS Mss A/Y21b/Folder 105.

43. Enid's attention to one field of study and profession was documented in "How an American Girl Has Astonished the Art World," FHS Mss A/Y21b/Folder 105. "The Work of an Artist," *Louisville Courier-Journal,* January 18, 1889.

44. A letter of ca. May 20, 1889 from Enid to Grannie about an impending visit ("I am very tired & hope you and I will be all alone") indicates that they were leaving for New York on the first of June. At the close of the trip, Enid penned a letter on December 1, 1889, from London indicating the familiarity of Europe in her announcement that "We sail on Wednesday two more days only in this dear old land!" See FHS Mss A/Y21b/Folder 16.

45. Letter from Enid to Grannie, December 1, 1889. Written from London, Enid wrote: "We sail on Wednesday two more days only in this dear old land!" The note was postmarked December 15 to Eliza in Louisville (FHS Mss A/Y21b/Folder 16). Enid toured Europe with mother and two sisters in 1889. Her planned departure was noted in the papers alongside a review of her exhibit in 1889, noting that she was to depart on June 1.

46. Consider, for example, the experiences of Anne Whitney (1821–1915), who went to Italy at age forty-six, having already established a career in the United States. In 1875, Whitney entered a national competition from the Boston Art Committee to create the sculpture of Charles Sumner, an abolitionist and political figure. She won the competition, but her invitation to create the work was rescinded when the judges realized she was a woman. The competition was instead awarded to Thomas Ball, although many years later Whitney's version was cast as well. Rich materials focusing on Anne Whitney may be found in the Wellesley College Archives.

47. Identities were kept secret except for Peyton Clarke, who was Chief Satellite and general manager of the organization. During the festivals, Satellite members wore masks to protect their identity. They also kept secret the pageant themes and parade routes to build anticipation.

48. Ben-Hur was the fictionalized hero of Lew Wallace's book *Ben-Hur: A Tale of the Christ* (1880), a wildly popular novel of the time that chronicles the life of a Jewish prince-turned-charioteer in parallel to that of Jesus. The story highlights themes of redemption, love, and compassion, making its relevance to the Louisville pag-

eant slightly vague, though the Christian connection may have been intentional. It is worth mentioning that *Ben-Hur* was so wildly popular that its publisher, Harper and Brothers, spotlighted the volume in the literary exhibit at the Manufactures and Liberal Arts Building at the 1893 World's Fair in Chicago.

49. FHS Mss A/Y21b/Folder 94 is a scrapbook compiled by Yandell. On page 46 is the clipping from the 1890 program.

50. *Twice-a-Week Messenger* (Owensboro, KY), September 25, 1890, 2.

51. *Louisville Courier-Journal*, October 3, 1890, 2–4. The connection of the theme to the overall narrative of the parade portended that Mercury "had appeared after the lapse of another year of peace and prosperity to attest his appreciation of the efforts of his faithful subjects to keep the wheels of progress moving" (p. 2). The description of Enid's outfit draws from the photograph of Enid in the text, where she stands in front of a carved, gold chair, which may have been used in the pageant.

52. See Enid's scrapbook with a white calling card of her studio for Friday, July 3 [1891]. On her home setting, see Briney, "A Gifted Bachelormaid." Regarding her use of her home as a studio as early as 1891, see FHS Mss A/Y21b/Folder 94, glued on p. 49, along with entries around 1891.

53. My description of the attire of lawyer, manuscript and book collector, and author Reuben T. Durrett (1824–1913) and its import for Enid's visual communication are based on my direct study of the plaster of Durrett at the Filson Historical Society and the photograph of Enid's original from 1891, which was shown at the Art Institute. Information on the books comprising the pedestal are taken from an undated clipping in FHS Mss A/D965c/Folder 94, which discusses the 1891 exhibition that Enid held at her studio on July 3. Durrett was an avid collector of materials about his native state. Following his tenure as editor of the *Louisville Courier* from 1857 to 1859, he continued to serve as a lawyer until retiring from the bar in 1880. Thereafter, he devoted much of his efforts to historical study and its promulgation. He "made it an object to secure every book about Kentucky or Kentuckians, or that was written by a Kentuckian or even printed in Kentucky." During his life, Durrett was said to have collected some 50,000 items. See "Reuben T. Durrett" in *The Builders of the Nation: A History of the University States, Including Portraits and Biographies of Presidents, Cabinet Officers, Statesmen, Legislators, Jurists, Educators, Authors, Editors, and Divines* (Stanley-Bradley Publishing Co., 1892), 450–453 (quotation on 453). See "The Collector: Colonel Durrett's Collection," *Art Collector: A Journal Devoted to the Arts and the Crafts* 2 (1889): 133. When part of Durrett's collection was sold to the University of Chicago in 1913, the contents of 20,000 bound volumes in addition to 250 file folders of pamphlets along with numerous manuscripts, newspapers, and maps. The contents filled 287 large packing crates. See "Guide to the Reuben T. Durrett Collection—Richard H. Collins Papers, 1761–1873," University of Chicago Library, Special Collections Research Center, https://www.lib.uchicago.edu/e/scrc/findingaids/view.php?eadid=ICU.SPCL.COLLINSR. At the University of Chicago, several collections bearing Durrett's name exist, including his personal papers, ca. 1850-1912, as well as documents and correspondence with

areas of emphases relating to material type or subject. See https://www.lib.uchicago.edu/scrc/finding-aids/?searchq=Durrett.

54. *Louisville Courier-Journal,* July 5, 1891, 10.

55. William Dodd, one of the designers of the Louisville Trust building, had worked with William LeBaron Jenney and Solon S. Beman, two of the founders of the Chicago School of architecture. National Register of Historic Places, Reference Number 77000624.

56. Having established a working relationship with Maury and Dodd by 1891, Enid pursued a collaboration of a different sort—one in which she was the lead—for the Confederate Monument, which she undertook in 1894.

57. While much of the interior of the Trust Building has been renovated, the exterior is largely original. Because SIRIS and Darst point out that Enid created "capitals" for the building, we might assume that the exterior columns are by Enid's hand. If these indeed are the elements that she created, they remain in situ today and give us a clear indication of Enid's skill in carving stone—in this case, granite.

58. An anecdote about ordering beer appears in Enid Yandell, "A Corner in Kentucky," in FHS Mss A/Y21b/Folder 73.

59. FHS Mss A/Y21b/Folder 73.

60. Ibid.

61. "A Corner in Kentucky" mentions Burlington, the farm, and an old-fashioned Kentucky home. See FHS Mss A/Y21b/Folder 73. (The town of Burlington is not to be confused with the Elliston property in Nashville, also called Burlington.) Enid signed the piece with a pen name that corresponds to her initials: El Ysium. This approach to signing written works with attributes of her own name is characteristic of Enid's work; it appears again when she coauthored *Three Girls in a Flat,* a semiautobiographical work of fiction that gives accounts of women working at the World's Columbian Exposition in Chicago. It is unclear if "A Corner in Kentucky" was ever published during Enid's lifetime.

For assistance on the Yandell-Dinsmore connections, I am grateful to Cathy Callopy of the Dinsmore Homestead. See Catherine T. Callopy, "Julia Stockton Dinsmore," unpublished manuscript at the Dinsmore Homestead, Burlington, Kentucky. See also "A Trip Back in Time—Dinsmore Homestead Takes Visitors Back to NKY's Past," *Sunday Challenger,* October 24, 2004, 4c, Dinsmore Family Papers, Dinsmore Homestead, Burlington, Kentucky. Enid's larger circle of friends included Patty Flandrau Selmes (1861–1923), who was associated with Benjamin Pitman of the art school in Cincinnati. It may have been Patty who introduced Enid to Julia. Enid created a bas-relief in plaster and bronze of Julia; the plaster is in the collection of Dinsmore Homestead, and is discussed in more detail in Chapter 8.

62. For Enid's text about the river view, see FHS Mss A/Y21b/Folder 73.

63. Founded in 1881 as the Cincinnati Museum Association, the Cincinnati Art Museum is among the oldest museums of art in the United States. Quotes from the *Louisville Courier-Journal,* May 6, 1889, 2.

64. As least four books currently at Dinsmore are related to the relationship

between the Yandells and the Dinsmores, and one of these refers to the diary entry above. I am indebted to Cathy Collopy for assistance in the collections of Dinsmore Homestead.

65. On November 6, 1897, an accident occurred with Amy Campbell, Enid, Geysa de Braunecker, and a few others. The account appeared in the *Cincinnati Enquirer,* with news of a lawsuit against Yandell et al. (November 28, 1897, 35). In the article, Enid is associated with the character she created in *Three Girls in a Flat* and is identified (erroneously) as traveling secretary to a Mrs. Palmer. Campbell is identified as a horsewoman and sister of William Campbell, cashier of the Commercial Bank in Cincinnati. See also "Motorman: Will Ask $10,000 Damages for That Tallyho Collision," *Louisville Courier-Journal,* November 29, 1897, 2.

66. The term was popularized through a novel written in 1894 by Constance Cary Harrison, whose tale discloses the dilemma that faces Marion Irving and her betrothed, Alexander Gordon. See Constance Cary Harrison, *A Bachelor Maid* (New York: Century Co., 1894). See also Melville O. Briney, "Enid Yandell, Louisville's Gifted Bachelormaid," *Louisville Times,* July 28, 1949, 16.

67. Evidence of Enid's travels may be pieced together from clippings in her scrapbook, FHS Mss A Y21b Folder 76, as well as census records.

68. Geysa was born on June 23, 1869, and died January 16, 1960, at the age of ninety. She is buried in Swan Point Cemetery in Providence, Rhode Island (Plot 355-23570), https://www.findagrave.com/memorial/27810052/geysa-hortense-de_braunecker. Her obituary is the sole reference that points to Geysa having been married. See *Bridgeport Post,* January 18, 1960, 46, which referred to the her as the "widow of Mortimer Adye." Letters from Louise to Enid, while Enid was in Paris, often mention Geysa (or Geyza) Hortense de Braunecker along with allusions to their "bohemian" lifestyle. See, for instance, FHS Mss A/Y21b/Folder 23, with correspondence from 1897.

69. See FHS Mss A/Y21b/Folder 34 for the telegram, dated January 3 or 13, 1896, and an October 1896 note to Enid. See FHS Mss A/Y21b/Folder 23 for a letter dated November 14, 1897, from Louise in Louisville to Enid in New York, who was then receiving mail at 28 East Twenty-Second Street, in care of Mrs. Leonard. In this letter, discussion is made of a Mrs. Hite's wanting to send pickles to Enid and Geysa, another reminder, as with Durrett's cider, of the comforts of home.

70. In 1898, Enid sculpted a bust of Geysa; its whereabouts are unknown. The bust is listed as one of three works in David Gray, *Catalogue of the Exhibition of Fine Arts* (Buffalo: Pan-American Exposition, 1901), 72. Item 1665 was *Baroness de Braunecker*; 1666, *Mermaid and Fisher Boy* (*Pewter Tankard*); and 1667, *Bust of the Honorable John G. Carlisle.* In addition, Enid exhibited the plaster of the Carrie Brown Memorial Fountain, which will be discussed in Chapter 5.

Enid and Geysa were said to "arrive in Louisville the last of this week on a short visit to Miss Pauline May. They are on their way to Boyle county [*sic*] where they will join Mrs. Louise Yandell at her cottage." See *Louisville Courier-Journal,* May 2, 1906, 6.

Geysa's relaying of Enid's health may be found in a letter from Patty Selmes to Julia Dinsmore, March 10, 1906 (file 1402), which noted that "Enid was operated on for appendicitis today and Geysa, the Baroness, has just telephoned me that she is all right. E[nid] has had very bad what she thought was indigestion for two years, she fainted from it the other day and Dr. Bull told her it had been her appendix all the time. I hope she will be well now." Dinsmore Family Papers, Dinsmore Homestead, Burlington, Kentucky. I am grateful to Cathy Collopy for locating and sharing this letter.

71. The literature on these relationships is vast and varied. A seminal article is Carroll Smith-Rosenberg's study of thirty-five relationships between the 1760s and the 1880s focusing on emotional ties among women in highly structured relationships. See "The Female World of Love and Ritual: Relations between Women in Nineteenth-Century America," *Signs* 1, no. 1 (Autumn 1975): 1–29.

72. Letter from Enid Yandell to Reuben Durrett, July 5, 1899. The additional note was added by Idell Scheider, and another note was added by Geysa, who sent her affection. See FHS Mss A/D965c.

2. Caryatids and Clay

1. See FHS Mss A/Y21b/Folder 2 for the letter from Enid to Eliza Bland Yandell, August 16, 1886. The word "Gunther" is illegible; however, the firm did have outlets from 1886 to 1871 in the city and had customers in Louisville.

2. On Durrett, see Thomas D. Clark, "Reuben T. Durrett and His Kentuckiana Interest and Collection," *Filson Club History Quarterly* 56 (October 1982): 353–378; Edward M. Walters, "Reuben T. Durrett, the Durrett Collection, and the University of Chicago," *Filson Club History Quarterly* 56 (October 1982): 379–394. For the Durrett letter, see FHS Mss A/D965c/Folder 73. Palmer, a writer and businesswoman, was also musically gifted and politically engaged. At the age of twenty-one, she married forty-four-year-old business mogul Potter Palmer. The quotation is from Mrs. M. P. Handy, "The Women of the World's Fair City," *Munsey's Magazine* 8, no. 6 (March 1893): 610. On the bifurcation of women's work between those stressing women's social usefulness and those seeking the vote in the context of the Woman's Building, see *The Fair Women: The Story of the Woman's Building, World's Columbian Exposition, Chicago, 1893* (Chicago: Academy Chicago, 1981); Wanda M. Corn, Charlene G. Garfinkle, and Annelise K. Madsen, *Women Building History: Public Art at the 1893 Columbian Exposition* (Berkeley: University of California Press, 2011). An interesting facet of the Board of Lady Managers' work is its intersection with suffrage and literary exhibition, in the form of library displays; see *Right Here I See My Own Books: The Woman's Building Library at the World's Columbian Exposition*, edited by Sarah Wadsworth and Wayne A. Wiegand (Amherst: University of Massachusetts Press, 2012).

3. Trumbull White and William Igleheart, *The World's Columbian Exposition, Chicago, 1893* (Boston: Standard Silverware Co., 1893), 561; Robert W. Rydell, *All*

the World's a Fair: Visions of Empire at America's International Expositions, 1876–1916 (Chicago: University of Chicago Press, 1984); Robert W. Rydell, John E. Findling, and Kimberly D. Pelle, *Fair America: World's Fairs in the United States* (Washington, DC: Smithsonian Institution Press, 2000).

4. See the William F. Cody Archive: Documenting the Life and Times of Buffalo Bill (website), *Buffalo Bill (Hon. Wm. F. Cody) and His Wild West Companions, Including Wild Bill, Texas Jack, California Joe, Capt. Jack Crawford and Other Famous Scouts of the Western Plains* (Chicago: M. A. Donohue & Co., 1893), http://codyarchive.org/texts/wfc.bks00018.html.

5. This theme coincided with the Kentucky Building and the dedication of the Daniel Boone statue. See "Kentucky, Dedication of Its Home at the World's Fair," *Louisville Courier-Journal,* June 2, 1893, 1. See Rossiter Johnson, ed., *History of the World's Columbian Exposition Held in Chicago in 1893*, 4 vols. (New York: D. Appleton and Co., 1897–1898); Richard Harding Davis, "The Last Days of the Fair," *Harper's Weekly* 37 (October 21, 1893): 1002; and Johnson, *History of the World's Columbian Exposition,* vol. 1: 292–293, 306.

6. FHS Mss A/D965c/Folder 81; Folder 97 for the letter dated April 15, 1892.

7. In a letter to Edward Freiberger, Enid wrote that she had a bust of Durrett on view at an exhibition in Chicago. Freiberger was a playwright, poet, and critic who wrote reviews for the *Chicago Times* and *Tribune.* Letter from Enid Yandell to Edward Freiburger, November 5, 1891. See autograph letter of Enid Yandell, Yandell, Enid, 1870–. 5 A.L.s. to Edward Freiberger, Houghton Library Repository, Harvard University. For Durrett, See FHS Mss A/D965c/Folders 81 and 97.

8. *Starchitect* is a portmanteau word that combines *star* and *architect* to connote a practitioner of remarkable fame who designs museums, civic, and other sizable structures the look of which has become so familiar that the architect and his or her work has been popularized by works of a similar style.

9. Janet Scudder, *Modeling My Life* (New York: Harcourt, Brace & Co., 1925), 54–55, 58. Since Scudder's time, the names of women artists employed at the fair have emerged from the pages of Scudder's account and, as a result of the work of art historians and historians, their profiles have been raised; in addition to Scudder and Enid, these include Julia Bracken, Carol Brooks, Ellen Rankin Copp, Helen Farnsworth, Margaret Gerow, Mary Lawrence, Zulime Taft, and Bessie Potter Vonnoh. See Maude Howe Elliott, ed., *Art and Handicraft in the Woman's Building of the World's Columbian Exposition, Chicago, 1893* (New York: Goupil & Co., 1893); Jeanne Madeline Weimann, *The Fair Women: The Story of the Woman's Building, World's Columbian Exposition, Chicago, 1893* (Chicago: Academy Chicago, 1981). While some details regarding Enid's travel to Chicago and work at the fair, including her connection with Bertha Palmer, may be obtained from Weimann, the best accounts come from piecing together materials from primary documents in the Art Institute, Chicago History Museum, and the Filson Historical Society.

10. Letter from Thomas S. Noble to Whom It May Concern, February 27, 1893, FHS Mss A/Y21b/Folder 32. Earlier than this, however, in order to secure indepen-

dent work, Enid also obtained a letter dated August 18, 1891, from John B. Castleman. Although the contents of this letter are unknown, a response dated August 21, 1891, from Bertha Palmer on behalf of the Board of Lady Managers to Castleman indicated the board's pleasure at receiving it: "I read with great pleasure your testimonial to her unusual talent and ability as a designer. . . . thanking you for the pleasant information in regard to the remarkable work done by Miss Yandell" (Chicago History Museum, World's Fair Collection). Enid applied for an award, for which she secured an additional three letters of recommendation from fellow sculptors Karl Bitter (1867–1915) and Philip Martiny (1858–1927) and Henry Watterson, editor of the *Louisville Courier-Journal*—all of whom affirmed Enid's abilities. See FHS Mss A/Y21b/Folder 32.

11. The construction of the Woman's Building, which is beyond the scope of this study, pays heed to the ways in which women competed with one another as part of the fair work. As Erik Larson recounts, construction of the Woman's Building had "become an ordeal, both for Burhnam and its young architect, Sophia Hayden, mainly because of modifications demanded by . . . Palmer." Put simply, Bertha Palmer orchestrated every aspect of the design as soon as the foundation was laid. Hayden produced final drawings for the building in Chicago, leaving her plans with Burnham. Construction began July 9, 1891, with the final coat of staff applied in October. However, in September, without Hayden's knowledge, Palmer invited women to contribute architectural ornaments for the building and in response "had received a museum's worth of columns, panels, sculpted figures, window grills, doors, and other objects." Erik Larson, *The Devil in the White City* (New York: Crown, 2003), 142–143. Enid's caryatids were among these uninvited enhancements to the building. However, they were favorably reviewed and earned her a gold medal.

12. Letter from Enid Yandell to Bertha Honoré Palmer, October 14, 1891, Chicago History Museum, Worlds Fair Collection, Box 48, folder 9. The final sentence in the letter reads: "Mr Phillipson is anxious to begin the casting at once." The *New York Sun,* February 27, 1898, later recounted that "Miss Yandell is, in a way, one of Mrs. Potter Palmer's discoveries; though probably her light wouldn't have been hidden under a bushel long even if Mrs. Palmer had not removed the bushel." See FHS Mss A/Y21b/Folder 94.

13. The other two women earning gold medals were Bertha Palmer and Sophia Hayden, the architect of the Woman's Building. Enid's medal is now in the collection of the Speed Museum in Louisville. Letter from Daniel Burnham to Enid Yandell, October 11, 1892, FHS Mss A/Y21b/Folder 31.

14. See FHS Mss A/Y21b/Folder 32 for this undated letter (perhaps December 28, 1891) from Cooke addressed to Enid in Louisville.

15. FHS Mss A/Y21b/Folder 32, Letter from Bertha Palmer to Enid Yandell, August 29, 1891. Palmer had learned of Enid through Alice Barbee Castleman, a member of the Board of Lady Managers and fellow Kentuckian.

16. Scudder, *Modeling My Life,* 59.

17. Ibid. Although Enid completed works prior to Chicago, as recounted in the

previous chapter, it is unclear if any of these, such as the bust of Reuben T. Durrett, was actually purchased or sold, rather than given or gifted.

18. Durrett owned a portrait of Daniel Boone by Chester Harding, the only artist who painted Boone from life. For the Filson Boones (which were in the possession of Durrett at the time of the Chicago Fair), see Otto A. Rothert, "Chester Harding's Two Portraits of Daniel Boone" *Filson Quarterly* 8 (1934): [n.p.]. A handwritten letter dated April 25, 1893, from R. T. Durrett to Enid asks for the return of Boone items, referring to them as "relics": "If you are done with the Boone relics had you not better send them to me?" FHS Mss A/Y21b/Folder 59. This religious connotation in conjunction with Enid's work, and essentially Kentucky pioneerism, comes up again in an undated clipping, where the prominent figures marking the site at Harrodsburg for the Pioneer Monument tread on sacred soil for Kentuckians. Enid was among the group of six that "drove the stakes that marked the site." From the context, this clipping could be attributed to around 1924 as held in FHS Mss A/Y21b/Folder 95, p. 27. A surprising find as part of this research was the location of a typescript in the collection of the Speed Museum in Louisville, inscribed on the cover sheet "BOONE— Enid Yandell" (all underscored). I am grateful to Chuck Pittenger and Lisa Rolfe Parrott for their knowledge of the typescript item and efforts in locating it for my use during a visit in July 2017.

19. FHS Mss A/D965c/Folder 97 Durrett, Reuben T. 1824–1913, Added Papers, 1883–1910; see also FHS Mss A/Y21b/Folder 59.

20. The construction of the building was an early collaboration between William James Dodd and Mason Maury, who formed a partnership in 1889 and built the Louisville Trust in 1891, for which they hired Enid to carve capitals on the façade. Dodd is also credited with designing St. Paul's Episcopal Church (1895–1897), Enid's home church. See FHS Mss A/Y21b/Folder 59 for the agreement between the members of the Filson Club and Enid for the Boone subscription. Pledges were received from nineteen participants, whose contributions ranged from $25 to $100 each.

21. While very little is known of Enid's working method from the 1890s, we can make assessments based upon information disclosed in letters, documentation from reviews and reports of her exhibitions, as well as extant works. Like many contemporary sculptors, Enid's method involved modeling in clay so as to work with a malleable substance. Then, works could be crafted in plaster to preserve a certain handling. In the case of the world's fair sculptures, the clay was often converted directly to staff, skipping the plaster stage. In some instances, the plaster was conceived of as the "final" product, and a number of Enid's plasters exist both as preparatory works and as finished products. To give the appearance of finished material, plasters could have been tinted. If a plaster work was to be preserved and retained long term, the patron may have requested the work be cast in bronze or carved in stone. The role of sketches is less possible to know, as few sketches by Enid exist. And the role of photography, as documentary of the process, is discussed in Chapter 5. See FHS Mss A/D965c/Folder 114 for the letter, dated April 29, 1893.

22. *Inter-Ocean,* April 30, 1893, pasted on p. 65 of the scrapbook contained in FHS Mss A/Y21b/Folder 94.

23. See FHS Mss A/D965c/Folder 114 for the letter dated May 20, 1893. For the date of June 2, 1893, see FHS Mss A/Y21b/Folder 66.

24. Staff was inexpensive composite material made with concrete, plaster and hemp or other readily available organic filler. "By Kentucky Belles," *Chicago Herald,* June 2, 1893, FHS Mss A/Y21b/Folder 66.

25. Ibid.

26. *Louisville Commercial,* June 2, 1893, FHS Mss A/Y21b/Folder 66.

27. *Louisville Courier-Journal,* June 2, 1893, FHS Mss A/Y21b/Folder 66.

28. Enid's Boone was exhibited at the Columbian Exposition (1893), the Pennsylvania Academy of Fine Arts (1899), and the Louisiana Purchase Exposition in St. Louis (1904). Today the bronze Daniel Boone sculpture is a historic fixture of Louisville's Cherokee Park, part of the Olmsted Parks designed by architect Frederick Law Olmsted. See *Louisville Courier-Journal,* June 16, 1906; *Inter-Ocean,* June 16, 1906, 12.

29. Pauline King, "American Women Sculptors," *Harper's Bazaar* 32 (March 4, 1899): 180; Scudder, *Modeling My Life,* 58. See also scrapbooks in FHS Mss A/Y21b/Folders 76–78 and 94–97.

30. FHS Mss A/Y21b/Folder 69. The article continues, "She has a special gift for portraiture, and has made successful busts of Dr. D. W. Yandell, Mr. A. V. Dupont, Col. Durrett, Mrs. Locked, of New York, Mrs. F. S. Peabody of Chicago, and many others" (p. 324). The article also remarks on Enid's work on a Confederate monument, presumably the commission for Louisville that was later revoked.

31. See article by "C" entitled "The Bachelor Maid in Art," *Southern Magazine,* February 1895: 504; *Chat-Nash* clipping, which Enid dated June 14, 1894, in FHS Mss A/Y21b/Folder 66. The *Chat-Nash* clipping makes reference to the *Louisville Courier-Journal*'s description of Enid, her moving "from triumph to triumph" and the quote by Saint-Gaudens.

32. For this, Enid earned a Gold Medal, one of only three given to women at the fair. The other two gold medals awarded to women were received by the organizer of the Woman's Building, Bertha Honoré Palmer (aka Mrs. Potter Palmer) who, like Enid, was a native of Louisville, and Sophia Hayden, architect of said building. The invitation, dated October 11, 1892, from Daniel Burnham to Enid "in recognition of the services of the Architects, Artists and Designers of the World's Columbian Exposition," is found in FHS Mss A/Y21b/Folder 32.

33. *Three Girls in a Flat* fits into the genre of female artists in literature and the even narrower genre of fictionalized accounts. In this vein, consider *Little Women,* which recounts the tales of a painter named "Amy," who is purported to refer to the author's own sister, May. (Note the play on the first names as anagrams of each other.) The similarity between this framing and Enid's framing of one of the characters, Duke Wendell, (which sounds similar to Enid Yandell) cannot be overstated. See Enid Bland Yandell, Laura Hayes, and Jean Loughborough, *Three Girls in a Flat*

(Chicago: Bright, Leonard & Co., 1892). Enid's other writings include "Sculpture at the World's Fair," *Current Topics,* April 1893: 251–255; and an account of her visit to Boone using a pen name, "El Ysium" (bearing similarity to her own initials). This account, a story called "A Corner in Kentucky," described in Chapter 1, focused on Julia Dinsmore's homestead and life on the farm, as well as a view of the city (FHS Mss A/Y21b/Folder 73).

34. See brief mention of this history in Joan Bradley Wages and Doris Weatherford, Foreword, *Right Here I See My Own Books,* xi–xii. On the framing of scholarship around world's fairs and gender, see T. J. Boisseau and Abigail M. Markwyn, "World's Fairs in Feminist Historical Perspective," in *Gendering the Fair: Histories of Women and Gender at World's Fairs,* edited by T. J. Boisseau and Abigail M. Markwyn (Urbana: University of Illinois Press, 2010), 1–16. Deserving of further attention, particularly in light of Enid's work on for the Tennessee Centennial (1897) is the note of "woman's work" by the president of the Woman's Department, Katherine (Kate) Kirkman, in her address at the opening of the Woman's Building in Nashville on May 3, 1897, where she linked "sanctity" and the state's "freedom" and called upon "woman's work" to preserve one and ensure the other. See Elisabeth Israels Perry, "Memorializing the 1897 Tennessee Centennial Woman's Building," in *Gendering the Fair,* 149–165, esp. 157.

35. Such identifiers may be confirmed with a simple glance into the photographic records of Yandell's youth, a number of which are included in this book. The Duke was also known as Miss Wendell, further reflecting Enid through the similarity of their last names. Moreover, a cursory glance at Enid's genealogy reveals an uncle, David Wendel Yandell, a doctor and professor at the University of Louisville Medical Department, as well as a family connection to a branch of her Tennessee family, that of Enid's paternal grandmother, whose maiden name was Wendel. See Nancy Disher Baird, *David Wendel Yandell: Physician of Old Louisville* (Lexington: University Press of Kentucky, 1978). "Three Girls in a Flat," undated article from *New York World* pasted on p. 69 of the scrapbook in FHS Mss A/Y21b/Folder 94.

36. The association between Durrett and Rogers was first observed in Juilee Decker, "Enid Yandell (1869–1934): Kentucky's Frontier Sculptor and 'Bachelor-Maid,'" in *Kentucky Women,* edited by Melissa A. McEuen and Thomas H. Appleton, (Athens: University of Georgia Press, 2015), 196–218. In the present volume, I have expanded the discussion with regard to cider, cigars, and clay, although it merits much further investigation. While the Duke was not commissioned to make a bust of Rogers, Enid did undertake such a task by preparing the aforementioned bust of Durrett, a painted plaster completed in 1891 that was exhibited at the Art Institute of Chicago that year. It should be noted, too, that Enid inscribed a copy of *Three Girls in a Flat* to Durrett. The inscription reads: "With a merrie Xmas for my dear Colonel Durrett—Enid Yandell/92." This volume is in the Chicago History Museum.

37. *Three Girls in a Flat,* 27–28.

38. Ibid., 65–66, 75.

39. Ibid., 101, 104–105. Louis T. Rebisso (1837–1899) was a Cincinnati-based

artist whom Enid certainly knew from her training at the Academy. The sculpture of Grant was dedicated in 1891, and more than 200,000 people attended the unveiling ceremonies, including Enid. Bertha Palmer's sister, Ida, was married to Lt. Col. Frederick Dent Grant, and thus was daughter-in-law to President Ulysses S. Grant and Julia Dent Grant.

40. Ibid., 104–105.

41. "Three Girls in a Flat," undated article from *New York World* pasted on p. 69 of the scrapbook in FHS Mss A/Y21b/Folder 94.

42. Enid Yandell, "Sculpture at the World's Fair," *Current Topics,* April 1893: 251–255; *Buffalo Commercial,* May 24, 1893, 4.

43. "A Kentucky Girl's Art: Miss Enid Yandell Tells of Her Work as a Sculptor," *New York Sun,* February 27, 1898, 4.

44. "Some American Women Sculptors," *Richmond Item,* January 23, 1904, 6. Within this article, the existing bias is acknowledged: "Then there is unfortunately still considerable mediaeval masculine prejudice to be overcome."

45. Enid Yandell, "Talent for Sculpture," in *What Women Can Earn: Occupations of Women and Their Compensation,* edited by Grace H. Dodge, Thomas Hunter, et al. (New York: Frederick A. Stokes, 1898), 226–228 (quotations on p. 226; emphasis mine).

46. For the full article, see Alfred T. Goshorn, "The World's Fair and Industrial Art," *Engineering Magazine* 4, no. 5 (February 1893): 645–653, quotations on page 652 (emphasis mine). In addition to his activities in Philadelphia, Goshorn organized the Cincinnati Industrial Expositions from 1870 on and served as director of the Art Museum for at least one year (1889–1890). See Art Academy of Cincinnati Records, Mary R. Schiff Library and Archives, Cincinnati Art Museum, Cincinnati, Ohio.

47. Yandell, "Talent for Sculpture," 227.

3. Commemoration and Controversy

1. The earliest mention of Decoration Day in the extant Yandell household letters to Enid occurred in an undated letter of circa 1887 when Louise mentioned that she was to visit Cave Hill to make the graves beautiful with "white and purple lilacs": FHS Mss A/Y21b/Folder 3. For Maude's letter about Decoration Day, see her letter to Enid on May 27, 1888: FHS Mss A/Y21b/Folder 12. Enid's mother reported her visits to her husband's grave as well, on multiple occasions. See, for instance, a letter from Louise Yandell to Enid Yandell, June 7, 1894, FHS Mss A/Y21b/Folder 18.

The earliest mention of Decoration Day in the *Louisville Courier-Journal* occurred in its April 22, 1868, issue (p. 1), while accounts of the history of Decoration Day may be found in the pages of *Confederate Veteran,* a monthly publication founded in 1893 that was published of, for, and by Confederates and associated lineage organizations, including the United Confederate Veterans, the United Daughters of the Confederacy, the Sons of Confederate Veterans, the Confederated Southern Memorial Association, and others. Enid was recognized in the November 1893 issue for her work at the World's Fair.

2. "A Southern Girl at the World's Fair," *Confederate Veteran* 1 (1893): 324. David Yandell served as medical director for the armies of Albert Sidney Johnston and was with Johnston at his death on the first day of the battle at Shiloh (April 6, 1862). Yandell was very influential in education and requirement for doctors, becoming president of the American Medical Association and other organizations. See Nancy Disher Baird, *David Wendel Yandell: Physician of Old Louisville* (Lexington: University Press of Kentucky, 1978). For data regarding statuary and its imagery of the ordinary soldier, see Gaines Foster, *Ghosts of the Confederacy: Defeat, the Lost Cause, and the Emergence of the New South, 1865–1913* (New York: Oxford University Press, 1988), 129 and appendix.

3. The differentiation between working *for* men and *alongside* men contrasts Enid's reproducing another's designs with creating her own designs and seeing them through to completion. In the latter category, although Enid might report to a male superior, she was developing agency as an artist, as a maker who envisioned her own ideas. In the former category, consider the work Enid did "pointing up" sculpture at the Fair in Chicago. In the latter, consider her design for desk panels for the Royal Insurance Comapny (1890, oak and maple, location unknown), the capitals for the Louisville Trust Building (granite, 1891), commissioned busts, and her statue of Daniel Boone.

4. Foster, *Ghosts of the Confederacy,* 44. The classic work situating Kentucky and Southern women in these larger currents of American culture of this era is Anne Firor Scott, *The Southern Lady: From Pedestal to Politics, 1830–1930* (Chicago: University of Chicago Press, 1970); for a more current and readily applicable example, see Melissa A. McEuen and Thomas Appleton, eds., *Kentucky Women: Their Lives and Times* (Athens: University of Georgia Press, 2015), for which I authored a chapter on Enid Yandell.

5. I first remarked upon the connections between Enid's sculptural forms and Kentucky predecessors in 2012. See Juilee Decker, "Sculpting a Postwar Identity: Enid Yandell and Louisville's Confederate Dead," presentation at Civil War Conference, University of Louisville, March 8, 2012. Since then, I have developed a typology of Confederate monuments and have codified Kentucky monuments within this framework, which I presented through a series of lectures. See Juilee Decker, "Re-Presenting the Civil War: Monuments and Public Memory Then and Now," presented as part of "Legacy of the Civil War: Changing Memories over Time," National Endowment for the Humanities Landmarks of American History and Culture Workshop, June 30 and July 14, 2016, http://legacyofthecivilwar.org/speakers/.

6. See Kirk Savage, *Standing Soldiers, Kneeling Slaves: Race, War, and Monument in Nineteenth-Century America* (Princeton: Princeton University Press, 1997), 176. While Savage's analysis focuses on race, his use and popularization of the term "citizen-soldier" has impacted scholarship of public monuments, particularly with regard to identity and memory, which are the focus here.

7. On the Ladies' Memorial Associations, which formed from 1865 until 1900 when they confederated, see Caroline E. Janney, *Burying the Dead but Not the Past: Ladies' Memorial Associations and the Lost Cause* (Raleigh: University of North Carolina Press, 2008). On the United Confederate Veterans (or the Confederate Veterans, which was succeeded by the Sons of Confederate Veterans), see the periodical *Confederate Veteran* and historical records, such as the Minutes of the United Confederate Veterans, available online through the Internet Archive (http://archive.org) as well as Larry M. Logue and Michael Barton, eds., *The Civil War Veteran: A Historical Reader* (New York: New York University Press, 2007). For the United Daughters of the Confederacy and an associated group, Children of the Confederacy, see Karen L. Cox, *Dixie's Daughters: The United Daughters of the Confederacy and the Preservation of Confederate Culture*, New Perspectives on the History of the South (Gainesville: University Press of Florida, 2003).

8. LeeAnn Whites, *Gender Matters: Civil War, Reconstruction, and the Making of the New South* (New York: Palgrave, 2005), 88–89.

9. Confederated Southern Memorial Association, *History of the Confederated Memorial Association of the South* (New Orleans: Graham Press, 1904), 29. In support of this sense of spirit emboldened through memorial work, Margaret Cary Green Davis, historian of the Confederated Southern Memorial Association, acknowledged a connection among the women of the South, people of the future, and the sons and daughters of the women of the Confederacy, "who first banded themselves together in memorial work."

10. Ibid., 29–30; Foster, *Ghosts of the Confederacy,* 37. Elsewhere in his book Foster also addresses the Ku Klux Klan within this context of "ghosts." A different take on ghosts comes from William Faulkner, who in his novel *Absalom! Absalom!* (1936) remarked upon the role women played in the dissemination of varied, incredibly personal narratives of the war: "Years ago we in the South made our women into ladies. Then the War came and made the ladies into ghosts. So what else can we do, being gentlemen, but listen to them being ghosts." William Faulkner, *Absalom! Absalom!* (New York: Modern Library, 1936), 12. See also Anne Firor Scott, *Natural Allies: Women's Associations in American History* (Chicago: University of Chicago Press, 1991); and historical sources, including the publications of the Confederated Southern Memorial Association and the monthly *Confederate Veteran.*

11. *William Campbell Preston Breckinridge, 1837–1904* (Louisville: J. P. Morton & Co., printers, 1887), 5, 7; also John W. Petrie, "Noted Characters Memorable to Louisville: Number 26—Susan Preston Hepburn," *Louisville Courier-Journal,* June 25, 1916, 46, 49.

12. Hepburn lived in Louisville from the 1860s until her death in 1897. The monument is inscribed with the words "Our Confederate Dead, 1861–1865" making clear the purpose of the memorial. Petrie reported that "it was she who conceived the idea of honoring in bronze the dead of the Confederate army, and it was she who waged a personal and successful campaign for $20,000 and the Confederate monument on Third street." Petrie, "Noted Characters Memorable to Louisville,"

46. Hepburn's motivations were many: she was the sister of General William Preston, who served in the Confederate Army. Her motivation to memorialize came on the heels of his death in 1887. Moreover, Hepburn was the sister-in-law of General Albert Sidney Johnson, the highest-ranking fatality of the war perished at the Battle of Shiloh on April 6, 1862, an event that dealt a significant blow to the morale of the Confederacy. Upon Hepburn's death, the Confederate Association of Kentucky, a benevolent society based in Louisville, unanimously passed resolutions that reflected the importance of her work to the community, noting that her contributions "won for her the affection of all its [the association's] members" and that it was her wise counsel and encouragement that were "largely instrumental" in erecting "that beautiful monument which commemorates the courage, devotion, gallantry and renown of those who fought and died for the precious principles maintained and defended by the Confederate armies." See "Confederates Pay a Tribute to Mrs. Hepburn's Memory: Fitting Resolutions Adopted," *Louisville Courier-Journal,* October 13, 1897, 5.

13. "Probably the greatest sums were raised at four entertainments, a baza[a]r at the residence of Mrs. W. N. Haldeman, the Kindersymphony. Ben Hur and the World's Fair, the latter having been given at Music Hall in May, 1894. The order for the monument was given a few days after the fair at Music Hall and Mrs. Hepburn's dream assumed definite proportions." See Petrie, "Noted Characters Memorable to Louisville," 46. Letter from Louise to Enid, ca. January 7, 1899, FHS Mss A/Y21b/ Folder 14.

14. Petrie, "Noted Characters Memorable to Louisville."

15. See, e.g., *Louisville Courier-Journal*, September 30, 1894, 6: "For Sale—A beautiful lot just opposite the Confederate monument at intersection of Third st. and Boulevard." After the dedication, notices continued to mention the monument. See October 12, 1894, 8, for mention of a fountain put up by the Humane Society, which stated it was "placed near the site of the Confederate monument." See also *Louisville Courier-Journal,* October 16, 1894, 6 (wheelmen's celebration of the boulevard), and August 25, 1895, 6 (a listing for a property "on the west site of Third st., directly facing the beautiful Confederate Monument").

16. The call for submissions identified the site as Third Street at an intersection, within a circle. See undated clipping in Enid's scrapbook, FHS Mss A/Y21b/Folder 94. The deadline was set for September 15, 1894. The offer was made by Henry S. Tyler, Basil W. Duke, John B. Castleman, J. Stoddard Johnston, Jno. H. Leathers.

17. See undated clipping affixed to scrapbook pages in FHS Mss A/Y21b/Folder 94.

18. The gathering included Mrs. John Cabell Breckinridge as president, Mrs. W. C. P. Breckinridge as secretary, and Miss Mary Desha on the executive board. The Breckinridges and Deshas were friends of the Yandells. Information about the history of public statuary related to the Confederacy in Kentucky may be found in several sources; see, e.g., National Register of Historic Places, "Civil War Monuments in Kentucky, p. 11 (website), https://npgallery.nps.gove/pdfhost/docs/NRHP/Text/64500229.pdf. Despite inclination and intent to memorialize, during the 1860s, it was not until 1884 that a Civil War memorial was erected in a public

place in the Bluegrass State. This was the Union Soldiers' Monument in Vanceburg, Kentucky, which was placed on the Lewis County courthouse lawn. See Stuart C. McConnell, *Glorious Contentment: The Grand Army of the Republic, 1865–1900* (Chapel Hill: University of North Carolina Press, 1992), 185–193; and Rev. O. G. Rogan, *History of Lewis County* (Cincinnati: Press of Jennings and Graham, 1912), 93, 364.

19. Gaines Foster, in the conclusion to his book *Ghosts of the Confederacy,* calls attention to the ways in which the Confederate celebration following Southerner Woodrow Wilson's election to the White House was "a cultural movement . . . [that] helped create . . . 'patterns of deference'" (195). On the context for patterns of deference, see Lawrence Goodwyn, *The Populist Moment: A Short History of the Agrarian Revolt in America* (New York: Oxford University Press, 1978). Goodwyn addresses problems facing agrarian organizers in light of such patterns that had been "instilled in working Americans over generations" (99).

20. The intent, from the announcement of Enid as the winner of the competition, was to have the sculpture ready for the Grand Army of the Republic (GAR) Encampment. The politics of positioning a Confederate monument in advance of the national gathering of Union veterans who were scheduled to meet in Louisville in 1895 are an integral part of understanding civic space and the Lost Cause, as well as commemoration, but are beyond the focus of this chapter. See Caroline E. Janney, *Remembering the Civil War: Reunion and the Limits of Reconciliation* (Chapel Hill: University of North Carolina Press, 2013); Drew Gilpin Faust, *This Republic of Suffering: Death and the American Civil War* (New York: Knopf, 2008); Anne E. Marshall, *Creating a Confederate Kentucky* (Chapel Hill: University of North Carolina Press, 2010).

21. In his discussion of world's fairs, Burton Benedict has further linked patriotism to economic growth. See Burton Benedict et al., *The Anthropology of World's Fairs: San Francisco's Panama Pacific International Exposition of 1915* (Berkeley: Scolar Press and the Lowie Museum of Anthropology, 1983), 6–7.

22. FHS Mss A/Y21b/Folder 94, scrapbook, loose telegrams. The friend, "Langston," is unfamiliar in any other context of the letters, scrapbooks, and other extant materials related to Enid.

23. *Louisville Post,* September 21, 1894, affixed to scrapbook pages in FHS Mss A/Y21b/Folder 94.

24. Clipping from the *Louisville Times*, October 2, 1894, FHS Mss A/Y21b/Folder 66.

25. *Louisville Courier-Journal*, October 2, 1894, 6. This meeting was adjourned until Friday, October 5, 1894.

26. The Confederate Soldiers and Sailors Monument in Libby Hill Park in Richmond features a shaft with a Corinthian capital and a single solder on top. The thirteen cylinders comprising the column represent the thirteen Confederate states. It was dedicated May 30, 1894, and was designed by William Ludwell Sheppard. The monument at Raleigh was designed by Ferdinand Von Miller II, as was Louisville's. The cornerstone was laid May 20, 1894, and dedicated on May 20, 1895. See Smith-

sonian American Art Museum, "Art Inventories Catalog" (website), https://siris-art-inventories.si.edu/, control number 75006509. In the end, the Raleigh monument was installed prior to the Louisville monument.

27. *Louisville Courier-Journal,* October 2, 1894, 6. A report from the *Louisville Post* recorded the results of the October 1 vote to de-select Enid's monument and choose the proposal from Muldoon was affirmed: "It seems after all that there will be no further controversy over the selection of a design for the Confederate monument. The meeting Monday [October 1] ended in confusion, but it is now said the vote taken on that occasion will stand and that the Muldoon design, with the soldier surmounting the shaft, will serve for the monument. Charges of ballot-box stuffing have been withdrawn. It is now claimed that the explanation of why there were more ballots than voters is that some of the ladies left the room immediately after casting their ballots." Clipping from *Louisville Post,* October 3, 1894, FHS Mss A/Y21b/Folder 68.

28. Whites, *Gender Matters.* Whites argues that women gave over many public activities to men and "constituted no assertion of women's individual rights, autonomy, or equality with men" (90). She continues by noting how women had to dedicate their efforts toward seeing to the care of Confederate widows and orphans.

29. Undated clipping affixed to scrapbook pages in FHS Mss A/Y21b/Folder 93.

30. Wolfe, in her article on the absent stories of and about women over the two hundred years of Kentucky history, notes that their experiences offer a cross-section that "cuts through time, race, class, and circumstance." See Margaret Ripley Wolfe, "Fallen Leaves and Missing Pages: Women in Kentucky History," *Register of the Kentucky Historical Society* 90, no. 1, Focus Issue: "The Kentucky Image" (Bicentennial Issue): 64–89 (quotation on 64).

31. Ibid., 65; Whites, *Gender Matters,* 3.

32. Mary Elizabeth Massey, *Bonnet Brigades: American Women and the Civil War* (New York: Knopf, 1966), 367; Anne Firor Scott in *The Southern Lady* references the opening of doors and opportunities in her chapter title "Door after Door Is Being Flung Open" and throughout chapter 5, pp. 105–133; Massey, *Bonnet Brigades*, 367. Contrasting Scott's view, see Drew Gilpin Faust, who has argued that the loss of life during the war disrupted the domestic life of Confederate women, rendering them less, not more, emboldened: Drew Gilpin Faust, "Confederate Women and the Narratives of War," in *Divided Houses: Gender and the Civil War,* edited by Catherine Clinton and Nina Silber (New York: Oxford University Press, 1992), 171–199. See also Faust, *Mothers of Invention: Women of the Slaveholding South in the American Civil War* (Chapel Hill: University of North Carolina Press, 1996).

33. According to Gaines Foster, "approximately 75 percent were of funereal design—that is, they resembled cemetery statuary and evoked mourning rather than featuring a Confederate soldier" (*Ghosts of the Confederacy,* 41).

34. "Mr. Muldoon Says a Word, Miss Yandell and Mr. Dodd Explain Their Specifications and Offer to Amend," *Louisville Courier-Journal,* October 5, 1894, 6.

35. Records regarding the Muldoon collaboration, with Michael Muldoon, the

Ferdinand von Miller studio, and the Royal Bronze Foundry in Munich, are located in Phyllis Profumo, *Muldoon Monument Company, Kentucky, Sales Records* (Louisville, KY: The Compilers, 1895). Details regarding Enid's commission may be found in Enid's scrapbook, FHS Mss A/Y21b/Folder 94. The quoted passage comes from an undated clipping in the scrapbook.

36. "Women and a Monument," *Memphis Commercial-Appeal*, n.d. (ca. September 24, 1894), undated clipping in Enid's scrapbook, FHS Mss A/Y21b/Folder 94.

37. *Times*, October 6, 1894, clipping in Enid's scrapbook, FHS Mss A/Y21b/Folder 94.

38. Petrie, "Noted Characters Memorable to Louisville," 46.

39. Federal Writers' Project of the Works Progress Administration for the State of Kentucky, "Kentucky: A Guide to the Bluegrass State," typescript, 1939, in University of Kentucky Libraries; Federal Writers' Project of the Works Progress Administration for the State of Kentucky, *Kentucky: A Guide to the Bluegrass State* (Lexington: University of Kentucky, 3rd printing, 1942), 193 and 119; and *Louisville: A Guide to the Falls City* (Louisville: Louisville Automobile Club, 1940), 99.

40. Schaefer also acknowledged the usefulness of newspaper clippings and the generosity of Enid's relatives, including James Henning, who was of the same family line that forged the connection between the Trask and Speed families. These primary materials were important resources, because she could not view the plasters in the possession of the Speed at the time of her research. As Schaefer noted, "at the time of this writing they were stored in a warehouse in another part of the city." See Mary Phyllis Schaefer, "Enid Yandell, 1870–1934," bachelor of arts thesis, University of Louisville, 1948, n.p. Justus Bier, "Found: The Sculptor," *Louisville Courier-Journal,* June 11, 1954, 101–103. As a specialist on the German sculptor Tilman Riemenschenieder (ca. 1460–1531) and an art critic for the *Courier-Journal,* Bier felt some duty to research and correct the misinformation that his student had uncovered.

41. FHS Mss A/Y21b/Folder 27, letter from Louise to Enid dated October 6, 1899, Enid's thirtieth birthday and addressed to her in New York (13 East Twenty-Second Street).

42. Enid's grandmother died on October 4, 1897. Letter from Louise to Enid, ca. August 9, 1898, FHS Mss A/Y21b/Folder 25.

43. *New York Sun,* March 12, 1924, featuring the headlines "Bronze and Marble Worker Sun Dial's Enthusiastic Sponsor: Miss Enid Yandell, Sculptor, Has Done Meritorious Work, Gaining for Her Sex Recognition in this Field. Many of Her Best Known Pieces are Designed for the Out-of-Doors." FHS Mss A/Y21b/Folder 95, between pages 4 and 5.

44. The text on the marker indicates that it was "presented by the families of David Yandell Wood and Ian Yandell Henderson" and "Kentucky Foundation for Women and ENID: Generations of Women Sculptors" in 2004, as marker 2133. It is situated on a traffic circle at 2100 Eastern Parkway near the sculpture of Daniel Boone at Cherokee Park.

4. Fairs and Figureens

1. See clipping, ca. 1900, FHS Mss A/Y21b/Folder 105. Throughout this article, particular mention was made of Enid's Boone sculpture for the Columbian Exposition (1893)—which attracted not only the admiration of Kentuckians, but of art critics from every part of the world—and the enormous figure of Athena for the replica of the Parthenon that was built for the Centennial in Nashville. (Athena was also referred to by the goddess's Roman name, Minerva.)

2. According to art historian Linda Kim, Vonnoh's work is best understood in terms of the "qualities of the miniature, the feminine, and the domestic" that were "folded into her work." "Separate Spheres: Potterines, Gender, and Domestic Sculpture in Turn-of-the-Century America," *American Art* 28, no. 2 (Summer 2014): 3–25.

3. Following the European excursion after Enid's graduation from the Art Academy at Cincinnati in 1889, Enid seems to have relocated to Paris as early as February 1895. The earliest dated letter that mentions Paris is February 13: FHS Mss A/Y21b/Folder 19.

4. Enid would have completed sculptures of Louise Yandell and may have been at work on any of the following: Elsie Yandell, David Yandell, Alfred Victor du Pont (1894, bronze); Mayor Henry G. Lewis (in conjunction with architect Richard Hunt, 1895). For the letters from Rodin, see FHS Mss A/Y21b/Folder 33 in addition to related materials in folders 36 and 72. Details of Enid's daily life in Paris do not exist, but some elements can be pieced together through reading her letters and adding in context from Janet Scudder's biography. See Janet Scudder, *Modeling My Life* (New York: Harcourt, Brace, & Co., 1925), 101. Although Scudder does not mention Enid as being employed in the Atelier des Anges (Studio of Angels), a drawing class of American women, a photograph from the period described as such does include Enid in the group.

5. On Rodin's work, see Albert Elsen, *Rodin's Sculptural Studies for the Monument to the Burgers of Calais from the Collection for the Cantor, Fitzgerald Group* (Beverly Hills: Cantor Fitzgerald Group, 1977); Albert Elsen, *Pioneers of Modern Sculpture Exhibition, Hayward Gallery, July 20–September 23, 1973* (London: Hayward Gallery, 1973). "A Kentucky Girl's Art: Miss Enid Yandell Tells of Her Work as a Sculptor," *New York Sun,* February 27, 1898, 4.

6. "A Kentucky Girl's Art." It is unclear what contact Rodin may have had with Enid's teachers in the United States. However, all of the sculptors mentioned in this chapter would have come into contact with Rodin's work, at least through the World's Fair in 1893, thus setting the stage for the pipeline of students making their way to Paris and returning to the United States fueled by what they saw and experienced.

7. FHS Mss A/Y21b/Folder 25.

8. Susan Martis, "Famous and Forgotten: Rodin and Three American Contemporaries," PhD diss., Case Western Reserve University, 2005. See 160, notes 8, 9. Martis examines George Grey Barnard, Lorado Taft, and Malvina Hoffman. At the time of the 1876 exhibition, Rodin was living in Belgium, and his works were

assigned to the Belgian section of the exhibition. For more on Taft and 1876, see Ada Bartlett Taft, *Lorado Taft: Sculptor and Citizen* (Greensboro, NC: Mary Taft Smith, 1946), 4.

9. Martis, "Famous and Forgotten," 38–53.

10. "Tennessee Centennial Exposition," *Confederate Veteran* 5, no. 2 (February 1897): 88. In fact, closer to two million people attended, far fewer than the number at Chicago. Nonetheless, the fair was considered a successful showcase and measure of civic pride overall.

11. The builder was Robert T. Creighton; the structure was made of wood and plaster. After the fair, the Parthenon remained the only remnant of the fair. By 1920, it was deemed beyond repair, and plans were made to replace it with an exact replica of the Parthenon in Athens. See National Register of Historic Places, February 23, 1972, NHRP 72001236, db0a0b39–976b-43da-a351-f62f172136d5.

12. A portion of the 132-acre park belonged to Enid's mother's family, the Ellistons, and was known as the Burlington plantation. The family's mansion was built in 1859 by William R. Elliston, with William Strickland as the architect. (Strickland was from Philadelphia and also designed the Tennessee state capitol. He drew up plans for the expansion and renovation of Burlington, but died before construction began.) For letters from Louise Yandell to Enid Yandell dated March 1, 1896, see FHS Mss A/Y21b/Folder 20; letters dated February 1, 1897 through February 8, 1897, see FHS Mss A/Y21b/Folder 21.

13. Letter from Louise Yandell to Enid Yandell, March 21, 1898, FHS Mss A/Y21b/Folder 24; October 30, 1896, FHS Mss A/Y21b/Folder 20.

14. Letter from Louise Elliston to Enid Yandell, March 1, 1896, FHS Mss A/Y21b/Folder 20. The events at the fair are recounted in Herman Justi, ed., *Official History of the Tennessee Centennial Exposition* (Nashville: Allied Printing, 1898), 103, 85, 100.

15. These details were recounted by Joseph May, who wrote an article on Enid in an American publication, *The Paris World,* ca. 1902. See FHS Mss A/Y21b/Folder 89. Afterward, Enid commented on the affair, "We were a merry party but we were also somewhat weird. Our voices sounded strangely within the statue, and our faces glowed in the lamplight." Ibid. This story is one of many detailed by Marion Porter on the occasion of the donation of works by Enid to the Speed Art Museum in 1941. See Porter, "This Girl Sculptor Was of Uncommon Clay," *Louisville Courier-Journal,* February 9, 1941, 67.

16. FHS Mss A/Y21b/Folder 89, article, pp. 19–20.

17. Letter from Louise Elliston to Enid Yandell, March 7, 1897, FHS Mss A/Y21b/Folder 22.

18. Justi, *Official History,* 101 and passim. Justi's guidebook to the fair reproduces a photograph of Enid at work in the studio as she stands beside Athena's face in profile, beneath a scaffold, and in front of the larger torso of the sculpture. The image is captioned "Pallas Athena in the Studio," suggesting that Enid herself is Athena. Ibid., 118.

19. Letter from Louise Yandell to Enid Yandell, May 3, 1897, FHS Mss A/Y21b/Folder 22. The ground floor plan for Burlington, also known as the Elliston-Ferrell Home, may be seen at the Tennessee State Library and Archives, Nashville (Image 601, Houses; Floor Plans, "Ground floor plan for Burlington," Library Collection, Drawer 3, Folder 146), along with a number of interior views (including Image 607, Bedrooms, Ma's Room, "Elizabeth Boddie Elliston's Room, at Burlington," Library Collection, Drawer 3, Folder 152).

20. A clipping from Program of the Tennessee Centennial, 7, in FHS Mss A/Y21b/Folder 94. See also Herman Justi, *The Official Catalogue of the Tennessee Centennial Exposition* (Nashville: Burch & Hinton, 1897); Justi, *Official History*; and Don H. Doyle, "Tennessee Centennial Exposition of 1897," in *The Tennessee Encyclopedia of History and Culture,* edited by Carrol Van West (Knoxville: University of Tennessee Press, 2002). The poster for the opening day included an image of Athena, although Enid is not attributed as the creator. And the cover of Justi's official history of the exhibition featured a gold embossing of Pallas Athena. For more on the Nashville fair, see Bruce G. Harvey, *World's Fairs in a Southern Accent: Atlanta, Nashville, and Charleston, 1895–1902* (Knoxville: University of Tennessee Press, 2014).

21. Letters from Louise to Enid, January 4, 1897, and January 12, 1897, FHS Mss A/Y21b/Folder 21.

22. The Official Catalogue identified the following items in the exhibition of statuary as Enid's: 997, *Indian Praying* (also known as *Allah il Allah*); 998, Portrait of M'Fargo; 999, Portrait of Miss Yandell; 1000, Mrs. Outhwaite; 1001, Mr. Barker; 1002, Mrs. Kuhn; 1003, Miss McPherson. See Justi, *Official Catalogue,* 100. In addition to this selection of statuary in the Fine Arts exhibition that was organized by artist, two additional sculptures by Enid were on view at the fair. The bust of Landon Cabell Garland (identified as number 629, in Justi, *Official Catalogue,* 95) was on view in the Parthenon, in the section for loaned collections, since it was lent by the alumni of Vanderbilt University. The bust of Kirkman, which was an exemplar of Enid's figureen type, was on view in the Woman's Building. See Justi, *Official History*, 459.

23. Louise wrote to Enid about the Boone: "He wants me to send down the Daniel Boone—Can you give me any idea which boxes it is in[?] Col. Durrett doesn't want to send his. Will I have to open all the boxes to get the other things out?" See Letter from Louise to Enid, March 7, 1897, FHS Mss A/Y21b/Folder 22. This suggests that there were at least two Boone statues by this time, if Durrett had one and another was in Enid's studio.

24. *Nashville American* [n.d.], p.10, FHS Mss A/Y21b/Folder 94.

25. Justi, *Official History,* 459, for the reference to *Allah-il-Allah* and the bust of Mrs. Van Leer Kirkman; reference to Elsie and Garland, see *Nashville American* [n.d.], p. 10, FHS Mss A/Y21b/Folder 94.

26. As of 2017, the "second" bust is located in Stevenson Hall (Science Library); its predecessor was on view outside the chancellor's door on the second floor of Kirkland Hall. Email from Joseph S. Mella, Director of Vanderbilt University Fine Arts

Gallery, and Teresa Gray, Public Service Archivist, Vanderbilt University, April 14, 2017. See also Robert Lagemann, "Alumni Business Meeting," *Vanderbilt University Quarterly* 7, no. 3 (July 1907): 208, which described the action to replace the bust as being swift.

27. Painted plaster models for the bronze panels are in the collection of the Speed Museum, Louisville, Kentucky (1941.14.2, 1941.14.3, 1941.14.4). On July 13, 2017, upon my own inspection of the bas relief plasters for the Thomas Monument, I was able to observe the nature of Enid's construction. The back of each panel was grooved, non-smooth plaster with wooden stretcher bars at the top and bottom for support and hanging, presumably for display in Enid's studio. An additional, larger set of plasters, retained by Enid in her studio, are in the collection of the city of Edgartown, Massachusetts, as they await conservation work. For some time, at least one of these was view in the Edgartown School. Upon my visit to Edgartown in August 2017, the plasters were unable to be located, though their presence in Edgartown was recounted in newspaper reports as well as anecdotes.

28. Letter from D. B. Kelly to Louise Yandell, February 10, 1902, FHS Mss A/Y21b/Folder 35; *Woman's Work in Tennessee* (Memphis: Tennessee Federation of Women's Clubs, 1916), 143.

29. "President McKinley Favors Reciprocity," *New York Times,* September 6, 1901, 1; and Robert W. Rydell, *All the World's a Fair: Visions of Empire at American International Expositions, 1876–1916* (Chicago: University of Chicago Press, 1984), 6. It should be noted that Enid and her colleagues, in the fictionalized account *Three Girls in a Flat,* mentioned "woman as the inventor of the industrial arts and the first maker of the home": Enid Bland Yandell, Laura Hayes, and Jean Loughborough, *Three Girls in a Flat* (Chicago: Bright, Leonard & So., 1892), 76.

30. "Miss Yandell, Sculptor," *New York World,* September 5, 1897, FHS Mss A/Y21b/Folder 94.

31. Enid explained her interest in securing the Boone in a letter to Reuben T. Durrett, July 23, 1899. In a later letter to Durrett, Enid noted that the French "are much interested in our American pioneers": Enid Yandell to Reuben T. Durrett, January 10, 1900, Reuben Thomas Durrett Papers, 1821–1931, Filson Historical Society, Mss A D965.

32. While Enid held her own, "the vast majority of women who succeeded professionally as sculptors in 19th-century France did not comport themselves, nor did they produce work according to the individualistic, traditionally male model offered by [Camille] Claudel." The work of Camille Claudel (1864–1943) has recently been re-presented within the context of equal attribution and contribution, rather than disserved as mistress and muse of Rodin. Nevertheless, it is not known whether Claudel and Yandell knew one another, although certainly their paths may have crossed in studio circles, given Enid's travels and studies in Paris in conjunction with Claudel's intersection with Rodin beginning in 1883. For more on Claudel, see Anastasia Louise Easterday, "Charting a Course in an Intractable Profession: Women Sculptors in 19th-Century France," Ph.D. Dissertation, UCLA, 1997, 14.

33. John G. Carlisle (1835–1910) served in the Kentucky House and Senate and was also lieutenant governor of the state. On the federal level, he served as Speaker of the House and served as President Grover Cleveland's Secretary of the Treasury from 1893 to 1897. Enid knew Carlisle and enlisted his assistance in 1901 to defeat a case against her landlord, Charles R. Stein, who owned the studio building where Enid lived in New York (at 23 East Seventy-Fifth Street). At issue was the condition of Enid's fourth-floor apartment, specifically a problem with roof leaks, "when snow melted and ruined some of her pictures" and her inability to get water on the top floor. Neither Carlisle nor the defendant appeared in court with Enid, so the case was dismissed. See "Miss Yandell Wins Her Case," *Brooklyn Daily Eagle,* March 6, 1901, 3.

34. John M. Carrère, "The Architectural Scheme," in *Art Hand-Book: Official Handbook of Architecture and Sculpture and Art Catalogue to the Pan-American Exposition,* edited by David Gray (Buffalo, NY: David Gray, 1901), 16.

35. Karl Bitter, "The Sculpture Plan," in *Art Hand-Book,* 78.

36. See David Gray, *Catalogue of the Exhibition of Fine Arts/Pan-American Exposition, Buffalo, 1901* (Buffalo: D. Gray, 1901), 72, for the listings of items 1665, 1666, and 1667, along with the title of each work: *Baroness de Braunecker*; *Mermaid and Fisher Boy* (pewter tankard); and *Bust of the Honorable John G. Carlisle* (lent by Hon. J. G. Carlisle), respectively.

37. The description of the Boone concludes with notice of the artist's name; however, Enid's association is with New York in this instance. See Mark Bennitt, *History of the Louisiana Purchase Exposition: Comprising . . . a Full Account of the Great Exposition, . . . Comp. from Official Sources* (St. Louis: Universal Exposition Pub. Co., 1905), 80. In the description of the sculpture leading from the exposition's lower ground up to the Colonnade of the States, Marshall Everett draws attention to the portrait statues and their context. See *The Book of the Fair: The Greatest Exposition the World Has Ever Seen Photographed and Explained, a Panorama of the St. Louis Exposition* (Philadelphia: P. W. Ziegler, 1904), 483.

38. Bennitt, *History of the Louisiana Purchase Exposition,* 539.

39. See FHS Mss A/Y21b/Folder 94.

40. In a letter from Enid to F. Edwin Elwell written from Paris on September 9, 1902, Enid thanks Elwell for his letter of August 6 and sends some information that Elwell had asked for. Accompanying the letter are two handwritten pages, including a list of Enid's commissions to date. The handwriting appears not to be Enid's but rather Geysa's. The letter describes some of Enid's travel to and from Paris. See "Yandell, Enid—Correspondence," Item b1724662, Metropolitan Museum of Art, New York, New York. A clipping of a photograph of Enid's *Mermaid and Fisher-Boy* in bronze (identified as a cast by Jno. Williams Bronze Foundry) is also in the possession of the museum. The two items may have been related, perhaps having to do with the museum acquiring one of Enid's work, such as the *Kiss Tankard.*

41. See AWH, "Woman's Work: Enid Yandell, Sculptor," *New Century Path* 7,

no. 8 (January 3, 1904): 6; "A Southern Sculptress and Some of Her Work," *New York Journal*, September 5, 1898.

5. Passions and Pursuits

1. Letter from Louise Yandell to Enid, September 20, 1896, FHS Mss A/Y21b/ Folder 20.

2. Enid's career is anchored in two significant moments in art history, the World Columbian Exposition in 1893 and the Armory Show of 1913, of which the latter has been recognized as a catalyst for American artists who became more independent and created their own "artistic language" as independent, though springing from, their European roots. The show was on view in New York City on Lexington Avenue between Twenty-Fifth and Twenty-Sixth Streets, from February 17, and remained on view until March 15, 1913. Enid's works here included a work of unknown medium (likely plaster or staff) entitled *Indian and Fisher,* which was exhibited in Gallery A, American Sculpture and Decorative Art. Moving from documentation to allegory, Enid's other contribution, a bronze vase sculpture entitled *The Five Senses,* bore witness to classical subject through its relief of allegorical figures representing the five senses as figures hold flowers, a ball, a conch shell, a mirror, and grapes (for smell, touch, hearing, sight, and taste).

3. Nancy Disher Baird noted: "The Parisian firm Rudier properly cast the tankard in bronze for a yachting trophy, but when Tiffany and Company of New York made the vessel in silver for the 1899 Christmas market, the silversmith miscalculated. . . . Despite the error [of the boy overshooting the mermaid's lips] Yandell gave one of the silver cups to her sister Elsie as a wedding gift." See Baird, "Enid Yandell: Kentucky Sculptor," *Filson Club History Quarterly* 62, no. 1 (January 1988): 19. In her discussion of the wedding gift Enid made for Elsie, Désirée B. Caldwell noted, "This version of the tankard is possibly the one owned by the Rhode Island School of Design Museum, but the evidence is not certain." See Désirée B. Caldwell, "A Brief Account of the Life and Works of Enid Yandell," honors thesis, Brown University, May 15, 1978, 26.

4. The correspondence comes from the Files for Enid Yandell, RISD Museum, Providence, RI. Given that I have seen neither of the silver versions firsthand, I can only rely upon auction records for information. I believe these two silvers are not the same. At Bonham's in 2017, lot 36 was described as "An American Sterling Silver Art Nouveau Style Figural Tankard" by Enid Yandell of Louisville, Kentucky, and New York, New York. This item was part of "The Elegant Home: Select Furniture, Silver, Decorative and Fine Arts," an auction held on June 6, 2017. The other silver was sold in "The Jerome Rapoport Collection of American Aesthetic Silver" on June 20, 1996, at Sotheby's New York as lot no. 82, where it sold for $5,750 including premium. This tankard was described as *The Kiss,* ca. 1890, with a provenance from the Historical Design sale in New York, October 22, 1988.

5. Enid refrained from using the tankard design after her work on the *Kiss Tankard*, and made few vessels in her career. She created a mug or stein bearing symbols of Kentucky for William Edmund Halsey in 1904. For more on this, see Chapter 8.

6. The description of the grottos may be found in Herman Justi, ed., *Official History of the Tennessee Centennial Exposition* (Nashville: Allied Printing, 1898), 101; the work of the Lapini Brothers in Justi, *Official Catalogue of the Tennessee Centennial Exposition* (Nashville: Burch & Hinton, 1897), 29; that of Moretti in Justi, *Official Catalogue,* 100, 187. See FHS Mss A/Y21b/Folder 23 for letters from Enid's mother before and after the fair, which refer (in November) to a visit from Geysa and Enid as well as her mother's caring for Enid's dog, Thias, later in the year, once Enid had settled in her New York studio.

7. "American Art in Modeling in Silver," *Jewelers' Circular and Horological Review* 37, no. 24 (January 11, 1899): 1. This periodical was published by Jewelers' Circular Publishing Company. "Cincinnati," *Jewelers Review* 32, May 31, 1899: 693; June 1899 *Illustrated Kentuckian* pasted in Enid's scrapbook, in FHS Mss A/Y21b/Folder 94.

8. The mention of a "silver" loving cup for Elsie throws into question whether the *Kiss Tankard* was the item that Enid had created for Elsie, because Gorham had cast ten silver pieces in the 1898 season, meaning they would have appeared a year prior to Elsie's wedding. Second, Enid's brother, Lunsford, wrote about expenses and the potential purchase of a tankard from Gorham that had been cast in bronze. Enid forwarded information she had received from the foundry on June 14 in a July 21 letter to Lunsford. In his reply, Lunsford wrote to Enid on July 24, 1918, in agreement to purchase a "loving cup." See FHS Mss A/Y21b/Folder 36. For Elsie's wedding, see "Matrimonial Matters," *Stanford (KY) Interior Journal,* November 24, 1899, 1. The Yandell-Barber wedding occurred at noon on November 23, 1899, at Christ Church Cathedral and was officiated by Bishop Thomas Underwood Dudley. The wedding party included sister Maude as the bridesmaid, with brother Lunsford as one of the groomsmen.

9. Letter from Maude Yandell to Enid, November 23, 1899. Enid was staying at 17 Rue Davioud in Paris. Maude's reference to Sunshine is interesting here, as that was their maternal grandmother's pet name for Enid. Maude's use of that term was probably intentional. See FHS Mss A/Y21b/Folder 27 for both letters and the clipping.

10. In various publications, Carrie's death has been reported as early as 1892 and as late as 1919. The specifics of this, along with insight into the relationship between Paul and Carrie may be found in Rush C. Hawkins, *A Tribute to the Memory of Carrie Matilde Bajnotti* (New York: Devinne Press, 1893), located in John Hay Library, Brown University, Providence, Rhode Island. Hawkins was married to Annmary Brown, Carrie's sister.

11. This project was overseen by the Carrie Brown Memorial Fountain Commission, which included the mayor of Providence, who presided as chair (Democrat

William Cotter Baker served in this capacity January 1898–January 1901, succeeded by Daniel L. D. Granger); John Carter Brown; lawyer John C. Pegram; and artist Sidney R. Burleigh. The administration of the commission was handled by Daniel F. George, secretary of the commission; and James A. George, secretary pro tem. The commission invited eighteen sculptors and architects to submit designs. In addition, at least two other professionals submitted designs. See "The Brown Fountain," *Providence Journal,* June 27, 1901, 4.

12. Letters from Enid Yandell to Daniel F. George, March 13 and May 2 1899, RG 33 Series AN 20086, Carrie Brown Memorial Fountain, City Archives, Providence, Rhode Island. A number of letters with affirmations, queries, and declinations from other sculptors are also held in the City Archives.

13. Invitations were sent out to sculptors and architects, who were asked to prepare designs and models. Architects were asked to submit a plan, one elevation, and a perspective sketch, with a scale of 2 inches :1 foot. Sculptors were asked to furnish a model for their designs on the same scale. No prize was awarded for the accepted design, other than the commission itself and the funds for it ($9,500). It is unclear why the invitations from the city stipulated a $9,500 award, rather than the full $10,000 award from Bajnotti; perhaps the difference went to the awards that were granted. Awards were given to the better designs, including $100 to the first prize (H. L. Hubert); $75 for the second (Oscar L. Lenz); and $50 for the third (William W. Mannatt). See RG 33 Series AN 20086, Carrie Brown Memorial Fountain, City Archives, Providence, Rhode Island.

14. "No Decision: Commission on Bajnotti Memorial Fountain Talk Over the Designs," *Providence Journal,* July 18, 1899. Kraus also submitted a second design, which appeared in the July 23, 1899, issue of the *Providence Journal*, p. 8.

15. The announcement read "Enid Yandell's Design for Bajnotti Fountain," *Providence Journal,* July 22, 1899, 2. Letter from Enid Yandell to Reuben Durrett, July 30, 1899. See Reuben Thomas Durrett Papers, 1821–1931, Filson Historical Society, Mss A D965. Later in life Enid referred to her relationship as "having worked with" Rodin, rather than being his pupil. For this context, see "Talks on Sculpture" *Vineyard Gazette,* August 30, 1924, a photocopy of which is in the Nancy Disher Baird Manuscript Collection, Box 7, Folder 4, Western Kentucky University, Bowling Green, KY.

16. Regarding the backlash, see *Boston Globe,* July 28, 1899, 4.

17. "Mr. Kraus' View," *Boston Evening Record,* July 28, 1899.

18. The two pages with an article and the handwritten comments can be found in a scrapbook owned by Enid Yandell. The handwriting does not appear to be Enid's. This scrapbook was given to the Speed Museum by Elsie Barber Trask in 1941 and is now in the collection of the University of Louisville Special Collections.

19. Unidentified clipping, "Design for Memorial Pleases the Donor," located in RG 33 Series AN 20086, Carrie Brown Memorial Fountain, City Archives, Providence, Rhode Island.

20. On the day before the fountain's debut, Enid traveled to Providence; while there, she inspected the fountain herself. See the image "Miss Yandell Inspecting the Fountain," *Providence Journal,* June 27, 1901, 4.

21. RG 33 Series AN 20086, Carrie Brown Memorial Fountain, City Archives, Providence, Rhode Island.

22. A number of issues arose with the fabrication of the basin and the support of the bronze central figure group. Part of this may be due to Enid's innovative design, but part may also be due to the number of collaborators and their need to communicate with the city, which was overseeing the project. See RG 33 Series AN 20086, Carrie Brown Memorial Fountain, City Archives, Providence, Rhode Island.

23. Some accounts indicate that there are just four figures: three men and the Angel of Truth. I see two women, however, one exposing her face and the other exposing her back. The presence of five figures is also in keeping with Enid's text, which identifies five discrete individuals. The base of the fountain, when treated as an independent unit, is referred to as *The Passions.* See FHS Mss A/Y21b/Folder 88 and Richard Ladegast, "Enid Yandell, the Sculptor," *Outlook* 70, no. 1 (1902): 81–84.

24. Commission Minutes, June 26, 1901, RG 33 Series AN 20086, Carrie Brown Memorial Fountain, City Archives, Providence, Rhode Island.

25. Enid completed more than twenty works over this period. In addition, the full-scale plaster model of the fountain was exhibited at the Pan-American Exposition in Buffalo in 1901, where it earned an honorable mention, and was exhibited at the New York Florists' Club and the National Sculpture Society exhibit at Madison Square Garden in 1902.

26. A photograph in the collection of the Filson Historical Society suggests that Enid employed a model as part of her creation process for the fountain. See FHS 987PC52.x.93, which shows the plaster of the fountain; an inscription in Enid's hand reads, "A ma modelle Marcelle avec mes compliments Enid Yandell sculptor" ("To my model, Marcelle, with my compliments Enid Yandell sculptor").

27. Status updates from Enid provide context, including a November 14, 1900, letter from Enid to Secretary George regarding the cast's state and a later letter from Enid to Mayor Baker regarding the long travel time due to the size of the sculpture. Enid herself also traveled to the United States, arriving in mid-December and writing Secretary George about a meeting in Providence. Regarding the meeting, see letter from Enid to Daniel F. George, December 19, 1900, RG 33 Series AN 20086, Carrie Brown Memorial Fountain, City Archives, Providence, Rhode Island. She attended a meeting of the Commission at City Hall on December 28, 1900.

28. See FHS Mss A/Y21b/Folder 94, scrapbook, p. 34. Based in Providence, Gorham had previously cast bronze doors, weighing 1,000 pounds apiece, in 1898. For a history of the firm, see Charles H. Carpenter, *Gorham Silver* (San Francisco: Alan Wofsy Fine Arts, 1997).

29. Letters from Enid Yandell to Daniel F. George, January 6 and July 12, 1900, RG 33 Series AN 20086, Carrie Brown Memorial Fountain, City Archives, Providence, Rhode Island.

30. Letters from Enid Yandell to Daniel F. George, January 6 and May 24, 1900, RG 33 Series AN 20086, Carrie Brown Memorial Fountain, City Archives, Providence, Rhode Island.

31. Letter from Enid Yandell to Daniel F. George, April 18, 1900, RG 33 Series AN 20086, Carrie Brown Memorial Fountain, City Archives, Providence, Rhode Island.

32. Regarding "marble," see letter and telegram from Enid Yandell to Daniel F. George, both dated July 19, 1899, RG 33 Series AN 20086, Carrie Brown Memorial Fountain, City Archives, Providence, Rhode Island. Enid's methods as outlined here are aspects of her working process heretofore unresearched due to the dearth of material in terms of correspondence from "the other side"—those who commissioned her to make particular pieces—and merits fuller attention.

33. "The Brown Fountain," *Providence Journal,* June 27, 1901, 4.

34. Commission Minutes, October 28 and December 4, 1901, RG 33 Series AN 20086, Carrie Brown Memorial Fountain, City Archives, Providence, Rhode Island. Bajnotti was present at the October meeting. The December 4 meeting was the final convocation of the Carrie Brown Memorial Fountain Commission. Both amounts were paid to Enid. The $1,000 was paid as a note in Louise Elliston Yandell's name at Enid's mother's bank, while the $351.91 was paid through the city auditor's office to Enid in November 1901.

35. "Going to Paris Soon to Complete Fountain Model," *Providence Telegram,* July 29, 1899; Louise Hall Tharp, *Saint-Gaudens and the Gilded Age* (Boston: Little, Brown & Co., 1969), 304–305; and Lorado Taft, *The History of American Sculpture* (New York: Macmillan, 1930), 451.

36. Saint-Gaudens gave his work the title *The Mystery of the Hereafter and the Peace of God that Passeth Understanding.* The memorial is also known by a third title, *Grief.* On this monument, see Cynthia J. Mills, "Casting Shadows: The Adams Memorial and Its Doubles," *American Art* 14, no. 2 (Summer 2000): 2–25.

37. The equestrian statue of Burnside, by Launt Thompson, was created in 1887 and sited at Exchange Place before its relocation to the site described in the text in 1906. In other words, during Enid's day, this plot of land would have been landscaped, but otherwise fairly empty.

38. "Miss Yandell's Design for Bajnotti Fountain," *Providence Journal,* July 25, 1899; Ladegast, "Enid Yandell, the Sculptor," 83; George D. Laswell, *Corners and Characters of Rhode Island* (Providence: Oxford Press, 1924), as printed in the *Providence Evening Bulletin,* April 24, 1924. Also see handwritten note on the top portion of a newspaper clipping located in an interleaved book by Hawkins, *A Tribute to the Memory of Carrie Matilde Bajnotti,* located in the John Hay Library, Brown University.

39. Enid's studio address is known through letterhead that she used in communication with the Carrie Brown Memorial Fountain Commission. Borglum's address is found on a printed business card as well as letterhead from several years later, his 1915 letters to Enid. See FHS Mss A/Y21b/Folder 36.

40. Enid's residence may be gleaned from her emergency passport application of February 8, 1915, where she named Edgartown as her permanent residence, thus affirming the need for an address at the service of Borglum. She also indicated that she left the United States in November 1913 and had been temporarily living at 10 Villa St. Jacques Boul., St. Jacques, Paris. See Emergency Passport Applications, Argentina–Venezuela, 1906–1925, ARC Identifier 1244183/MLR no. A1 544, Box 4534, vol. 150, National Archives and Records Administration (NARA), Washington, DC. The letter from Borglum is located in FHS Mss A/Y21b/Folder 36.

41. Borglum left the project in 1924 due to disputes with his patrons.

42. See FHS Mss A/Y21b/Folder 36.

43. The *Vineyard Gazette,* January 6, 1916, reported: "Miss Enid Yandell, the well known sculptor, who is a valued summer resident of Edgartown is, we are told, under a three years' contract, with other American sculptors, to work under the direction of Gutzon Borglum, the distinguished American sculptor, who will carve Stone Mountain, near Atlanta, Ga., into a monument to the Southern Confederacy." This is the only mention known to date that authorized Enid's acceptance of the invitation from Borglum. The project, and Borglum's role in it, did not take off until several years later, after World War I. See Western Kentucky University, Box 7, Folder 4.

44. Enid's scrapbook is both diary and archive. Pages 49–50 (loose) contain Gutzon Borglum, "Carving Mountains into Monuments," *New York Herald Tribune,* August 21, 1927: FHS Mss A/Y21b/Folder 67. Enid also retained two copies of Lord Guthrie's writing on Gutzon Borglum, which was mistyped as "Gorglum" (on the second copy, Enid corrected his name to "Borglum"): FHS Mss A/Y21b/Folder 73. *Centaur and Centauress* is a tabletop plaster in the Speed Museum, 1941.14.16. No other versions of the work are known to exist in plaster; however, one or more may be extant and catalogued by another title, such as *Centaurs* or *Two Centaurs.* For instance, a work of Borglum's described as "one group of Centaurs" is described in an exhibition review that appears in the *Topeka Daily Capital,* November 6, 1905, 4. A larger marble, 43½ inches high, titled *Centaurs,* recently sold at Sotheby's in the American Paintings, Drawings, and Sculpture show on October 10, 2007, lot 250.

45. Information about Borglum's two marriages (to Elizabeth Janes Putnam 1899–1908, although they separated in 1903; and Mary Montgomery Williams from 1909 on) and his artistic development may be found in a number of scholarly and popular treatments of the artist and his art. See Robert J. Casey and Mary Borglum, *Give the Man Room: The Story of Gutzon Borglum* (New York: Bobbs-Merrill, 1952); and Mervyn Davies, *The Man Who Stood Alone* (Chester, CT: Pequot Press, 1974).

6. Edgartown and Education

1. It is unclear why Enid chose Edgartown to visit in 1907. No one from her family appears to have gone there prior to her stay, although newspaper accounts report that family and friends, including Enid's sister Maude and Maude's friend, Pauline May of Louisville, visited in 1908. In addition, Enid's sister Elsie visited

with her husband Donn and their three daughters from at least 1919. Enid's mother's death in 1908 perhaps facilitated the sculptor's commitment to live in New York and Edgartown, without regular visits to Kentucky or Tennessee, where her parents had roots. (Enid's siblings Maude and Lunsford had remained in or near Louisville and were thus able to help their aging mother as needed). For the quotes by Elsie, see unpublished manuscript by Nancy Baird, undated (1977–1988?), which the author kindly shared with me.

2. A report from the year 1924 of the Dukes County Historical Society showed Enid as a member for 1922–1923: FHS Mss A/Y21b/Folder 64. Regarding the 1908 exhibit, see "A Delightful Evening," *Vineyard Haven Gazette,* October 15, 1908. Regarding the lecture, see FHS Mss A/Y21b/Folder 60. The 1916 event was held on March 25, as part of the Woman's Press Club program. In a letter from Paris dated July 27, 1914, Enid addressed "My dear friends in Edgartown." In this note, she recounted a trip taken with dogs and suitcases and questions behavior during the war, especially the destruction of architecture: "Why will the people destroy beauty when they come in power! Or was it the church they hated?" FHS Mss A/Y21b/Folder 36. On her birthday following Enid's death, October 6, 1934, Enid's friends gathered to consecrate a silver lavabo in the church. It had the following inscription: "To the Glory of God, in Memory of Enid Yandell, from Her Loving Friends." *Vineyard Gazette,* October 12, 1934. The silver cup is still owned, and often used, by St. Andrew's Episcopal Church, Martha's Vineyard.

3. The earliest obituary for Enid appeared the day after her death and focused primarily on her work and accomplishments; a second, more personal, notice appeared a few days later in Massachusetts. See "Enid Yandell Dies: A Noted Sculptor," *New York Times,* June 13, 1934, 23; "Woman Who Designed Many Memorials Dead: Miss Enid Yandell of Edgartown Won World Wide Fame, Career Ends," *Vineyard Gazette,* June 15, 1934, 1-2. The latter of these provides details about her work practice, including mention of her studio having been designed by her brother-in-law Donn Barber, a New York architect. See "Woman Who Designed Many Memorials Dead," 2. While both point out that Enid may have taken a residence in Boston, the notice in the *Vineyard Gazette* pointed out that Enid died in a Boston sanitarium following an illness of several months (since December 1933), which included a nervous breakdown followed by a heart attack (ibid.). In addition, a receipt in FHS Mss A/Y21b/Folder 44 shows a piece of stationery with an address in Boston and a date of November 11, 1929. Further research is needed in this area of Enid's life and work (ca. 1929 on). On at least one occasion a notice of a program appeared in the Martha's Vineyard paper for Christmas at the Yandell Studio, Friday, December 26, 1924. The text included a note that "Miss Yandell furnished the studio for the occasion," suggesting that sometimes Enid was in Edgartown in the wintertime. See FHS Mss A/Y21b/Folder 66.

4. The chapters following this one further address Enid's life and work, but thematically, focusing on her advocacy and activism, her pioneerism, and her legacy.

5. Several documents from FHS Mss A/Y21b/Folder 43 include a purchase

agreement and leases on Enid Yandell's Branstock property, Edgartown, Mass.., 1919–1929.

6. The properties that Enid owned in Edgartown included Branstock and two adjacent houses, one of which was on Summer Street opposite the *Vineyard Gazette,* according to Helen Allen, "An Essay on 'Aunt Enid' in Honor of Elsie Barber Trask, Enid's Favorite Niece" (unpublished manuscript, ca. 2003–2007).

7. Enid was friends with performers of theater and opera, including Julia Marlowe (a calling card of Marlowe's is located in FHS Mss A/Y21b/Folder 32; see also correspondence from Marlowe in FHS Mss A/Y21b/Folder 33, 38, 94) and Augusta Holmes (see letter dated July 20, 1902, located in FHS Mss A/Y21b/Folder 35, and notations that Enid made to an article in FHS Mss A/Y21b/Folder 89). Enid also took notice of opera through the work of Andreas Pavley (FHS Mss A/Y21b/Folder 57). The mention of European travel occurs in a letter ca. March 1, 1889, in FHS Mss A/Y21b/Folder 75.

8. See, for instance, an exhibition listing of Leo F. Dorn's work at The Vineyard Weaver, August 5–12 [n.d.], in FHS Mss A/Y21b/Folder 75.

9. Arthur R. Freedlander was an instructor at the Martha's Vineyard School of Art. Thomas Hart Benton spent his summers on Martha's Vineyard from 1920 until 1975. See *Thomas Hart Benton* (New York: Harry N. Abrams, 1974) cited in Karal Ann Marling, *Wall-to-Wall America: Post Office Murals in the Great Depression* (Minneapolis: University of Minnesota Press, 1982), 74n22. For the Provincetown Art Association, see "Biggest Art Colony in the World Near Boston," *Boston Globe,* August 27, 1916, 1. A bit further afield was the Nantucket Art Colony, which was in operation 1920–1945; see https://nha.org/digitalexhibits/artistcolony/index.htm.

10. John H. Dryfhout, "The Cornish Colony," in *A Circle of Friends: Art Colonies of Cornish and Dublin* (Durham, NH: University Art Galleries, 1985), 33.

11. Commissioned in 1883 and dedicated in 1897, the Shaw Memorial honors the first Civil War regiment of African-Americans enlisted in the North. See Lindsay R. Harris, *Tell It with Pride: The 54th Massachusetts Regiment and Augustus Saint-Gaudens' Shaw Memorial,* exhibition catalogue, National Gallery of Art, Washington, DC, September 15, 2013–January 20, 2014 (Washington, DC: National Gallery of Art, 2013).

12. See FHS Mss A/Y21b/Folders 89–91 and FHS Mss A/Y21b/Folder 75. For the *Craftsman* ad (1910), see FHS Mss A/Y21b/Folder 91, p. 8a. For the 1911 advertisement, see *Arts and Decoration* magazine, April 1911, 237; also note mention of that year as "the beginning of the fourth year of the Branstock School of Art . . . with Miss Yandell at the head of the Sculpture department and John C. Johansen at the head of the painting." (265). Johansen was born in Copenhagen and came to the United States at a very young age, settling in Cincinnati. He studied at the Academy there under Frank Duveneck. He also visited Paris, studying at the Académie Julian around 1919. Johansen also contributed to the St. Louis Exposition. It seems that he and Enid may have met through Paris contacts, or perhaps through their studios (both had studios in New York). Sterner was born in London and established roots

in Chicago. He opened a studio in New York in 1885 and then sought further training in Paris around 1888, remaining there, on and off, until 1918. It seems likely that Sterner and Yandell became acquainted from their days in Paris. See "What Artists Are Doing," *New York Times*, June 20, 1909.

13. For information on atmosphere and the nickname, see *Martha's Vineyard: The Isle of Health* (Martha's Vineyard Chamber of Commerce, 1926), 3–5. Of the air and the studio, Enid wrote ca. 1926, "The climate of the Island is so ideal, cool in summer and warm in winter. The air coming off the great Atlantic is life-giving and nerve-soothing." Quoted in *Vineyard Gazette*, June 15, 1934, 2.

14. "What Artists Are Doing."

15. These materials may be found in FHS Mss A/Y21b/Folder 51–53; reference photos are located in Folder 54.

16. FHS Mss A/Y21b/Folder 52; sketch of the crab is located in FHS Mss A/Y21b/Folder 51.

17. FHS Mss A/Y21b/Folder 52. Also retained among presumed instruction material were books, including W. M. Hunt's *Talks on Art*, First Series, ca. 1875; "Drawing Models Album No. 33 Easy," a booklet with twelve folios for landscape drawing. FHS Mss A/Y21b/Folder 53.

18. See FHS Mss A/Y21b/Folder 53; sketches of the trees are located in FHS Mss A/Y21b/Folder 51.

19. See "Edgartown" announcement for exhibition, *Vineyard Gazette*, July 22, 1909; and WCN, "Our Artist Colony," *Vineyard Gazette*, July 29, 1909, pasted in the scrapbook located in University of Louisville Special Collections.

20. For the excursions, see Blanche I. Goel, "Tramping on Martha's Vineyard," lecture to Dukes County Historical Society, October 29, 1925, reprinted as a pamphlet by the society. See references to this talk in *Martha's Vineyard: The Isle of Health*, 4.

21. "Opening of the Tea Room," *Vineyard Gazette*, June 24, 1909 (emphasis mine), pasted in a scrapbook given to the Speed Museum by Elsie Barber Trask in 1941, now in the collection of the University of Louisville Special Collections.

22. Hogan's Fountain, 1905, bronze by Alexis Rudier Fondeur, J. S. Clark Company as contractor; *Daniel Boone*, 1906, bronze by Henry-Bonnard; *John R. Thomas*, 1907, bronze by Henry-Bonnard with contracting by Winsboro Granite. In addition were other works: *General John B. Castleman*, 1905, plaster; *Mademoiselle Deckert de la Meillaie*, 1905, marble; *William T. Bull*, 1907, bronze.

23. No remnants in Enid's studio nor extant correspondence of hers bears witness to this work and its commission. However, we are fortunate to know of it from information gleaned from Julia Dinsmore's diary. According to that source, over the period of just over a week, it appears that Enid created a profile relief of Julia in 1920. See Dinsmore Family Papers, Arizona Historical Society, Roll 7, in the collection of Dinsmore Homestead, Burlington, KY.

24. By 1930, she had taken up work with the Roman Bronze Works/General Bronze Corporation.

25. An undated list offers insight as to an uptick in prices, perhaps due to the increasing demand of the bronzes. See FHS Mss A/Y21b/Folder 65.

26. Mary Bronson Hartt, "Women and the Art of Landscape Gardening," *Outlook*, March 28, 1908, 695–704. Judith B. Tankard, "Defining Their Turf: Pioneer Women Landscape Designers," *Studies in the Decorative Arts* 8, no. 1 (2000): 31–53.

27. Hartt, "Women and the Art of Landscape Gardening," 699.

28. The thistle panel calls to mind a number of works of Enid's academy days, the heyday of carved decoration in Cincinnati, as illustrated in Benn Pitman, *A Plea for American Decorative Art with Illustrations and Designs Showing Examples of Artistic Wood Carving, China and Pottery Painting, Mural Decoration, Etching, Etc., by the Girls and Women of Cincinnati* (Atlanta: Cotton States & International Exposition, 1895). Two other linens are in the collection of Rhode Island School of Design Museum. These embroidered hand towels include an "EY" initial treatment in gold on white linen and the name "Enid" in blue letters on a hand towel, with fifteen oblong trefoil knots, or triquetra, dispersed as two or three knots per row from top to bottom.

29. See Charles de Kay, "A Word or Two on Sculpture," *Flower and Sculpture Exhibition*, 1902, a copy of which is located in FHS Mss A/Y21b/Folder 81. The quoted passages appear on pages 30 and 32 respectively.

30. A photograph of Enid in her Edgartown studio at a table with finished works, among them the *Birthday Beasts,* dated 1921. On the table to Enid's right are at least two of the *Birthday Beasts,* Badger (behind Daniel Boone) and Rat in front of Boone, in Enid's hand. For a second photograph, see ["Birthday beasts"] by Enid Yandell, n.d. Enid Bland Yandell Photograph Collection, 987PC52-x-135, Filson Historical Society, Louisville, KY.

31. In the 1920s, Enid's work led her to Butler, a legislator for the state of Massachusetts in the 1890s who turned his attention to the national political scene, serving as manager of Calvin Coolidge's 1924 campaign for the presidency, member of the US Senate 1924–1926, and chair of the Republican National Convention 1924–1928. Butler's Republican politics were aligned with Enid's, particularly in relation to women's reform, including suffrage. For example, Enid attended a dinner, reported in the *Washington Post* of March 6, 1925, at the home of Senator and Mrs. William M. Butler, for members and friends of the National Republican Committee. See FHS Mss A/Y21b/Folder 95, scrapbook, pp. 41–42. In 1921, William Butler acted as intermediary between Enid and the author Kenneth Grahame, who had created the fictional account that inspired Enid to create her next body of work. For the letter regarding Butler's intersession with Grahame, see FHS Mss A/Y21b/Folder 37.

32. The exhibition was on view in New York on Lexington Avenue between Twenty-Fifth and Twenty-Sixth Streets February 17–March 15, 1913; the other venues continued the show's run, keeping it on view through May.

33. The Armory Show brought modern European art, within the context of American contemporary art, to the fore, including Cubism and Futurism. According to Roberta Tarbell, the treatment of sculpture at the exhibition varied. Roberta K. Tarbell, "The Impact of the Armory Show on American Sculpture," *Archives of*

American Art Journal 18, no. 2 (1978): 2–11; see also Holland Cotter, "Rethinking the Armory Show," *New York Times*, October 25, 2012, F1. For the Roosevelt article, see Theodore Roosevelt, "A Layman's Views of an Art Exhibition," in *For and Against: Views on the Infamous 1913 Armory Show* (Tucson: Hol Art Books, 2009), originally published in *Outlook*, March 29, 1913: 718–719.

34. Locating primary documents about Enid Yandell and her work at exhibitions is complicated by the misspellings of her name (and incorrect use of her first name). See "Americans Abroad," November 15, 1893, which mentions Mrs. Stoddard and Miss Yardell [*sic*] (see FHS Mss A/Y21b/Folder 66). On May 19, 1895, the *New Haven Register* included an image of Enid and identified her as "Enid Yandel" both in the caption and throughout the accompanying article. "A Day among Girl Artists" [n.d.] gives her last name as Yandle. The *New York World* for September 5, 1899, uses the correct spelling of her last name in the heading "Miss Yandell Sculptor," but the text of the article has her first name as "Ella"; yet the captions with illustrations of Enid, one of her works, and the artist in her studio print her name correctly. See clippings in FHS Mss A/Y21b/Folder 66.The Indiana exhibition has gone unnoticed in the Yandell literature; it is mentioned in Ella Bond Johnston, "Art in Indiana," *Outlook*, June 24, 1911, 433–440. See also "Art and the Nation," *Art and Progress* 2, no. 12 (October 1911): 370–371, quotation on 371; George T. Settle, *Catalog of Art in the Louisville Free Public Library: Paintings, Statuary, Etchings, Prints, Photographs, and Bronze Tablets* (Louisville: n.p., 1928), 29.

35. "Woman Who Designed Many Memorials Dead," 2.

36. The latest document related to lessons, though perhaps not affiliated with Branstock, is dated November 11, 1929. This notice was for twelve lessons for Elizabeth "Betty" Hazard. In addition, Enid leased property to the Hazards in 1928 and 1930. For both of these documents, see FHS Mss A/Y21b/Folder 44. A letter from Linda E. Norton to Christopher Monkhouse, June 22, 1982, details how Norton reported that a current resident of Edgartown took lessons from Enid and that one of Enid's neighbors, "Uncle Joe," was asked to pose as a model for Enid and/or her courses, calling to mind Enid's own training and the training she sought to provide her students. See RISD Museum of Art Curatorial Files, RISD Museum, Providence, RI.

37. See "Miss Yandell's Pupil Sends Statue Here," *Louisville Courier-Journal*, October 19, 1930, 9. Enid and Elizabeth ("Betty") had met a few years earlier when summering in Edgartown. According to the *Louisville Courier-Journal* article, Enid had taken an interest in Betty's work, and the two were to travel to Paris together. According to an undated clipping from the *Vineyard Gazette*, Betty (along with Mrs. Butler and her daughter, Molly) was with Enid when she took ill in Paris. See Nancy Disher Baird Manuscript Collection, Box 7, Folder 4, Western Kentucky University, Bowling Green, KY. See also the obituary for Elizabeth Hazard, *The Hour*, November 1, 1994.

38. The whereabouts of *Boy with a Snail* are unknown. See "Miss Yandell's Pupil Sends Statue Here." As noted throughout this book, the original Boone was made for the World's Fair in Chicago in 1893 and took on a new life as a plaster cast that

traveled to several fairs and was loaned out before being cast in bronze for the citizens of Louisville in 1906.

39. Also consider the foundries that sculptors relied upon to realize their visions. Both Enid and Mary worked with Roman Bronze Works. See Roman Bronze Works Archives, Amon Carter American Art Museum Archives, Ft. Worth, TX. I am grateful to Warren Payne and Julie Payne for their generosity in sharing their material related to this collection. Regarding Mary Knollenberg, see obituary for Mary Tarleton Knollenberg, *New York Times,* January 7, 1993. See also John Caldwell, "Sculptures at the Wall Focus Gallery," *New York Times,* September 6, 1981.

40. "Helen G. Sahler, Sculptor, Artist," *New York Times*, December 4, 1950. John E. D. Trask, *Official Catalogue of the Department of Fine Arts, Panama-Pacific International Exposition (with awards), San Francisco, California* (San Francisco: Wahlgreen Co., 1915), 244.

41. On details about Enid's mannerisms, see email from Nancy Baird to the author, July 7, 2014, in which she recounts her experiences visiting Edgartown and interviewing friends and students of Enid's in August 1981.

42. A full set of the plasters consisting of Citizenship, as well as Philanthropy and Railroading, is in the collection of the Speed Museum. It is presumed that this plaster of Citizenship is also from a set of three, although the whereabouts of the other two are unknown.

43. For this recollection, I am grateful to a local resident who shared her remembrances, as well as those of her mother and grandmother (who attended from 1935 to 1948 and does not remember seeing the work on view in the school during those years). Email from Elyce Bonnell to author, August 15, 2017.

44. Edgartown Historic District Commission Minutes, November 5, 2013, 2–3.

45. The tabletop sculpture has been misidentified as "Frank Worthington" in Darst's catalogue and subsequently in the Smithsonian Institution's database of American art. As part of the research for this book, I have uncovered that this work is actually a sculpture of Frank Worthing, the actor, and may very well relate to his performance in *The Cavalier,* a Civil War saga wherein a Southern belle mistakenly marries a spy and simultaneously is in love with a Confederate soldier. The play was George Middleton's first work, which he adapted for the stage with fellow playwright Paul Kestor and the novel's author, George Cable. The show ran in New York City from December 2, 1902, through February 1, 1903, and it is likely that Enid saw the play. Enid was a lifelong fan of the theatre and the performing arts, and she was in New York at the time. Enid inscribed the sculpture "To my friend/ Frank Worthing/Enid Yandell 1902 Sc," connoting a measure of familiarity. Worthing also starred with Julia Marlowe, one of Enid's close friends. According to Elsie Trask, Julia Marlowe, a "great friend" of Enid's, was in Louisville in 1897 and may have met Enid there. See note from Elsie Barber Trask to Nancy Baird, July 31, 1981, FHS Mss A Y21b Folder 71. For information on *The Cavalier,* see Donald J. Stubblebine, *Early Broadway Sheet Music: A Comprehensive Listing of Published Music from Broadway and Other Stage Shows, 1843–1918* (Jefferson, NC: McFarland, 2010),

36–37. For the listing of the playbill for this show, see http://www.playbill.com/show/detail/11881/the-cavalier.

7. Advocacy and Activism

1. For instance, Louise wrote to Enid, who was away at school in Cincinnati at the time, "As soon as I mail this I shall begin painting on the Crittenden portrait. I must give it my undivided attention for the next two weeks—I will probably not write tomorrow as I have to go to the Orphanage in the morning & of course must hear [Episcopal Reverend] Phillips Brooks in the evening." FHS Mss A/Y21b/Folder 5.

2. Rather than continuing her education, she was executing works for hire for high-profile clients. "A Kentucky Girl's Art: Miss Enid Yandell Tells of Her Work as a Sculptor," *New York Sun,* February 27, 1898, 4.

3. Rucker Hall was completed in 1895, as the fifth significant building on campus, after Giddings, Pawling, Highbaugh, and the Old Chapel. Enid's bronze bust of Rucker is part of Georgetown College's permanent art collection and is on view in the Colbert Room in the Student Center.

4. The address is identified as an "Alumni address" at Commencement to be followed by "a banquet to be given by the Students' Association," according to a note from Professor of History and Politics to Durrett, May 2, 1894. FHS Mss A/D965c/Added Papers, 1883–1910, Folder 138; FHS Mss A/D965/Box 21/Folder 269, "Address delivered at Georgetown College, 1894, June 13" in Durrett, Reuben Thomas, 1824–1913, Papers 1821–1931, Correspondence.

5. "Address delivered at Georgetown College, 1894, June 13," 8, 30.

6. Fannie Tucker Summers (1855–1943) sought to pay tribute to Rucker by beautifying the hall's parlor, which served as a community area as well as seating for private entertainment. See *The Georgetonian,* January 1898, p. 4.

7. Ibid., 4 (Metcalf) and 5 (Lewis).

8. Ruth Crocker, *Mrs. Russell Sage: Women's Activism and Philanthropy in Gilded Age and Progressive Era America* (Bloomington: Indiana University Press, 2006), 97.

9. Ibid. For the memorial's early mention, see "The Emma Willard Memorial," *Churchman,* September 5, 1891, 298; multiple entries by Florence Montgomery Taylor, ed., in *Chicago Woman's News*; Mary Allen West, "Memorial to Mrs. Emma Willard by the Women of America," at the World's Columbian Exposition, Chicago, 1893. These items may be found in "Emma Willard School. Emma (Hart) Willard Collection, 1809–2004," series: Memorials, Box 7, folder 6, Emma Willard School Archives, Emma Willard School, Troy, New York.

10. "Miss Yandell's Fine Bust of Mrs. Emma Willard," *Louisville Courier-Journal,* May 14, 1899, 13.

11. "Woman's World and Work Menu for Friday," *New Orleans Daily Picayune,* May 18, 1899, 3; the article also recounts the bust's viewing at Tiffany's, the flagship "palace of jewels" store at 15 Union Square West, Manhattan.

12. On the reception, see "Northern Budget, Troy NY, July 2, 1899," clipping in FHS Mss A/Y21b/Folder 94; "A Wealthy Woman's Life: Mrs. Russell Sage Devotes Herself to Works of Philanthropy," *New York Times,* November 12, 1899, 12.

13. *Louisville Courier-Journal,* May 14, 1899, 13, in which the May 11, 1899, *New York Sun* is quoted.

14. Pauline King, "American Women Sculptors," *Harper's Bazaar,* March 4, 1899, included as clipping in FHS Mss A/Y21b/Folder 69.

15. Ibid.

16. A thorough description of the library around 1888 is reported in the *Library Journal,* March–April 1888, 93–94. On the fire, see Brian Keough, University of Albany, SUNY, email to author, September 7, 2012. Janet Scudder recounted a story from Frederick MacMonnies about how he found the destruction of art not a problem, but a means of justification for starting over and making one's best work after such a loss. See Janet Scudder, *Modeling My Life* (New York: Harcourt, Brace, & Co., 1925), 68.

17. Details from Lunsford's life may be found in FHS Mss A/Y21b/Folder 21, specifically a letter from Louise to Enid, January 4, 1897, which mentions Avery Plow Factory. Lunsford was also in charge of the Avery exhibit at Nashville (April 8, 1897 letter). He also communicated to Enid with regard to property after their mother's death in 1908. See FHS Mss A/Y21b/Folder 42.

18. Woman's editions were published by *Albany Argus, Albion Recorder, Chicago Baptist Union, Elmira Advertiser, Kansas City Journal* (taken charge by the WCTU) *Lisbon Leader,* and *Port Jervis Daily Union.* See *The Fourth Estate: A Weekly Newspaper for Publishers, Advertisers, Advertising Agents and Allied Interests* (New York: Fourth Estate Publishing Co., 1895), esp. 5, 7, 8, 11.

19. See FHS Mss A/Y21b/Folder 19 for the letter dated February 13, 1895, and an article by Elsie as noted in the *Louisville Courier-Journal,* March 27, 1895, 17.

20. For more on woman's editions, see "It Sold Well: Getting Out a 'Woman's' Edition of a Paper," *Fourth Estate,* April 25, 1895, 5.

21. Anne Firor Scott, *The Southern Lady: From Pedestal to Politics, 1830–1930* (Chicago: University of Chicago Press, 1970), 177. The organized women's rights movement began with two conventions, held two weeks apart from one another in July and August of 1848 in Seneca Falls and Rochester, New York, respectively. On July 19–20, 300 women and men gathered to discuss the rights of women. A "Declaration of Sentiments" was prepared, calling for equal treatment of women on a range of issues, including the right to vote.

22. Once her grandmother and mother had passed away, Enid's reasons for writing home were fewer, as Maude navigated a world of her own and Elsie and Lunsford were engaged in the affairs of their growing families. No extant correspondence with the family mentions Enid's participation in the suffrage effort. However, exhibition records and a photo from a suffrage parade disclose Enid's role in these events and, presumably, the broader efforts ongoing in New York City, her adopted home outside of Kentucky. In her article, Josephine Henry included extracts from letters writ-

ten by women who gave their opinions on the matter. See Josephine K. Henry, "The New Woman of the New South: A Feminist Literature Classic," *Arena* 11 (1895): 353–362. For instance, the four Clay sisters—Mary, Anne, Sallie, and Laura—supported suffrage and practically served as "a suffrage organization in themselves," due to their political power. Yet, as Anne Firor Scott so poignantly stated, "the antisuffrage arguments drew heavily on the old image of southern woman in danger of becoming unfeminine if she dared to step out of her natural sphere." Anne Firor Scott, *The Southern Lady*, 170.

23. I discovered this photograph on a visit to the Museum of Art at the Rhode Island School of Design in early August 2017, when I was reviewing its collections files and curatorial documentation related to Enid Yandell. Enid Yandell Curatorial Files, RISD Museum, Providence, RI. The photograph, of which no one on staff was aware, was tucked in a white envelope, which was itself tucked inside a yellow manila envelope postmarked 1982. I am grateful to the staff of the museum for allowing me permission to use this photograph in this book, where it is published for the first time. For more on the move for New York state suffrage, see Susan Goodier and Karen Pastorello, *Women Will Vote: Winning Suffrage in New York State* (Ithaca: Cornell University Press, 2017). While Goodier and Pastorello do not address women sculptors as part of this effort for woman suffrage, their perspective on the transition from ridicule to referendum as a case study of the broader movement is insightful.

24. Although Beals opened her own studio on Sixth Avenue in New York City in 1905, she moved to a Greenwich Village studio in 1920. It is likely that the parade route was "in her neighborhood" around 1915, meaning Sixth Avenue. See Alexander Alland Sr., *Jessie Tarbox Beals, First Woman News Photographer* (New York: Camera/Graphic Press, 1978). For more information on Beals, particularly the collection of her photographs at the New-York Historical Society, see "Jessie Tarbox Beals Photographs [1900–1940], Bulk 1904–1920, PR 4" http://dlib.nyu.edu/findingaids/html/nyhs/beals/beals.html.

25. John William Leonard, ed., *Woman's Who's Who of America: A Biographical Dictionary of Contemporary Women of the United States and Canada, 1914–1915* (New York: American Commonwealth Co., 1914), 909.

26. See various accounts, including *New York Times*, October 22, 1915.

27. The description of Enid in her role as Queen in 1890 is repetitive, including adjectives such as "wealthy, educated, traveled and beautiful" as well as her being a "beautiful, cultured, traveled, wealthy lady" who, "though connected with a prominent family, has not been much known in what is called society." See "Carnival Programme," *Louisville Courier-Journal*, September 17, 1890, 10.

28. This exhibition should not be confused with the one featuring the work of Mary Cassatt and Edgar Degas, which also benefited the suffrage cause. See Rebecca A. Rabinow, "The Suffrage Show of 1915," in *Splendid Legacy: The Havemeyer Collection*, edited by Alice Cooney Frelinghuysen, Gary Tinterow, et al. (New York: Metropolitan Museum of Art, 1993), 89–95; "Art Sale to Aid Suffrage: Prominent Women Offer Works for an Exhibition Here," *New York Times*, September 9, 1915,

12; *San Antonio Light*, October 17, 1915; Mariea Caudill Dennison, "Babies for Suffrage: The Exhibitions of Painting and Sculpture by Women Artists for the Benefit of the Woman Suffrage Campaign," *Woman's Art Journal* 24, no. 2 (Autumn 2003–Winter 2004): 24.

29. On Sahler's listing as a student of Art Students League and Enid Yandell, see John E. D. Trask, *Official Catalogue of the Department of Fine Arts, Panama-Pacific International Exposition (with awards), San Francisco, California* (San Francisco: Wahlgreen Co., 1915), 244.

30. See FHS Mss A/Y21b/Folder 94, scrapbook, pp. 41–42; p. 46 for the invitation and pass, dated March 4, 1925. It is unclear if Enid attended. In addition, notices that Enid attended a luncheon given by Mrs. Butler and more presidential clippings are located in the scrapbook.

31. See Edith Wharton, ed., *The Book of the Homeless* (New York: Scribner, 1916); Mary Alice Heekin Burke and Lois Marie Find, *Elizabeth Nourse, 1859–1938: A Salon Career* (Washington, DC: National Museum of American Art and the Smithsonian Institution Press, 1985); and Emma Anderson, *Elizabeth Nourse: A Sketch* (Cincinnati: Anderson, 1922).

32. See FHS Mss A/Y21b/Folder 36. A letter from Enid, written from Paris to her friends in Edgartown, was dated July 27, 1914. Some documentation lists Enid's involvement in relief work in Paris as far back as 1913. For instance, the *Vineyard Gazette* stated that Enid was director of the Bureau of Communications for the New York branch of the Red Cross 1913–1919. See "Woman Who Designed Many Memorials Dead: Miss Enid Yandell of Edgartown Won World Wide Fame, Career Ends," *Vineyard Gazette*, June 15, 1934, 1–2. Stephanie Darst and Nancy Disher Baird claim that these activities consumed almost all her time and that she largely gave up her work as a sculptor to help others. While her artistic production did decrease, she was still considered an active sculptor.

33. See FHS Mss A/Y21b/Folder 54 for Enid's role as secretary. "Americans Aid French Artists," *New York Times*, May 30, 1915, 20–21. In addition, the founding of the organization is noted in *American Art News* 12, no. 38, September 19, 1914. This publication noted that the honorary committee included Henry Clews (an artist who moved to France in 1914), Antoine Mercié, Paul-Albert Besnard, Max Blondat, and Leon Bonnat.

34. The story of the cable's arrival in Harriman's hands is detailed by Enid and recounted in the *New York Times* article, although no direct quotes are provided by Harriman.

35. FHS Mss A/Y21b/Folders 64 and 66; and "Americans Aid French Artists," *New York Times*, May 30, 1915, 66. The heading appearing in the *New York Times* read: "100,000 Meals Given to Destitute Artists and Families of Artists at the Front by Cantine System."

36. One of the medals in the Speed's collection is a bas-relief and plaque in bronze affixed to board that has a tooth-shaped foot on the back so that the plaque could be stood on a table. The bronze features a woman facing left and looking off

into a distance. Behind her is a scene that appears to be French, specifically, a Parisian landscape as indicated by the faint silhouette of the Eiffel Tower. The figure is draped in a long cloth gown and veil with her right hand up to her chin and her left hand extended and holding a scroll. Beneath the figure is the word "Meditation." Beneath the entire scene is a dedication plaque, which reads: "A Miss Enid Yandell En Souvenir de l'Appui aux Artistes Cantine No. 1 1914," thus connoting a remembrance of Enid's work.

37. "An Appeal from Paris," *American Magazine of Art* 7 (1916): 211. It is unclear how long the activities of Appui lasted.

38. See "Americans Aid French Artists," 66. A photograph of two small dolls accompanies the article, with the following caption: "Dolls Made by Polish Artists and Sold through the 'Appui aux Artistes' for the Sufferers in Paris." Although it is unclear what role Enid had in the actual administration of this event, it is worth noting the proximity of dates (November 1915) for the doll sale and Enid's own lecture circuit in Chicago that year and her work in support of suffrage around the same time.

39. The content of this speech is documented by a 17-page typed and annotated manuscript in the Yandell collection at the Filson Historical Society. See FHS Mss A/Y21b/Folder 49 for the document, entitled "Lecture by Miss Enid Yandell, Concerning her Work in the Universitie [*sic*] Populaire at Paris; Delivered at the home of Mrs. Robert McGann, 120 Pearson Street, Chicago, November 11, 1915." For information on the McGanns, see *The Chicago Blue Book: Selected Names of Chicago and Suburban Towns Containing the Names and Addresses of Prominent Residents* (Chicago: Chicago Directory Co., 1915), 136.

40. See FHS Mss A/Y21b/Folder 49 for the speech, specifically pp. 1–6.

41. Ibid., p. 10.

42. Ibid., pp. 12–13.

43. This article, "North Shore Society Women to Provide for French War Orphans: Mrs. Arthur Aldis and Two Others 'Adopt' Homeless Children; Seek Funds to Aid Paris Artists," appearing on November 18, 1915, in the *Chicago Evening Post*, mentioned Enid's going from house to house to make speeches and solicit money for aid efforts.

44. Letter from Henry Watterson to the American Red Cross, October 10, 1918, FHS Mss A/Y21b/Folder 36. The quote within the letter comes from a poem by Thomas Gray. See also letter from Enid Yandell to Henry Watterson, October 5, 1918, Watterson Papers, FHS Mss A/W344a.

45. Letter from Ethan Allen to Henry Watterson, November 16, 1918, FHS Mss A/Y21b/Folder 36.

46. "Listing 200,000 Wounded Doughboys," *New York Times*, July 6, 1919, 68.

47. Enid is shown wearing this pin in a photograph of Enid with *The Pioneer* taken ca. 1924 or later, discussed in Chapter 8. The medal is in the collection of Speed Museum. In addition, a typed list of "Sculpture Awards and Social Service Recognitions" is located in FHS Mss A/Y21b/Folder 63.

48. Stephanie Wilding Darst, *The Sculpture of Enid Yandell* (Louisville: J. B. Speed Art Museum, 1993), 9.

8. Pioneer and Promoter

1. On this page, in Enid's handwriting, is "Washington Post"; however, I have been unable to locate a reference to that article in this newspaper. Given the content, it seems the article is from the mid-1890s because it contains no mention of Nashville or later commissions. In addition, the article notes her Louisville work on interiors and exteriors, which is not mentioned in later articles. FHS Mss A/Y21b/Folder 94, scrapbook, p. 67.

2. Here I have drawn from the Dinsmore Family Papers at the Arizona Historical Society, Roll 7, in the collection of Dinsmore Homestead.

3. Edmund T. Halsey had wanted "something typical of Kentucky so Enid used corn, hemp, and tobacco in the design," according to Halsey's sister-in-law, who gave the plaster model for this cup to the Speed Museum. In a letter to Hattie Speed, the museum director, Mary Lee Halsey noted that the design was created in 1904 and the silver was cast in 1907. She wrote, "Enid had the work done by a silversmith in Paris, and sent the cup to Mr. E. T. Halsey's English namesake, William Edmund Halsey." See Enid Yandell, item 1927.19.1, Registrar Files, Speed Museum, Louisville, KY.

4. Thomas D. Clark, *Agrarian Kentucky* (Lexington: University Press of Kentucky, 1977), 15; see also Mark V. Wetherington, "'Buried in Original Records, Government Reports, Statistical Tables, and Obscure Essays'? Kentucky's Twentieth-Century Agricultural History," *Register of the Kentucky Historical Society* 113, nos. 2–3 (Spring–Summer 2015): 271–306.

5. The display was held in the Palace of Agriculture at the St. Louis World's Fair. At the time, 90 percent of the hemp in the United States was grown in Kentucky. See "Kentucky at the World's Fair Agriculture," *Louisville Courier-Journal*, September 4, 1904, 2. More general information may be found in US Census Bureau, Census of Agriculture, https://www.census.gov/library/publications.html. Detailed reports for census information may be found in the agriculture reports from 1880 through 1930, such as Volume 3 of the 1883 census: https://www.census.gov/library/publications/1883/dec/vol-03-agriculture.html.

6. For quote on hemp, see Mark V. Wetherington, "Buried in Original Records, Government Reports, Statistical Tables, and Obscure Essays," 278. On hemp generally, see Clark, *Agrarian Kentucky*, 15, 23; James F. Hopkins, with a foreword by Thomas D. Clark, *History of the Hemp Industry in Kentucky* (Lexington: University Press of Kentucky, 1998). As Hopkins notes in his introduction, Kentucky was a border state during the Civil War, which reflects its position as not "completely southern" in terms of its disapproval of enslavement and its disregard for a single-crop economy (in contrast to the dominance of cotton in the deep south), among other

contexts. Hemp production required extensive use of enslaved labor. Hopkins, *History of the Hemp Industry,* 4.

7. The Confederate Monument, the history of which was discussed in Chapter 3, was later removed from its original location on Third Street and relocated to Brandenburg, Kentucky. It was rededicated there on the banks of the Ohio River in 2017.

8. See H. Addington Bruce, "The Romance of American Expansion: Daniel Boone and the Opening of the West," *Outlook* 88 (January 25, 1908): 202–212.

9. The three letters over this affair were written by Enid from her studio in New York (Fifty-Sixth Street, Eighth Avenue, the Van Dyck Studio Building). See letters from Enid Yandell to John W. Thomas, February 15, 1898, February 22, 1898, and March 8, 1898, Tennessee Centennial and International Exposition (1897) Collection 1895–1900, Box 5, Folder 21, Tennessee State Library and Archives, Nashville, TN.

10. This reference is to the USS *Kentucky* (BB-6), which was commissioned on May 15, 1900. Letter from Enid Yandell to Reuben Durrett, April 25, 1899. FHS Durrett Collection, Mss A/D965c/.

11. Letter from Enid Yandell to Reuben Durrett, February 7, 1903, FHS Durrett Collection Mss A/D965c/. In this letter, Enid also mentions cider that Durrett had sent to her. In the second letter, dated April 28, 1903, Enid asked Durrett to measure the Boone for casting purposes. Several other letters from Enid to Durrett recounted issues with the casting (including the rifle being broken).

12. "Welcome Home, Kentuckians!" *Louisville Courier-Journal,* June 13, 1906, 1; "Fifty Thousand Do Honor to Kentucky's Backwoodsman," *Louisville Courier-Journal,* June 16, 1906, 1. The *Washington Post* reported that a parade, floats, and dance were part of the Daniel Boone "glorification," which included a reunion of "about a dozen lineal descendants of the local pioneer." See "Glorification of the Great Pioneer by Kentuckians at Louisville," *Washington Post,* June 16, 1906, 9. The *Courier-Journal* gave a much higher number of descendants, upwards of 100 individuals: "Fifty Thousand Do Honor," 4.

13. "Fifty Thousand Do Honor." Durrett's call for a movement in outdoor art unfortunately did not come to pass.

14. The work is inscribed on the back "Enid Yandell Sc 1924." In addition, a woman named Emily (last name unknown), from the White House, also received one such plaster; her thank-you note identifies it as *The Pioneer.* For the Coolidge letters and this one from Emily, see FHS Mss A/Y21b/Folder 95, scrapbook, p. 31.

15. As outlined earlier, Enid purchased the Branstock property in 1907: FHS Mss A/Y21b/Folder 75.

16. "To Restore Harrod's Fort," *New York Sun,* March 26, 1925, clipping in FHS Mss A/Y21b/Folder 67.

17. This information comes from a typed document that appears to be a press release for the *Louisville Herald,* April 30, 1924; FHS Mss A/Y21b/Folders 61 and 62. Erroneously, this document, and others, refer to Enid as the first woman to be

elected to the National Sculpture Society. She was in fact among the first. Theo Alice Ruggles Kitson was elected in 1893; Yandell and Bessie Potter Vonnoh were elected in 1898 and appear on the member roster starting in 1899.

18. Enid had returned to Kentucky on occasion over the years, while her mother was living in Louisville (until 1908), at least. On these return trips home, Enid often acknowledged her love of the state. For instance, in a letter to Reuben Durrett she wrote, "There I am at last and oh Kentucky is a beautiful state! I am glad to be at home." Letter from Enid Yandell to Reuben Durrett, August 14, 1901. She also occasionally returned home for horse shows. Letter from Enid Yandell to Reuben Durrett, September 4, 1901; FHS Mss A/D965; Nancy Disher Baird Collection, WKU, Box 7, Folder 5; FHS Mss A/Y21b/Folder 62.

19. See Enid's sketchbook in FHS Mss A/Y21b/Folder 96. The inclusion of Lewis and Clark may be tied to the Lewis and Clark Centennial and American Pacific Exposition and Oriental Fair, which was held from June 1 to October 15, 1905, in Portland, Oregon. This Centennial Exposition was not international in its focus, as many previous fairs had been; instead, it was a regional fair that celebrated the acquisition of lands that ultimately became the states of Idaho, Montana, Oregon, Washington, and Wyoming. Like the Louisiana Purchase centennial celebration of 1904, the Lewis and Clark exposition held to overarching themes, including "the expansion of the United States, the conquest of the wilderness, and the expansion of international commerce." Nancy J. Parezo, *Anthropology Goes to the Fair: The 1904 Louisiana Purchase Exposition* (Lincoln: University of Nebraska Press, 2007), 382. See also undated typed manuscript about Enid's Pioneer Monument, FHS Mss A/Y21b/Folder 73.

20. Many of the children from Edgartown posed for Enid's statue. Linda E. Norton of the Edgartown Library, as part of a series of letters with Christopher Monkhouse, Curator of Decorative Arts at the RISD Museum, provided context for Enid's working methods based upon her own study and familiarity with Enid's works in the library's collection. Enid Yandell Curatorial Files, RISD Museum, Providence, RI. In a letter dated July 2, 1981, Norton wrote, "Several Islanders who were children then posed for it and wondering where the statue is now and what national monument it represents." See undated typed manuscript about Americans and Kentuckians that is written in the first person and annotated in Enid's hand. FHS Mss A/Y21b/Folder 73.

21. On westward expansion, see Abbott's article which appeared in the *Outlook* on January 10, 1925. In it, he did not mention the form of the work, although from Enid's sketchbook we know that she had intended to have roundels or profiles of Lewis, Clark, Harrod, and Boone. See FHS Mss A/Y21b/Folder 96. On the selection of Enid for major projects, see "Bronze and Marble Worker Sun Dial's Enthusiastic Sponsor: Miss Enid Yandell, Sculptor, Has Done Meritorious Work, Gaining for Her Sex Recognition in This Field. Many of Her Best Known Pieces Are Designed for the Out-of-Doors," *New York Sun*, March 12, 1924, FHS Mss A/Y21b/Folder 95, between pp. 4 and 5.

22. FHS Mss A/Y21b/Folder 95, p. 19. The program is dated May 6, 1924; the announcement in the *New York Sun* appeared on April 30 of that year. FHS Mss A/Y21b/Folder 73. A typescript draft of Enid's speech is also located in this folder. A write-up about the event appeared in the *Louisville Courier-Journal* on June 29, 1924; see "Kentucky's Historic Past Pictured in Pageant for Home Comers at Harrodsburg," which notes the prominent figures marking the site as "sacred soil for Kentuckyians," including Enid Yandell. A badge inscribed "150th Celebration of the Founding of Kentucky, Harrodsburg, June 16, 1924" was kept among Enid's possessions. For the badge, see FHS Mss A/Y21b/Folder 63. In her talk, Enid invited the attendees to the sesquicentennial of statehood, the pioneer celebration to be held the following month, June 1924. This conflation of statehood (1792) and settlement at Harrodsburg (1774) often occurred and, while factually wrong, may reveal insights into the Kentucky imaginary of Enid and others.

23. See "Obituary: Donn Barber, FAIA," *Journal of the American Institute of Architects* 13, July 7, 1925: 274.

24. See Juilee Decker, "Enid Yandell (1869–1934): Kentucky's Frontier Sculptor and 'Bachelor Maid,'" in *Kentucky Women*, edited by Melissa A. McEuen and Thomas H. Appleton (Athens: University of Georgia Press, 2015). See also the *New York Sun* article "To Restore Harrod's Fort."

25. Quoted in "Woman Who Designed Many Memorials Dead: Miss Enid Yandell of Edgartown Won World Wide Fame, Career Ends," *Vineyard Gazette,* June 15, 1934, 2.

26. Enid was familiar with firms who were recognized as leading domestic and landscape architects, just as was her earlier collaborator, Donn Barber. Barber and Olmsted are included in a listing of domestic and landscape architects of 1922. See Architectural League of New York, *Year Book of the Architectural League of New York* (New York: Secretary of the League, 1922). The Olmsted Brothers, for instance, designed Cherokee Park, home to Enid's bronze Daniel Boone of 1906 and Hogan's Fountain in 1905; see archives of the Office of Metro Parks, Louisville. The designs and sketches, as well as architectural plans by the Olmsted firm for the Pioneer Monument at Harrodsburg deserve further study. One blueprint, identified by the Olmsted Firm as File No. 7660, Plan No. 6 and dated June 2, 1927, is located in FHS Mss A/Y21b/Folder 62. Other blueprints, drawings, and documents related to this project are held by the Frederick Law Olmsted National Historic Site, Brookline, MA.

27. Bobbi Dawn Rightmyer and Anna Armstrong, *Harrodsburg*, Images of America Series (Charleston, SC: Arcadia Publishing, 2011); "Harrodsburg" in John E. Kleber, *The Kentucky Encyclopedia* (Lexington: University Press of Kentucky, 1992), 414. The model for the completed sculpture is located in the Kentucky State Office Building.

28. For more on Anne Pogue McGinty, see Catherine Fosl, "Anne Pogue McGinty and Anne McCarty Braden (c. 1735–1815; 1924–2006): The Power of Place across Four Centuries," in *Kentucky Women*, edited by Melissa A. McEuen and Thomas H. Appleton, (Athens: University of Georgia Press, 2015), 33–58. Fosl

articulates McGinty's role in the "pioneer" world of Fort Harrod and expertly situates McGinty as pioneer, innovator, and entrepreneur. While interpretation at this historic site has changed over the years, as Fosl notes, "the public presentation of Anne Pogue is still evolving along with the status of women in Kentucky history" (43).

29. See Lewis Collins and Richard H. Collins, reviser, *Collins' Historical Sketches of Kentucky: History of Kentucky*, vol. 1 (Covington, KY: Collins & Co., 1874), 18. This edition, from which Enid's transcript was taken, was prepared by Richard H. Collins (1824–1888), a lawyer and journalist who, like his father, had an interest in Kentucky history.

30. See Frederick Jackson Turner, "The Significance of the Frontier in American History," in *Annual Report of the American Historical Association for 1893* (Washington, DC: Government Printing Office, 1894), 208; Robert Spencer Cotterill, *History of Pioneer Kentucky* (Cincinnati: Johnson & Hardin, 1917), 62.

31. See Margaret Ripley Wolfe, "Fallen Leaves and Missing Pages: Women in Kentucky History," *Register of the Kentucky Historical Society* 90, no. 1 (1992), Focus Issue: The Kentucky Image/Bicentennial Issue: 64–89; Robert Morgan, *Boone: A Biography* (Chapel Hill: Algonquin, 2007), esp. 62–63, 187–88.

32. The literature on heritage tourism crosses many disciplines, including public history, anthropology, sociology, hospitality and tourism, folklore, and history. Among many relevant sources, see: Bob McKercher and Hilary du Cros, *Cultural Tourism: The Partnership between Tourism and Cultural Heritage Management* (New York: Haworth Hospitality Press, 2002); Philip Scranton and Janet F. Davidson, *The Business of Tourism: Place, Faith, and History* (Philadelphia: University of Pennsylvania Press, 2007); Patricia Mooney-Melvin, "Harnessing the Romance of the Past: Preservation, Tourism, and History," *Public Historian* 13, no. 2 (Spring 1991): 35–48; and Richard D. Starnes, ed., *Southern Journeys: Tourism, History, and Culture in the Modern South* (Tuscaloosa: University of Alabama Press, 2003). On the Pioneer Monument's ties to tourism, see William D. Moore, "'United We Commemorate': The Kentucky Pioneer Memorial Association, James Isenberg, and Early Twentieth-Century Heritage Tourism," *Public Historian* 30, no. 3 (Summer 2008): 51–81.

Epilogue

1. This surmising by Professor Giese was reported in an unpublished manuscript by Helen Allen, "An Essay on 'Aunt Enid' in Honor of Elsie Barber Trask, Enid's Favorite Niece," which I obtained in 2012 from David Yandell Wood, a relative of Enid's descended from her father's brother, Dr. David Wendel Yandell. Because the undated document was written before Trask's death (otherwise it would have been "in her memory"), the text likely was written ca. 2003–2007.

2. Ibid. Also, see handwritten notes from historian Nancy Baird regarding a conversation with Enid's niece Elsie Barber Trask, in the collection of the Filson

Historical Society: Notes by Nancy Baird regarding E. B. Trask, July 31, 1981, FHS Mss A/Y21b/Folder 71.

3. At the time of my research, the museum was in the midst of a capital campaign and its relocation to a new facility at the Marine Hospital (in 2018–2019), so I was unable to consult its research materials and the minutes of the society to ascertain Enid's possible role in the museum's establishment. Regarding the DAR, Enid made application on March 3, 1909. Her relation to the American Revolution comes from the Boddies. One of her ancestors was Nathan Boddie of Edgecombe County, North Carolina. He was born in 1732 and served in that war.

4. No museum records detail the donation from Elsie Trask to the museum, although it is presumed that the donation occurred sometime in the decade following Enid's death, in line with Trask's donation to the Speed Museum in 1941.

5. Established in 1925, the museum was formerly known as the J. B. Speed Memorial Museum. It is unclear if Enid ever visited the museum, though she could have visited upon her return to Kentucky in 1924 for the Harrodsburg project. Moreover, the museum was in a neighborhood she knew, due to its proximity to her former home in Old Louisville (about one mile from the museum) and the site of the Confederate Monument, the commission that she won in 1894 though had to give up. The museum was established in 1925 by Harriet "Hattie" Bishop Speed.

6. See Kathleen D. McCarthy, *Women's Culture: American Philanthropy and Art, 1830–1930* (Chicago: University of Chicago Press, 1991), xi, 150. Hattie Speed's role here stands in contrast to McCarthy's assessment that "rather than founding or managing the nation's great Gilded Age museums, they [women] remained 'on the borders,' neither 'fully at home in male houses of power, though seeking to live there,' nor fully in command" (115). Yet it is useful to view Speed and the museum she founded as authorizing memorial culture as part of female cultural custodianship. See letter from Mrs. John J. Trask to Mrs. J. B. Speed, March 19, 1940, Curatorial Files for Enid Yandell, Speed Art Museum, Louisville, KY. In this letter, part of the early correspondence between the women, Trask identifies a point of connection between the two. Josephine Henning (Elsie's cousin) had spoken to Hattie Speed about the works in Enid's studio and the potential donation.

7. Letter from Mrs. John J. Trask to Mrs. J. B. Speed, March 19, 1940, and draft of a note from Speed to Trask, April 1 [?], 1940, Curatorial Files for Enid Yandell, Speed Art Museum, Louisville, KY.

8. Trask arranged for a gallerist in Boston to send staff to look at the plasters in Enid's studio (for which the Speed reimbursed Trask). See "Works by and related to Enid Yandell, 1941.14.1–17," Speed Art Museum, Louisville, KY; and J. B. Speed Memorial Museum, *Exhibition of Recent Acquisitions and Loans* (Louisville: Speed Museum, 1941), 18. Letter from Mrs. John J. Trask to Mrs. J. B. Speed, January 11, 1941, described the fees associated with crating and packing Enid's work in Edgartown for shipment to the Speed for this exhibition.

9. The photographs are mentioned in J. B. Speed Memorial Museum, *Exhibition of Recent Acquisitions and Loans* 14. Page 9 mentions an "Antique Arm Chair—Eng-

lish from Studio of Enid Yandell (gift of Mrs. J. J. Trask)" (item 56); page 5 mentions *Three Girls in a Flat* as part of the exhibition of books (item 15).

10. From the installation photographs that I have viewed, it is unclear if Enid's book and the Halsey Cup were exhibited in this display. Enid's medals, discussed in Chapter 7, were donated in 1945 as a result of Elsie Trask's initiative.

11. Letter from J. B. Speed Memorial Museum to Mrs. John J. Trask, Norwalk, CT, July 20, 1945, Curatorial Files for Enid Yandell, Speed Art Museum, Louisville, KY.

12. The J. B. Speed Memorial Museum, *Exhibition of Recent Acquisitions and Loans,* 17.

13. Letter from Christopher Monkhouse to Mrs. John Trask, August 17, 1977, unpublished material in the Curatorial Files on Enid Yandell, RISD Museum, Providence, RI.

14. The Trask donation consisted of a thistle panel, early twentieth century, mahogany (83.215.4); linen embroideries and crossed-stitch hand towels (83.215.1, 83.215.2A, and 83.215.2B); *Maquette of the Indian Sachem, Ninigret* (usually referred to as *Chief Ninigret*), 1912, plaster (83.215.5); bas-reliefs titled *Relief* (usually referred to as *Les Tres Amis*), 1922, plaster (83.215.6), *Woman in Profile*, 1919, bronze (83.215.7), and *Betty Brown,* 1918, bronze medallion (83.215.8); and *The Five Senses*, ca. 1909, bronze cast by Gorham (83.215.12). These nine works are in addition to the gift from Hazard and two pieces donated by the Edgartown Free Library, bringing the total number of Enid's pieces in the museum's collection to twelve. Other works from the 1982 exhibition have been retained by the museum on long-term loan.

15. While the museum has assigned that these belonged to Enid, they may be early works created by her, given that she had begun working with her hands by the age of four. Alternatively, they may have been given to her by one of her students at Branstock or as gift from a friend.

16. Desiree Caldwell, Introduction, in "Enid Yandell and the Branstock School," unpublished catalogue, RISD Museum, Providence, RI, 1982, 1, 9. As a result of more current research and the important work by Nancy Baird (1988) and Stephanie Darst (1993), some of the information presented in the catalogue can be corrected.

17. Desiree Caldwell, a student at Brown University, also undertook an honors thesis under the direction of Christopher Monkhouse, the RISD Museum's Curator of Decorative Arts, and Professor William H. Jordy, an architectural historian at Brown. In the thesis, for which the exhibition at RISD was a part, Caldwell included a list of major exhibitions to which Enid had contributed, a chronological list of her works, and a bibliography. However, copies of this publication were limited.

18. See Nancy Baird, "Enid Yandell: Kentucky Sculptor," *Filson Club History Quarterly* 62, no. 1 (January 1988): 6. According to Baird, "Apparently letters to her [Enid's] family were forwarded to Nashville for her grandmother's enjoyment. . . . However, an Elliston descendant remembers hearing about the gargantuan task of cleaning 'Burlington' after its sale in the 1920s. She recalled that three generations of

correspondence and ephemera were burned." These letters were microfilmed by the Archives of American Art before finding their eventual home at the Filson Historical Society, with Enid's documents catalogued as FHS Mss A/Y21b/. In addition, nineteen nitrate negatives sent to the Archives of American Art in 1983 for microfilming were disposed of due to the harmful nature of the nitrate stock. Because these negatives had severely deteriorated, they could not be printed from, and their contents are lost forever. Regarding the nitrate negatives, see letter from Erica Ell to Elsie Trask, August 3, 1983, Curatorial Files for Enid Yandell, RISD Museum of Art, Providence, RI.

19. Some of the details of this connection are relayed in a letter from Christopher Monkhouse to Nancy D. Baird, June 27, 1981; Curatorial Files for Enid Yandell, RISD Museum, Providence, RI; and various publications on the Yandells by Baird (see bibliography).

20. Emphasis in the original, as typed underscore. Letter from Nancy Baird to Elsie Trask, February 15, 1982. See also Robert F. Brown to Christopher Monkhouse, February 2, 1983, unpublished material on Enid Yandell, RISD Museum, Providence, RI.

21. A letter from the AAA to Elsie Barber Trask (Mrs. John J. Trask) indicates that one carton of miscellaneous papers and photo reproductions were sent to the Archives on May 21, 1980, for which Trask signed a deed of gift. The contents do not appear to include autograph letters or other manuscript material. See letter from Dzvinia Orlowsky to Mrs. John J. Trask, May 28, 1980, unpublished material on Enid Yandell, RISD Museum, Providence, RI. On the family records, see Baird, "Enid Yandell: Kentucky Sculptor." On history, see Barbara Tuchman, "Biography as a Prism of History," address to symposium on the Art of Biography, National Portrait Gallery, Washington, DC, November 14, 1978, published in Tuchman, *Practicing History* (New York: Knopf, 1981), 80–90. On the article and book by Baird, see letter from Nancy Baird to Christopher Monkhouse, February 17, 1988, unpublished material on Enid Yandell, RISD Museum, Providence, RI.

22. See handwritten notes from historian Nancy Baird regarding conversations with Elsie Barber Trask that are held in the collection of the Filson Historical Society and a copy of handwritten note from E[lsie] B[arber] Trask July 31, 1981 to Nancy Bayard [*sic*] regarding the deposition of papers in FHS Mss A/Y21b/Folder 71. The Enid Bland Yandell papers were given to the Filson Historical Society and cataloguing was undertaken there January 3–March 2, 1989.

23. See Stephanie Wilding Darst, "Art's Bachelor Maid: The Sculpture of Enid Yandell," MFA thesis, University of Louisville, Louisville, Kentucky, 1993). Darst's thesis informed the presentation of the exhibition "The Sculpture of Enid Yandell" at the Speed Museum. The accompanying catalogue raisonné was a key source for the Smithsonian American Art Museum's initiative called "SIRIS," or the Smithsonian Institution Research Information System; see http://siris-artinventories.si.edu. Entries in the database are cataloged with references to document the paintings, sculptures, and so on. In the case of Enid's works, Darst's thesis serves as a key ref-

erence. Unfortunately, however, the database has become stagnant, and corrections have not been made in a number of years, thus promulgating incorrect information. For instance, Enid's birthday is listed in the database as 1870, the date used by Darst and others, rather than 1869, Enid's actual birth year, as documented in Chapter 1 of this volume.

24. See *The Sculpture of Enid Yandell* (Louisville: J. B. Speed Art Museum, 1993), 1 for the quoted material. The sections are defined and described over pp. 1–10. A few of the works in the catalogue were misidentified. See page 18, entries 8, 9, 10 addressed Isaac Shelby (Kentucky Historical Society, Frankfort); Governor William Goebel (Kentucky Historical Society, Frankfort), and Professor J. J. Rucker (Georgetown College, Georgetown, Kentucky). The images for each are incorrect, with the image of Goebel identified as Figure 8; the image of Rucker identified as Figure 9, and the image of Shelby identified as Figure 10. The catalogue did give Enid's birth year as 1869 (which, as noted elsewhere in this book, is often misreported).

25. The 1993 exhibition also spurred interest in restoring Daniel Boone and Pan (also known as Hogan's Fountain), two of Enid's works in Cherokee Park. See "Neighborhoods Join Effort to Restore Historic Park Statues," *Louisville Courier-Journal*, April 29, 1993, B4.

26. Linda Nochlin, "Why Have There Been No Great Women Artists?" in *Women, Art, Power, and Other Essays* (Boulder: Westview Press, 1971), previously published in *ArtNews* 69, no. 9 (January 1971): 22–39, 61–71. See also, e.g., Norma Broude and Mary D. Garrard, *Feminism and Art History: Questioning the Litany* (New York: Harper & Row, 1982); Norma Broude and Mary D. Garrard, "Feminist Art History and the Academy: Where Are We Now?" *Women's Studies Quarterly* 15, nos. 1–2 (Summer 1987): 10–16; Thelma Gouma-Peterson and Patricia Mathews, "The Feminist Critique of Art History," *Art Bulletin* 69, no. 3 (September 1987): 326–357; and Lisa Tickner, "Feminism, Art History, and Sexual Difference," *Genders* 3 (Fall 1988): 92–128.

27. While Weimann was in contact with RISD as well as the Speed Museum with regard to their respective collections of Enid's works, her research and publication were distinct from the efforts of these institutions, including the efforts of Elsie Trask, in sculpting Enid's legacy. See Jeanne Madeline Weimann, *The Fair Women: The Story of the Woman's Building, World's Columbian Exposition, Chicago, 1893* (Chicago: Academy Chicago, 1981).

28. Griselda Pollock, "Feminist Interventions in Art's Histories," in Eric Fernie, ed., *Art History and Its Methods* (London: Phaidon, 1988); Rozsika Parker and Griselda Pollock, *Old Mistresses: Women, Art, and Ideology* (London: Routledge and Kegan Paul, 1981; reprint, Pandora Press, 1986), 3.

29. Gerda Lerner, "Priorities and Challenges in Women's History Research," *Perspectives on History: The Newsmagazine of the American Historical Association*, April 1, 1988, which was based on a talk she gave at the AHA in 1987; see https://www.historians.org/publications-and-directories/perspectives-on-history/april-1988/priorities-and-challenges-in-womens-history-research. The assessment of Lerner's call

as taking a "more feminist approach" is asserted by Sara Alpern, Joyce Antler, Elisabeth Israels Perry, and Ingrid Winther Scobie, eds., *The Challenge of Feminist Biography: Writing the Lives of Modern American Women* (Urbana: University of Illinois Press, 1992), 5. See Joan W. Scott, "Gender: A Useful Category of Historical Analysis," *American Historical Review* 91, no. 5 (1986): 1053–1075; and reviews of this concept in the focus issue of *American Historical Review* entitled "Revisiting: Gender a Useful Category of Analysis," 113, no. 5 (2008): 1344–1430, where Scott offered an update. See her "Unanswered Questions?" *American Historical Review* 113, no. 5 (2008): 1422–1429. Scott maintains that gender is a useful category "because it requires us to historicize the ways sex and sexual difference have been conceived." (1428). The use of the phrase "feminist interventions" borrows from Pollock and asserts the notion of an intervention over "feminist art" and feminist art history. Alternative expressions might include art "informed by feminism" (Mary Kelly), the "feminist problematic in art history (Lisa Tickner), or myriad other phrasings, each with its own, intentional grounding, purpose, and function.

30. Enid was said to be the first woman member of the National Sculpture Society. However, she was in fact not the first female member of the society, as explained in a letter from Claire A. Stein to Elsie Trask, October 27, 1982, unpublished material on Enid Yandell, RISD Museum, Providence, RI. For information on ENID and its mission of support, see Pyro Gallery, "Pyro Gallery presents ENID—Generations of Women Sculptors," April 12, 2017, https://pyrogallery.com/pages/enid-generations-of-women-sculptors.

31. The account by Ewing Fahey was provided in a letter to the author, October 15, 2013.

32. The group's beginnings, like Enid's foray into the field professionally, may be traced to Louisville and the Ohio Valley region. On the emergence of the group and their first group exhibition, see Albertus Gorman, "ENID—Generations of Women Sculptors," in *ENID—Generations of Women Sculptors*, exhibition catalogue, Louisville Visual Art Association, November 5, 1999–January 2, 2000, 4. Ewing Fahey, letter to author, October 15, 2013.

33. I am grateful for the time, since 2013, that I have been able to spend with ENID through exhibitions as well as gallery talks, including two that I offered in 2013 and 2014 amidst the work of the group at the Cressman Center for the Arts in Louisville and the Morlan Gallery at Transylvania University in Lexington, Kentucky. I am indebted also to members of the group who participated in an evening of first-person interviews with members of the collective at the home of Caren Cunningham on July 19, 2017.

34. "The COP Guide to Etiquette," exhibition on view August 12–September 4, 2011, Strychnin Gallery, Berlin, http://www.strychnin.com/News.html?articles=the-cop-guide-to-etiquette.

35. The makers of the adult education quilt include Krystal Anderson, Chandra Baughman, Barbara Hopkins, Betty Price, Harmony Prosser, Stephanie Reid, Melissa Rolph, John Terrell, and Shelia Trosper. See Kentucky Historical Society

files, 2002.31, Frankfort, KY. Two other Enid-related quilts are in the collection. The older is a "mission," or friendship, quilt in red and white cotton, containing names and Bible verses embroidered in many of the white blocks with red letters. The quilt's exact origins are unknown, although reference is made on one of the blocks to First Presbyterian Church, Louisville (Kentucky Historical Society 80.44). The second quilt was made by Jane Burch Cochran, with the assistance of Michelle Lustenberg. Measuring 81 by 78 inches, "Coming Home: Kentucky Women Quilt" features the names of 200 historically significant Kentucky women, stamped with paint on fabric, machine pieced, and embellished with beads, buttons, and other materials (Kentucky Historical Society 2015.54).

36. *Yes, I Cut Marble, Mrs. Grant* was originally commissioned by Pleiades Theatre Company, Louisville, Kentucky. It is included in the anthology *Women of the 15th State*, written with support from the Kentucky Foundation for Women. An archival typescript is in the International Centre for Women Playwrights Collection at the Ohio State University, Columbus, OH. The play was produced by Pleiades at its Stars of the Future New Play Festival, October 26–November 5, 2000. I am grateful to the author, Nancy Gall-Clayton, for meeting with me and sharing the play with me in July 2014.

37. Gall-Clayton, *Yes, I Cut Marble, Mrs. Grant*, 15, 17.

38. Ibid., 9.

39. When I asked Chase about the choice of the sriracha maple flavor for Enid, I had anticipated a response that might have connected in some way to Enid's life, work, or attributes. She had lived near Maple Street in Edgartown; her stationery, early on in 1888, had a maple leaf on it; and she carved in maple on at least one occasion, the Royal Insurance Company Desk Panel, which she created in 1890. He said that the choice had nothing to do with any of these ideas; he said it was just a solid taste. Interview with Stanley Chase III, July 17, 2017. For the description of the flavor, see http://lvjco.com/flavor/enids-perfect-pepperoni/.

40. Joe Creason, "All's Quiet, for Now, on Dan'l Boone Front," *Louisville Courier-Journal,* May 14, 1967. The article also pointed out that the Boone in Cherokee Park was removed for eight or nine months so that the EKU bronze could be created from that original bronze cast. See also Vincent Crowdus, "Dan'l to Be a Model—If He'll Stand for It," *Louisville Courier-Journal,* September 1, 1965, A14.

41. "Eastern Unveils Its Boone Statue," *Louisville Courier-Journal*, May 4, 1967, 47; "Traditions that Unite Us," *Eastern Kentucky University Magazine,* Spring 2017, 30–36, shares information on this and other university traditions. See also https://www.eku.edu/photo/celebrating-281-years-daniel-boone.

42. The application process is managed by the Kentucky Historical Society. The marker is number 2133 of the Historical Marker Database for Kentucky Department of Highways.

43. Sheldon S. Shafter, "Louisville Has Honored 'Hometown Heroes' with a Banner since 2002. Now It's Ending," *Louisville Courier-Journal*, October 9, 2017, https://www.courier-journal.com/story/news/local/2017/10/09/louisville-home-

town-hero-banner-campaign-ending/737216001/. For more information on the project and the ways that the banners are funded through partnerships with local organizations, see http://louheroes.org/. The banner is located in downtown Louisville at Seventh and Main Streets.

Selected Bibliography

Collections Consulted

Manuscripts, Documents, Photographs

Amon Carter Museum of American Art, Ft. Worth, TX
Archives of American Art, Smithsonian Institution, Washington, DC
Arkansas State Archives, Little Rock
Art Academy of Cincinnati, Cincinnati, OH
Art Institute of Chicago, Chicago, IL
Bolton Archives and Special Collections, Georgetown College, Georgetown, KY
Chicago History Museum, Chicago, IL
City of Louisville, Parks Department, Louisville, KY
City of Providence, RI
Dinsmore Homestead, Burlington, KY
Duke University, Durham, NC
Edgartown Town Hall, Edgartown, MA
Filson Historical Society, Louisville, KY
Gale Huntington Research Library, Martha's Vineyard Museum, Vineyard Haven, MA
Harvard University, Cambridge, MA
John Hay Library, Brown University, Providence, RI
Juniata College, Huntingdon, PA
Kentucky Historical Society, Frankfort
Library of Congress, Washington, DC
Louisville Free Public Library, Louisville, KY
Mary R. Schiff Library and Archives, Cincinnati Art Museum, Cincinnati, OH
Metropolitan Museum of Art, New York, NY
Newberry, Chicago, IL
New-York Historical Society, New York, NY
New York State Library and Archives, Albany
Providence Public Library, Providence, RI
RISD Museum, Providence, RI
Speed Art Museum, Louisville, KY

St. Louis Art Museum Archives, St. Louis, MO
Tennessee State Libraries and Archives, Nashville
University Archives, University at Buffalo Libraries, Buffalo, NY
University of Kentucky, Lexington
University of Louisville, Louisville, KY
Vanderbilt University, Nashville, TN
Watch Hill Memorial Library and Improvement Society, Westerly, RI
Western Kentucky University, Bowling Green

Works of Art, Drawings, Inscribed Volumes

Collection of Wendy Bell
City of Providence, RI
Dinsmore Homestead, Burlington, KY
Filson Historical Society, Louisville, KY
Georgetown College, Georgetown, KY
John Hay Library, Brown University, Providence, RI
Kentucky Historical Society, Frankfort
Louisville Free Public Library, Louisville, KY
Martha's Vineyard Museum, Vineyard Haven, MA
Collection of Warren and Julie Payne
RISD Museum, Providence, RI
Speed Art Museum, Louisville, KY
University of Kentucky, Lexington
University of Louisville, Louisville, KY
Vanderbilt University, Nashville, TN
Westerly Historical Society, Westerly, RI

Interviews

Nancy Baird, July 7, 2014, and July 18, 2017
Elyce Bonnell, August 8, 2017
Beth Carter, July 11, 2017
Stanley Chase III, July 17, 2017
Cathy Collopy, July 15, 2017
Geoff Edwards, July 10, 2017
ENID—Generations of Women Sculptors, July 19, 2017
Ewing Fahey, March 25, 2014
Diana Y. Fisher, November 11, 2018
Nancy Gall-Clayton, July 8, 2017
Joe Leduc, August 10, 2017
Peter Morrin, March 6, 2012, February 26, 2013, July 17, 2017, and July 21, 2017
Julie Payne, March 6, 2012, July 20, 2012, and July 17, 2017
Warren Payne, March 6, 2012, July 20, 2012, and July 17, 2017

Chuck Pittenger, July 12, 2017
Kristy Rose, August 8, 2017
Carter Wood Sartor, February 26, 2013, and July 8, 2014
Ardi Schneider, August 9, 2017
Kim Spence, July 21, 2017
Bow van Riper, August 7, 2017
David Yandell Wood, February 26, 2013, July 8, 2014, and July 14, 2017

Books and Articles

Alland, Alexander, Sr. *Jessie Tarbox Beals, First Woman News Photographer.* New York: Camera/Graphic Press, 1978.

Allen, Helen. "An Essay on 'Aunt Enid' in Honor of Elsie Barber Trask, Enid's Favorite Niece." Unpublished manuscript, ca. 2003–2007.

Alpern, Sara, Joyce Antler, Elisabeth Israels Perry, and Ingrid Winther Scobie. *The Challenge of Feminist Biography: Writing the Lives of Modern American Women.* Urbana: University of Illinois Press, 1992.

American Art News 12, no. 38 (September 19, 1914).

American College and Public School Directory. Chicago: C. H. Evans & Co., 1893.

American Studies at the University of Virginia, Virtual Armory Show website. "I Prefer the Navajo Rug: Locating an American Primitive." http://xroads.virginia.edu/~museum/armory/primitivism.html.

Anderson, Emma. *Elizabeth Nourse: A Sketch.* Cincinnati: Anderson, 1922.

"An Appeal from Paris." *American Magazine of Art* 7 (1916): 211.

Architectural League of New York. *Year Book of the Architectural League of New York.* New York: Secretary of the League, 1922.

"Art and the Nation." *Art and Progress* 2, no. 12 (October 1911): 370–371.

"Art in France: The Chauchard Collection at the Louvre." *Burlington Magazine* 18 (1911): 194–195.

Artists in Ohio, 1787–1900: A Biographical Dictionary. Edited by Mary Sayre Haverstock, Jeannette Mahoney Vance, and Brian L. Meggitt. Kent, OH: Kent State University Press, 2000.

"Artists' Statement." In *ENID—Generations of Women Sculptors.* Exhibition catalogue. Louisville Visual Art Association, November 5, 1999–January 2, 2000.

Baird, Nancy Disher. "'Been Pretty Good': The Diary of an Eight-Year-Old." *Filson Club History Quarterly* 66, no. 2 (April 1992): 252–264.

———. *David Wendel Yandell: Physician of Old Louisville.* Lexington: University Press of Kentucky, 1978.

———. "Enid Yandell: Kentucky Sculptor." *Filson Club History Quarterly* 62, no. 1 (January 1988).: 5–31.

———. "There Is No Sunday in the Army: Civil War Letters of Lunsford P. Yandell, 1861–1862." *Filson Club History Quarterly* 53, no. 3 (July 1979): 317–327.

Baird, Nancy Disher, and Carol Crowe-Carraco. "A 'True Woman's Sphere': Motherhood in Late Antebellum Kentucky." *Filson Club History Quarterly* 66, no. 3 (July 1992): 369–394.

Barryte, Bernard, and Roberta K. Tarbell. *Rodin and America: Influence and Adaptation, 1876–1936.* Stanford, CA: Iris and B. Gerald Cantor Center for Visual Arts, 2011.

Beach, Damian. *Civil War Battles, Skirmishes, and Events in Kentucky.* Louisville: Different Drummer Books, 1995.

Benedict, Burton, et al. *The Anthropology of World's Fairs: San Francisco's Panama Pacific International Exposition of 1915.* Berkeley: Scolar Press and the Lowie Museum of Anthropology, 1983.

Bennitt, Mark. *History of the Louisiana Purchase Exposition: Comprising . . . a Full Account of the Great Exposition, . . . Comp. from Official Sources.* St. Louis: Universal Exposition Pub. Co., 1905.

Birchfield, James D. "Thomas Satterwhite Noble: 'Made for a Painter.'" Pts. 1 and 2. *Kentucky Review* 6, nos. 1 (Winter 1986): 35–60; and 2 (Summer 1986): 45–73.

Bitter, Karl. "The Sculpture Plan." In *Art Hand-Book: Official Handbook of Architecture and Sculpture and Art Catalogue to the Pan-American Exposition,* edited by David Gray. Buffalo, NY: David Gray, 1901.

Blyth, Alan. *Wagner's Ring: An Introduction.* London: Hutchinson, 1980.

Boisseau, T. J., and Abigail M. Markwyn. "World's Fairs in Feminist Historical Perspective." In *Gendering the Fair: Histories of Women and Gender at World's Fairs,* edited by T. J. Boisseau and Abigail M. Markwyn, 1–16. Urbana: University of Illinois Press, 2010.

Bratcher, Kathryn Anne. "The Satellites of Mercury, 1888–1892." *Filson Newsmagazine* 5, no. 1, website, http://www.filsonhistorical.org/archive/news_v5n1_mercury.html.

Brenneman, Chris, and Sue Boardman. *The Gettysburg Cyclorama: The Turning Point of the Civil War on Canvas.* El Dorado Hills, CA: Savas Beatie, 2015

Broude, Norma, and Mary D. Garrard. *Feminism and Art History: Questioning the Litany.* New York: Harper & Row, 1982.

———. "Feminist Art History and the Academy: Where Are We Now?" *Women's Studies Quarterly* 15, nos. 1–2 (Summer 1987): 10–16.

Bruce, H. Addington. "Daniel Boone and the Opening of the West." *Outlook,* January 25, 1908.

Buffalo Bill (Hon. Wm. F. Cody) and His Wild West Companions, Including Wild Bill, Texas Jack, California Joe, Capt. Jack Crawford and Other Famous Scouts of the Western Plains. Chicago: M. A. Donohue & Co., 1893. Website: http://codyarchive.org/texts/wfc.bks00018.html.

Burke, Mary Alice Heekin, and Lois Marie Find. *Elizabeth Nourse, 1859–1938: A Salon Career.* Washington, DC: National Museum of American Art and the Smithsonian Institution Press, 1985.

Butler, Ruth. *Rodin: The Shape of Genius.* New Haven: Yale University Press, 1993.

"C." "The Bachelor Maid in Art." *Southern Magazine,* February 1895: 504.

CMK. "Art in the South." *Art Union: The Official Journal of the American Art Union* 1, nos. 8–9 (August–September 1884): 145.

Caldwell, Désirée B. "A Brief Account of the Life and Works of Enid Yandell." Honors Thesis, Brown University, May 15, 1978.

———. Introduction. In "Enid Yandell and the Branstock School." Unpublished catalogue. RISD Museum, Providence, RI, 1982.

Callopy, Catherine T. "Julia Stockton Dinsmore." Unpublished manuscript, Dinsmore Homestead, Burlington, KY.

Carpenter, Charles H., Jr. *Gorham Silver.* San Francisco: Alan Wofsy Fine Arts, 1997.

Carpenter, Charles H., Jr. "Nineteenth-Century Silver in the NY Yacht Club." *Antiques,* September 1977: 496.

Carrère, John M. "The Architectural Scheme." In *Art Hand-Book: Official Handbook of Architecture and Sculpture and Art Catalogue to the Pan-American Exposition,* edited by David Gray. Buffalo, NY: David Gray, 1901.

Casey, Robert J., and Mary Borglum. *Give the Man Room: The Story of Gutzon Borglum.* New York: Bobbs-Merrill, 1952.

Catalogue of Copyright Entries. Part 4. Works of Art, etc. New Series. Washington, DC: Government Printing Office, 1931.

The Chicago Blue Book: Selected Names of Chicago and Suburban Towns Containing the Names and Addresses of Prominent Residents. Chicago: Chicago Directory Co., 1915.

"Cincinnati." *Jewelers Review* 32, May 31, 1899: 693.

Cincinnati Art Museum. "History," website, http://www.cincinnatiartmuseum.org/visit/info/history.

Cincinnati Museum Association Art School Circular. Cincinnati: Robert Clarke & Co. for the Museum Association, 1884.

A Circle of Friends: Art Colonies of Cornish and Dublin. Durham, NH: University Art Galleries, 1985.

Circular and Fifth Annual Catalogue of the Art Academy of Cincinnati, 1889–1890. Cincinnati: Woodrow, Baldwin, and Co., 1889.

Cladel, Judith. *Rodin: The Man and His Art.* Translated by S. K. Star. New York: Century Co., 1917.

Clark, Thomas D. *Agrarian Kentucky.* Lexington: University Press of Kentucky, 1977.

———. "Reuben T. Durrett and His Kentuckiana Interest and Collection." *Filson Club History Quarterly* 56 (October 1982): 353–378.

"The Collector: Colonel Durrett's Collection." *Art Collector: A Journal Devoted to the Arts and the Crafts* 2 (1889): 133.

Collins, Lewis, and Richard H. Collins, reviser. *Collins' Historical Sketches of Kentucky: History of Kentucky,* vol. 1. Covington, KY: Collins & Co., 1874.

Confederated Southern Memorial Association. *History of Confederated Memorial Associations of the South.* New Orleans: Graham Press, 1904.

Corn, Wanda M., Charlene G. Garfinkle, and Annelise K. Madsen. *Women Building History: Public Art at the 1893 Columbian Exposition.* Berkeley: University of California Press, 2011.

Cotterill, Robert Spencer. *History of Pioneer Kentucky.* Cincinnati: Johnson & Hardin, 1917.

Coulter, E. Merton. *Civil War and Readjustment in Kentucky.* Chapel Hill: University of North Carolina Press, 1926.

Cox, Karen L. "Dixie's Daughters: The United Daughters of the Confederacy and the Preservation of Confederate Culture." New Perspectives on the History of the South. Gainesville: University Press of Florida, 2003.

Creighton, Wilbur F. *The Parthenon in Nashville from a Personal Viewpoint.* Nashville: [n.p.,] 1968.

Crocker, Ruth. *Mrs. Russell Sage: Women's Activism and Philanthropy in Gilded Age and Progressive Era America.* Bloomington: Indiana University Press, 2006.

Current Literature 8 (1891): 182–183.

Dabakis, Melissa. *A Sisterhood of Sculptors: American Artists in Nineteenth-Century Rome.* University Park: Pennsylvania State University Press, 2014.

Darst, Stephanie Wilding. "Art's Bachelor Maid: The Sculpture of Enid Yandell." MA thesis, University of Louisville, 1993.

———. *The Sculpture of Enid Yandell.* Louisville: J. B. Speed Art Museum, 1993.

Davies, Mervyn. *The Man Who Stood Alone.* Chester, CT: Pequot Press, 1974.

Davis, Louise L. "The Parthenon and the Tennessee Centennial: The Greek Temple That Sparked a Birthday Party." *Tennessee Historical Quarterly* 26, no. 4 (1967): 335–353.

Davis, Richard Harding. "The Last Days of the Fair." *Harper's Weekly* 37 (October 21, 1893): 1002.

Decker, Juilee. "Enid Yandell (1869–1934): Kentucky's Frontier Sculptor and 'Bachelor Maid.'" In *Kentucky Women,* edited by Melissa A. McEuen and Thomas H. Appleton, 196–218. Athens: University of Georgia Press, 2015.

———. "Re-Presenting the Civil War: Monuments and Public Memory Then and Now." Presentation at "Legacy of the Civil War: Changing Memories over Time," National Endowment for the Humanities Landmarks of American History and Culture Workshop, June 30 and July 14, 2016, website: http://legacyofthecivilwar.org/speakers.

———. "Sculpting a Postwar Identity: Enid Yandell and Louisville's Confederate Dead." Presentation at Civil War Conference, University of Louisville, March 8, 2012.

Dennison, Mariea Caudill. "Babies for Suffrage: 'The Exhibition of Painting and Sculpture by Women Artists for the Benefit of the Woman Suffrage Campaign.'" *Woman's Art Journal* 24, no. 2 (Autumn 2003–Winter 2004): 24–30.

Doyle, Don H. "Tennessee Centennial Exposition of 1897." In *The Tennessee Encyclopedia of History and Culture,* edited by Carrol Van West. Knoxville: University of Tennessee Press, 2002.

Dukes County Historical Society. *Walking Tour of Historic Edgartown.* Edgartown: Dukes County Historical Society, 1988.

Easterday, Anastasia Louise. "Charting a Course in an Intractable Profession:

Women Sculptors in Nineteenth-Century France." PhD diss., University of California, Los Angeles, 1997.

The Elegant Home: Select Furniture, Silver, Decorative and Fine Arts. San Francisco: Bonhams and Butterfields, 2017.

Elliott, Maude Howe, ed. *Art and Handicraft in the Woman's Building of the World's Columbian Exposition, Chicago, 1893.* New York: Goupil & Co., 1893.

Elsen, Albert. *Pioneers of Modern Sculpture Exhibition.* London: Hayward Gallery, 1973.

———. *Rodin's Sculptural Studies for the Monument to the Burgers of Calais from the Collection for the Cantor, Fitzgerald Group.* Beverly Hills: Cantor Fitzgerald Group, 1977.

Everett, Marshall. *The Book of the Fair: The Greatest Exposition the World Has Ever Seen Photographed and Explained, a Panorama of the St. Louis Exposition.* Philadelphia: P. W. Ziegler, 1904.

Faulkner, William. *Absalom! Absalom!* New York: Modern Library, 1936.

Faust, Drew Gilpin. "Altars of Sacrifice: Confederate Women and the Narratives of War." In *Divided Houses: Gender and the Civil War,* edited by Catherine Clinton and Nina Silber. New York: Oxford University Press, 1992, 171–191.

———. *Mothers of Invention: Women of the Slaveholding South in the American Civil War.* Chapel Hill: University of North Carolina Press, 1996.

———. *This Republic of Suffering: Death and the American Civil War.* New York: Knopf, 2008.

Federal Writers' Project of the Works Progress Administration for the State of Kentucky. "Kentucky: A Guide to the Bluegrass State." Typescript. Lexington: University of Kentucky, 1939.

———. *Kentucky: A Guide to the Bluegrass State.* 3rd printing. Lexington: University of Kentucky, 1942.

Fisher, Julie A., and David J. Silverman. *Ninigret, Sachem of the Niantics and Narragansetts: Diplomacy, War, and the Balance of Power in Seventeenth-Century New England and Indian Country.* Ithaca: Cornell University Press, 2014.

Foster, Gaines. *Ghosts of the Confederacy: Defeat, the Lost Cause, and the Emergence of the New South, 1865–1913.* New York: Oxford University Press, 1988.

Francis, David Rowland. *The Universal Exposition of 1904.* St. Louis: Louisiana Purchase Exposition Co., 1913.

Georgetown College. *Georgetown College Bulletin.* Georgetown, KY: Georgetown College, 1952.

Gilder, Jeannette L. Review of Henry James, *Life of William Wetmore Story. The Critic* 44, no. 2 (February 1904): 175–177.

Goel, Blanche I. "Tramping on Martha's Vineyard." Lecture to Dukes County Historical Society, October 29, 1925. Reprinted as a pamphlet by the society.

Goodier, Susan, and Karen Pastorello. *Women Will Vote: Winning Suffrage in New York State.* Ithaca: Cornell University Press, 2017.

Goodwyn, Lawrence. *The Populist Moment: A Short History of the Agrarian Revolt in America.* New York: Oxford University Press, 1978.

Gorman, Albertus. “ENID—Generations of Women Sculptors.” In *ENID—Generations of Women Sculptors,* exhibition catalogue, Louisville Visual Art Association, November 5, 1999–January 2, 2000.

Goshorn, Alfred T. “The World’s Fair and Industrial Art.” *Engineering Magazine* 4, no. 5 (February 1893): 645–653.

Gouma-Peterson, Thelma, and Patricia Mathews. “The Feminist Critique of Art History” *Art Bulletin* 69, no. 3 (September 1987): 326–357.

Gray, David. *Catalogue of the Exhibition of Fine Arts.* Buffalo: Pan-American Exposition, 1901.

Handy, Mrs. M. P. “The Women of the World’s Fair City.” *Munsey’s Magazine* 8, no. 6 (March 1893): 607–613.

Harris, Lindsay R. *Tell It with Pride: The 54th Massachusetts Regiment and Augustus Saint-Gaudens’ Shaw Memorial.* Exhibition catalog. National Gallery of Art, Washington, DC, September 15, 2013–January 20, 2014. Washington, DC: National Gallery of Art, 2013.

Harrison, Constance Cary. *A Bachelor Maid.* New York: Century Co., 1894.

“Harrodsburg.” In John E. Kleber et al., *The Kentucky Encyclopedia.* Lexington: University Press of Kentucky, 1992.

Hartt, Mary Bronson. “Women and the Art of Landscape Gardening.” *Outlook,* March 28, 1908.

Harvey, Bruce G. *World’s Fairs in a Southern Accent: Atlanta, Nashville, and Charleston, 1895–1902.* Knoxville: University of Tennessee Press, 2014.

Hawkins, Rush C. *A Tribute to the Memory of Carrie Matilde Bajnotti.* New York: Devinne Press, 1893.

Henry, Josephine K. “The New Woman of the New South: A Feminist Literature Classic.” *Arena* 11 (1895): 353–362.

Hopkins, James F. With a foreword by Thomas D. Clark. *History of the Hemp Industry in Kentucky.* Lexington: University Press of Kentucky, 1998.

“It Sold Well: Getting Out a ‘Woman’s’ Edition of a Paper.” *Fourth Estate,* April 25, 1895: 5.

J. B. Speed Memorial Museum. *Exhibition of Recent Acquisitions and Loans.* Louisville: Speed Museum, 1941.

Jacobs, Michael. *The Good and Simple Life: Artist Colonies in Europe and America.* Oxford: Phaidon, 1985.

James, Henry. *Life of William Wetmore Story.* New York: Houghton, Mifflin & Co., 1903.

Janney, Caroline E. *Remembering the Civil War: Reunion and the Limits of Reconciliation.* Chapel Hill: University of North Carolina Press, 2013.

Jewelers’ Circular and Horological Review, 37, no. 24 (January 11, 1899): 1.

Johnson, Rossiter, ed. *History of the World’s Columbian Exposition Held in Chicago in 1893.* 4 vols. New York: D. Appleton and Co., 1897–1898.

Johnston, Ella Bond. “Art in Indiana.” *Outlook,* June 24, 1911: 433–440.

Journal of the Regular Session of the House of Representatives of the Commonwealth of Kentucky, volume 1. Frankfort, KY: Capital Office, 1891.

Justi, Herman. *The Official Catalogue of the Tennessee Centennial Exposition*. Nashville: Burch & Hinton, 1897.

———, ed. *Official History of the Tennessee Centennial Exposition*. Nashville: Allied Printing, 1898.

Karson, Robin S. *A Genius for Place: American Landscapes of the Country Place Era*. Amherst: University of Massachusetts Press, 2007.

Kentucky State Parks. "Fort Harrod." https://parks.ky.gov/parks/recreationparks/fort-harrod/history.aspx.

Kentucky Women Artists: 1850–2000. Exhibition catalog. Owensboro, KY: Owensboro Museum of Art, 2001.

Kim, Linda. "Separate Spheres: Potterines, Gender, and Domestic Sculpture in Turn-of-the-Century America." *American Art* 28, no. 2 (2014): 3–25.

Klotter, James C. *The Breckinridges of Kentucky, 1760–1981*. Lexington: University Press of Kentucky, 1981.

Kolloff, Fred C., and Paul J. Ramsey. "Daniel Boone." EKU Television, 2002. https://youtu.be/BO_-xHY0YOU.

Ladegast, Richard. "Enid Yandell, the Sculptor." *Outlook* 70 (January 1902): 80–83.

Lankford, Lyle. "Women to the Rescue." Presentation to the Vanderbilt Aid Society, April 19, 2007, reprinted in *Vanderbilt Magazine*, August 6, 2009. https://news.vanderbilt.edu/vanderbiltmagazine/women-to-the-rescue/.

Larson, Erik. *The Devil in the White City*. New York: Crown, 2003.

Laswell, George D. *Corners and Characters of Rhode Island*. Providence: Oxford Press, 1924.

Lefebvre-Laboulaye, Éduoard René. *Abdallah or The Four-Leaved Clover*. Translated by Mary L. Booth. New American Edition. Chicago: A. C. McClurg & Co., 1889.

Leonard, John William, ed. *Woman's Who's Who of America: A Biographical Dictionary of Contemporary Women of the United States and Canada, 1914–1915*. New York: American Commonwealth Co., 1914.

Lerner, Gerda. "Priorities and Challenges in Women's History Research." *Perspectives on History: The Newsmagazine of the American Historical Association*, April 1, 1988.

Logue, Larry M., and Michael Barton, eds. *The Civil War Veteran: A Historical Reader*. New York: New York University Press, 2007.

Louisville: A Guide to the Falls City. Louisville: Louisville Automobile Club, 1940.

"The Marine World Modeled in Silver." *Jewelers' Circular and Horological Review* 37, no. 15 (November 9, 1898): 1.

Marling, Karal Ann. *Wall-to-Wall America: Post Office Murals in the Great Depression*. Minneapolis: University of Minnesota Press, 1982.

Marshall, Anne E. *Creating a Confederate Kentucky: The Lost Cause and Civil War Memory in a Border State*. Chapel Hill: University of North Carolina Press, 2010.

Martha's Vineyard: The Isle of Health. Martha's Vineyard: Martha's Vineyard Chamber of Commerce, 1926.

Martha's Vineyard Business Directory, 1910–11. Boston: Union Publishing Co., 1910.

Martha's Vineyard Informer. N.p.: Littlefield & Co., 1929.

Martis, Susan. "Famous and Forgotten: Rodin and Three American Contemporaries." PhD diss., Case Western Reserve University, 2005.

Massey, Mary Elizabeth. *Bonnet Brigades: American Women and the Civil War.* New York: Knopf, 1966.

McCarthy, Kathleen D. *Women's Culture: American Philanthropy and Art, 1830–1930.* Chicago: University of Chicago Press, 1991.

McConnell, Stuart C. *Glorious Contentment: The Grand Army of the Republic, 1865–1900.* Chapel Hill: University of North Carolina Press, 1992.

McEuen, Melissa A., and Thomas Appleton, eds. *Kentucky Women: Their Lives and Times.* Athens: University of Georgia Press, 2015.

McKercher, Bob, and Hilary du Cros. *Cultural Tourism: The Partnership between Tourism and Cultural Heritage Management.* New York: Haworth Hospitality Press, 2002.

Mercer, Paul, and Vicki Weiss, for the Friends of the New York State Library. *The New York State Capitol and the Great Fire of 1911.* Charleston, SC: Arcadia Publishing, 2011.

Mills, Cynthia J. "Casting Shadows: The *Adams Memorial* and Its Doubles." *American Art* 14, no. 2 (Summer 2000): 2–25.

Mooney-Melvin, Patricia. "Harnessing the Romance of the Past: Preservation, Tourism, and History." *Public Historian* 13, no. 2 (Spring 1991): 35–48.

Moore, William D. "'United We Commemorate': The Kentucky Pioneer Memorial Association, James Isenberg, and Early Twentieth-Century Heritage Tourism." *Public Historian* 30, no. 3 (Summer 2008): 51–81.

Morgan, Robert. *Boone: A Biography.* Chapel Hill: Algonquin, 2007.

Munson-Williams-Proctor Institute. *1913 Armory Show: 50th Anniversary Exhibition.* Utica, NY: Munson-Williams-Proctor Institute, 1963.

Nantucket Historical Association. "Nantucket Art Colony, 1920–1945" (website). https://nha.org/digitalexhibits/artistcolony/index.htm.

National Agricultural Statistics Service, US Department of Agriculture. https://www.nass.usda.gov/AgCensus/.

National Register of Historic Places. "Civil War Monuments in Kentucky" (website), https://npgallery.nps.gov/pdfhost/docs/NRHP/Text/64500229.pdf.

———. "Nomination form for Louisville Trust Building." National Register of Historic Places, ref. no. 77000624, April 18, 1977. https://npgallery.nps.gov/NRHP/AssetDetail?assetID=6d66af91-3bdd-446e-ad29-b9832fcd5eaa.

"New York, Passenger Arrival Lists (Ellis Island), 1892–1924." FamilySearch (website). https://familysearch.org/pal:/MM9.1.1/JJWF-5JM.

New-York Historical Society Museum and Library. "Guide to the Jessie Tarbox

Beals Photographs: Jessie Tarbox Beals Photographs [1900–1940], Bulk 1904–1920, PR 4." http://dlib.nyu.edu/findingaids/html/nyhs/beals/beals.html.

"The New York State Library." *Library Journal,* March–April 1888: 93–94. (Reprinted from *New York Times,* February 27, 1888.) Website: https://babel.hathitrust.org/cgi/pt?id=njp.32101076204963;view=1up;seq=93.

Ninth Annual Catalogue of the Hampton College. Louisville, KY: John P. Morton and Co., 1886–1887.

Nochlin, Linda. "Why Have There Been No Great Women Artists?" In *Women, Art, Power, and Other Essays.* New York: Harper & Row, 1988, 145–178. (Reprint of essay appearing in *ARTnews,* January 1971: 22.)

Norton, Henry Franklin. *Martha's Vineyard.* Hartford, CT: Henry Franklin Norton and Robert Emmett Pyne, Publishers, 1923.

Nutter, Krista Atkins. "Tracing the Paths of Interior Design Education." Master's thesis, University of Cincinnati, 2001. http://rave.ohiolink.edu/etdc/view?acc_num=ucin990129600.

"Obituary: Donn Barber, FAIA." *Journal of the American Institute of Architects* 13, July 7, 1925: 274.

Parezo, Nancy J. *Anthropology Goes to the Fair: The 1904 Louisiana Purchase Exposition.* Lincoln: University of Nebraska Press, 2007.

Parker, Rozsika, and Griselda Pollock. *Old Mistresses: Women, Art, and Ideology.* London: Routledge and Kegan Paul, 1981.

Perry, Elisabeth Israels. "Memorializing the 1897 Tennessee Centennial Woman's Building." In *Gendering the Fair: Histories of Women and Gender at World's Fairs,* edited by T. J. Boisseau and Abigail M. Markwyn, 149–165. Urbana: University of Illinois Press, 2010.

Pitman, Benn. *A Plea for American Decorative Art with Illustrations and Designs, Showing Examples of Artistic Wood Carving, China and Pottery Painting, Mural Decoration, Etching, etc., by the Girls and Women of Cincinnati.* Atlanta: Cotton States & International Exposition, 1895.

Pollock, Griselda. "Feminist Interventions in Art's Histories." In *Art History and Its Methods,* edited by Eric Fernie. London: Phaidon, 1988, 300–313.

Pope, William F. *Early Days in Arkansas.* Little Rock: Frederick W. Allsopp, 1895.

Profumo, Phyllis. *Muldoon Monument Company, Kentucky, Sales Records.* Louisville, KY: The Compilers, 1895.

Pyro Gallery. "Pyro Gallery presents ENID—Generations of Women Sculptors." April 12, 2017. https://pyrogallery.com/pages/enid-generations-of-women-sculptors.

Rabinow, Rebecca A. "The Suffrage Show of 1915." In *Splendid Legacy: The Havemeyer Collection,* edited by Alice Cooney Frelinghuysen, Gary Tinterow, et al., 89–95. New York: Metropolitan Museum of Art, 1993.

Report and Catalogue of the Woman's Department of the World's Exposition Held at New Orleans, 1884–1885. Boston: Rand, Avery, and Co., 1885.

"Reuben T. Durrett." In *The Builders of the Nation: A History of the University States,*

Including Portraits and Biographies of Presidents, Cabinet Officers, Statesmen, Legislators, Jurists, Educators, Authors, Editors, and Divines. New York: Stanley-Bradley Pub. Co., 1892, 450–453.

"Revisiting: Gender a Useful Category of Analysis," *American Historical Review* 113, no. 5 (2008): 1344–1430,

Ridpath, John Clark. *The Life and Work of James A. Garfield.* Cincinnati: Jones Brothers & Co., 1881.

Right Here I See My Own Books: The Woman's Building Library at the World's Columbian Exposition, edited by Sarah Wadsworth and Wayne A. Wiegand. Amherst: University of Massachusetts Press, 2012.

Rightmyer, Bobbi Dawn, and Anna Armstrong. *Harrodsburg.* Images of America Series. Charleston, SC: Arcadia Publishing, 2011.

Rogan, Rev. O. G. *History of Lewis County.* Cincinnati: Press of Jennings and Graham, 1912.

Roosevelt, Theodore. "A Layman's Views of an Art Exhibition" *Outlook* 29 (March 1913): 718–720.

Rothert, Otto A. "Chester Harding's Two Portraits of Daniel Boone." *Filson Quarterly* 8 no. 4 (1934): frontispiece.

Rydell, Robert W. *All the World's a Fair: Visions of Empire at America's International Expositions, 1876–1916.* Chicago: University of Chicago Press, 1984.

Rydell, Robert W., John E. Findling, and Kimberly D. Pelle. *Fair America: World's Fairs in the United States.* Washington, DC: Smithsonian Institution Press, 2000.

Sander, Kathleen Waters. *The Business of Charity: The Woman's Exchange Movement, 1832–1900.* Urbana: University of Illinois Press, 1998.

Savage, Kirk. *Standing Soldiers, Kneeling Slaves: Race, War, and Monument in Nineteenth-Century America.* Princeton: Princeton University Press, 1997.

Schaefer, Mary Phyllis. *Enid Yandell, 1870–1934.* Undergraduate thesis, University of Louisville, 1948.

Schermerhorn, Henry A. "The Bajnotti Trust Fund for the Encouragement of the Family." In Rush C. Hawkins, *A Tribute to the Memory of Carrie Matilde Bajnotti.* New York: Devinne Press, 1893.

Scott, Anne Firor. *Natural Allies: Women's Associations in American History.* Chicago: University of Chicago Press, 1991.

———. *The Southern Lady: From Pedestal to Politics, 1830–1930.* Chicago: University of Chicago Press, 1970.

Scott, Joan W. "Gender: A Useful Category of Historical Analysis." *American Historical Review* 91, no. 5 (1986): 1053–1075.

———. "Unanswered Questions?" *American Historical Review* 113 no. 5 (2008): 1422–1429.

Scranton, Philip, and Janet F. Davidson. *The Business of Tourism: Place, Faith, and History.* Philadelphia: University of Pennsylvania Press, 2007.

Scudder, Janet. *Modeling My Life.* New York: Harcourt, Brace, & Co., 1925.

Settle, George T. *Catalog of Art in the Louisville Free Public Library: Paintings, Statuary, Etchings, Prints, Photographs, and Bronze Tablets.* Louisville: [n.p.,] 1928.

Smith-Rosenberg, Carroll. "The Female World of Love and Ritual: Relations between Women in Nineteenth-Century America." *Signs* 1, no. 1 (Autumn 1975): 1–29.

Smithsonian American Art Museum (SIRIS), "Art Inventories Catalog" (website), https://siris-artinventories.si.edu/.

Sotheby's. *The Jerome Rapoport Collection of American Aesthetic Silver.* New York: Sotheby's, 1996.

"A Southern Girl at the World's Fair." *Confederate Veteran* 1 (1893): 324.

Starnes, Richard D., ed. *Southern Journeys: Tourism, History, and Culture in the Modern South.* Tuscaloosa: University of Alabama Press, 2003.

Strychnin Gallery. "The COP Guide to Etiquette" (website), http://www.strychnin.com/News.html?articles=the-cop-guide-to-etiquette.

Stubblebine, Donald J. *Early Broadway Sheet Music: A Comprehensive Listing of Published Music from Broadway and Other Stage Shows, 1843–1918.* Jefferson, NC: McFarland, 2010.

Taft, Ada Bartlett. *Lorado Taft: Sculptor and Citizen.* Greensboro, NC: Mary Taft Smith, 1946.

Taft, Lorado. *The History of American Sculpture.* New York: Macmillan, 1930.

Tankard, Judith B. "Defining Their Turf: Pioneer Women Landscape Designers." *Studies in the Decorative Arts* 8, no. 1 (Fall–Winter 2000–2001): 31–53.

Tarbell, Roberta K. "The Impact of the Armory Show on American Sculpture." *Archives of American Art Journal* 18, no. 2 (1978): 2–11.

Terborg-Penn, Rosalyn. *African American Women in the Struggle for the Vote, 1850–1920.* Bloomington: Indiana University Press, 1998.

Thomson, D. Croal, Herbert E. Butler, and E. G. Halton, eds. "The Paris Exhibition, 1900." *Art Journal.* London: Art Journal Office, 1901.

Tickner, Lisa. "Feminism, Art History, and Sexual Difference." *Genders* 3 (Fall 1988): 92–128.

"Traditions That Unite Us." *Eastern Kentucky University Magazine,* Spring 2017, 32.

Trask, John E. D. *Official Catalogue of the Department of Fine Arts, Panama-Pacific International Exposition (with awards), San Francisco, California.* San Francisco: Wahlgreen Co., 1915.

Trubeck, Anne. "Edith Wharton Recruited the World's Greatest Artists to Raise Money for WWI Refugees." *Smithsonian.com,* May 30, 2017 (website), https://www.smithsonianmag.com/arts-culture/edith-wharton-recruited-worlds-greatest-artists-raise-money-wwi-refugees-180963493/.

Tuchman, Barbara. "Biography as a Prism of History." Address to symposium on the Art of Biography, National Portrait Gallery, Washington, DC, November 14, 1978. In Tuchman, *Practicing History,* 80–90. New York: Knopf, 1981.

Turner, Frederick Jackson. "The Frontier in American History." In *Annual Report of the American Historical Association for 1893.* Washington, DC: Government Printing Office, 1894, 197–227.

"University News." *Vanderbilt University Quarterly* 7, no. 3 (July 1907): 208.

University of Chicago Library, Special Collections Research Center. "Guide to the Reuben T. Durrett Collection of Richard H. Collins Papers, 1761–1873" (website), https://www.lib.uchicago.edu/ead/rlg/ICU.SPCL.COLLINSR.pdf.

US Commission to the Paris Exposition. *Official Illustrated Catalogue: Fine Arts Exhibit, United States of America Paris Exposition of 1900.* Boston: Noyes, Platt & Co., 1900.

Villamil, Victoria Etnier. *From Johnson's Kids to Lemonade Opera: The American Classical Singer Comes of Age.* Boston: Northeastern University Press, 2004.

Visscher, William Lightfoot. *Snap Shots of the Saint Louis Exposition, 1904: Commemorating the Louisiana Purchase of 1903, One of the Greatest Events in the History of Our World.* Chicago: White City Art Co., 1904.

Walters, Edward M. "Reuben T. Durrett, the Durrett Collection, and the University of Chicago." *Filson Club History Quarterly* 56 (October 1982): 379–394.

Weimann, Jeanne Madeline. *The Fair Women: The Story of the Woman's Building World's Columbian Exposition Chicago 1893.* Chicago: Academy Chicago, 1981.

Wetherington, Mark V. "Buried in Original Records, Government Reports, Statistical Tables, and Obscure Essays?: Kentucky's Twentieth-Century Agricultural History." *Register of the Kentucky Historical Society* 113, nos. 2–3 (Spring–Summer 2015): 271–306.

Wharton, Edith, ed. *The Book of the Homeless.* New York: Scribner, 1916.

White, Trumbull, and William Igleheart. *The World's Columbian Exposition, Chicago, 1893.* Boston: Standard Silverware Co., 1893.

Whites, LeeAnn. *Gender Matters: Civil War, Reconstruction, and the Making of the New South.* New York: Palgrave, 2005.

William Campbell Preston Breckinridge. 1837–1904. Louisville: J. P. Morton & Co., printers, 1887.

Williams, Alice L. *Treasures New and Old.* Chicago: Belford, Clark & Co., 1884.

Wolfe, Margaret Ripley. "Fallen Leaves and Missing Pages: Women in Kentucky History." Focus Issue: The Kentucky Image/Bicentennial, *Register of the Kentucky Historical Society* 90, no. 1 (1992): 64–89.

Woman's Work in Tennessee. Memphis: Tennessee Federation of Women's Clubs, 1916.

"Woman Who Designed Many Memorials Dead: Miss Enid Yandell of Edgartown Won World Wide Fame, Career Ends." *Vineyard Gazette,* June 15, 1934, 1–2.

Women's Culture: American Philanthropy and Art, 1830–1930. Chicago: University of Chicago Press, 1991.

Yandell, Enid. "Sculpture at the World's Fair." *Current Topics,* April 1893: 251–255.

———. "Talent for Sculpture." In *What Women Can Earn: Occupations of Women and Their Compensation,* edited by Grace H. Dodge, Thomas Hunter, et al., 226–228. New York: Frederick A. Stokes, 1898.

Yandell, Enid Bland, Laura Hayes, and Jean Loughborough. *Three Girls in a Flat.* Chicago: Bright, Leonard & Co., 1892.

Index

Page numbers in italics refer to illustrations.

TOPICS IN KENTUCKY HISTORY
James C. Klotter, Series Editor

Books in the Series

The Family Legacy of Henry Clay: In the Shadow of a Kentucky Patriarch
Lindsey Apple

Kentucky and the Great War
David J. Bettez

George Keats of Kentucky: A Life
Lawrence M. Crutcher

Enid Yandell: Kentucky's Pioneer Sculptor
Juilee Decker

A History of Education in Kentucky
William E. Ellis

Madeline McDowell Breckinridge and the Battle for a New South
Melba Porter Hay

Committed to Victory: The Kentucky Home Front During World War II
Richard Holl

Alben Barkley: A Life in Politics
James K. Libbey

Henry Watterson and the New South: The Politics of Empire, Free Trade, and Globalization
Daniel S. Margolies

Murder and Madness: The Myth of the Kentucky Tragedy
Matthew G. Schoenbachler

How Kentucky Became Southern: A Tale of Outlaws, Horse Thieves, Gamblers, and Breeders
Maryjean Wall

Madam Belle: Sex, Money, and Influence in a Southern Brothel
Maryjean Wall